Voices from the Rocks

Voices from the Rocks

Nature, Culture & History
in the Matopos Hills
of Zimbabwe

TERENCE RANGER

Emeritus Rhodes Professor of Race Relations
University of Oxford

Visiting Professor
University of Zimbabwe

Baobab
HARARE

Indiana
University Press
BLOOMINGTON & INDIANAPOLIS

James Currey
OXFORD

James Currey Ltd
73 Botley Road
Oxford
OX2 0BS

Baobab Books
PO Box 1559
Harare

Indiana University Press
601 North Morton Street
Bloomington, Indiana 47404

British Library Cataloguing in Publication Data
Ranger, T. O. (Terence Osborn), 1929–
  Voices from the rocks : nature, culture & history in the
Matopos Hills of Zimbabwe
1. Matopo Hills (Zimbabwe) – History   2. Matopo Hills
(Zimbabwe) – Civilization
I. Title
968.9´1
          ISBN   0–85255–654–3 (James Currey cased)
                 0–85255–604–7 (Jamese Currey paper)

Library of Congress Cataloging-in-Publication Data
A catalog record for this book is available from the Library of Congress

          ISBN 0–253–21288–x (Indiana paper)
          ISBN 0-253-33527-2 (Indiana cloth)

Set in 10/11.6 pt Ehrhardt, the Monotype revival of a seventeenth-century Leipzig face,
by Long House Publishing Services, Cumbria
Printed in Great Britain by Villiers Publications, London N3

Contents

List of Photographs & Maps

Photographs

(All photographs are reproduced with the permission of the National Archives of Zimbabwe unless otherwise stated)

Maps

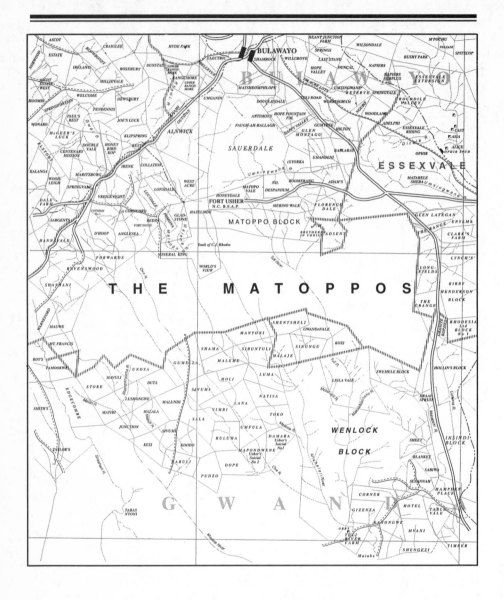

Map 1 This map, made in 1909, shows the large 'reserved' area of the Matopos. To the north lie Rhodes's lands – Sauerdale, Westacre, Lonsdale, Lucydale, Hazelside, Honeydale, Matoppo Vale and the rest. To the east lies the Matopo Mission of the Brethren in Christ and Absent Farm. To the south-west lie the farms of the Mapani belt; to the south-east lies Wenlock.

Introduction

In 1985 my book *Peasant Consciousness and Guerrilla War** was published. It dealt with the agrarian history of Makoni district in eastern Zimbabwe. Makoni district was unusual because conditions there were particularly favourable to African peasant production. I wanted to make a comparison with another district. The question was where it should be. In the same year I organised a conference in London on the research which was then being carried out or planned by expatriate researchers on Zimbabwe. As those present made their reports, I put pins in a map of the country. Two-thirds had worked or were planning to work in the eastern third of Zimbabwe; one third had worked or hoped to work in the middle third. Except for two or three projects in Bulawayo, no research of any sort was then planned for Matabeleland. I began to think that I should choose a district in Matabeleland in order to compare and contrast it with Makoni.

It was easy enough in 1985 to understand why no researchers wanted to work in Matabeleland. There was in effect a state of war, with the 'dissidents' being hunted by the Security Forces and the civilian population caught in the middle. It was impossible to carry out field research. So in 1985 and for the next two years I had to content myself with working in the National Archives in Harare. I first identified a district in Matabeleland for which there seemed to be a great deal of archival material and in this way I chose Matobo district in southern Matabeleland. Then I worked for three years on the massive archival deposit relating to that district.[1] At last, with the amnesty of May 1988, it became possible to work in the field. Less than two months after the surrender of the 'dissidents', I was travelling freely around Matobo and carrying out interviews.[2]

* Terence Ranger, *Peasant Consciousness and Guerrilla War in Zimbabwe*, James Currey, London, 1985.
[1] After the first two months' work in 1985 I wrote a long draft account: 'Promises, Promises. An Alternative History of the Rhodes Matopos Park', August 1986. On the basis of my archival work and before I had gone into the field I wrote 'Whose Heritage? The Case of the Matobo National Park', *Journal of Southern African Studies*, 15, 2, January 1989.
[2] The situation in Matobo just after the amnesty is described in Terence Ranger, 'Matabeleland Since the Amnesty', *African Affairs*, 351, 88, 1989.

1

I was able to go there again in 1989, 1990 and 1991, and more briefly in 1992, 1993, 1994 and 1995.[3]

As a result of this field experience two things became clear. One was that Matobo certainly made a sharp contrast with Makoni. There was only briefly a chance of a 'peasant option' in Matobo. In 1988 I met a white Catholic nun at Minda Mission. She had previously worked in Makoni district but had found it much too pleasant to test her vocation. So she had moved to Matobo instead: 'You really have to be tough to survive here.' The then District Adminstrator, Livingstone Mashingele, told me that Matobo was a 'Cinderella District', with no towns, too little rain, no resettlement schemes, and few markets for peasant produce. He was glad I had come to work on its past, he said. The people of Matobo had almost nothing. They might as well have some history.

But the second thing that became clear was that I could not really base my research on a comparison or contrast with Makoni. Makoni district more or less occupied the area of the pre-colonial paramountcy of Maungwe and had considerable coherence. Matobo was very different. In 1988 I met Stephen Nkomo, the member of parliament for the district, and told him that I was planning a history of Matobo. He was astonished and dismissive. 'Matobo is a mere geographical expression', he said. 'Now, if you were to write the history of Cecil Rhodes in the Matopos hills *that* would really make a book worth reading.' At first I thought that Stephen Nkomo had too old-fashioned a view of history. But as I came to work in southern Matabeleland I more and more appreciated his point of view. Matobo district *has* been a mere geographical expression, its boundaries constantly changing. Its African population have time and time again been evicted and resettled in the far south or the far north.

I came to realise that the real historical unit south of Bulawayo was not the district but the Matopos hills, which fall into three districts, Gwanda and Mzingwane as well as Matobo. So this book has come to be about the hills: not only about Cecil Rhodes, though my narrative begins with him in Chapter 3, but about their whole history over the past hundred years. And since it has come to be about the hills, it is the hills themselves which have determined its emphases. It has ceased to be a comparison with the agrarian history of Makoni and come to be about landscape, religion, conservation, political symbolism and war.

Almost all visitors and many Zimbabweans think of the Matopos hills as they are presented to them in the National Park – as wild nature. The purpose of this book is to re-instate culture and history into nature. The hills, including the area of the National Park, have been the home of men and women for at least 40,000 years. It is only since

---

[3] Four chapters which draw upon my Matobo field-work are 'Power, Religion and Community: The Matobo Case', *Subaltern Studies VII*, OUP, Delhi, 1992, which discusses the rain shrines in the Matobo Communal Area; 'The Invention of Tradition Revisited: the Case of Colonial Africa', in Terence Ranger and Olufemi Vaughan, eds, *Legitimacy and the State in Twentieth-Century Africa*, St Antony's/Macmillan, 1993, which deals with Ndebele ethnicity; 'African Identities: Ethnicity, Nationality and History. The Case of Matabeleland, 1893–1993', in Joachim Heidrich, ed., *Changing Identities. The Transformation of Asian and African Societies under Colonialism*, Center for Modern Oriental Studies, Berlin, 1994; with Mark Ncube, 'Religion in the Guerrilla War. The Case of Southern Matabeleland', in Ngwabe Bhebe and Terence Ranger, eds, *Society in Zimbabwe's Liberation War*, University of Zimbabwe, Harare, and James Currey, London, 1995.

1962 that cultivators and hersdmen have been removed from the Park itself, and the human history of the hills continues to this day in Kumalo and Gulati and Matobo Communal Areas, which are as beautiful as the Park itself with all the added interest and depth of an environment still subject to the social imagination.

This is why the book is called *Voices from the Rocks*. By this I do not mean the objective messages that scientists have wrung from the rocks by geological or archaeological study in the Matopos. I refer rather to the idea that the rocks themselves speak and I also refer to the speech of the men and women who live among them. 'Gulati' is a compression of a Kalanga term which means 'The Voice from the Rock' and the hills have long been the home for shrines of the High God, Mwali, at which the voice of the deity has been heard by pilgrims as though emanating from the rocks themselves. I shall try in this book to unriddle the messages of the cave shrines and to show that they contain statements about environment, history and politics which have influenced not only the inhabitants of the hills but also hundreds of thousands of people throughout Matabeleland and beyond.

Such supernatural voices have been seconded by the rejoicing and lamenting and protesting voices of the human occupants of the hills themselves. The book will reflect how they have spoken about their history, their economy, their relationships, their aspirations and their grievances. It will recount how in the late 1940s the people of the hills created the most effective rural protest associations in Zimbabwe – the *Sofasonke* and *Sofasihamba* movements. These associations called upon the help of the aptly named African Voice Association so as to deliver a challenge to colonial authoritarianism. In the late 1950s and early 1960s the peoples of the Matopos, whether they remained in the hills or were evicted to the north or south of them, took this legacy of self-assertion and confrontation into the mass nationalist movement. These are voices from the rocks which are well worth listening to.

Religion and politics have thus been central to the history of these apparently 'wild' and 'remote' hills – and white religion and politics as much as black. The hills have been the site of an intense symbolic struggle, with mission schools thrust up against every Mwali shrine, and with the grave of Cecil Rhodes standing to this day as a sign of the white endeavour to capture and embody the spirit of the land. White settlers came on pilgrimage to Rhodes's grave – and to the other memorials of white achievement and sacrifice which were erected in the hills – just as blacks journeyed as pilgrims to Mzilikazi's grave and to the shrines. Such white and black travellers have come from all over Southern Africa. These introverted hills, with their locked valleys, have been at the centre of two great international symbolic systems, each proclaiming its own myth of the sacred history of the Matopos.

But whites have not relied only on a symbolic assertion of control over the hills. They have also called upon 'science' – geology, pre-history, archaeology and, above all, ecology. By these means they have proclaimed their rights (and duties) as guardians of the land. White pre-historians have produced a version of the history of the hills in which there was long and benevolent occupation by Stone Age Africans, who lived in the hills among and like the animals. They were succeeded by Iron Age agriculturalists and cattle keepers. Stone Age men did not impose themselves upon the hills; Iron Age farmers, with their wasteful 'traditional' methods, wreaked wanton destruction upon them. African farmers, in short, could not strike a proper balance between man and nature. White science, on the other hand, could either ensure a proper and fruitful exploitation of the land, or else intervene dynamically to conserve it. Science was needed in the Matopos to save nature from African humanity.

Yet this 're-invention of nature' (because the environment which we see today in the National Park is *not* 'wild' but the result of centuries of interaction with human beings and their grazing domestic animals) has been countered in the Matopos by an African ideology of the land, which states a quite different relationship between nature and culture. In the High God cult the shrines represent a quintessential natural *source* of culture; the two are inseparable, so that human society bears no meaning without the rocks and pools and caves, and they in turn are given meaning only by the residence among them of human beings. This confrontation continues today, as black 'experts' replace white 'experts'. The Matobo Communal Area is the only place left in Zimbabwe today where a number of major shrines interact with each other and with the agricultural economy. It is also top of the list of the areas which ecological experts are determined to clear altogether of human occupation.

The hills have not only been the scene of symbolic, ideological and political conflict. They have also been the site of the violent confrontations of armed struggle. They were a bastion for the regiments of the Ndebele state in 1896; they were a stronghold for both ZIPRA and ZANLA guerrillas in the 1970s; they witnessed many clashes between 'dissidents' and government forces in the 1980s. At the end of this book I shall try to show how these armed conflicts related to the religious, symbolic, ideological, political and ecological history of the hills.

During these intense moments of strife, of course, the history of the hills has been a crucial part of the history of the African peoples of Zimbabwe as a whole. The late Reader Ncube, then Chairman of Mzingwane District Council, told me in 1988 that armed men had fought decisive battles in the Matopos not only because of their rugged environment. The hills, he said, were the fontanelle of the nation, and the site of the most critical events in its history. Things literally came to a head there – 'when the fighting of 1896 reached the hills peace had to be made; when the guerrilla war of the 1970s reached the hills the whites had to concede; when the dissidents of the 1980s reached the hills the government had to make a settlement.'

The people of the Matopos see themselves as central rather than as remote. They value their special relationship to a unique environment, their 'ownership' of the shrines, their very particular form of agriculture. But they also value their connections with the Ndebele state – commemorated in the hills by Mzilikazi's grave at Entumbane and by the Mzilikazi Memorial; they value their links with adepts of the Mwali cult who live far to the south, to the north and to the east. All this makes the question of 'identity' a fascinating one in the Matopos. The hill people were once 'Banyubi'; there was then a movement into the hills of fragments of all the people who were caught up into the Ndebele state; these fragmented peoples were ruled over in the twentieth century by Ndebele *indunas*; all of them, together with the descendants of the Ndebele regiments stationed around the hills, came to observe the ecological rules of the pre-Ndebele

Mwali cult; in protest against the conservationist ideologues who planned to evict them the people of the hills stressed a political Ndebele identity. Ethnicity in the Matopos has been constantly re-invented and re-imagined. It is a theme which is traced throughout this book.

The book, then, has ceased to be a district study, though I hope it will have a good deal to say about the history of Matobo, as well as of Gwanda and Mzingwane districts. It has become a study of many of the questions crucial to the history of Matabeleland as a whole, and some of those central to the history of Zimbabwe – the right relationship of men and women to the land, of nature to culture; the dynamics of ethnicity; the roots of dissidence and violence; the historical bases of underdevelopment. The Matopos are a 'locality' but they are a very special and privileged locality, to which both in imagination and action people far outside the hills have given significance. I believe that this enables a historian of the Matopos to tell a story which has a resonance far beyond the local.

I hope this book also goes some way to redress a damaging imbalance in Zimbabwean historiography. Together with the forthcoming study of Nkayi and Lupane districts in northern Matabeleland by Jocelyn Alexander, JoAnn McGregor and myself, it documents the modern history of Matabeleland. For far too long the only history of Matabeleland known to Zimbabweans has been the bloody saga of Mzilikazi and Lobengula, with its emphasis on the Ndebele as invaders, raiders and conquerors. This book is about Ndebele-speakers as the conquered but resilient subjects of colonialism. As a stranger to Matabeleland I could not have begun to understand its history without a great deal of help. I owe much to the advice, help and friendship of the leading historian of modern southern Matabeleland, Professor Ngwabi Bhebe.[4] I have also drawn on research by students of the History Department at the University of Zimbabwe.[5] Pathisa Nyathi, author of a recent Sindebele history, lent me an unpublished manuscript about the Matopos.[6] I have enjoyed a most fruitful partnership and debate with other students of southern Matabeleland, especially with Dr Jocelyn Alexander, Dr JoAnn McGregor and Professor Richard Werbner.[7] Jeremy Brickhill gave me his

[4] Professor Bhebe's first book, *Christianity and Traditional Religion in Western Zimbabwe, 1859–1923*, Longman, London, 1979, initiated the study of the interactions between the Mwali shrines and mission Christianity; his *B. Burombo. African Politics in Zimbabwe, 1947–1958*, College Press, Harare, 1989, throws much light on African resistance to eviction in the Matopos and elsewhere; his forthcoming study of the experience of the Lutheran missions of Mberengwa and Gwanda during the 1970s will become a classic among guerrilla war studies.

[5] S. J. Mhabi, 'The Effects of and African Responses to the Land Husbandry Act of 1951 with Special Reference to Ntabazinduna Communal Land', BA Honours thesis, 1984; Sibongile Mlotshwa, 'The Matopos Research Station: Origins and Contribution to the Agrarian Development of Zimbabwe', BA Honours thesis, 1984; T. V. Ncube, 'Aspects of Agrarian Labour in Matabeleland South from 1899 to 1948', BA Honours thesis, 1985; Faith Ntabeni, 'The Under-development of Mzingwane District', BA Honours thesis, 1985; A. R. M. Ruwitah, 'Matopo National Park and Rhodesdale Estate: a Comparative Study of African Under-development in a colonial state, Rhodesia 1890–1960', MA thesis, 1987.

[6] Pathisa Nyathi, *Igugu Likamthwakazi: Imbali Yamandebele, 1820–1893*, Mambo, Gweru, 1994. The unpublished manuscript is a novel about the Matopos which is remarkable for its fusion of royal Ndebele and Mwali cult history.

[7] Richard Werbner's *Tears of the Dead. The Social Biography of an African Family*, International African

material on the guerrilla war in Matobo. Preben Kaarsholm accompanied me on a grand tour of all the shrines in Matobo Communal Area. Wendy Urban-Mead has made available to me her work on the Brethren in Christ in the Matopos.

I was supported at the University of Zimbabwe by the late Mutero Chirenje, by Victor Mashingaidze and by Gilbert Pwiti. As always, the staff at that magnificent institution, the National Archives of Zimbabwe, did everything they could to lay its treasures before me. At the Historical Reference Library in Bulawayo I was helped first by Paddy Vickery and then by Peter Genge. Sir Garfield and Lady Todd have given me much encouragement and hospitality both in Harare and Bulawayo. Judith Todd has shown me unstinting friendship. Yvonne Vera has encouraged me to think that historians as well as novelists can be imaginative creators of past lives. In Matobo I was warmly welcomed by District Administrators Livingstone Mashengele and Lancelot Moyo. In Oxford my numerous seminar papers were energetically debated by Jocelyn Alexander, William Beinart, Jeremy Brickhill, Marieke Clarke, Phyllis Ferguson, JoAnne McGregor, Geoffrey Manase, Stella Makanya, Nyasha Masiwa, David Maxwell, Arthur Mutambara, Bella Mukonyora, Josephine Nhongo, Heike Schmidt, Ossie Stuart and Ken Wilson, among others. They share no blame for my errors and perversities – especially those I have persisted in after their rebuke – but it has been marvellous to share their commitment to and fascination with Zimbabwe.

But overwhelmingly my greatest research debt is to Mark Ncube, friend, oral historian and archivist. Mark made available to me the texts of his own interviews; he carried out interviews for me in Sindebele and translated them into English; he accompanied me on expeditions into the hills and far to the south and the west; he and his wife Judith made me warmly welcome in their home. But he did much more than all this. He became my fellow historian of the hills and though he has no responsibility for the views expressed in this book, it could not have existed without him. In 1994 Mark expressed his love for the hills and their sacred history by applying for and being granted a rocky and forested patch of land in Kumalo Communal Area, within sight of the senior Mwali shrine at Njelele mountain. I hope to be able to visit him there and to go on hearing the voices from the rocks.

This book itself has been long – perhaps too long – in the writing. It has been interrupted several times by other work.[8] It was still unwritten in August 1996, more than ten years after I began work on Matobo. On August 18 I went to climb a new hill in the Matopos Communal Area with Dr Michael Gelman and his wife Ann, great lovers of the mountains and good walking friends. Michael realised that I was having a

---

[7] (cont.) Institute, Edinburgh University Press, 1991, is a classic account of the experience of an extended Kalanga family in twentieth-century southern Matabeleland. Jocelyn Alexander's doctoral thesis, 'The State, Agrarian Policy and Rural Politics in Zimbabwe. Case Studies of Insiza and Chimanimani Districts, 1940–1990', Oxford University, 1993, is a magisterial account of the politics of land.

[8] Most particularly by the research and writing of my family biography, *Are We Not Also Men? The Samkanges and African Politics in Zimbabwe, 1920–64*, James Currey 1995; by the editing of Ngwabi Bhebe and Terence Ranger, eds, *Soldiers in Zimbabwe's Liberation War* and *Society in Zimbabwe's Liberation War*, University of Zimbabwe and James Currey, 1995; and by the research and writing with Jocelyn Alexander and JoAnn McGregor of our study of Nkayi and Lupane districts.

heart attack; walked me down the hill; and after a series of misadventures with burst tyres and inoperative jacks, drove me to the Intensive Care Ward at Mater Dei Hospital in Bulawayo. It is much more than a conventional piety to say that this book would not exist but for Michael.

For two weeks I lay in hospital wondering why this should have happened to me in the Matopos. It had happened too far away from Rhodes's Grave for it to be a plausible spiritual revenge by 'The Founder of Rhodesia'. But nor did I think it was another of Mwali's punishments for white intrusion which are recorded in this book. It was true that Sitwanyana Ncube, charismatic priest at Njelele, had long before prohibited me from entry to the shrine. Mwali would not tolerate anything sharp and bright, he said, like camera and tape recorder. And when I said I would abandon all such equipment, Sitwanyana still refused. 'White *minds* are sharp and bright.' Maybe it was because I had lost something of my sharpness and brightness, but as I dozed in Intensive Care I was sure that I was being supported rather than castigated by the spirits of the hills. Father Odilo Weeger, who erected the great cross that can be seen opposite Rhodes's Grave, came to see me in hospital. 'God is not punishing you, you understand', he told me. 'He is telling you that you can do even greater things with Him than you have done without.' I thought that this probably *was* God's message, in His manifestation as Mwali. I was not being punished for writing this book, but being told to get on with it!

I
Nature & Culture
in the Matopos

1

Seeing the Matopos

The Nineteenth Century

For most white visitors to the Matopos the hills are pre-eminently 'scenery'. When I lectured at the National Gallery in Bulawayo in February 1995 I had the impression that every second member of my audience was a water colourist or landscape painter of the Matopos. To white Rhodesians the Matopos above all other places came to represent Nature; as Eric Nobbs, the author of the first *Guide to the Matopos*, wrote in 1924, the hills were

> a collection of broken masses of granite stretching for some fifty miles north-east and south-west and some twenty-five miles in depth.... The region consists of wild granite hills with narrow gorges in between.... The country is untouched by civilised man and remains in its natural state of wild grandeur, with only occasional kraals and native gardens, just as it has been from time immemorial.[1]

The Matopos country had an unrivalled capacity to touch 'civilised man', in his Rhodesian settler manifestation. The hills became a place of meditation and communion with Nature; more than anywhere else they symbolised the white Rhodesian's special relationship with the landscape. In 1980, when so many Rhodesians left Bulawayo and Matabeleland to go into exile in South Africa, they often took with them a water colour of the Matopos to remind them of what they had lost.[2]

But this sort of intimacy with landscape is not, of course, just given. It has to be worked for. When whites first saw the Matopos in the nineteenth century, they saw a confusing jumble of rocks rather than scenery. It took a long time for whites to turn the

---

[1] Eric Nobbs, *Guide to the Matopos*, Maskew Miller, Cape Town, 1924, pp. iii and 64.
[2] The most poignant expression of these emotions has been provided by the poet and novelist John Eppel, now back in Bulawayo. His collection of poems, *Spoils of War*, which express all the sadness of exile, contain many set in the Matopos. His Bulawayo saturnalia, *Hatchings*, Carrefour, Cape Town, 1993, begins and ends in innocence and peace, at Mtshelele Dam in the Matopos, 'a land in which it always seemed to be afternoon' and 'where there is no joy but calm.' I was told about the brisk business in water colours of the Matopos in 1980 while on an expedition to Matobo Communal Area in January 1995 with Dr and Mrs Gelman, themselves lovers of the hills.

Matopos into landscape and even longer for them to turn them into their own particular beloved place. Meanwhile Africans possessed their own various visions of the hills. I shall devote two chapters to white and black imaginations of the Matopos, the first to the nineteenth century process by which whites 'saw' the hills and the second to the twentieth century process by which they 'appropriated' them.[3]

Water Colourists and the Problem of the Matopos

In the second half of the nineteenth century the route to the capital of the Ndebele state ran through the Matopos. European travellers – hunters, traders, concession-seekers, missionaries – passed through the western edges of the hills, by way of the Mangwe Pass and Manyami's kraal, where they waited for the king's permission to proceed. Then they passed 'through the beautiful and hilly country of the Makalaka' and finally reached 'Matabele ground'.[4] The journey through the 'wild' Matopos – along what was in reality a well-beaten track – provided a chapter in most nineteenth-century travellers' tales of Matabeleland.

But although this part of the Matopos became very familiar to Europeans, they found it difficult to know quite what to make of the hills; to work out how to see them. Some of the nineteenth-century travellers were landscape artists, but they did not paint the Matopos. Thomas Baines, whose pictures have so much shaped our image of nineteenth-century Zimbabwe, passed through the Matopos in 1869 but did not stop to make a sketch. Frank Oates, naturalist and water colourist, journeyed through the hills in 1873 and 1874 but he did not paint them either. Yet both men painted the Victoria Falls, in pursuit of which Oates died of fever.

It is instructive to ask why this should have been. The Falls, one would suppose, are technically more difficult than the hills. But the Falls could be classified in an instantly recognisable category. As Eduard Mohr wrote, in describing the awe of his San guide when they reached the Zambezi: 'The eloquent language of Creation, though it speaks not in words, is intelligible to all nations of the earth!'[5] The Falls, in other words, are one of the rare marvels of Nature which transcend culture and history and are there to be marvelled at and recorded.[6] The hills do not enter this category. They struck the first artist travellers as *almost* picturesque. But to be fully picturesque, and therefore

---

[3] For a general discussion of capitalist and imperial making of the landscape see D. Cosgrove, *Social Formation and Symbolic Landscape*, Barnes and Noble, New York, 1985. A particularly stimulating discussion of a Zimbabwean case is Heike Schmidt, 'Penetrating Foreign Lands: Contestations over African Landscapes. A Case Study from Eastern Zimbabwe', *Environment and History*, 1, 3, October 1995. A first version of what follows is Terence Ranger, 'Making Zimbabwean Landscapes: Painters, Projectors and Priests', *Paideuma*, 43, 1997.

[4] John Smith Moffat's journal, 30 August 1863, MO 1/1/6, National Archives, Zimbabwe. All files cited hereafter are in the National Archives unless otherwise stated.

[5] Eduard Mohr, *To the Victoria Falls of the Zambesi*, Sampson Low, London, 1876, p. 318.

[6] It was pointed out to me in Harare by Pip Curling that pictures of the Victoria Falls were in high demand in nineteenth-century Europe and hence very much worth painting. There was no such European demand for pictures of the Matopos.

paintable as landscape, they needed something which seemed lacking to European eyes. They needed a castle, or a hermitage, or some of the other signs of culture and history which marked the great nineteenth-century paintings of the picturesque. Without such human signs the Matopos were hard to see.

Frank Oates is the most illuminating guide here. Oates was a Fellow of the Royal Geographical Society, and a traveller to Guatemala and California before his Southern African expedition. He was also a proficient water colourist. His diary shows him in deep debate and confusion about the Matopos. In September 1873, as he approached the hills from the south, he wrote:

> What a wonderful difference is made to one's feelings by fine scenery! South Africa is sadly dull and monotonous, and I believe the influence is a bad one, and the loss of scenery has a depressing effect on one's spirits; one's imagination is never called into play.

The Matopos almost, but not quite, brought Oates out of this aesthetic depression. 'There is something here which might remind one a little of Central America', he noted at Mangwe, 'but somehow the charm is wanting.' Next day 'there was a lovely moon as we trekked, but after all it is South Africa and one cannot feel poetical'.[7] Still, by 13 September he was into the Matopos proper and was forced to admit that there was 'really fine country here; kopjes on every side, rising into fine crags, with huge stones strewed on the ground. In the distance more ranges of kopjes are to be seen, becoming blue against the horizon.' He noted that 'S could have made a picture here', but he was not yet ready to make one himself.[8]

On his return journey in January and February 1874 the Matopos further undermined his scepticism. On 29 January 'we went through some really beautiful scenery ... The sun set and the sunset was a lovely one. I can now fancy that South Africa may have much fine scenery.' He began to see the hills in terms of colour:

> In the foreground was undulating and broken ground, covered with long grass, showing in some places a silver white colour, in others a yellow, and in others a green one. Beyond, the deep green of the trees ... rose distinct against the deep violet kopjes on the horizon and the sunset sky. The upper part of the sky was blue with large lilac clouds; lower down, the blue was streaked with pale yellow, and this again, as it approached the kopjes, became golden streaked with lilac ... and ere the sunset hue had faded from the sky, the moon was shedding a clear light over the romantic scene.

Oates even came on a 'lovely spot' where the 'ground was open and park-like'.

On 1 February he came close to surrender. Man was vile – Africans he thought 'to a man dishonest, lazy and impudent.' But all in Nature pleased. 'The scenery about here *is* pretty, I admit', he wrote,

> [and] wakened a little enthusiasm and thoughts of former days, such as the usual dull uniformity of South African scenery fails to elicit. The ground is broken up into rugged crags, piled one upon the other in such a manner that you can't help wondering how the mischief they ever got there.

[7] C. G. Oates, ed., *Frank Oates, Matabeleland and the Victoria Falls*, Kegan Paul, Trench and Co, London, 1889, pp. 46–7.
[8] *Ibid.*, p. 55.

But Oates was still not enthusiastic enough to paint the hills.[9]

Thomas Baines had less metaphysical reasons for his failure to make a pictorial record of the Matopos. Baines was an adventurer rather than a naturalist, and a concession seeker before he was a painter. (It was no accident that his Rhodesian master work is that great projector's picture of Henry Hartley discovering gold beside the corpse of a huge elephant – a true icon of man's dominance over animate and inanimate Nature.) As he passed through the mountains in 1869 he was hurrying to reach Lobengula to extract a gold mining concession. So although 'some of the scenes presented at various turnings of the road were indeed most beautiful, and I would fain have sketched them, the rate at which we are travelling forbids any attempt of that kind.' Baines rested content with word pictures in which, significantly enough, he imported castles and church furniture into the 'hill scenery':

> Our road lay over an undulating country between granite hills, some of which were of considerable magnitude and most picturesque form, grey or sometimes nearly white masses of rock rising like gigantic pillars, pinnacles or castles, while others were balanced like immense logans (rocking-stones), while their rugged sides were in some places bare and grey and in others clad with thick forest.... A rock, almost as perfectly simulating an eagle as some of the brass lecterns in our churches, was balanced on another rock, on apparently as small a base as the real bird would require to stand upon.[10]

If the African inhabitants of the Matopos had neglected to build castles or to carve eagles, Baines and other European travellers were prepared to let erosion and imagination do the job for them. In 1876 Eduard Mohr described the Matopos as a 'sea of rocks' out of which stood 'solitary rocks, looking like half-fallen towers or huge old deserted fortresses.'[11] As E. P. Mathers contemplated the Matopos in 1891, he was led to historicise them for himself, since Africans, he thought, had not done so:

> You begin to enter the seething mass of granite kopjes; it has been likened to a storm-tossed sea of granite ... sometimes looking like the ruins of old castles perched on crags unassailable by aught but time. Then others take the fantastic shape of animals, or stand up like obelisk monuments.[12]

Missionaries and the Problem of the Matopos

For the painter, land needed historical and cultural associations in order to become landscape. For the missionaries it needed to be redeemed before it could be admired.

[9] *Ibid.*, p. 125.
[10] J. P. R. Wallis, ed., *The Northern Goldfields Diaries of Thomas Baines, 1869–1872*, Chatto and Windus, London, 1946, pp. 66–7. For an illuminating discussion of Baines's 'preoccupation with the picturesque' and his 'difficulty' in 'articulating frontier space in picturesque terms' see P. R. Anderson, 'The Human Clay: An Essay in the Spatial History of the Cape Eastern Frontier, 1811–1835', M. Litt. thesis, Oxford, 1993, pp. 73–5.
[11] Mohr, *To the Victoria Falls*, p. 187.
[12] E. P. Mathers, *Zambesia. England's El Dorado in Africa*, London, 1891, p. 188.

The London Missionary Society pioneer, T. M. Thomas, believed that failure by African man to master the environment had left it delightfully but immorally 'natural', literally in a state of original sin. There was 'no park, nor even a road of any description' to be seen; 'no traces of art, or even of civilization', Mzilikazi's own court being 'primitive in the extreme' and swallowed up 'in the forest.' But:

> Among these [Amadobo] mountains, there are countless hills and dales, cliffs and deep ravines, perennial fountains and wandering brooks, green fields of pasturage and gardens, full of ripe maize, and various indigenous grains.... And while the beauty of the scene entrances the lover of nature, and leads even the Christian to forget, for the time, the moral and spiritual waste, the latter soon feels his spirit stirred within him [and longs for] these dark places of the earth [to be] filled with the knowledge of the Lord.[13]

The Jesuit missionaries, entering Matabeleland by way of the Matopos in 1879, saw their evangelical task as bringing Christian culture into unredeemed and primeval Nature, thus freeing Africans from their abject dependence on it. The Jesuits became aware that the hills were the site of an African religion – the oracular cult of the High God, Mwali – but so far from humanising the Matopos in their eyes, this diabolised the landscape:

> This God lives in a subterranean cave in a labyrinth of rocks.... In this cave is a deep, black well, the well of the abyss. From time to time dull sounds like thunder come forth from this well. The faithful trembling with fear, place offerings on the edge of the abyss – wheat, corn, poultry, cakes and other gifts – to appease the hunger of the terrible God and to make him propitious.... They seek information about hidden things, future happenings, the names of people who have bewitched them.... After a few moments of deep silence, they hear, in the midst of the subterranean noises, inarticulate sounds, strange words, broken and incomprehensible, which the accomplices of the makers of thunder explain to the credulous devotees ... This is the bliss of the children of nature ... the people whose beliefs, ideas, traditions, habits and customs, we must attempt to change completely.... It is obvious that we shall meet with terrible opposition, with an uprising of primeval passions.[14]

These were voices from the rocks which the Jesuits had no desire to interpret.

Instead they took steps to claim the Matopos for Christ. They offered their first Mass in a cave in the hills, as an artefact of Christian culture and a promise of salvation for unredeemed Nature:

> There, with an altar of rock and the 700 foot pyramid as canopy, we offered to God the sacred sacrifice of Calvary. At that solemn moment it seemed that the mountain itself, together with the Holy Angels surrounding us, was trembling with joy and adoring the Eucharistic God.[15]

The Jesuits passed on, and for nearly twenty years the Matopos were left to their 'terrible God'. But when missionaries returned to the hills, their vision was much the

[13] T. M. Thomas, *Eleven Years in Central Africa*, Snow, London, 1872, pp. 64 and 81.
[14] Letter of 28 March 1880, *Journey to Gubulawayo. Letters of Frs H. Depelchin and C. Crooneberghs, S.J., 1879, 1880, 1881*, ed., R. S. Roberts, Books of Rhodesia, Bulawayo, 1979, pp. 264–5.
[15] *Ibid.*, Letter of 28 August 1879, p. 155. For an account of Christian appropriation of an African landscape, see Terence Ranger, 'Taking Hold of the Land: Holy Places and Pilgrimages in Twentieth Century Zimbabwe', *Past and Present*, 117, November 1987, pp. 158–84.

same. Frances Davidson of the Brethren in Christ mission, arriving in the eastern
Matopos in July 1898 to establish what became the Matopo Mission, noted first that
they had been placed in 'a beautiful valley among the Matoppa Hills' and second that
the inhabitants were 'sunk so low in sin and degradation'. Hence their arrival had made
'the devil angry because his stronghold in these Matoppos is being assailed and [he] is
raging in his fury.'[16]

African Landscapes in the Matopos

Underlying the responses of both travellers and missionaries was the belief that the
African inhabitants of the Matopos were making no use of the hills. No roads, no parks,
no towns, no mines, no castles, no cathedrals, no attempts to exploit the forests – in
short, no command over Nature. It worried Europeans that Africans seemed to have
left no mark on the hills. Because of this, it was assumed that Africans could not possess
any objective view of the Matopos as landscape. 'The eyes of a heathen tribe are
holden', wrote the missionary, Carnegie, about the Ndebele, 'for they see no beauty or
variety in earth or sky. The book of Nature is shut up and sealed; there is no music in
the moaning of the wind ... nor loveliness in the golden-tinted sunsets. Nature's
messengers inspire only fear and distrust'.[17]

Some nineteenth-century European observers were perceptive enough to see that
the Banyubi people of the hills were rich in cattle and reaped good crops. But they
knew nothing of the history of these cattle owners and cultivators. Nor did they know
that hunter-gatherers had left many marks on the hills. Baines knew all about 'Bushmen
paintings' in South Africa – one of his most virtuoso works being a reproduction of
'Bushmans Krantz, Baviaans River', complete with its cave paintings of men and
animals.[18] In the Cape the 'Bushman' had resisted settler occupation fiercely, and their
caves were thought of as bandit lairs. In the Matopos San peoples had long been
replaced or assimilated by African cultivators, and nineteenth-century white travellers
caught no echo of them. This was ironic. Baines and Oates didn't paint in the Matopos
but generations of San *had* painted there.

The long-sighted pre-historian may remark that 'it is only in the last 150,000 years
or so that people have consistently used the hills', but this is certainly long enough to
give the Matopos a lived-in feel. Even the 14,000 years in which 'people began to focus
increasingly on the local resource strengths' and to make the hills 'a focus for human
settlement' with 'a relatively dense and stable population' offers an adequate time-
depth. Zimbabwe's oldest human skeleton – a woman found at Nswatugi cave – dates
back some 10,000 years. For thousands of years, in short, the Matopos have offered an

---

[16] Entries for 5 June and 14 September 1898, Frances Davidson Diaries, Volume 3, pp. 51 and 54. I am much
indebted to E. Morris Sider, Archivist of the Brethren in Christ, for this reference.

[17] D. Carnegie, *Among the Matabele*, Religious Tract Society, London, 1894, p. 43.

[18] This painting is reproduced in David Bunn, 'Our Wattled Cot. Mercantile and Domestic Space in Thomas
Pringle's African Landscapes', W. J. T. Mitchell, ed., *Landscape and Power*, Chicago, 1994, p. 159.

extraordinarily rich environment – 'a mosaic of some 8 different habitat types ... a wide range of plant and animal food resources [is still] available in the area today ... at least 60 edible plant species of primarily fruit-bearing trees.' The cave paintings began in this environment some ten thousand years ago.[19]

But it is hard to know in what way the cave paintings reflect their context. Peter Garlake asserts that

> the granite country of Zimbabwe provides surroundings of extraordinary variety and splendour ... Every hill in sight seems to have a more dramatic and extraordinary shape than its neighbour ... It takes little imagination to recreate the landscape of the painters themselves. This landscape was the setting of the paintings.[20]

But it is more difficult to tell how the painters saw that landscape.

Their paintings are not in any sense landscape paintings. As Garlake writes, 'space is never suggested. Conventional perspective ... is, of course, not found. There is no landscape background to any painting.' Garlake suggests that the paintings do not set out to mirror nature, but to control it. He asserts that they express 'supernatural potency' and the urge 'to control many aspects of the natural world, from rain to animals.'[21]

Nick Walker points out that the painters did not even reflect the animal species which were common in the hills and on which they themselves lived. They focused on big game – giraffe, koodoo, etc. – which they rarely were able to kill. The paintings are more about masculine status than they are about the fauna of the Matopos.[22] In short, the paintings were a way of mastering nature rather than being subjected to it.

The fruits of the Matopos attracted cultivators and stock keepers as well as hunter-gatherers. By the third century AD the people of the caves were interacting with the people of the homesteads.[23] The first farmers we can identify, however, are the Banyubi, whose descendants still live in the Matopos today. Banyubi groups have been in the hills for at least four hundred years. According to their oral traditions, they were at first attracted to the Matopos because they 'had plenty of *mapfura* (marula nuts)' – a reminder that farmers are gatherers too. To this day the inhabitants of the hills say that they provide unique nourishment and can feed their people even when drought has destroyed crops. '*Dombo linetshilenga*, the rocks have something to offer. One would not fail to get a water melon at least. The hills are fruitful.'[24]

But in most years there is plenty of water in the hills too, with perennial pools and

[19] N. J. Walker, 'Late Stone Age Research in the Matopos', *South African Archaeological Bulletin*, 35, 131, June 1980; 'Dassie Hunters of the Matobo Hills', *Zimbabwe Wildlife*, June 1989.

[20] Peter Garlake, *The Painted Caves*, Modus, Harare, 1987, pp. 3, 9 and 63.

[21] *Ibid*, pp. 3, 9, 63. Garlake's argument is based on studies of San myth and ritual in desert country, which plainly have limitations in helping us to enter into their visions of the hills. Although rain is just as important to hunter-gatherers as it is to farmers and herders, and despite all the work that has been done on the Stone Age archaeology of the Matopos, we know nothing of San rain rituals there.

[22] Nick Walker, 'Dassie Hunters of the Matobo Hills', p. 23.

[23] Walker, 'Late Stone Age Research in the Matopos'.

[24] Interview with Denge Sibindi Mbezhi, Kumalo, 26 July 1988. Mbezhi is a Nyubi, a hereditary messenger to the Dula Mwali shrine and custodian of the Mashakambayo cave.

springs and with the granite rocks acting as water-courses. As the oral historian of the Matopos, Dawson Munjeri, writes: 'The *sipiti* (small springs of water) provided good pasturage which in turn encouraged the Nyubi to keep large herds of cattle'.[25] A prosperous agriculture grew up in the valleys and on the *vleis*. E. P. Mathers, whose imported castles and obelisks I cited above, noticed in passing that the Banyubi possessed numerous, if small, cattle, and that

> their mealie gardens in the rich soil of these valleys produce good crops. Their method of cultivation is to cut down the trees to within three feet of the ground, or merely to strip the lower bark and so kill the tree. They thus obtain the necessary light; then with their mattocks they raise the ground into ridge and furrow two feet high and the same apart. On the ridges they plant corn. The Shashani River has water still running through rocky pools and the large mealie gardens on its banks testify to the richness of the soil.[26]

The Banyubi certainly *used* the hills. But usable arable and grazing was widely scattered. As Munjeri writes: 'The settlements in the Matombo were small though numerous and so co-ordination by the rulers was not easy.' There were no powerful chiefs in the Matopos nor large chiefly towns. Successive state systems based themselves close to the mountains and exercised devolved authority over them – the Torwa state, the Rozwi Mambos, the Ndebele state under Mzilikazi and Lobengula. Except in times of emergency, the dominant peoples of these states did not live in the Matopos. But they also used the hills. They extracted either in tribute or trade the various products of the Banyubi – grain, cattle and iron hoes or spears.[27] And they imposed themselves by renaming the rocks.

When Eric Nobbs produced the first guide to the Matopos in 1924 he included a section on 'The Names of the Hills'. His list contains Banyubi names; Rozwi names; Ndebele names. Nobbs recorded several name changes. The Banyubi 'Ntabakaikingwa', or 'the hill which is not to be pointed out', became Fumukwe. Later, under the Europeans, it became Mount Francis. Igambinga became Ingwena. In other cases, as with Bambata hill, old names were retained but were explained by new stories, involving the Ndebele kings. (Mzilikazi is said to have found himself unable to descend Bambata hill and to have been 'obliged to climb down on all fours, in doing which he caressed the hill with his hands, *ugubambata* in Zulu.')[28] White appropriation by renaming, which I record in the next chapter, was merely the latest in a series of appropriations of the hills. When I interviewed Headman Mnindwa Moyo in Gulati Communal Area in 1988, he told me that he knew all the old Banyubi names but used the Sindebele ones. 'This hill here has a Banyubi name which means a man without

---

[25] Dawson Munjeri, 'Oral Traditions and the Matopo Hills', in C. K. Cooke, *The Matopo Hills. A guide*, National Museums and Monuments of Zimbabwe, Harare, 1986, p. 11.

[26] E. P. Mathers, *Zambesia. England's El Dorado in Africa*, 1891, p. 188.

[27] For iron working in the Matopos see C. K. Cooke, 'Account of Iron-smelting Techniques Once Practiced by the Manyubi of the Matobos District of Rhodesia', *South African Archaeology Bulletin*, 21, Part 2, 82, June 1966.

[28] Nobbs, *Guide to the Matopos*, pp. 84–92. Nobbs points out that the word for 'pat' was in fact the same in Banyubi as in Sindebele.

covering. That's my language you see, but I don't wish it to be taught to the people'. He didn't wish it because everyone in the Matopos now spoke Sindebele and to recall the old names would be to divide the people into competing identities.[29]

And if chiefs and kings did not build towns or towers in the Matopos, they certainly made use of the rocks and caves themselves for their memorials. 'The bones of the rulers of the indigenous natives (not the Matabele) were placed in a cave [in the Matopos] known as Murindidzimu, the bones being covered with stones.'[30] Mzilikazi himself was buried in Entumbane cave, a 'cleft among great boulders situated on the very edge of the hills overlooking the Umzingwane valley.' His personal bodyguard, the Inyati regiment, was appointed guard of honour at the grave, to keep away intruders, to prevent veld fires and to sing the King's praise songs. 'Black cattle too were regularly sacrificed to his spirit and mourners paid pilgrimages.'[31]

When the white travellers and painters passed through the hills, then, and thought them so unsubdued by the human imagination, they were ignoring millennia of occupation, centuries of cultivation, the paintings in the caves, the graves and the places of pilgrimage. They did not ignore, as we have seen, the existence of cave shrines, but they interpreted these as evidence of the fearful tyranny of Nature. In fact, had they listened to the voices from the shrines, they would have been presented with an African perception of landscape.

Religion and Landscape in the Matopos

The unique formation of the Matopos makes them a natural site for rain shrines. The hills are full of pools and springs; they are the source of the rivers of southern Matabeleland; thunder and lightning are yet more terrifying and impressive among the granite crags and whale-backs. Yet to the south and north lie areas of uncertain rainfall, subject to periodic drought.

It is hardly surprising that a Shona myth of 'the creation of water' is situated in the Matopos. God's messenger, Mudzanapabwe, came into a 'hot and dry' country, where 'nothing grew, and there were no animals or any other living things.' God had provided him with a bow and arrows and a red needle, and had told him to remember 'that there is life in the big rocks.' So:

Standing on a rock he stamped his foot, and at once a large dust-cloud rose to the sky. Mudzanapabwe looked up and saw huge rocks towering in the heavens ... He shot an arrow into the sky which hit a rock. There was a great noise, the heavens shook, and the rocks turned black. Mudzanapabwe shot once more at the rocks but this time the red needle sewed together the large rocks and the land in which Mudzanapabwe now lived. Then it started to rain and went on raining until the whole country was flooded. Mudzanapabwe was at a loss

[29] Interview with Mnindwa Moyo, Gulati, 21 July 1988. Gulati itself comes from the Banyubi 'Guwa Lati', 'The cave has said we should do so and so', Interview with Obadiah Mlilo, Mpopoma, 3 August 1988.
[30] W. R. Benzies, 'Funeral of Cecil John Rhodes', *Native Affairs Department Annual*, 1964, p. 38.
[31] Nobbs, *Guide to the Matopos*, p. 38.

what to do and again shot an arrow into the sky. This separated earth and heaven again. The rain stopped and trees, grass and vegetables began to grow.

The rocks remained 'stitched' to the land, but where 'the needles had made a seam, rivers formed.'[32]

There have probably been rain ceremonies in the Matopos for thousands of years. Garlake believes that many of the cave paintings were linked with rain making.[33] Agricultural peoples performed rain dances in the hills, sometimes in the painted caves, long before the establishment of the Mwali shrines. R. N. Hall, Rhodesia's first pre-historian, found that the Banyubi regarded many hills in the Matopos as 'rain-dance hills'.[34] Tredgold's *The Matopos* reported that 'rain dances are held in various parts of the hills' and quoted a 'very old' informant:

> The dancers were young girls about twelve years old who wore a small apron only when they danced; old women danced, too. They danced to the music of drums and woman clapped their hands, whistles were not allowed. All the men had to go away when the dance was on. As they danced, they threw water up into the air.

Tredgold's conjecture that 'this ceremony has roots far back in the past and is very much older than the Mlimo [Mwali] cult' seems a reasonable one.[35]

These rain dances of pre-pubertal and post-menopausal Banyubi women continued into the twentieth century side by side with the more elaborate rituals of the Mwali shrines. In December 1913 the Native Commissioner, Fort Usher, reported that people were fearful of a third year of drought. 'About 50 women and girls assembled near this office 10.12.13 and went through the *Amabizana* ceremony for rain and similar dances have taken place in many other parts of the district.'[36] When I visited Nswatugi cave – with its San paintings and its evidence of ten thousand years of occupation – in September 1985, the guard told me that in the early 1960s, when he was young, 'women from the villages used to come to Nswatugi to rain-dance in the cave and present beer, but now all villages have been removed and no-one comes. Old women still perform ceremonies at Silozwane cave, where my grandmother used to be custodian.' Neither Nswatugi nor Silozwane had been Mwali shrines.[37]

Nevertheless, by the time that Baines and Oates and Thomas and the Jesuits entered

---

[32] Herbert Aschwanden, *Karanga Mythology*, Mambo, Gweru, 1990, p. 11. The 'Karanga' live to the east of the Matopos but send messengers there regularly. Aschwanden stresses that 'real rocks' figure in this myth, which refers to 'the Matopo Hills (a mountain-range in the south-west)'. He adds that by 'life in the rocks' the 'water in the Matopo caves is meant as well as the rain-clouds.'

[33] There may have been a continuity between hunter-gatherer and agricultural rain ceremonies. Thus Matthew Schoffeleers has argued that the Mbona rain cult in southern Malawi originated in hunter-gatherer times. J. M. Schoffeleers, *River of Blood, The Genesis of a Martyr Cult in Southern Malawi, c. AD 1600*, University of Wisconsin Press, Madison, 1992.

[34] Nobbs, *Guide to the Matopos*, p. 63.

[35] Robert Tredgold, ed., *The Matopos*, Federal Department of Printing, Salisbury, 1956, p. 85. Tredgold speculates that 'because of its hold on the minds of the ordinary people, the organisers of the Mlimo cult grafted this very ancient fertility cult on to the more spiritual aspects of their own observances.'

[36] Monthly Report, Fort Usher, December 1913, N 9/4/27.

[37] Interview with Malaki Sithole, Nswatugi, 1 September 1985.

the Matopos, the hills were the home of the wide-ranging oracular cult of the High God, Mwali. The senior shrine, Njelele, lay on the south-western edge of the hills; two other important shrines, Dula and Dzilo, operated in the eastern Matopos. Scholars are divided on the antiquity of this cult. Tredgold thought that it 'came to these hills well over five hundred years ago',[38] and the oral traditions of the cult's interaction with the various state systems of western Zimbabwe suggest such a long history. Julian Cobbing argues that the Mwali cult only came into the Matopos from Vendaland in the nineteenth century.[39] I incline myself to the view that the Mwali cult is many centuries old. But the important thing is that at whatever date the Mwali shrines developed in the hills, the cult came to express the essence of their extraordinary landscape.

The rocks of the Matopos became a symbol of God's endurance – 'It always has to be a stone', the Njelele adept, Obed Masuku, told me. 'A stone can keep something better. A tree rots.'[40] The great rocks stand for Mwali's authority – 'No-one can rule this country unless he comes to the rock', the priests say. In the cult's myths, the Voice of Mwali – which in fact sounded from within the shrine caves – speaks from the rock itself. A myth of Mwali's return to earth, after a period of withdrawal and punishment, tells how Mwali took pity on creation, 'and then the sky became pregnant by the clouds and God's voice came like a needle which sewed up the earth, and a stone began to speak.'[41]

Yet, stable as they seemed, the rocks could not be easily grasped. One of the praise-names of Njelele mountain was *Dombo letshipoteleka*, the shifting or turning rock. Adepts today comment how different it looks as one walks round it; the variety of meanings which it communicates. But no-one can, should, walk right round Njelele on pain of death; no human should aspire to grasp its full meaning. The rock walls above the cave compel submission; gentler slopes draw pilgrims up to the dancing ground on the summit, where they pitch their fires around the perennial pools. Particularly dramatic messages are communicated when rocks break away from the summit of a hill and come crashing down – the shrine of Bembe in the eastern Matopos was founded in 1964 because its priestess first dreamt that a great rock would fall and then went to tend the rock when her dream came true.[42]

---

[38] Tredgold, *The Matopos*, p. 82.

[39] Julian Cobbing, 'The Ndebele Under the Khumalos, 1820 to 1896', PhD thesis, University of Lancaster, 1976, Chapter 6, 'Ndebele Religion'. Cobbing relied heavily upon the 1968 research of District Commissioner I. C. Cockcroft, a condensed version of which was published in *NADA*, 10, 4. However, in 1973 another Internal Affairs official, A. Latham, drew up a 'Shamanism Book' to inform administrators on African religion. He thought Cockcroft had made a 'penetrating investigation', but nevertheless found that the 'Mwari cult in the Matopo hills is of great antiquity ... associated with a very great past.' I consulted the 'Shamanism Book' in the office of the District Administrator, Esigodini.

[40] Interview with Obed Masuku, 19 July 1989.

[41] Aschwanden, *Karanga Mythology.*, p. 217.

[42] Annual Report, Umzingwane, 1969; *Chronicle*, 1 June 1971; *Sunday News Magazine*, 26 October/8 November 1988. Mark Ncube and I visited Bembe on 27 July 1989 and interviewed the priestess, Mdingene Ncube, and her husband, Melusi Sibanda. She told how she had three times dreamed of a great rock falling; how she had informed the chief; how he had summoned her when the rock fell from Bembe hill; how her rain-making powers were then tested by the District Commissioner and she made so much rain that he begged her to stop. Melusi Sibanda took us to the shrine which is formed by the overhang of

The rocks were not only solid and massive but also, against all expectation, they gave water. 'Water from the rock' became the key metaphor of God's mercy. A variant creation myth tells how Musikavanhu, Mwali's emissary, fell from the heavens to land 'softly onto a white stone. The first spot his feet touched softened and emitted water. Touching the stone, Musikavanhu heard God's voice coming from it. This place became the stone of the pool (*mabwe adziva*, today called Matopos).'[43] A Mwali praise poem, collected in 1935, hails God as 'the stone from which the rain comes ... the great pool from which mist rises when one stirs the water.'[44] The perennial pools in the shrine caves are identified with the uterus and amniotic fluid of a pregnant woman, and as the source of all life. 'When people in the Matopos pray for fertility the seed is sprinkled with water from the cave. It is water of life, they say, for it comes from the rock, and so from God.'[45]

A young Zimbabwean scholar, Oliver Zvabva, has analysed the landscape of an oracular cave, not this time in the Matopos, but at Nyachiranga on the mountain frontier between north-eastern Zimbabwe and Mozambique. In a cave in Nyachiranga mountain is heard the Voice of Dzivaguru, eastern Zimbabwe's High God. Zvabva describes what the cave contains:

> The structures inside the cave are very symbolic and have a bearing on agricultural fertility. In the cave is a stream which has its source in the cave, which flows into a ninga, or bottomless pit; a Baobab tree; a dome-shaped pillar; mipfura trees with bee-hives; two expansive rock dwalas, one close to the entrance and the other at the far back of the cave.

He adds:

> In the cave, scenery is attractive, full of life: biological as well as social. It has an independent existence, hence paradisial – like Adam in the Garden of Eden, the people are seen living in a paradise of their own.[46]

Of course, I have quoted Zvabva because of his invocation of the 'alien' ideas of 'scenery' and of 'paradise'. But he uses them legitimately to make his point. *This* cave is not a place where fearful, trembling and credulous worshippers turn their back on landscape to propitiate the terrible God of the abyss. It is, writes, Zvabva, 'natural, undomesticated' but also the 'source of all biological and social life'. It is the focus of history – past chiefs are buried in the *ninga*; the stone in the cave 'stands as the seat of the Voice, the centre of all instructions, and the highest point of authority.' Many of

---

[42] (cont.) the fallen rock, around which a stockade has been erected. The *Chronicle* of 23 October 1967 described a rain ceremony at Bembe on 22 October, attended by hundreds of people, including the leaders of the Nyanga Association of Central Africa. The Voice of Mwali was heard speaking from the rock at Bembe as late as the mid-1980s.

[43] Aschwanden, *Karanga Mythology*, p. 31.

[44] F. W. T. Posselt, *Fact and Fiction*, Bulawayo, 1935, pp. 80 ff.

[45] Aschwanden, *Karanga Mythology*, p. 217.

[46] Oliver Zvabva, 'Nyachiranga Regional Cult', BA Honours thesis, Religious Studies, University of Zimbabwe, November 1988.

these instructions concern people's relations with and obligations to the land. The cave is the nucleus of a living and active landscape.[47]

All these points can be made for the Matopos shrines. They possess their own interior landscapes of pools and rocks and trees. They are 'natural'. People possessed by the cult spirits sweep the shrines with their hands and not with brooms; stone tools rather than metal one are used to cut grass.[48] Their priests mount to the heights clad in skins:

> The right man should put on leopard skins and stay in the hills with the leopards. He should not even plough, let alone trade.... A priest at Njelele should not cut his hair. When you look at him you'd think he was a madman. He should be able to patrol the Matopos and leopards wouldn't touch him. Even the baboons he could control.[49]

Sitwanyana Ncube, several times chief priest at Njelele, speaks of his induction, spending 'three months living with a lion, leopard, baboon, snake in Sihazabana cave ... where I was taught the traditions of the shrine. I was talking directly to a snake which is the one which showed me all the caves.'[50]

Yet this entry to a state of nature empowered the priest or priestess to guarantee the prosperity of agriculture. This was symbolised in the test, reportedly still carried out, to determine the true successor as guardian of the shrine. The most vivid account among many comes from Thenjiwe Lesabe:

> A number of those who claim to be possessed are put together in a house. Certain words are pronounced ... and they are each given rapoko seed to hold in their hands. They must not open their hands. There are men who are put to guard, actually guarding like a soldier guards the king, on twenty-four hours guard, that these people don't open their hands. Even if you want to go and wee-wee you must ask for permission. You are escorted. In the morning there are certain things that happen. This man is heard screaming, whatnot, and when they open his hand they find the rapoko is germinated. This is the person who takes responsibility for the shrine.[51]

The 'natural' guardians at the 'natural' shrine control the environment. 'There were areas considered sacred, hence no cultivation could take place – *inyutha*, a swampy area. These swamps were used to determine whether the rains would fall or not.'[52] At Njelele, says Obed Masuku, lions used to be on guard. The Voice of Mwali would tell the people: 'You can drink from this water but not from that, that is for my wild animals. You can cut trees here but not there. If anyone had a project with land he would have to acknowledge that the land is Mwali's and put it up to Him.'[53]

The shrine guardians also control agriculture. Seeds soaked in the water of the rock are bound to be fertile. The shrines lay it down when planting can start and where;

---

[47] The close parallels between Nyachiranga cave and the Matopos shrines suggest that there is no need to invoke a Venda origin to explain the character of the Mwali cult. The Venda anthropologist, Victor Ralushai, insists that the worship of Mwali orginated among 'the Kalanga' and not in Vendaland.

[48] Interview between Mark Ncube and Obed Masuku, Bulawayo, 17 July 1989.

[49] Interview with Michael Ncube, Hlekweni, 21 July 1989.

[50] Interview with Sitwanyana Ncube, Mguza, 28 July 1988.

[51] Interview with Mrs Tenjiwe Lesabe, Bulawayo, 24 August 1988.

[52] Interview with Sitwanyana Ncube, Njelele, 19 August 1988.

[53] Interview with Obed Masuku, 19 July 1988.

where fire can be used for clearing the land and where not; what the rest days shall be; when harvesting shall commence. Even today in Matobo Communal Area in the eastern hills, where several shrines and sub-shrines interact with each other, the old controls still persist. In September 1988 Mark Ncube and I held a group interview there, arranged for us by the late Reader Ncube. Everyone agreed that the major prohibitions and injunctions of the cult are still followed. People do not plough or do any other field work on the Wednesday *chisi* rest day, and if anyone breaks the veto they are taken before the chief and fined, perhaps having their ox team and plough confiscated for a month. One is not supposed to plough in the first rains, or if there is a storm, or in the period from the last quarter of the moon to its first quarter. In each area there is an individual who inherits the role of *isitunywa*, or seed bearer. He collects seeds from everyone in his neighbourhood and hands them to a *hosana*, or shrine messenger, who in turn takes them to the shrine, where they are soaked in the water of the rock. The seeds are then returned, and the planting year begins with samples from the seeds of the whole neighbourhood being mixed together for sowing in a special field at the chief's or headman's place. The interrelation of the shrines is important to the success of the harvest. One shrine, Dula, represents Mwali in the male aspect; another shrine, Dzilo, represents the female aspect. Mwali as male rests in Bazubatumba grove on his way to the female shrine: the grove is protected from cutting or fire.[54]

Mwali's Voice from the rock issued commands and prohibitions which determined the whole pattern of land use in the Matopos:

> Njelele used to lay down everything – when to plant, when to eat certain plants, when to reap. In those days you didn't harvest until early August when the corn was really dry and mature. The land was protected for longer, the cattle did not stray on the land.[55]

Agriculture in the pre-colonial Matopos depended on the *vleis* and other wetlands. *Vlei* farmers used bedding and ridging systems in order to retain moisture and prevent flow and gully erosion. This involved 'an enormous investment of labour', largely performed by young men. Control of wet lands and of the labour of young men was the basis of differentiation of wealth and power. Young men worked for their fathers-in-law rather than paying bride-price: elders demanded 'the manual labour rather than the goods of the intended husband who has, in most cases, to till the ground of his future father-in-law for years.'[56]

Colonial agricultural officers fenced the *vleis* and prosecuted those who cultivated or grazed them. But the Mwali shrines monitored their use. The Matopos *vleis* are dry

---

[54] Group interview at Kumbudzi Clinic, Matobo Communal Area, 10 September 1988.

[55] Interview with Michael Ncube, Hlekweni, 21 July 1989. Ncube is Director of the Hlekweni Training Centre, a Catholic, a Kalanga and a trained agronomist. He contrasts 'the laws of Njelele' to modern 'scientific' agriculture, much to the advantage of the former. 'Now people harvest by May. We no longer get direction from Njelele so everything is chaos.'

[56] Annual Report, Malema, March 1898, NBE 7/1/1. Ken Wilson, 'The Importance of Vlei Farming in the Nineteenth Century', *ms*, n.d. As late as 1956 colonial officers, making a survey of the Matobo Reserve, described 'the local tribes' as having been 'in the habit of planting on ridges', by contrast with the Ndebele cultivation of 'one main food crop grown on the flat.' Provincial Agriculturalist, etc. to Provincial Native Commissioner, 1 October 1956, Internal Affairs, Box 100356.

from May to July; from August to October 'water begins to run from the rocks'; then in the rainy season they become waterlogged. Under the Mwali rotation, cattle were grazed on the *vleis* in the three dry months; crops were planted in August – pumpkins, green mealies, vegetables, rice. Dry land, rain-fed cultivation would begin in November for a harvest the next August. After the harvest cattle could move from the *vleis* to graze on cereal stalks in the harvested dry land. During the rainy season, when the *vleis* are waterlogged and the dry lands are under crops, the cattle had to be moved away to summer grazing. It was a system which demanded investment of labour throughout the year, but was sensitive to the needs and capabilities of the people:

> Njelele was always very sympathetic with the people. It let them use the vleis but advised them how to do it and controlled them. For example, it would not permit cultivation too close to the rocks.[57]

I may have drawn an over-static and over-idealised picture of the Mwali cult's relationship to landscape and environment; to nature and culture. In the nineteenth century the shrines interacted with political power and gave legitimacy to inequality; priests accumulated wealth and fought bitterly with each other to control shrines; there were many droughts, epidemics and failures of fertility to be explained away. But the point is that there existed in the nineteenth-century Matopos – unknown to their European visitors – a vision of landscape and an ideology of land use. By contrast with white assumptions that humanity needed to dominate nature or be dominated by it, Mwali ideology fused nature and society. People can live in the hills, Mwali adepts say, because the rocks provide water: the rocks provide water because people live in the hills.[58] The Matopos represents an original nature, but it is a nature which exists inseparably from human culture. Men and women are not just living *in* nature; nor are they operating *on* it. Nature and culture are in symbiosis in this African landscape of the Matopos.

Finally, the voices from the shrine rocks articulated a narrative of the history which white travellers assumed the hills to lack. This was not a history limited to the Matopos themselves. The shrines belonged especially to the mountains but emissaries came to them from far to the south, the north and the east. Rozwi and Sotho, Kalanga and Karanga, Venda and Ndebele were all received in the shrine villages; their supplications and Mwali's answers to them were translated by the gifted linguists who served the shrines.[59] 'God

---

[57] Interview with Michael Ncube, 21 July 1989.

[58] Michael Ncube told me on 21 July 1989 that 'water is a gift from the rock', but that if the people were moved out of the hills by conservationists who wanted to save the water table, 'the hills will dry up'.

[59] The Mwali cult has been seen as essentially 'Karanga' by scholars who have approached it from the east and as essentially 'Kalanga' by those who have approached it from the south. My own research in the Matopos has predisposed me to see it as essentially Nyubi and even Ndebele. Today it is all these and many more. For a 'Karanga' perspective see Martinus Daneel, *The God of the Matopo Hills*, Mouton, The Hague, 1970; M. Gelfand, *An African's Religion. The Spirit of Nyajena*, Juta, Cape Town, 1966. For a 'Kalanga' perspective see Richard Werbner, 'Continuity and Policy in Southern Africa's High God Cult', in R. P. Werbner, ed., *Regional Cults*, Academic Press, London, 1977; 'Regional Cult of God Above. Achieving and Defending the Macrocosm', in R. P. Werbner, *Ritual Passage, Sacred Journey. The Process and Organization of Religious Movement*, Smithsonian Institute, Washington, 1989.

is language' say the priests. The myths of the world's creation in the Matopos which I have quoted above come from the cult's Karanga zone. Mwali's doctrine of the environment was carried out to all these constituencies.[60] Cult historical narrative concerned the successive states which had dominated much, though by no means all, of its zone of influence.

It was a narrative of the rise and fall of regimes, each one in turn legitimated by its acceptance of Mwali and then falling from grace and power by flouting Mwali's commands. In the late twentieth century, as we shall see, this narrative of the rise and fall of regimes, of the legitimation and illegitimacy of power, became important to thousands of people as a way of understanding modern politics. But there is no doubt that the narrative was in place at the end of the nineteenth century. Missionaries and administrators collected traditions describing various parts of the narrative – how past kings had refused to pay tribute in cattle to Mwali, or even sought to silence the Voice by cutting down the trees and blasting the rocks from which it spoke.

An early colonial account which attempted to put a narrative sequence together was written in 1913 by E. G. Howman. Mwali, Howman thought,

> was essentially the god of the Warozwi, making himself heard through the medium of the *Dombo re-Mwari*, or the Boulder of God, from which his voice proceeded…. For many years the Mambos [Rozwi kings] were in the practice of sacrificing to Mwari at the rock.

In Howman's version, the Rozwi sinned by burning alive the last Torwa ruler, Tumbare, and then defying Mwali by dancing around the rock singing, 'Tumbare has burnt, why should you not also burn?' They then bought firewood and piled it around the rock, setting it on fire so that

> Mwari should be burnt in the rock. Next morning Mwari spoke from a tree that stood in the village and foretold the punishment that should come upon them, saying that as they had done this thing the land should be taken from them. A people calling themselves Swazi would arrive … and later another people [the Ndebele] would come, who would destroy them utterly.

And then would come the whites, 'a people called *Makiwa*, or the stiff-legged ones, to whom they would be slaves.' Mwali would punish the Ndebele in turn for Lobengula's disobedience to divine commands. But 'at the last, he, Mwari, would have mercy upon them and send a deliverer, or *Manganguhutari*, a man dressed in armour, who would drive the *Makiwa* out and restore them to their former prosperity.'[61]

---

[60] For the fullest elaboration of Mwali's ecological doctrines as they apply to the Karanga districts of Masvingo Province, see M. L. Daneel, *Earthkeeping at the Grassroots in Zimbabwe*, Sigma Press, Pretoria, 1991; 'Healing the Earth: Traditional and Christian Initiatives in Southern Africa', conference paper, Utrecht, 1992; 'Zimbabwe's Traditional Custodians of the Land and Environmental Reform', ms, n.d.

[61] Though written in 1913, Howman's account was not published until 1966 in the *NADA* volume of that year, under the title of 'Native Tribes of the South'. Howman spells Mwari and Tumbare in the Karanga form, replacing the l with an r. There are many variants of the early part of this story. In a version told by Peter Sebina to Bessie Head, Tumbale figured as the mad Rozwi Mambo, and himself the object of Mwali's vengeance. According to Sebina, 'life was peaceful' under the oversight of 'Ngwale', 'an ancient cave-god whose shrine was at Njelele.' But then Tumbale, 'the blasphemer', tried to destroy the Voice:

Conquering the Matopos

In the 1890s the contradictions between white and black notions of environment and how to exploit it led to open violence. The Ndebele state was overthrown in 1893. There followed a series of ecological disasters: drought, rinderpest, locusts. People flocked to the shrines in the Matopos for explanation and remedy. Meanwhile, much of the land in central Matabeleland was alienated to white fortune hunters and thousands of young men were press-ganged to work in the newly opened mines. In March 1896 a widespread uprising broke out in Matabeleland; many whites were killed and Bulawayo besieged; British troops were brought in; savage fighting took place; eventually Cecil Rhodes negotiated an end to the war with Ndebele *indunas*, to whom he made significant concessions.

There has been much debate about the role of the Mwali shrines in these events. Whites at the time believed that shrine priests had ordered their supplicants to drive out the whites, as the only way to end ecological disaster and restore peace to the land. E. G. Howman's 1913 account says that 'in 1896 the spirit medium gave out that the time for the arrival of the deliverer was drawing near, and that when they rose in insurrection *Manganguhutari* would at once appear and assist them.' He did not, but 'to this day the arrival of the deliverer is still anxiously looked forward to, and firmly believed in by the old people.'[62]

There are many oral traditions in Matabeleland today which also assert that Mwali played a leading role in 1896. In particular, at Dula in the eastern Matopos a new shrine is said to have emerged just before the uprising – the shrine of the Red Axe – which bestowed the powers of making war and making peace. According to Thenjiwe Lesabe, a prominent Ndebele military leader, Mtuwane Dlodlo,[63] was called to Dula by the Voice:

> He was given the power of war by the shrine.... At Dula there are two powers there. One is for the war and the kingdom of the Ndebele people.... This Mtuwane Dlodlo was given the power of war, really of war.... It was [also] this man who caused the stop of the war. The Voice came to Mtuwane and asked Mtuwane to stop the war. He did, and finally there was peace. And when you read the history of the Amadebele, Mtuwane features there very much. It was the Voice of the shrine. He was a warrior.[64]

---

[61] (cont.) 'Ngwale became uncontrollable; his voice was heard from everywhere – in the air and in every part of the earth. The blasphemer, Tumbale, was struck dumb with fear [and] fled from his people.' The Swazi and then the Ndebele fell upon the people. 'Once their life had been a daily rhythm of sweet and courteous communication [under] the laws of Ngwale'; now 'human bones littered the land.' Bessie Head, *A Bewitched Crossroad*, Ad. Donker, Craighall, 1984, pp. 11-19.

[62] Howman, 'Native Tribes', p. 37.

[63] Marieke Clarke, who has been working on a biography of Mtuwane's sister, Lozigeyi, most powerful of Lobengula's queens, tells me that during her field work in 1996 his name was rendered to her as 'Umuntuwani', 'human being for what?' I employ the most common administrative usage in this book.

[64] Interview with Thenjiwe Lesabe, Bulawayo, 24 August 1988. I have discussed this tradition, and its confirmation by other informants, in 'The Politics of Prophecy in Matabeleland', Satterthwaite Seminar on

I accepted that the Mwali shrines played a crucial role in the 1896 uprising when I published an account of it in 1967.[65] Since then Julian Cobbing has made very effective criticisms of my account, and argued that the uprising can readily be explained in terms of the continued authority of the Ndebele military leaders.[66] But whatever uncertainties there are about the role of the shrines, there can be no doubt that the Matopos themselves became central to the making of war and peace. Their normal population was swollen by the incursion of Ndebele fighting men and of refugees from white reprisals.

The London Missionary Society missionary from Hope Fountain, David Carnegie, set off towards the end of 1896 to find his school children and their parents who had fled to the Matopos. He descended deep gorges, climbed stony kopjes, crept through narrow passes, 'going up and down, round about, threading our way as if we had been in some ancient city made by man.' He found the Hope Fountain people in 'a lovely ravine', where women were 'digging their gardens' and 'a beautiful stream of clear water ran beside the garden.'[67] Carnegie's narrative reflects the responses of earlier nineteenth-century travellers to the Matopos, combining as it did the sense of natural beauty with the importation of extra-African historical imagery – that 'ancient city made by man.' But by the time Carnegie wrote there had been a very different white response to the hills. This came from British soldiers entering the Matopos to fight rather than to succour refugees.

The military engagements in the Matopos came indelibly to mark white ideas about the history of the hills. In Eric Nobbs's 1924 guide an account of them takes up more pages than are devoted to all the earlier African occupation of the hills. Nobbs describes for the benefit of tourists the location of the ring of British forts around the Matopos. He lists the battles which took place there, ranging from 'a skirmish' on 19 July 1896 in the Mtshelele Valley, to the assault on Nkantolo mountain on 20 July, to the Ndebele dawn attack at Inungu on the same day, the second battle of Inungu on 25 July, and finally to 'the most severe fight in the rebellion' at Umlugulu in the eastern Matopos on 5 August.[68]

Participating in these engagements gave British soldiers a much more thorough and much less romantic idea of the hills. As Frank Sykes, a trooper in Colonel Plumer's regiment, wrote, the soldiers had to fight in country which was 'to all intents and purposes *terra incognita*, into which very few white men have yet penetrated.' Sykes did

---

[64] (cont.) African Religion and Ritual, 18–21 April 1989. Rhodes himself thought that Mtuwane played a critical role in the peace negotiations. Calling him 'the man whom we considered would fight to the last' and 'the Mlimo's [Mwali's] mouth-piece', Rhodes told Grey on 21 September 1896 that now Mtuwane had come in 'the matter is over as far as the hills are concerned'. LO 5/6/4.

[65] T. O. Ranger, *Revolt in Southern Rhodesia, 1896–7. A Study in African Resistance*, Heinemann, London, 1967.

[66] Julian Cobbing, 'The Absent Priesthood: Another Look at the Rhodesian Risings of 1896-7', *Journal of African History*, 17, 1977.

[67] Carnegie's account was published in the LMS children's magazine *News From Afar* in 1898. It is cited in Iris Clinton, *Hope Fountain Story*, Mambo, Gwelo, 1969, pp. 35-6.

[68] E. A. Nobbs, *Guide to the Matopos*, Maskew Miller, Cape Town, 1924, pp. 41–54.

not see the Matopos as picturesque. To him they were a terrible, hard place in which to have to fight. Nor did he see them as unpeopled, or see those people as mere slaves of nature. His description of the landscape sees it as belonging to the Ndebele enemy. He wrote of:

> Tiers upon tiers of gigantic granite boulders ... thrown together as it were carelessly by the forces of nature. It is in these mountain fastnesses that the Matabele always have their strongholds. Another kind of mountain slope, frequently met with in the Matopos, is that in which a smooth rock rises upward without a vestige of vegetation on its surface ... gradually rounding off gently until the broad flat top is reached. It is along these elevated plateaux that the Matabele have their highroads from stronghold to stronghold. The valleys are all splendidly watered [and] in these valleys of the Matopos alone there is ample ground for the growing of sufficient crops to supply the whole Matabele race.

Sykes claimed that his book on the 1896 campaign was different from most accounts of Southern African adventures. These contained illustrations as mere decoration. *His* illustrations were essential to a sober description of the war. So his book does not present picturesque landscapes. Instead it provides the first real notion of what the Matopos look like. Sykes carried out what he called 'the Matoppographic work of taking views among the hills.' He set off with two horses, a pack-mule, four companions, and a cumbrous camera, 'in search of photographic spoil'. His book is full of photographs – of soldiers, of forts, of the enemy, and of particular hills in the Matopos as sites of battle. There is no hint of the picturesque but this is certainly in its own way landscape humanised.[69]

I believe, indeed, that the fighting of 1896 was critical to the European imaginative appropriation of the Matopos. When Sykes's book was reprinted much later in the Rhodesiana Reprint series, the blurb claimed that it was 'an invaluable companion on outings to the Matopos.... With Sykes as a guide the reader is able to appreciate that there is as much of historical interest in these intriguing hills as there is of beauty.' History came late to the Matopos in this view – in 1896 – but now that it had come the 'beauty' of the hills had all the resonance which Oates had been vainly seeking. The Jesuits re-entered the Matopos in 1896, when Father Barthelemy accompanied the British troops through all their encounters in the mountains as chaplain (thus earning himself a special chapter, and photo, in Sykes's book). Barthelemy wrote in 1898 of this 'country unique in the world for its weirdness', in which British soldiers had 'written with their blood on these imperishable rocks a glorious and authentic page of *English* history.'[70]

---

[69] Frank Sykes, *With Plumer in Matabeleland*, Constable, London, 1897, pp. 168, 279. The closest Sykes came to the picturesque was his citation of a description by another soldier of the country around in Taba zi ka Mambo: 'It was a beautiful morning and as one took in the full beauty of the surrounding scenery, it seemed hard to realise that the day and the place were being totally devoted to the work of slaughter.' This observer came to terms with the slaughter by comparing it to 'a day amongst the "birds" at home.' *Ibid.*, pp. 141–2.

[70] Fr M. Barthelemy, 'During the Matabele Wars', *Zambesi Mission Record*, 1, 1, May 1898, p. 21, my italics.

Cecil Rhodes sees the Matopos

The Jesuits were soon able to rhapsodise over a definitive occupation of the hills by a British heroic legend. With Rhodes's interment in the Matopos on 10 April 1902, 'a man stronger than Mzilikazi ... even in death holds the land. From his vantage point his spirit will keep watch over his conquest.'[71]

Rhodes had long planned to be buried in the country which bore his name. But he looked for a site which would recall the glories of its remote history. At first he thought that Great Zimbabwe would be the ideal place. He arranged for the bones of the Allan Wilson patrol, killed to a man by the Ndebele in 1893, to be interred at Zimbabwe, there to await his own death and burial. Zimbabwe would then become a 'Rhodesian Valhalla'. In 1896, however, Rhodes 'saw' the Matopos. At Umlugulu in the eastern Matopos on 21 August 1896 Rhodes held his famous *indaba* with the Ndebele leaders in the hills – 'one of those moments in life', he said, 'that makes it worth living.' Soon he came to think of the Matopos as a place that made it worth dying. After the *indaba*, writes Robert Rotberg, Rhodes 'over and over again rode unarmed into the Matopos, on one occasion stumbling upon the granite dome of Malindudzimu.... He chose it then for his place of burial'.[72]

It is often said that Rhodes chose the site because it commanded one of the 'views of the world'. Nobbs's guide described that view ecstatically: 'A world is exposed to view, a world of chaotic grandeur, of mystical distance and minute detail.'[73] Yet it is clear that for Rhodes the real advantage of the site was that it combined a view with ease of access – as Nobbs puts it, the 'feeling is conveyed of loneliness generally associated with great heights and unwarranted by the short climb.' Or as Rhodes put it, the ascent to the top of Malindudzimu was easy enough for a grandmother to manage. From the beginning, in short, he planned his grave as a place of pilgrimage. Mzilikazi's tomb at Entumbane, disturbed and looted by British troopers, had been in Rhodes's mind. Now he planned to replace the Ndebele king as master of the land.

When Rhodes died six years later nothing was spared in installing him as the 'spirit' of the land. At his interment on 10 April 1902 the Bishop of Mashonaland intoned Rudyard Kipling's pantheistic elegy celebrating Rhodes as ancestor deity:

> It is his will that he look forth
> Across the world he won,
> The granite of the ancient North,
> Great spaces washed with sun.
> There shall he patient make his seat
> (As when the Death he dared)
> And there await a people's feet
> In the paths that he prepared.

[71] Anon,'The Graves in the Matoppo Hills', *Zambesi Mission Record*, 2, 24, April 1904, pp. 496–500.
[72] R. I. Rotberg, *The Founder. Cecil Rhodes and the Pursuit of Power*, OUP, 1988, p. 572.
[73] Nobbs, *Guide to the Matopos*, p. 12.

> The immense and brooding Spirit still
> Shall quicken and control.
> Living he was the land, and dead
> His soul shall be her soul.

Rhodes's appropriation of the land was carefully impressed upon the minds of local Africans. The burial was watched by 'a great concourse of natives'. Three weeks later Colonel Frank Rhodes, accompanied by the Chief Native Commissioner of Matabeleland, Herbert Taylor, and the Native Commissioner of Matopo district, H. M. Jackson, met the chief *indunas* of the Ndebele and explained why his brother had desired to be buried there:

> 'And as a proof', continued Colonel Rhodes, speaking with feeling, 'that I know the white man and the Matabele will be brothers and friends for ever, I leave my brother's grave in your hands. I charge you to hand down this sacred trust to your sons that come after you and from generation to generation and I know if you do this my brother will be pleased.[74]

Like Mzilikazi's grave, Rhodes's was to be guarded by Ndebele warriors. But at the grave site an exhibition was erected, showing photographs of Ndebele 'atrocities' against the whites in 1896, dramatising the passage of the people and their land from 'barbarism' to imperial custody.

Rhodes's burial was a tremendous challenge to African concepts of the Matopos landscape. There is no reason to suppose that Rhodes himself knew, when he chose the Malindudzimu site, that 'the bones of the rulers of the indigenous natives (not the Matabele) were placed in a cave only a few hundred yards from Mr Rhodes' tomb.' But the African observers of the funeral certainly knew it. The young W. R. Benzies was chosen to be one of the firing party, which 'in full uniform, with their bandoliers packed with live cartridges, marched the whole way with arms reversed, to the strains of the various dead marches, played by the band.' But when it arrived at the grave, 'the firing party was merely ordered to present arms instead of the usual volley ... due to the fact that the Chiefs had requested Mr Taylor, the CNC, that there should be no shooting as we were on sacred ground.'[75]

Both white and black came to see Rhodes's burial as a conscious usurpation. The Rhodesian poet, Cullen Gouldsbury, described Rhodes as reshaping the landscape and triumphing over the African spirit guardians of the hills:

> 'Twas his to have fashioned the valleys
> In semblance of subsequent weal –
> And, braving the ghosts and their malice
> To summon their spirits to heel –
>
> 'Twas his to have braved, in a measure,
> The pulse of their primitive wrath
> To clutch from the silence the treasure
> En Route for the Uttermost North.[76]

---

[74] Nobbs, *Guide to the Matopos*, p. 18.

[75] W. R. Benzies, 'Funeral of Cecil John Rhodes', *NADA*, 1964, pp. 37–8.

[76] Cullen Gouldsbury, 'A Reminder', *Rhodesian Rhymes*, Philpott and Collins, Bulawayo, 1932, p. 157. The poem was written in the 1910s.

Sitwanyana Ncube told me in 1988 that

> there is a bad place. Where Rhodes was buried. What is below that rock? Of Rhodes? No-one will know that cave and I will not show anyone until the country's traditions are restored.... There is a big thing, a wonderful phenomenon. [Rhodes' Grave] is fine for the whites but not for us. That is where we were brain-washed. That grave is at the fontanelle of the nation. There were sell-outs who revealed the secrets of the nation.[77]

Yet Rhodes did not clutch from the silence all of its treasure. Even after 1902 there were African voices from the rocks, though few Europeans heard them.

[77] Interview with Sitwanyana Ncube, 28 July 1988.

1 Mwali priests and adepts in chains in Bulawayo Gaol during the 1896 uprising

2 Rhodesian settlers amusing themselves at World's View, later the site of Rhodes's grave, in July 1898

3 African workers opening up the rock for the burial of Rhodes in 1902

4 European artisans finishing off Rhodes's Grave in 1902

5 Refreshment camp in the Matopos

6 'Queen Victoria', Whitewaters

7 *The London Missionary Society church at Whitewaters*

8 *The pilgrimage to Rhodes's Grave in 1927*

9 The Rhodes Scholars pilgrimage in 1953

10 A Cyrene representation of the life of Christ set in the Matopos by Livingstone Sango

2

Appropriating the Matopos

1897–1946

Recreation and Inscription in the Matopos

Once the Matopos had been conquered and Cecil Rhodes buried there, the mountains became a white playground. They were seen as 'wild' and domesticated at the same time. Rhodes himself set out this combination of splendour and recreation in his will. 'I admire the grandeur and loneliness of the Matoppos in Rhodesia', he wrote, and instructed that a railway line be built so that 'the people of Bulawayo may enjoy the glory of the Matopos.'[1] The scenery of the hills was now eminently available for depiction. As Nobbs wrote:

> To the photographic enthusiast the Matopos have special attractions. Apart from the graves and monuments the natural features of the landscape are eminently picturesque in the sense of making charming pictures. The mountains are not too large for the ordinary camera. The artist can both get and give great pleasure from the pursuit of his talent in the Matopos, the scenery lending itself to a peculiar degree to pictures and sketches.[2]

Many photographs of the early colonial period in the Matopos have survived and some are reproduced in this book. They show 'refreshment camps' out in the hills; the mail coach at the Matopos Hotel; settlers playing at holding up the boulders at Malindudzimu, and other scenes of the 'people of Bulawayo' sporting among the rocks. The landscape was confidently appropriated. There were, of course, the battle sites of the 1896 war. In 1919 Eric Nobbs drew up a list of places in the Matopos to be marked as historic: the sites of the battles at Inungu Hill and Inungu Gorge in July 1896, with the names of the white soldiers killed there; the site of the Nkantola fight; the site of the great *indaba*. The only pre-colonial African memory to be recorded was that of Mzilikazi, the state founder whom Rhodes had superseded. Nobbs's 1924 guide suggested a number of different 'excursions' to the battlefields.[3]

---

[1] I cite the text of the will as given in file S 246/245.
[2] Nobbs, *op.cit.*, p. 3.
[3] File G 1/7/3/6. Nobbs's Route IV took visitors past the 'base camp for military operations in 1896' at Fort

But appropriation went further. Rocks which struck whites as having a resemblance to this or that person, animal or thing were confidently renamed, with none of the Mwali adepts' sense of ambiguity. One great rock in the south-western Matopos, in what came to be called Whitewaters, was renamed after its resemblance to the widowed Queen Victoria. Nobbs informed tourists returning from Rhodes's Grave that close to the southern Park gates were 'a number of very fantastically shaped rocks to which such descriptions as the elephant, the frog, the seal, the sleeping man and the old woman in the chair are given, and these will be readily recognised when seen.'[4] The remarkable perennial water holes, sunk deep in the granite on the northern edge of the eastern Matopos – which for centuries have been the site of rain-making ceremonies – came to be called, with spurious classical resonance, Diana's Pool, after the Native Commissioner's wife. Nor was the appropriation and renaming of the hills only a business for romantically inclined elders. The Rhodesian schoolboys of the Matopos Farm School, who treated the hills as their personal playground, imposed more earthy names upon the rocks and caves, one becoming known as 'The Devil's Arse-hole'.[5]

We possess a vivid account of how Whitewaters was given its new name. Whitewaters will figure prominently in this book as the home of the leading Christians, cattle owners, entrepreneurs and political activists in the Matopos; the senior Mwali shrine, Njelele, lay just to the south, and a subsidiary shrine was sited in Whitewaters itself; it had long enjoyed a flourishing rotation of cultivation and cattle-grazing on its valley bottoms and *vleis*. In 1984 one of Mark Ncube's oral informants recalled that:

> The name Whitewaters was inscribed by the whites while we were still herdboys. There was a swampy area where cattle were not allowed to graze on. This area was always green. One day a white man on his motor bike asked for drinking water. We told him not to go to that area since it was very wet. It was so deep that one could disappear. The white man went to drink on the other side of the hill. When the white man came back he inscribed the name 'Whitewaters' on a tree with a knife.... The tree was cut down [but] the name is now inscribed upon a rock.[6]

As we shall see, this casual triumph of white inscription over local ecological knowledge makes a good metaphor for the area's twentieth-century experience.

Inscription on the rocks turned the Matopos into the monumental centre of the white Rhodesian 'nation'. Rhodes directed in his will that the remains of the Allan Wilson patrol should be exhumed from Great Zimbabwe and reburied at the 'Rhodesian Valhalla' in the Matopos. In March 1904 their remains were transferred and in July the Shangani Monument was dedicated by the Bishop of Mashonaland. In May 1920 Rhodes's right-hand man in the conquest of the territory, Leander Starr Jameson,

---

[3] (cont.) Usher; his Route V reached 'the very fig tree under which Mr Rhodes slept the night prior to his indaba with the Matabele' and also 'Nkantolo Mountain, five miles away and the scene of an important engagement in 1896 [which] can be reached by car or cart, but the services of a guide are desirable'. From Rhodes's grave could be seen Inungu, site 'of two engagements during the Matabele rebellion.' Nobbs, *op.cit.*, pp. 87, 111, 112.

[4] Nobbs, *Guide to the Matopos*, p. 109.

[5] I owe this information to Jeremy Brickhill, once himself a pupil at the school.

[6] Interview by Mark Ncube with G. A. Dube, Kezi, 22 November 1984.

was buried at World's View. In March 1935 the Bulawayo Boy Scout Association asked for a training ground to be set aside in the Matopos 'within a few miles of our Founder's grave'. This would be apt, it was urged, because 'Lord Baden-Powell acknowledges that it was in the Matopos Hills that he was first inspired with the idea of the Boy Scout organisation', during the 1896 fighting. In the training camp 'a large rock should have a face smoothed (such as was done at the entrance to the consecrated ground on the way to Rhodes's grave) and an inscription cut' saying that B. P. had been 'inspired in those hills to start the marvellous idea of the Boy Scouts.' They were granted the use of a site on World's View Farm and allowed to cut their inscription; they were also allowed to erect a plate at Fort Usher to record the fact that it had been built by Baden-Powell in 1896.[7] In May 1946 the Memorable Order of the Tin Hats asked permission to put up a memorial to the war dead at Rhodes's grave. They were allowed instead to erect the MOTH memorial shrine which is still to be seen by the side of the Circular Drive in the National Park. It had become accepted, in short, that 'the granite of the ancient North' had been predestined for European inscription.

All these additional commemorations, though unproblematic as documents in white Rhodesian history, raised some awkward questions so far as black memory was concerned. Africans were supposed to remember their 'surrender' to Rhodes and their pledge to guard his grave, but to forget their military achievements in 1893 (when they had wiped out the Shangani Patrol) or in 1896 (when their resistance had forced Rhodes to negotiate at the *indabas*). Thus in June 1916 the Administrator, Sir Drummond Chaplin, told a representative of 'Mr Schlesinger's cinematographic scheme' that:

> under present conditions it would be quite impossible for us to give any facilities for the reproduction of the scene of Wilson's last stand or to allow any such scene to be publicly represented in a film in this territory, even if it were made up elsewhere. I also told him that we could not give facilities for the assemblage of a large number of natives to enable him to reproduce the Indaba in the Matopos, but that as regards the reproduction of Mr Rhodes's funeral, the Superintendent of Natives will assist him by furnishing a limited number of natives. Having regard to the appearance of unrest among some of the Matabele ... it would be highly inexpedient to do or sanction at the present time anything which might revive among these people memories of the Rebellion.[8]

White concern to document both the European conquest of the hills and black acceptance of it continued into the 1930s. In March 1935, for example, 'Young Matabelelander' deplored in a letter to the *Chronicle* that Rhodes's grave was being guarded by 'a coloured man' in contravention of Colonel Frank Rhodes's pact with the *indunas*. He proposed that the Native Commissioner 'should select each year two full-blooded Matabele men of the "warrior class" to act as guards.' The man on guard 'would always be in full Matabele war dress' and every sunset he 'would give the royal salute and in a loud voice proclaim that he handed over the safe keeping of the grave of the friend of the Matabele people to the Almighty during the hours of rest.' 'Young Matabelelander' thought that such a ceremony would:

[7] Robert Gordon to Minister, Lands, 13 March 1935; Under Secretary, Lands, to Boy Scouts Association, 20 April 1938, S 1194/190/7.

[8] Drummond Chaplin to Lewis Michell, 30 June 1916, CH 8/2/2/12.

become as impressive as the changing of the guard before the Palace ... a source of great attraction to tourists ... [and] help make the World's View more sacred and impressive for the natives and the white people.[9]

This ceremony was not instituted but guides to the painted caves in the Matopos *were* kitted out in full Ndebele war dress.

Using the Matopos

Rhodes did not intend the Matopos to be set aside only for leisure and for monument. They were also to be used. As we shall see, he gave orders for a dam to be built on his land north of the hills, which was designed to irrigate large stretches of arable. He also laid it down in his will that part of his land on the northern fringe of the Matopos 'be planted with every possible tree', and that 'an experimental farming forestry market' be established on his estate. An arboretum was set up and Nobbs's 1924 *Guide* described how 'experimental plantations of exotic trees and shrubs' were developed, together with nurseries 'where the plants required are raised from seed and the surplus sold at very moderate prices to farmers for the purpose of beautifying their homes and encouraging afforestation.'[10]

Scientific forestry was one of the master disciplines of nineteenth-century white relationships to the land in Southern Africa.[11] In 1902 the distinguished South African forest officer, James Sim, was brought up to report on the prospects of Rhodes's Arboretum and on the need for a Rhodesian Forestry Department.

Soon surveyors were at work, cutting up the Matopos into farms so that Rhodes's example could be followed. Survey was another of the key colonial sciences. There were few white travellers in nineteenth-century Southern Africa who could not produce maps so as to impress themselves on the country through which they passed. Such amateurs gave way to professional surveyors. These first laid down frontiers between territories – 'In olden times ... we never spoke about boundary lines', complained Lobengula to Khama, as the frontier between Bamangwato and southern Matabeleland was being determined. 'It is only now they talk about boundaries.'[12] Then they mapped out farms. Everywhere there was laid on the land the network of straight lines and rectangles which defied the chaos of rock and river. In the Matopos, too, surveyors set up their metal trig points on sacred hills, even on Njelele – 'the utmost corruption and disrespect' say the Mwali priests.[13] The surveyors began to carve out estates. By 1908 the hills had been entrenched upon on all sides by the squares and oblongs of farms:

[9] *Chronicle*, 26 March 1935.
[10] Nobbs, *Guide to the Matopos*, p. 73.
[11] R. H. Grove, 'Early Themes in African Conservation: the Cape in the Nineteenth Century' in D. Anderson and R. Grove, eds, *Conservation in Africa: People, Policies, and Practice*, Cambridge University Press, Cambridge, 1987; 'Scottish Missionaries, Evangelical Discourses and the Origins of Conservation Thinking in Southern Africa, 1820–1900', *Journal of Southern African Studies*, 15, 2, January 1989.
[12] Lobengula to Khama, *Parliamentary Papers*, C.5237, LIX, 1887.
[13] Interview between Mark Ncube and David Ndlovu, Njelele, 23 November 1988.

Absent, the huge Matoppo Block, World's View farm itself, the optimistically named Mineral King, the less optimistically named Excess, all running across the northern zone of the Matopos; Mauwe, St Francis, Famockwe, Mount Edgecombe to the west; Man-yoni, Shentsheli, Gwandavale, Kozi, Malaje, Inungu, Wenlock and others to the south.

After forestry and surveying came a third key colonial science – geology. Geologists 'annexed the landscapes of the past' just as colonialists annexed those of the present. They 'proved extraordinarily successful in imposing scientific order upon the overseas wilderness.' As Robert Stafford tells us, the distinguished geologist Roderick Murchison held that southern Africa had retained the same physical features 'during countless past ages'; its ancient rocks held abundant mineral riches for whites to exploit, while at the same time its 'unique physical quiescence ... offered an anthropological corollary, arguing that the Negro race had likewise languished in cultural statis for many millenia.'[14] The Matopos with their extraordinary granites traversed by quartz and felspar veins, offered much room for both theoretical and practical geologists. Prospectors combed the hills, and the 'Geology' section contributed by H. B. Maufe to the 1924 *Guide*, noted that 'prospecting is in progress and there are quite a number of registered claims', and concluded with 'the possibility that one day further gold may be found and worked successfully on a large scale.'[15]

Early Colonial African Uses of the Matopos

Meanwhile the African inhabitants of the hills were also being encouraged to make a 'modern' use of them. The many Native Commissioners who administered the Matopos and the neighbouring areas in the early colonial period came to recognise the industry and productivity of the inhabitants. But they were also highly critical of Banyubi 'conservatism'. There seemed ample opportunity for missionaries to teach their converts how to exploit the Matopos environment in a properly progressive way.

Because the Matopos had been the focus of African resistance several Native Department stations were established in and around them. Reports survive from Native Commissioners or Assistant Native Commissioners for Matopo, Mawabeni, Malema and Mlugulu. These men were busy in the late nineteenth and early twentieth century riding through the hills hunting down rebels, enforcing disarmament, collecting intelligence on the Mwali shrines, recruiting labour for the mines. As they did so, they noticed to their surprise how much cultivation was going on. 'I rode into the hills passing over the ground where General Carrington's forces fought the final engagement against the Matabele on the 9th August 1896', wrote the Assistant Native Commis-sioner, Mlugulu. 'Large patches of land are tilled and sown. There is no doubt the wily native puts out all his energy and strength when working for himself.'[16]

---

[14] Robert Stafford, 'Annexing the Landscapes of the Past: British Imperial Geology in the Nineteenth Century', ms.

[15] Nobbs, p. 73. This prediction was dropped from the geology section of Tredgold's 1956 guide.

[16] Assistant Native Commissioner, Mlugulu to Native Commissioner, Matobo-Mawabeni, Monthly report for October 1898, NBE 7/2/1, vol. 3.

These administrators saw much more of the ordinary life of the Matopos than either the nineteenth century travellers or the soldiers campaigning in 1896. At first, in early 1897, they reported a 'continued state of famine' as a result of the deliberate destruction of standing crops during the 1896 fighting. But they came to realise that as soon as peace had been negotiated in August and September 1896 the Banyubi had planted large areas of ground. The 'crops look exceedingly well' and both 'friendlies and rebels are very quiet, the harvesting of their crops demanding their sole attention.'[17] The 1897 harvest provided enough food for the 'hill tribes'. An even greater effort was then put into planting for the coming year. The Assistant Native Commissioner, Mawabeni, reported in 1897 that men had joined women in hoeing and that 'already several disputes have arisen regarding fallow or disused land.'[18] The result was a very large harvest. 'The land is "picked" over by hand and only "turned" to a depth of about 6 inches' reported the Native Commissioner, Matopo/Mawabeni in March 1898, but 'alluvial soil in the river valleys yields a splendid crop in spite of the mode of cultivation.'[19] In 1898 'the rest of the District practially existed on these crops ... and a number of wagon loads of grain have been bought from these natives, both by white traders and by the natives themselves.'[20]

What was happening, in fact, was a brief flowering of a peasant option for the Banyubi of the Matopos. By 1899 the grain trade was in full swing in the hills. In March the Native Commissioner, Mawabane, reported that 'many natives sell a large quantity of grain and in this work (agriculture) do not deserve the usually true epithet of lazy'; in April the Malema monthly report recorded 'stern competition in the hills for the season's trade in grain.' Assistant Native Commissioner A. R. Wilson in Mlugulu found it 'positively wonderful the quantity of land these people turn over. These people live in these gardens the greater part of the year and are constantly working and improving their ground. They plant mealies, mabele, millet ... kafir beans, sweet potatoes, pumpkins ... and very rarely have a famine.'[21]

All this admiration was very different from later denunciations of African agriculturalists for ruining the Matopos. For a while the peasant option continued into the twentieth century. In 1900 parties of Banyubi from the hills were reported to be travelling as many as 20 miles 'carrying baskets of maize, millet, pink mountain rice, groundnuts, sweet potatoes, and onions for sale at distant stores and mines.'[22] Much grain was sold to traders in 1901 and 1902. Thereafter there were difficulties. Disarmament laid the Banyubi open to the depredations of baboons. Competition for fallows or unused land reached a peak. It became clear that there were too many farmers in the hills and a trek south into the *mapani* veld began. Nevertheless, in March 1906 the Native Commissioner, Matopo, was still reporting that Banyubi men greatly preferred to farm

[17] Monthly reports, Malema, for January, February and April 1897, NBE 7/1/1.
[18] Monthly report, Mawabeni, September 1897, NB 6/4/1.
[19] Annual Report, Matopo-Mawabeni, March 1898, NB 6/1/1.
[20] Native Commissioner, Malema to Chief Native Commissioner, Matabeleland, 24 January 1899, NBE 7/1/1.
[21] Monthly report, Matopo-Mawabeni, March 1899, NB 6/1/2; monthly report, Malema, April 1899, NBE 7/1/2; monthly report, Mlugulu, March 1899, NB 6/1/2.
[22] Quarterly report, Matopos, 30 June 1900, NBE 1/1/1.

than to go out for work and that 'good wages do not compensate for the loss of the produce of their fields.'[23]

This successful peasant production was based on a mixture of long-established methods and of carefully judged innovation. *Vleis* and alluvials were intensively farmed; sons-in-law worked on the land; big men held beer parties at harvesting time so that they could draw on the labour of their neighbours. At the same time, more labour – and especially male labour – was put into cultivation and new crops were grown to be traded for new commodities. The indigenous agriculture of the hills was proving its potentialities. So, too, was the traditional ideology.

In the immediate aftermath of the 1896 fighting the Native Commissioners in the Matopos could find no trace of Mwali shrine activity. Mwali adepts had been arrested in 1896 and some of them tried and sent to prison. The rest lay low. In March 1898 Charles Stuart at Malema even recorded that 'the Kalangas think that the Mlimo [Mwali] has left them and gone over to the whites.'[24] In fact, of course, the shrines were deeply involved in the newly intensive agricultural production. Before planting began in 1897 'a large function was held in the Matopo by a child of the Mlimo who blessed the seed corn of a large number and received gifts'; in March 1898 offerings were taken to a Mwali priest near Mtuwane Dlodlo's kraal; after the harvest began in 1899 'the gratitude of the inhabitants of the hills for the comparatively good crop' took 'the form of dances and offerings to the hereditary priest of the Mlimo who lives in the Matopo hills.'[25]

Like Banyubi farmers themselves, the Mwali shrines took peasant surplus production and trading in their stride. In September 1899 two female messengers from the shrines went eastwards into Belingwe 'with advice to cultivate much land'.[26] When drought made peasant production difficult or impossible, the shrines became more important to cultivators than in the years of plenty. The rains failed in 1905/6; desperate offerings were made to Mwali priests in the Matopos, who advised 'energetic planting to replace the former withered crop.' Archie Campbell, Native Commissioner of Insiza district, warned in January 1906 that the whole country 'has been in secret communication [to] make a concerted appeal [and] pilgrimages to the Matopo priests'. Remembering the uprising in 1896 he urged that 'the caves from which these voices come be demolished by dynamite, the priests be imprisoned and their kraals and people scattered.'[27] By this time, however, the Native Commissioners in the hills had come to think of the Mwali shrines more in terms of peasant production than of armed resistance.[28]

[23] Monthly report, March 1906, MB 6/1/6.

[24] Annual Report, Malema, 1898, NB 6/1/1.

[25] Monthly report, Matopo-Mawabeni, May 1899, NB 6/4/3; monthly reports, Bulalima and Mzingwane, March 1898, NB 6/1/1.

[26] S. N. Jackson, Native Commissioner, Belingwe to Chief Native Commissioner, Matabeleland, 6 September 1899, NB 1/1/8.

[27] Native Commissioner, Matopo to Chief Native Commissioner, Matabeleland, 17 January 1906, NBE 1/1/4; Native Commissioner, Insiza to Chief Native Commissioner, Matabeleland, 16 January 1906, NB 3/2/2.

[28] I have argued the case for the Mwali cult in the twentieth century as the articulator of 'peasant consciousness' in 'Religious Studies and Political Economy: the Mwari Cult and the Peasant Experience in Southern Rhodesia', in Wim van Binsbergen and Matthew Schoffeleers, eds, *Theoretical Explorations in African Religion*, KPI, London, 1985.

Progressive Christianity in the Matopos

Despite admitting that 'native crops are more uniformly successful than those planted by Europeans', the Native Commissioners were scornful of Banyubi conservatism.[29] They did not use manure; they did not possess carts or wagons; the men 'did the bulk of the heavy work ... by hand, a heavy and slow process', and only 'a few of the more advanced use ploughs drawn by oxen.'[30] Later, of course, plough cultivation was denounced as disastrous to the Matopos environment, but in the early twentieth century it was taken as the mark of progress. And it was missionaries who particularly preached the gospel of the plough.

Early in 1899 Donald Moodie, the Native Commissioner, Matopo-Mawabeni, once having admitted the intensity of grain production in the Matopos, gave vent to his prejudices against the Banyubi.

> The ordinary native of this country is the dirtiest and laziest specimen of his race I have ever encountered. They have no respect for themselves, no morals, no idea of truth and no sense of shame.... Instead of being raised in the scale by the advent of the Zulus with their good morals and cleanly customs, [they] have dragged the conquering race down to their own level.

What they needed was 'one simple religion', a straightforward version of Protestant Christianity, which would teach obedience.[31]

The first attempt to offer a loyal and simple Protestantism in the hills was made by the Anglicans. In June 1898 the Anglican chaplain in Bulawayo, Nelson Fogarty, set out to 'prospect for a likely "reef" of *Native* ore.'[32] Fogarty hoped to establish a mission 'in the heart of the famous Matoppo Hills, a most thickly populated part of the country.'[33] In the end a mission was set up under J. W. Leary just north of the Matopos on the huge Essexvale Estate. It was designed to minister to the Banyubi and Ndebele followers of the local *indunas*, many of whom were still living in the hills. Leary reported that the people had recently taken to hoe cultivation with enthusiasm:

> To the south of us, about four and a half miles distant, lie the now historic Matoppo Hills. The scene of Mr Rhodes's famous indaba is almost in sight.... The people in our neighbourhood are mainly Mandebele and quondam Mandebele slaves.... The Mandebele used to be entirely pastoral and warlike, most of the cultivation being done by slaves. In our days, owing to war and rinderpest having swept off almost all their cattle, the people are practically entirely agricultural.... Hoeing is done by both men and women.... Men, women and children spend a good deal of time in the lands.

[29] Annual Report, Matopo, 31 March 1901, NBE 1/1/2. Banyubi men were reported to work in their gardens for as much as nine months a year.

[30] Monthly report, Matopo, April 1903, NB 6/1/3–4.

[31] Annual Report, 1898/8, Matopo-Mawabeni, NB 6/1/2. Moodie was commenting on the influence of the Seventh Day Adventists in a neighbouring district, who were 'hopelessly confusing the natives'. There was no need for 'these fancy religions.'

[32] Bishop of Mashonaland's report, Bulawayo, 24 September 1898, *Mashonaland Quarterly Papers*, XXVI, November 1898, p. 4.

[33] Nelson Fogarty, Bulawayo, 25 June 1898, *Mashonaland Quarterly Papers*, XXV, August 1898, p. 20.

He aimed to introduce them to 'progressive' farming methods and his first action was to lay on 'a little ploughing.'[34]

In 1900, however, the Anglican station was abandoned due to Leary's capture in the South African war, the fever which afflicted his African assistants, and the lack of converts. It fell to more straightforwardly Protestant missions to modernise the Matopos. In 1902 Native Commissioner Stanley Jackson noted the presence of two sets of such missionaries in his annual report:

> Some American Missionaries who call themselves 'Brethren in Christ' have established a Mission Station in the Matopo Hills.... Amongst the younger natives they have a large number of eager and apparently apt pupils who are being taught to read and write the Matabele language. The natives from this Mission appear to have had instilled into their minds some idea of the 'dignity of labour'.... There are several native catechists or preachers (London Missionary Society) who hold services and also give lessons in reading and writing. On Sunday numbers of natives in gaudy, ill-fitting civilised dress, flood to the services and join in the singing of hymns most heartily.[35]

It was these two missions which produced the Protestant elites of the Matopos and who did their best to reshape the landscape.

The Brethren in Christ was very much a farmers' movement in the American mid-West. Its evangelists 'would often leave their little farms in care of their wives' and go off on 'missionary journeys through the US and Canada.' It had no overseas mission until 1897 when the *Evangelical Visitor* called for volunteers:

> The committee has not yet decided where the field shall be, but will decide when such workers present themselves as are believed to be called by God. South Africa has been spoken of; also South or Central America. No doubt God will direct.

It was in this spirit of invincible ignorance that the Brethren missionaries set off. The volunteers were all from Kansas and most had never seen the sea; they were astonished by their train journey from Liverpool to London, during which 'we were favoured with a glimpse of a hunting party in their brilliant coloured costumes in pursuit of the poor little animals in one of the game reserves'; during their three-week voyage from Southampton – since God had directed that Southern Africa should be the mission field – they were overwhelmed by the 'drinking, gambling, dancing and even grosser evils.' Exactly where they were to work remained 'a sealed book', though the liner's Chief Engineer produced a map and indicated where other missionaries were at work, showing a blank for central Matabeleland. A kindly patroness in Cape Town also recommended Matabeleland and 'especially the Matopo Hills, as there were no

---

[34] T. W. Leary, St Augustine's, Umlulugu, 23 June 1899, *Mashonaland Quarterly Papers*, X1X, August 1899, pp. 8–9.

[35] Annual Report, Matopo, April 1903, NB 6/1/3–4. Characteristically, the Native Commissioners were ambiguous even about simple Protestantism. Their own remedy for Banyubi deficiencies was to replace service marriage with bride price and Banyubi customs with 'Zulu law'. The 1907 Annual Report for Mzingwane remarked that under the influence of the LMS school at Hope Fountain, 'the whole district has taken to chanting psalms under the "Do Re Mi" method of vocal training. It is doubtful if their present imperfect knowledge of the air and key of "Old 100" is an improvement on the forsaken chants of their forefathers, or pink blouses and red sunshades preferable to the normal draped limbo.' NB 6/1/8.

missionaries in that locality'. But they still had no idea exactly *who* lived in the Matopos, nor that bloody fighting had only just ended there.[36]

In Cape Town the 59-year-old leader of the party, Jesse Engle, waited upon Cecil Rhodes, who gave him a characteristic letter of introduction to the Deputy Administrator in Bulawayo:

> This class I think is better than policemen and cheaper. The bearer impresses me as a good man. They wish to make a settlement in your country for American mission work. I think you might grant him a farm say fifteen hundred morgen in the middle of natives ... say in Matopos to deal with Umlugulu or Somabula.[37]

Delayed for months in Cape Town, the missionaries still did not know what language they were to speak in the Matopos.[38] Finally, they reached Bulawayo and in July 1898 set off for the 'mission valley' allocated to them in Chief Hluganiso's area of the northeastern Matopos. By this time they had learnt the stock version of Ndebele history – 'ruthlessly slaughtering and enslaving' – and had been warned by local whites that they were venturing into 'the enemy's stronghold':

> We were located in the very heart of these hills where no missionary had yet penetrated, and being surrounded by many of the rebels themselves ... still seething with discontent from the same cause which led to the rebellion ... far from other white people, among a class of natives who have never been subdued by the English soldiers ... kept in subjection only by forts of police stationed in the hills.[39]

The Brethren reacted to the Matopos much like earlier missionaries. The mountains constituted 'a city of rocks, covering a scope of 40 by 60 miles', riddled with 'thousands of crevices where [the Ndebele] could hide away.' Engle saw the Matopos as 'these benighted hills', Satan's stronghold.[40]

---

[36] H. Frances Davidson, *South and South Central Africa. A Record of Fifteen Years Missionary Labours Among Primitive Peoples*, Elgin, Illinois, 1915, pp. 19, 23, 26, 33, 35, 39. Wendy Urban-Mead's research paper, 'The Calling of an Unwomanly Woman: H. Frances Davidson and the Brethren in Christ Mission at the Matopo Hills, Rhodesia (Zimbabwe), 1897-1906', Columbia, October 1996, allows us to read Davidson's book rather differently. The book gives a delightful account, which I have followed, of innocent and unprepared missionaries. But Davidson herself was a much more forceful and well-equipped person. The daughter of the editor of the *Evangelical Visitor*, she was by far the best educated and qualified member of the Church, male or female. She had obtained both bachelor and master's degrees, specializing in languages, with a side qualification in surveying. The male elder in charge of the mission party, Jesse Engle, delegated to her the task of booking their overseas passages. It was evidently Davidson's preference for the 'raw natives' of Matabeleland which prevailed over Engle's idea of the Transvaal as a mission site. In her book Davidson conceals her own part in all this, since in Brethren theology 'as the man and the leader of the group Engle had to be allowed to make the decision'. See E. Morris Sider, 'Hannah Frances Davidson', *Nine Portraits. Brethren in Christ Biographical Sketches*, Nappanee, Illinois, 1978.

[37] Rhodes to Captain Lawley, January 1898, L 2/1/24. Umlugulu and Somabula were ex-'rebel' *indunas* whom Rhodes was very anxious to 'pacify'. In the event the Brethren were not sited among their followers.

[38] Once again this is the impression conveyed by Davidson's book. According to Urban-Mead, however, Davidson 'did not hesitate to acquire a Zulu grammar and Bible' in Cape Town, and to begin to equip herself to converse with the Ndebele. Engle, however, was more inclined to rely upon God's providence than on his colleague's linguistic skills.

[39] Davidson, *South and South Central Africa*, pp. 48, 49, 55, 56, 57.

[40] Jesse Engle in *Evangelical Visitor*, 30 March and 15 May 1899.

They found themselves 'without an interpreter and with no practical knowledge of mission work'; seeking to learn the language they were taught 'kitchen kaffir' by the locals, 'a jargon of their own, which they seemed to think especially adapted to the mental capacity of white people,' and which took years to unlearn.[41] The Brethren would not use either white or black medicines and fell victim to fever. There were many deaths among the missionaries. General ignorance of the language meant that they could not reach the Africans around them with their major evangelical weapon, 'the unadorned Word.' Yet in August 1899 they baptised nine boys and a girl 'in one of those sparkling streams', and 'during the dry season of 1900 an aggressive campaign against Satan and his followers among the rocks and strongholds was begun, for we felt that the Lord would have us press the battle to the gates.'[42]

Few missionaries can have been so ill-prepared. Yet in less than a year they had achieved more 'converts' than Protestant and Catholic missionaries combined had managed in Matabeleland in all the decades before 1890. Soon there were very many more. This was partly a matter of the effects of colonial conquest, of course – perhaps some of the inhabitants of the hills really did think that Mwali had gone over to the whites. But it was also because of the attraction of the gospel of the plough. From the beginning, the Brethren were confident in their agricultural skill. Looking out from the train in England, 'the methods employed in farming seemed somewhat antiquated to people fresh from the farms of Western America.' As they travelled north from Cape Town to Bulawayo, they thought 'parts greatly resembled Kansas prairies.'

The Matopos did *not* resemble prairies and as they struggled to reach the land allocated to them, their wagons mired in swamps and jolted among rocks, their farming hearts at first failed. Soon after they reached their valley one of them wrote home to describe its setting, 'surrounded by immense granite hills and boulders, some of which cover hundreds of acres, so that at first sight the rocks seem to constitute the chief part of the country.' But they soon regained confidence and saw in the landscape agricultural potentials which white conservationists were later to deny:

> A closer inspection showed us to what a beautiful place God had led us ... a beautiful rolling valley, of rich, dark earth, well supplied with an abundance of fresh water ... sparkling fountains of beautiful water, crystal clear, oozing from under the surface of the rocks, and flowing down the valley. Some contain delicate mosses and pretty water lilies, and surpass the Michigan lakes in transparency.[43]

The Brethren had no intention of leaving this idyllic scene to nature. They soon found themselves in a characteristic early Rhodesian dilemma. The administration had granted them the valley in the belief that it stood on an unalienated land. But it became

---

[41] Once again I follow Davidson's published account. But Urban-Mead, drawing on Davidson's diaries, shows that she 'was the only one who had acquired sufficient skills to communicate in Sindebele' and so was 'the school's head and its main teacher', as well as interpreter at religious services. Urban-Mead argues that her linguistic skills combined with her intellectual curiosity to produce 'extensive written accounts of the African social and cultural environment'.

[42] Davidson, pp. 72, 91, 110.

[43] *Ibid.*, pp. 33, 40, 55.

clear that in fact it had been granted by Jameson, during the period of 'creative survey', as part of the 11,946-morgen Matoppo Block, which in turn was part of 100,000 acres in Matabeleland passed to Robert Williams of the Bulawayo Syndicate. The Syndicate laid claim to the land which it wanted to administer like all the rest of its estate by letting it out for rent to the African residents.[44] The Brethren had a much more active notion of development. They 'climbed hills, went over precipices and waded swamps' so as to produce a map of their claim; they urged that the land was sanctified by the graves of two of their missionaries; and they challenged the moral position of the Bulawayo Syndicate. The Syndicate had no intention of *improving* the land; the Brethren had every desire to do so. In late 1902 they were successful and achieved a 99-year lease of their 3,000 acres. They could now confidently set about developing them.[45]

Engle had been 'alive to the value of the soil' from the beginning, had planted fruit trees and ploughed with two donkeys. In April 1899 fresh missionaries arrived with 'farm implements' and wagons. A mission farm was established, and Engle's successor, Stiegerwald, held a 'tea drink' (instead of the traditional beer party) to attract 164 local people to work with hoes on ten acres of arable land. Soon he began to convert the people from the hoe to the plough. He borrowed oxen, which he trained to pull the plough, used them for a period and then returned them so that their owners could themselves become ploughmen. By 1913 the initial ten acres of arable had been expanded into a densely settled valley, with the mission farm surrounded by African ploughmen. 'Every available place near the mission had been brought under cultivation'; every usable bit of the 3,000 acres had been taken up and much more land could have been made use of by those who wanted to join the mission's community of peasant ploughmen.[46]

'The natives continue to plough the small rich land in the valleys and on the river banks', reported the Acting Native Commissioner, Mzingwane, in 1909, 'but they are gradually increasing the size of their fields.' The spread of the plough and of literacy began to change the gender division of labour, many men ploughing their fields and then returning to paid employment, 'leaving the weeding and tending to their women.' White farmers, seeing the advantage to them, arranged 'for the absence of their servants for a sufficient period to plough their fields; one prominent farmer even lends cattle and implements for the purpose.'[47] In this way the plough revolution spread out from the missions into the hills and the lands around them.

Whatever reservations agricultural experts were later to have about farming in the Matopos, Education Inspectors in the 1920s and 1930s were very enthusiastic about the Brethren's gospel of improvement. The Brethren were permitted to set up a network of schools 'in the unsurveyed Matopos', each with 'more land than would be necessary for an ordinary Native School', because of 'an appreciable amount of industrial and

---

[44] Chief Native Commissioner, Matabeleland to Civil Commissioner, 13 June 1898; Frances Davidson to Cecil Rhodes, 31 May 1901, L 2/1/24.

[45] Davidson, *op.cit.*, pp. 119–25; Frances Davidson to Civil Commissioner, 8 July 1901, L 2/1/24. According to Urban-Mead, Davidson's earlier training in surveying 'proved crucial' in this controversy.

[46] Davidson, *op.cit.*, pp. 150, 211.

[47] Annual Report, Matobo, 1907, NB 6/1/8; Annual Report, Mzingwane, 1909, NB 6/1/10.

agricultural training.'[48] Inspectors' reports regularly praised farming – and scenic – development at the Matopos mission itself. 'Highly attractive, carefully planned', ran one description of it in 1922, 'among beautiful trees and even the rocks are fitted into the general scheme. Much of the best education given by the mission is that of general industry in farming, gardening, dairying, care of cattle and fowls ... draining of land,' though on the academic side 'the pupils appear to have little beyond reading in the native tongue, or rather in Zulu.'[49] In 1934 there was a similar balance of judgement. The Inspector did not think much of the Brethren's academic education – 'almost a year spent in reading *Pilgrim's Progress* is not conducive to a lasting belief in the joys of the language.... A knowledge of life in Canada and the Americas is less important than a knowledge of Rhodesian Native and European contact and development.' But 'the Matopos is so admirably equipped for farming life.'[50] A separate report on the practical agricultural examination for trainee teachers revealed a sharp difference of opinion between the Native Development department, which wanted them instructed only in basic 'four crop rotation as recommended for kraal schools', and the missionaries who were determined to produce 'fully trained farmers.'[51]

The Brethren, in short, remained determined to improve and transform the Matopos long after the state's emphasis had switched to protection and conservation. Their converts were equally committed to an entrepreneurial Christianity. Reared on such basic texts for self-improvement as *The Pilgrim's Progress* and school histories of North America, teacher-evangelists went out among the 'immense boulders', pledged to a war on the 'rock-bound customs' of their people. It was not going to be easy to convince these men that their beloved instrument, the plough, was an engine of destruction. These African converts were impressed by the opportunities of the Bulawayo food-market, but they were also impressed by the mission's atmosphere of miracle and its message of divine power. The mission's chronicler, Frances Davidson, tells how Engle raised a woman from the dead by anointing and prayer, and how 'the natives accept the miracles of healing, mentioned in the Scriptures, without question'. She also tells of the insistent message preached, 'until it is burned into the consciousness of the hearers [of] a Supreme Being who is holy, omnipotent, omniscient and omnipresent, and cannot look upon sin with any degree of tolerance, to whom all must render an account.' It was an atmosphere and a message which produced Protestant entrepreneurs convicted of sin and convinced of redemption.[52]

Frances Davidson tells us of one such early convert, Matshuba, one of the first handful in the school, who came to work at the mission herding donkeys, and who 'had many hard battles to fight' with the mission teaching:

> Often we have found him out among the rocks praying for help and victory. The day came when he saw himself as a great sinner and he repented in truth. He prayed openly before

[48] Chief Native Commissioner to Director, Land Settlement, 19 August 1915, N 3/5/1/3.
[49] R. McIntosh, Matopos Day School Report, 3 August 1922, N 9/5/8.
[50] C. S. Davies and A. R. Mather, Matopos Teacher Training School Report, 14 September 1934, S 605/34.
[51] H. Jowett, Director of Native Development, to Rev. L. B. Spreckley, 14 September 1935, S 605/34.
[52] Davidson, *South and South Central Africa*, pp. 74, 159.

the school ... Almost the hush of death fell upon all, for it was a new era to them.[53]

Matshuba became a teacher. By 1913 he could blacksmith, build and plough, just like a North American Brethren in Christ elder.

In this new era of victory among the rocks, Brethren in Christ converts confronted and defied the Mwali shrines, which stood for such different ideas of environment and community. In 1904 another convert teacher, Ndhlalambi, started Mpane sub-station south-west of the Matopos. Davidson visited him there in 1905. She heard of 'one special place' of Mwali worship – 'a large cave in the midst of the Makalanga country', where people went every year to 'dance and pray for rain'. Defying tradition, Ndhlalambi took Davidson and a woman convert, Setyokupi, to see the cave.[54] Davidson's report to the *Evangelical Visitor* in October 1905 offers an interesting account both of the post-conquest state of the Mwali shrines and of missionary response to them:

> According to the people, there were two of these mountains of worship and two Umlimos, the father and the son. One of these places is seven or eight miles from this mission.... This immense granite hill towers above all the surrounding ones and can be seen a long distance. No one has been able to climb its steep sloping sides to the top. We went over half way around the mountain and finally came to a cave up in the side where it was said the Umlimo dwelt.... We found ourselves in a fine large cave, high, broad and deep, with steeply sloping sides covered with the pictures of hundreds of animals, men, etc. supposed to be bushmen painting.

People took presents to this cave, which from its situation just north of the *mapani* veld was probably the senior shrine of Njelele. 'In return they would inquire of the Ulimo in regard to the condition of the country and whether they should go to war and so on.'

Davidson's visit was part of a general mission strategy of penetrating and defusing the shrines, which eventually led to mission schools and churches being built across the path to every important shrine in the Matopos. According to her 1905 account veneration of the shrines was already in decline. People 'no longer have responses from the cave'; ideas of Mwali's nature and power were 'quite vague'. When she pressed them, one man obligingly replied that 'since you tell us about the devil, we think this must have been he since he loved the things that Satan loves.' Davidson, who longed to win local youth from 'their wild, free life among the hills for the narrow confines of the schoolroom', prayed that 'while the worship of the Umlimo is losing ground among this people, that of the true God may take its place'.[55]

The Mwali adepts resisted the spread of Christian entrepreneurship and its display of contempt for the shrines as best they could. Davidson tells us that the rains of 1905/1906 were 'exceptionally late and the people were now becoming desperate'; diviners blamed the drought upon the visit to the cave and Ndhlalambi was in danger of his life. Several years later another drought was blamed upon Setyokupi.

[53] *Ibid.*, p. 81.

[54] *Ibid.*, pp. 157, 177.

[55] Frances Davidson, 'Progress of the Work in Mapane Land', 24 October 1905, in *Evangelical Visitor*, 15 December 1905, pp. 15–16. I am indebted to Wendy Urban-Mead for a photocopy of this report.

Ngwabi Bhebe describes a similar episode a long way south-west of the Matopos, at the Jesuit Empandeni station:

> The Jesuits' intensive methods of transforming the Empandeni community must have looked like a real threat to the god, for in 1906 one of his mediums displayed a somewhat aggressive atttitude towards the Catholics. In the spring of that year, Nina kaPanzi, 'Mother of the Ground', an influential priestess of Mwari, came and stayed in a hut a few miles outside Empandeni.... Before being driven away by the Catholics, Nina kaPanzi accused the people of ploughing before propitiating Mwari.... She called upon the people to bring offerings to her, to stop working on Saturdays and work on Sundays instead, and to bring seeds to her to be fructified. All these commands were obeyed. In 1912–13 Empandeni was unfortunate to have no rain when the rest of the country had it. The traditionalists took this to be a clear demonstration of the impotence of the missionary God and of the power of Mwari. Nina kaPanzi reappeared and called on the Empandeni people to return to their old ways.[56]

The Brethren's second mission at Mtshabezi, south-east of the Matopos, opened as a refuge for girls escaping forced marriages and developed into a girls' boarding school. Mtshabezi was thus a special offence to traditional patriarchy, and it was close to the stronghold of three particularly influential Mwali priests, Siginyamatshe, Dapa and Vudze. Siginyamatshe had been jailed in 1896 for inciting the uprising; when he was released in 1908 he turned to the Mtshabezi area and shortly after 'there was a seismic disturbance which he is claimed to have caused.' Both the missionaries and the administration were worried about his influence and in 1912 an African policeman, one Mbeyo, was sent to spy on the Mtshabezi priests. On his 'return to Fort Usher Mbeyo died. All the local natives knew the object of his visit and attribute his death to the displeasure of [Mwali]'. In 1911 a white policeman, Trooper Atfield, had entered Njelele cave, 'the headquarters of these natives', and removed some of the sacred objects. 'Six months later he died. Natives are convinced that his death resulted from this act.'[57]

Ideological warfare was being waged in the Matopos in the first 20 years of the twentieth century between the Mwali shrines and the spokesmen for 'progressive' Christianity.[58] It was a war about definition of community, patterns of production and hence about landscape. Although Christians were certainly still in a small minority, the Mwali adepts were being forced on to the defensive. Mission schools were sited right up against all the major shrines. And the Njelele priests could not prevent the development of a centre of African Christian initiative just to the north of them in 'Whitewaters'.

Whitewaters became, after Matopo Mission, the most important Protestant centre in the hills. It was a London Missionary Society out-station, but one founded by African Christians rather than by missionaries. The LMS minister Neville Jones described in 1937 the origin of the Whitewaters school:

---

[56] Ngwabi Bhebe, *Christianity and Traditional Religion in Western Zimbabwe, 1859-1923*, Longman, London, 1979, p. 125.

[57] Military Intelligence Report, Fort Usher, circa 1918, S 728/6A/4.

[58] This ideological war was not only with the Mwali shrines and their Banyubi adepts. The short-lived Anglican mission at Umlugulu met with high-caste Ndebele scorn: 'As Mr Leary was instructing a congregation of Matabele down at Umlugulu, he showed a lantern picture of the Crucifixion. A Matabele woman, proud mother and daughter of warriors, at once asked, "How could His dying like *that* save us?".' T. W. Leary, 23 June 1899, *Mashonaland Quarterly Papers*, X1X, August 1899.

The out-station, 'Whitewaters' in the Matopos Hills, is a spot of marvellous beauty. An evangelist lives there ... and the school is one of the biggest in the whole district. It has, moreover, a history. In 1915 I was at Betsa, on the fringe of the hills, for a week-end, and while I was there I was visited by a man named Bayane, who invited me to come and see 'my' school at Whitewaters. I replied that I had no school there nor had I ever heard of the place. His importunities, however, prevailed and I went with him to Whitewaters. To my great surprise, I found a flourishing little school, housed in a neatly built wattle-and-daub building. I was informed that this was one of my schools. The self-appointed teacher had himself built it and had for some time been carrying on unpaid and unknown.... I could hardly do otherwise than adopt the foundling and our now flourishing work at Whitewaters began.[59]

Thereafter Whitewaters was in the hands of an African evangelist, 'a man of outstanding personality and zeal', who 'built up an outstanding piece of work.' The people of the area were responsive but independent. In 1930 the missionary Isabel Ross went to Whitewaters with ten African women students trained as home improvement workers. They held a month's camp for local women, providing them with school-girl baby-sitters:

Most of the women were untidy and we told them that they should keep themselves clean. They said they had too much work to do. They were not like white people who had black boys to work for them.[60]

Other modernising instruction was accepted less critially. One of the LMS teachers, Boli Mashingele, had been born in Whitewaters in 1904, from where he had been taken by the Reverend Mtompe Khumalo for education and training. In 1933 Mashengele went to Domboshawa government school for an agricultural course. On his return he travelled constantly round the LMS schools, bugle at the ready to summon audiences. 'Boli is an adept at agriculture', wrote a missionary who accompanied him on one of these expeditions, 'and woe betide that teacher who has not got his plot in trim.'[61] Mashingele was assured of a warm reception in his Whitewaters home, where there was abundant water and where the motor road from Kezi to Bulawayo ran through the hills, making transport of produce easy. Headmaster Timothy Chadi had a rice paddy 'under the big rock' and Headman Captain Ngwenya cultivated 'beautiful big maize fields' as proof of the area's agricultural potential.[62]

In 1933 the proudly progressive LMS community at Whitewaters decided that they needed a proper stone church. They set about quarrying granite from the nearby hills, making bricks and cutting grass. They chose 'a spot at the foot of a pile of rugged rocks'. The African LMS evangelist and builder, Bhebe, whose son Micah served as a member of parliament after 1980, constructed the church. It was opened before a congregation of four hundred on Christmas Day 1935 by a local dignitary, Mlotjwa, 'a wonderful old woman and surely the oldest Christian in the country.' The altar was a slab

[59] Neville Jones, 'Whitewaters – a "Foundling" Church', *The Chronicle of the London Missionary Society*, May 1937, p. 106.
[60] Iris Clinton, *Hope Fountain Story*, Bulawayo, 1962, p. 87; Neville Jones to Native Commissioner, Fort Usher, 27 September 1934, S 605.
[61] Eric Wyatt, 'School in the Bush', *The Chronicle of the London Missionary Society*, May 1939, p. 111.
[62] Interview with Mac Partridge, Bulawayo, 22 July 1988.

of granite from the nearby hillside; the inscription round the top of the apse read in Ndebele 'I will lift up mine eyes to the hills'. From 1935 until its destruction in 1962, when everyone was driven out of the National Park, the much photographed stone church at Whitewaters was a focal point for Matopos Protestant progressives.[63]

In August 1988 I interviewed Mrs Tenjiwe Lesabe, now member of parliament, head of the united ZANU/PF Women's League and a Minister. She lived in White-waters in the 1940s as a girl. She remembers it as '*very* progressive and organised.... Up to now you can still identify my group that grew up in that place at that time by our behaviour. Moral behaviour, hard work.... The Christians of that time had houses with whitewash, outside and inside, they had windows, and wire gauze for mosquitoes and things, they had flowers, they had fruits, they had oranges, they were very much involved in gardening.'[64] With its church and orchards and whitewashed houses, Whitewaters was an ideal Christian landscape.

African Christians See the Matopos

By the 1940s African Christians were confidently at home in the Matopos. Some of them began to express their confidence by painting the landscape. This happened at the third important mission in the hills, the Anglican station at Cyrene which was founded in 1938 west of 'the strange ghostly Matopos'. Cyrene was intended to be an important centre for agricultural training, but there were a series of droughts. In 1942, wrote the priest-in-charge, Canon Ned Paterson, they 'harvested nothing': 'As the drought continues, day after day, week after week, month after month, one suffers with the slowly dying plant life. In such a time one grasps one's kinship with nature.' As Paterson's biographer comments, since 'the agricultural side of Cyrene proved disappointing, great stress was put on the artistic side.' Paterson reported in 1942 that 'every student draws and paints.'[65]

In particular they painted nature. 'The typical Cyrene picture', wrote Paterson, 'is a large imperial sheet crammed to the sky with every imaginable sort of detail: rocks, trees, animals, villages and people.' He denied that the results were landscapes in the European sense:

> A youngster is not interested in broad landscape, but only in the small details of which a landscape is made up ... My pupils at Cyrene have not attempted to paint landscape but rather the accumulative detail one gets after a picnic with children in the Matopos; detail added to detail until there remains room for only a thin line of empty sky.

[63] Neville Jones, 'Whitewaters', *The Chronicle*, May 1937, p. 106; Neville Jones to Cocker Brown, 15 and 28 December 1935, LMS, South Africa, 1936, School of Oriental and African Studies, London.

[64] Interview with Mrs Thenjiwe Lesabe, Bulawayo, 24 August 1988. Mrs Lesabe insisted, however, that close as it was to Njelele, Whitewaters also respected some of the ancient ecological wisdom. The *ijambobo* ritual was organised to protect the crops from birds, making use of medicines brought from Dula by 'an old man called Mbezhi', custodian of the Mashakambayo shrine. Old people in Whitewaters knew 'the secrets and ceremonies of the rains, the diseases, disunity and all those things.'

[65] David A. C. Walker, *Paterson of Cyrene*, Mambo, Gweru, 1985, pp. 32–3.

Nevertheless, he contrasted the impact the Matopos landscape made on his Shona and his Ndebele pupils. The Shona, he thought, 'chose the purely decorative approach to art; they are not interested in drawing a particular tree, but first pass the tree through the brain, turn it over and then paint a symbolic version of it'; by contrast, the Ndebele 'see things more photographically' and delight 'in recording the subtle differences which distinguish one rock from another.'[66]

It sounds as though these two styles in combination might come close to the Mwali adept's view of the ambiguities of the Matopos landscape. But Paterson insisted that all the paintings were 'modern'.

> It may come as a surprise to know that it is not everyone who is able to grasp a picture or a photograph. At a small exhibition in Essexvale, I was amazed to realise that not one of a small group of native chiefs and headmen could 'see' our water colour pictures; they held them at all angles, tried to be polite, and fled for refuge to our painted and carved wooden bowls.

Many of the watercolours were also specifically Christian, laying hold of the Matopos as a setting for the events of the Bible – 'the Gospel seen as though it had been delivered by a native Jesus to the native people of this country.' All of them were more self-assured renderings of the hills than Baines and Oates had been able to attempt, and some of them represented a remarkable appropriation of the water colour technique. John Balopi, wrote Paterson, 'is evidently conscious of deep rhythms in nature and paints his pictures of great rocks, tortured rivers and gnarled trees rapidly and with great confidence.'[67]

Conserving the Matopos

So far the twentieth-century history of the Matopos has been depicted as a combination of memorial and enjoyment, of inscription and representation, and of use by both black and white. But another theme came to combine with some of these and to clash with others. Increasingly, Europeans came to believe that the hills must be preserved rather than used. Preservation might be combined with memorial and enjoyment but not with mining or agriculture. Since small peasant cultivators, with their Mwali ideology, and entrepreneurial farmers, with their progressive Christianity, both depended on agriculture, conservation proved difficult to combine with either human habitation or religious culture. The rocks would be protected but deprived of their voices.

Colonial sciences, which had at first been directed toward the exploitation of the Matopos, increasingly contributed to the conservationist ideology. In the long run, indeed, the white claim to *exploit* nature in the Matopos was given less endorsement by these sciences than the white duty to *conserve* it. The geological image of the hills was one of a very ancient environment, appropriately either lived in by an ancient people (like the San hunter-gatherers) or preserved by a modern one (like the whites), but not appropriately farmed by African agriculturalists. It was geology, too, which first put erosion on the Matopan intellectual agenda. It challenged both the Mwali and the Christian creation myths, presenting the hills as the setting of a vast drama of

---

[66] Edward Paterson, 'Cyrene Art', *NADA*, 1949, pp. 45–50.
[67] *Ibid.*, p. 47; Edward Paterson, 'Cyrene Art in London', *NADA*, 1955, pp. 73–6.

'weathering', which over the millennia had produced the castles and monoliths and pyramids of the lay European imagination.

James Sim's report on the Arboretum and on forestry laid more emphasis on African destruction of the woods than on European establishment of plantations. Ignorant of the sacred groves protected by Mwali, he insisted that: 'In all countries inhabited by uncivilised tribes, destruction of timber is a characteristic feature. No value is placed on trees or timber, except such as contribute to their hand to mouth existence.' African agriculture, wrote Sim, burnt wood for ash fertiliser, 'leaving dead and charred stumps and ruined soil'. This drove back 'the magnificent big game for which the country has been justly famed ... into the still uninhabited tracts of forest.... Under present conditions the big game is doomed to extermination.'[68]

Sim's report – which recommended combined forest and game reserves – was one of the earliest Rhodesian conservationist documents. Although he did not include the Matopos in his list of woodlands to be preserved, his visit gave legitimacy to the idea that whites had a duty to protect indigenous trees in the hills. It also gave legitimacy to the idea that Africans were the enemies of such trees. In 1909, when Native Commissioners in Matabeleland were asked to report on the state of wood resources, only the Native Commissioner, Matopo, reported from Fort Usher that they were in danger. 'Thousands of indigenous trees are destroyed annually by natives', he complained, the worst offenders being Banyubi and Kalanga hoe cultivators. He recommended 'limitations being put on the expansion of native kraals, so that natives may be induced to cultivate in parts where there is no valuable timber.'[69] Thereafter there were regular criticisms of the inhabitants of the hills who were said to be destroying timber on a large scale both by farming and in order to provide charcoal for the Bulawayo market.

In fact the destruction of the indigenous trees of the Matopos was an idea in the European mind rather than a reality on the ground. In June 1912 A. G. S. Richardson reported to his employers, Willoughby's Consolidated, on the condition of their huge Wenlock Block estate, which ran from the 'foothills of the Matopos' southwards towards Gwanda township. The southern part of the estate lay in the gold belt and was traversed by innumerable woodcutters' tracks; in the northern granite country there were only two or three 'faint tracks'. In the south of Wenlock, where the gold mines had concessions to cut wood, 'timber has either been cut out or considerably thinned', but 'as one approaches the granite, distance from the mines begins to tell and the timber remains practically intact.' In the African inhabited areas of the Matopos foothills, 'there are a hundred thousand cords of firewood waiting for the axe', while 'close to the mines practically nothing is left.' The threat to indigenous woodland, then, clearly came from commercial mining rather than from African agriculture.[70]

Nonetheless, the view took hold that white science was needed in order to save the flora of the Matopos from black aggression or indifference. The African inhabitants of

[68] James Sim, 'Report on Forestry in Southern Rhodesia', 1902, GF 2/1/2.
[69] Native Commissioner, Fort Usher, 20 December 1909; Memorandum for the Administrator on Destruction of Timber by Natives, 9 February 1910, GF 2/1/2.
[70] A. G. S. Richardson, Report on Sheet, Wenlock and Zwemele, 11 June 1912, S 2823/13.

the hills gloried in the abundance and variety of fruits. Whites listed and classified them. Nobbs's 1924 *Guide* called upon botany as well as geology. It described the indigenous trees, flowering shrubs, flowers, mosses and lichens. 'The plant-collector will be stimulated to activity if he realizes that the flora of the Matopos is as yet only partially explored, and a keen hunter is bound to discover new species.' Yet 'the richest finds are likely to be made in remote nooks and shady corners', on the 'moist floor' of hidden grottoes, in 'damp patches of sand' filling 'the rocky hollows', and 'by the swamps' – in precisely those areas, in short, where white experts were to seek to prohibit Africans from cultivating or grazing.[71] By the 1930s the image of the white administration as protector of the indigenous plants of the Matopos had become firmly established. Rhodes's Arboretum came to be regarded as a source of contamination by 'exotics' rather than as an example of improvement. In 1935 the Boy Scouts were permitted the use of a camp in the Matopos provided that they planted no alien trees.[72]

Even the hard colonial science of survey was repulsed or itself faltered in the Matopos. A major battle was fought over survey in the Matopos between the exploitative, the developmental and the protective implications of colonialism, as these were articulated in the legacies of Rhodes. By supporting Jameson in his haphazard parcelling out of land in central Matabeleland between 1893 and 1896, Rhodes had turned a blind eye to what might be called the exploitative age of Rhodesian surveying, when huge blocks of land were marked out for concessionaries, their boundaries only vaguely recorded and capable of moving uncannily to and fro. As we have seen, Rhodes aimed at development on his land north of the Matopos. But in his will he also expressed his feeling for 'the grandeur and loneliness of the Matoppos'. It was this sentiment which was invoked to bring the age of exploitative surveying to an end and to limit white development of the Matopos.

In November 1902 one W. Whittaker applied to the Civil Commissioner for permission to peg 9,000 morgen in the hills. The matter was referred to the Administrator, Sir William Milton, who invoked Rhodes's view of the special character of the Matopos. Milton was 'pretty sure instructions were given 4 or 5 years ago that the Matoppos was not open for pegging', and ordered that 'if there was not a standing order to that effect on the Surveyor-General's books it should now be done.' As a result a 'reservation' was placed against any further survey or allocation of land in an area of some 144,750 morgen.[73]

This reservation was uncontested until 1908. In that year, however, the British South Africa Company's Land Settlement Department tried to take up Rhodes's option of development rather than his sentiment for protection. They argued that there was 'urgent need of giving some impetus to land settlement in Matabeleland.' Surely the Founder could not have intended to lock up so much land? The issue was reopened. When the Reserves Commission sat in 1914 they were urged to recommend a partition of the Matopos, with the eastern half set aside for Africans and the western half thrown

[71] Nobbs, *Guide to the Matopos*, pp. 74–8.
[72] Chief Forestry Officer to Secretary, Agriculture and Lands, 24 August 1935, S 11944 190/7.
[73] Memorandum by Administrator, 16 August 1908, L 2/2/117/32.

open. The Superintendent of Natives, Bulawayo, H. M. Jackson, told the Commission on 13 June 1914 that:

> The British South Africa Company has never collected rent from the Natives in the Matopos Hills which have consequently been treated more or less as a Reserve.... The suggestion has recently been made that that portion of the Hills to the East of the Mchelele or Tuli rivers should be made a Reserve and the remainder be open to white settlement. Originally the whole of the Hills was regarded as useless and there was some idea of regarding it as a National Park. But now land which was formerly useless has acquired a value for settlement.[74]

As we shall see, the Commission did recommend a Reserve in the eastern Matopos, and the Land Settlement Department pressed hard for a carve-up of the rest of the hills.

So at last, in 1917, the Department got a surveyor back into the Matopos. But Land Inspector Boyes was a very different figure from the piratical surveyors of the 1890s. His report was almost painfully responsible. He had travelled through the whole area of the western half of the Matopos 'between the Tuli River and bounded West by the surveyed farms.' Close to the Tuli River 'the country is extremely rugged and approximately 30 square miles of country could never be taken up in ranches due to the endless masses of granite rock bearing a very small acreage for grazing purposes.' Elsewhere he was able to demarcate 14 farms for ranching, but with little enthusiasm: 'In this area I estimate 80 kraals. The area with its small scrappy acreages for agriculture and suiting the native tastes might have been put aside as a Native Reserve.'

There were no prospects for irrigation; no marketable timber; no 'big game'; but 'millions of rock rabbits and thousands of troops of baboons'. Moreover, Boyes was impressed by the ceremonial character of the hills. Sentiment even stayed his surveyor's hand. One of the ranches demarcated was supposed to border on World's View farm, but Boyes purposely left a belt of land between then, since otherwise 'should this land be alienated, a homestead may possibly be built in full view of the Tomb which would be an eyesore to the tourist; even a sacrilege to the memory of Mr Rhodes.'[75]

All this was discouraging enough, but nevertheless in February 1919 the Company's London Board authorised the Land Settlement Department to put these new Matopos ranches on the market. It was really too late, however, for the development option in the hills. By 1919 the memorial character of the Matopos – their dedication to the inscription of Rhodesian heroism – had impressed itself on the minds of Rhodesian whites. Public opinion was inclined to agree with Boyes that active exploitation would be sacrilege. Moreover, all the legitimating sciences led in the Matopos to conservationist conclusions – geology as an admonitory melodrama of erosion; forestry with its emphasis on protection; botany with its revelation of the unspoilt Matopos glens as discovery sites for Rhodesian scientific pioneers. The first of the influential advocates for a Matopos National Park, Eric Nobbs, was able to put all this together.

---

[74] Evidence of H. M. Jackson, 13 June 1914, ZAD 3/1/1.
[75] R. C. Boyes to Director, Land Settlement, 31 July 1917, A 3/28/46.

Towards a National Park in the Matopos

Nobbs was himself a development scientist, holder of BSc and PhD degrees, and Director of Agriculture in Southern Rhodesia. No-one had a greater interest in the creation of a dynamic commercial agriculture than Nobbs. He could be tough-minded even in assessing the legacies of Cecil Rhodes, believing that his estates north of the Matopos had been badly managed; that the famous dam had been built in the wrong place and had never stood a chance of recovering the money spent on it; that the fringes of the Matopos were not at all a suitable place for an arboretum or an experimental farm. But as he looked out from the Rhodes Estates into the hills themselves, Nobbs experienced quite different emotions. Here was a land to which Rhodes's more sentimental impulses appeared totally appropriate, a land of nature and imperial history rather than of commerce and scientific agriculture. (Nobbs ignored Banyubi cultivation and the labours of the mission entrepreneurs.) In 1918 he put a good deal of effort into erecting 'stones at certain points in the Matopos to commemorate matters of interest' in the recent history of the hills.[76] At some point he became a passionate protagonist of the idea that the hills as a whole should be preserved for posterity.

Nobbs chose with great skill the moment to advance the idea of a Matopos National Park. Since Rhodes's funeral no-one else had been buried at World's View. But now in 1919 preparations were being made for the interment of Sir Leander Starr Jameson. On 11 June Nobbs escorted one of the Company's directors, the Duke of Abercorn, 'to inspect the site selected for Sir Starr Jameson's grave'. Forgetting that the London Board had authorised the subdivision of the land into farms, Abercorn was overwhelmed by the grandeur of the site. Nobbs pressed upon him the idea that 'a considerable tract of land in the neighbourhood of the grave' should be reserved perpetually; Abercorn agreed to present such a plan to the Board. On 12 June the Land Settlement Department was instructed 'to see that no further applications for land anywhere in the region are entertained.' Nobbs was asked to make detailed recommendations.[77]

Nobbs's report of October 1919 was the first major Rhodesian statement of colonial interventionism as conservation. But it looked back to the nineteenth-century idea that Africans merely lived in nature and were powerless to affect it, rather than forward to the later scientific condemnations of African land use. Nobbs began with a rebuff to those who thought the Matopos could be developed by whites using modern agricultural techniques:

> All this land is intrinsically poor in the extreme, excessively rugged ... too favoured by baboons for cropping and too tiger-haunted for stock, too water-logged in summer and too cold and exposed in winter ... for purposes of production of little or no value.

On the other hand, wrote Nobbs in language which invoked the Rhodesian self-image as pioneers, explorers and appropriators of land, the area was:

[76] G 1/7/3/6.
[77] Acting Commercial Representative to Acting Diector, Land Settlement, 12 June 1919; Administrator to Acting Treasurer, 24 June 1919, A 3/28/46.

scenically one of the most interesting and delightful tracts in Rhodesia, but although only a short distance from Bulawayo, it is at present inaccessible to the public. The prospect from the World's View is famous, but the Matopos are even more interesting and beautiful when seen from within, as can only be done by penetrating their recesses and traversing their remoter parts.

Nobbs went on to paint a picture of the Matopos as unspoilt Eden – but an Eden threatened by the industrial and urban Fall and needing an active protective inter-vention which the African inhabitants could not give:

This country is untouched by civilised man and remains in its natural state of wild beauty with only occasional kraals and native gardens, just as it has been from time immemorial.... The presence of natives would be a feature of interest to many visitors and there is no occasion to disturb them.... [By] the retention in its pristine condition for scientific interest of a large portion of the country not suited for other purposes, comparatively close to the centres of modern life, it would be possible to preserve in perpetuity the pristine conditions of South Africa – rapidly vanishing through the rest of the sub-continent. Sentiment and science alike support such a suggestion.

Nobbs was unusual not only in disregarding the criticisms of African attitudes to and uses of the land, which had already emerged by 1919, but also in paying some attention to African culture. This he saw not in terms of history but of 'tradition'. For Nobbs, this tradition was *part* of the 'pristine conditions' of the Matopos and should be open to white explorers just as much as the undiscovered blooms in the swamps. So he proposed, for instance, that a footpath be made to the main Mwali shrine at Njelele. As we have seen, Njelele was still very much part of a functioning, changing and contested religious and ecological history. But to Nobbs it was a monument of 'time immemorial'. Njelele *had* once been the headquarters of an age-old cult but the colonial conquest had ended all that. In times past, wrote Nobbs, Njelele was 'the scene of rain dances and the supposed home of the Mlimo.'[78]

Nobbs's report put an end to any further surveying and alienation of farms in the Matopos. But the British South Africa Company Board were reluctant to commit themselves to the expense of a formal National Park. A Park still had not been declared when Southern Rhodesia achieved Responsible Government in 1923. Nobbs's 1924 *Guide to the Matopos* was designed as an appeal to the newly dominant settler public opinion. I have quoted already from its historical, geological, topographical and other sections. For Nobbs, the key chapter was the concluding one on 'Future Possibilities – a National Park'. Much of this was taken word for word from his 1919 report, though with more emphasis on 'making this wonderful tract of country accessible as a holiday resort for Rhodesians, who cannot always get down to the coast for a change.' But Nobbs had not changed his patronising tolerance of the African inhabitants of the hills, whose continued presence still seemed desirable from a tourist point of view:

The few natives within the area need not be disturbed as their picturesque kraals, their

---

[78] E. A. Nobbs, 'Matopos', enclosed in Nobbs to Acting Treasurer, 31 October 1919, A 3/28/46.

costume, cattle, crops and customs would add features of interest to many visitors, and they might be usefully employed in preventing veld fires and maintaining roads and paths.[79]

The appeal was successful and on 19 November 1926 the new Rhodesian government proclaimed 224,000 acres of the Matopos – an area very much larger than the present park – 'for the purpose of a National Park and Game Reserve.' But there was still no legislation setting up a National Parks Authority. The huge proclaimed area in the Matopos was put under the undefined custodianship of the Forestry Department.

Nobbs's intervention had stopped surveying for farms and ranches in the Matopos; indeed, for many years after 1926 there was no surveying in the hills at all. When surveying *did* resume in the 1940s it was for a changed purpose and in a very different conservationist atmosphere. By the 1940s the African inhabitants of the hills no longer seemed to be 'few'; their 'cattle, crops and customs' no longer seemed 'picturesque' but a threat to the soil and water resources of the Matopos. The Christian ploughmen, whom Nobbs had ignored, were now seen as the greatest danger of all. Surveying was now employed for subdividing the hills for reclamation units; for enumerating human and animal populations; for mapping agricultural and pastoral 'incursions' on valley bottoms and swamps. Like the other sciences of colonialism, surveying had become an auxiliary of interventionist conservationism.

It was in fact partly the further development of the colonial sciences which ushered in the second conservationist age, so different in tone from Nobbs's romanticism. In 1956 Nobbs's guide was revised under the direction of Sir Robert Tredgold. Tredgold commented that Nobbs's original had been 'written at a time when … the specialised scientific knowledge of Rhodesia was much more imperfect…. In the passage of thirty years scientific knowledge has progressed. Whole sections, such as those dealing with the geology, archaeology, fauna and flora have been rewritten.' A new section on the now achieved National Park dramatised the survey of 1946:

> An exhaustive survey carried out on foot and horseback was made to determine the correct carrying capacity of the area in relation to African families and stock. This revealed that while there were some 1,750 families and 13,800 head of stock living in the park, its correct carrying capacity was 400 families and 4,000 head of stock. It was clear that unless this reduction was made it would be next to impossible to deal with the erosion and denudation that was going on.[80]

This language of 'carrying capacities' was very different from Nobbs's discourse. It arose, as we shall see in later chapters, out of the imperatives of the Rhodesian political economy and the need to evict the African peasants and pastoralists from 'white' land in central Matabeleland. It also arose out of developments in science. Two of these in particular affected the way in which whites came to look at the Matopos. These were prehistory and agronomy.

---

[79] Nobbs, *Guide to the Matopos*, pp. 64–65.
[80] Robert Tredgold, ed., *The Matopos*, Salisbury, 1956, pp. v, 25.

Prehistory, Agronomy and the New Conservationism

Tredgold's 1956 guide carried a chapter on 'The Archaeology and the Prehistory of the Hills', written by two Rhodesian experts whose type had not existed in 1924 – Roger Summers, FRAS, Keeper of Antiquities at the National Museum, Bulawayo, and C. K. Cooke, 'the well-known authority on Bushman paintings.' Their chapter began with a justified claim: 'The pre-history of Southern Rhodesia has been written almost entirely as a result of archaeological studies in the Matopos.' They rightly singled out the work of Dr Neville Jones, for many years LMS minister at Hope Fountain, whose cottage at Whitewaters had been the base for years of study of the Rhodesian Stone Age. Of course, Nobbs had known that there were 'Bushman paintings' in the hills. But Tredgold's *Matopos* gave a much fuller and more systematic account of millennia of hunter-gatherer occupation. It drew a sympathetic picture of 'straight-limbed people, fast walkers and great runners; of patience unthinkable to modern civilised men and having the most acute observation and visual memory.' These 'relatively few' hunters came into the hills only 'at certain seasons of the year'. But, as Summers and Cooke went on to say, much more was known about them than about their Iron Age agriculturalist successors. 'Between that period which properly belongs to the prehistorian and that which is recorded by the historian, there is … a curious twilight period.'[81]

The prehistorical work that had been done before 1956 – and virtually all the archaeological work that has been done in the Matopos since then – focussed entirely on the hunter-gathering economy of the Stone Age and ignored the agricultural and cattle-keeping economy of the Banyubi and their predecessors. Rhodesian pre-history – the colony's greatest claim to work of international scientific significance – thus gave the impression that hunter-gatherers had been the 'natural' inhabitants of the Matopos. It was they who had lived there since times immemorial and whose way of life was unthreatening to the ecology of the hills, while African agriculturalists, whose use of the environment remained completely unstudied, were 'relatively recent' interlopers. It was easy to pass from such pre-history to the agronomic conclusion that African crops and cattle, so far from being in age-old symbiosis with the hills, stood for Adamic original sin in the Eden of the Matopos. Up to today when one visits the great cave at Nswatugi, in order to marvel at its 'Bushman paintings', one finds outside it an ecological exhibit which announces that agriculture should *never* be carried on in the hills.

Many of the prehistorians developed a profound sympathy for the hunter-gatherers and an admiration for their relationship with nature which was a very long way from the nineteenth-century contempt for those who lived *in* nature rather than *on* it. Peter Garlake's admirable text, *Early Zimbabwe. From the Matopos to Nyanga*, which in its Matopos section focusses entirely on the Stone Age, represents the maturation of this attitude and paints an idyllic picture:

---

[81] Robert Tredgold, ed., *The Matopos*, Salisbury, 1956, pp. 39–61.

The last Stone Age people to hunt across Zimbabwe are known to us most vividly through the paintings they did on the rocks of many hundreds of our hills.... These people were far from being poor and homeless nomads wandering aimlessly. Their lives had a regular pattern. The country was rich in animals and wild fruits and vegetables. On these they lived, taking food and killing game as they needed it, moving with the herds and seasons across a territory recognised by all as theirs by right. In rich areas, like the Matopo Hills, many people could live and never have to move far. However, they did not have to put anything back into the land. They did not have to plan for future needs, keep food for the lean months or wait for the harvest. No one could sell his food or hoard it. No one could become wealthy ... There was no threat from people hungry for land and farms. Instead there was, for the time, a rich culture, an advanced economy, an easy and self-assured life.[82]

It was a great pity that the archaeologists of the Matopos were unable to write in this affectionate way about the hundreds of years of African agricultural occupation of the hills.

As it was, this kind of pre-history provided the new agronomic conservationists with the sort of past they needed. In the 1940s this school came to believe that the 'fragile' ecology of the Matopos required that no people live in it at all – or at least only people like those long-lost, happy hunter-gatherers. The focal point of this new conservationism was the Matopos Research Station, which had developed out of Rhodes's wish for an experimental farm and was situated on the Rhodes Matopos Estate, north of the hills. Tredgold's *The Matopos* contained a section on the Station, describing its 'animal husbandry work' during the 1930s and its focus on 'veld management', and noting that 'basic principles of conservation are involved in many of the experiments.'[83] It was from the Research Station, in fact, that the concept of 'correct carrying capacity' arose, and in particular from the experiments with 'Native' cattle carried out by Charles Murray.[84]

After Nobbs, Murray was the key figure in defining governmental attitudes to the Matopos. In fact, the Forestry Department, which had been in nominal charge of the National Park since 1930, had already been arguing for a total clearance of the African population from most of the Matopos, holding that 'the area should either be a National Park or a Native Reserve' and that it could not be both. In January 1935 the Chief Forestry Officer had proposed a compromise scheme of partition, whereby 42,000 acres adjacent to Rhodes's Grave should be entirely cleared of people, and had pressed this idea in 1938 and again in 1940. But his scheme would cost money, since land would have to be obtained outside the hills on which to settle those displaced, and no money was available. In any case, Forestry supervision of the Matopos was fitful and ineffective. Things changed in 1945 when Murray, a determined and qualified man of science, took the hills in hand.

Murray could articulate with authority the dogmas of a new ecological science, 'very exact, very recently developed and very difficult of appreciation by a native people.'[85]

[82] Peter Garlake, *Early Zimbabwe. From the Matopos to Nyanga*, Gweru, 1983, pp. 3–4.

[83] Tredgold, *The Matopos.*, pp.101–4.

[84] Sibongile Mlotshwa, 'The Matopos Research Station: Origins and Contribution to the agrarian Development of Zimbabwe', BA History Honours thesis, University of Zimbabwe, Harare, July 1984. Mlotshwa takes a much more positive view of Charles Murray's career than I do in this book.

[85] Advocate P. Lloyd, cross-examining Dr West, 18 March 1949, S 1561/6.

Nobbs's vague talk of preserving the Matopos for science now gave way to precise calculations of carrying capacity, siltage rates and erosion potential. Murray held an MSc in Agriculture; had initiated and managed the indigenous cattle experiment; and ran the Rhodes Matopos Estates. He had great confidence in his experiments, claiming them to be 'by far the largest and most important of their kind conducted anywhere in the world'. On the basis of their results, he presented with a largely spurious exactness those calculations of 'excess' human and cattle populations which lent 'scientific' justification to the mass eviction of Africans from central Matabeleland after 1945. He had no sympathy for Africans living on the Rhodes Matopos Estates or close by in the Matopos: 'We are running valuable experimental cattle ... and if they have any cattle at all we will get our work interfered with ... They used the place essentially for beer-drinks from Bulawayo.'[86] So far from the Matopos Africans living in a state of pristine picturesqueness, as Nobbs thought, Murray believed that the hills were used merely as a base for labour migrancy to Bulawayo or Johannesburg; for beer drinks and prostitution for workers coming out from Bulawayo; for destructive farming by women and old men; and for yet more destructive grazing by thousands of 'scrub cattle'. African 'traditional' methods of cultivation were bad enough, in Murray's eyes. Tradition corrupted by labour migration and urban influences was worse still.

The difference between Nobbs's attitude and Murray's partly reflected real changes in the economy of the hills. The early Banyubi 'peasant option', which involved so much investment of the labour of young men, had been undercut by drought and the rise of white agricultural production. By the 1930s the Matopos had become a typical migrant labour society. Moreover, cattle holdings had very greatly increased since the first decade of the century. Instead of depending on the sale of cereal surplus, many of the people of the hills subsisted on urban remittances with 'scrub' cattle as their 'bank'. What Murray looked at in the hills was different from what Nobbs had seen – but he also saw through different eyes.

During the 1930s Murray became fascinated by the Matopos – 'I often drove through the Park', he told the 1949 Commission of Inquiry. 'It always worried me that such vitally important land should be allowed to be destroyed at such a terrific rate.' To Murray the hills were 'important' not culturally, nor historically, nor even scenically. They were important as the source of the rivers which fed the ranching country of southern Matabeleland. In his view African occupation threatened these rivers through over-cultivation and over-grazing of the *vleis* and sponges. 'In other parts of the world', he insisted, 'parts like this Matopos National Park would not be made available for farming purposes under any conditions.'[87] Murray asked to be given the Matopos to sort out and in 1940 the Forestry Department handed over responsibility to him. It was Murray who appointed Ranger J. H. Grobler to carry out the detailed survey of 1946, which led to the recommendations for depopulating and destocking the Matopos.

[86] Evidence of Charles Murray, 21 March 1949, S 1561/46.
[87] *Ibid*.

Conclusion

I shall show in detail in later chapters the consequences of these recommendations. It suffices to say now that eventually depopulation and destocking were carried through; that a formally constituted National Parks Department came to manage the Matopos and sought to control African 'tenants'; that early in 1962 a partition was enforced by which the present area of the National Park was completely depopulated and the rest of the Matopos became Reserves. After 1962 the Parks Department had 107,645 acres all of its own, into which it could at last 're-introduce' big game and invent a pristine environment wl.:ch it could then conserve. It was to be back to the days of the hunter-gatherers, though with only their rock paintings surviving and carefully listed and protected as though waiting their seasonal return. A Wilderness Area was created in the eastern part of the new National Park, which could be entered only on foot or on horseback. Special Conservation Areas were closed to almost everyone. The Matopos National Park was now fully 'wild'; river bottoms which had for centuries been farmed by Africans had become 'secret valleys filled with rivers of long grass.' Close as it was to Bulawayo, the Park could now 'stamp itself indelibly on the mind as one of the wildest, loveliest and often strangest natural splendours in Zimbabwe.'[88]

These interventions sought to suppress the voices from the rocks – it is the silence of the hills which is most often remarked upon by white writers. But voices were nevertheless raised in opposition. Murray's policies were resisted first by the Christian entrepreneurs of Whitewaters, Matopo Mission and Mtshabezi, and later by the adepts of the Mwali shrines.

[88] Dick Pitman, *National Parks of Zimbabwe*, Harare, n.d., pp. 3, 67, 68.

II

The Struggle
for the Land

3

The Promises of Rhodes

So far I have been using words like 'seeing', 'inscribing', 'appropriating'. Despite my references to very real battles and evictions, perhaps it has all seemed to be constructed abstractly in the mind rather than acted out on the ground. But ways of seeing defined ways of acting. The previous chapters have set the context for critical economic and political – and, eventually, military – struggles between black and white. These were essentially struggles over land. In the second part of this book I want to show what happened to the peoples who were living in or around the Matopos in the 1890s and what happened to the land they were living on.

In this chapter I describe what happened to these people after the uprisings of 1896; the promises made to them that they would enjoy security on the land; and how those promises were broken. In the next chapters I describe what happened thereafter to the people of the *Nqameni* regiment, who lived in the 1890s on the northern edges of the Matopos and ended up south-east of them on Wenlock ranch; to the peoples of the area defined in 1923 as a National Park, and in particular to the Christians of Whitewaters; and to the peoples of what is today the Matobo Communal Area in the eastern hills. I then seek to bring together the responses of all these people to eviction and their creation of protest associations. Finally, I describe the aftermath of eviction and protest – the involvement of the Matopos peoples and of the Mwali shrines in nationalism, guerrilla war and the politics of the 1980s. Only then, in my conclusion, shall I return to questions of perception and the ways in which the Matopos are seen today.

Fearing the Matopos

I have already discussed many different ways of seeing the Matopos. But I have not yet described the dominant image of them in the minds of all whites and many blacks after the uprising of 1896. The Matopos were seen as *dangerous*. It had turned out to be impossible to defeat the Ndebele in the hills; it proved very difficult to track down 'murderers' in them; if Africans in Matabeleland were given too much ground for grievance, it was generally assumed that the Matopos would again become a redoubt for resistance. Native Commissioners in other districts were constantly reporting 'rumours of unrest', focussing upon 'a certain crowd in the Matopos.' In 1898 there were reports from Bubi in northern Matabeleland that Mwali priests from all over the country were joining the 'band of criminals and disaffected persons in the Matobos'; in July 1899 there were reports from Bulilima-Mangwe that an Ndebele king would be elected in the Matopos, that all royal cattle would be reclaimed, that whites would depart, and that Africans 'friendly' to them would also have to flee; in September of the same year the Native Commissioner, Belingwe, reported rumours emanating from the Matopos that all Africans were to be conscripted to fight the Boers, which he thought designed to provoke another uprising. In 1904 Kalanga in the south predicted that 'there will be a rising among chiefs in the Matopos when hut tax is collected', and in 1906 the Native Commissioner, Insiza, declaring that 'every native hates every whiteman', believed that Mwali priests in the Matopos were coordinating a 'combination of the whole country' against the Europeans.[1]

Even though the administrators in the hills themselves regularly discounted these reports – 'In spite of silly rumours to the contrary', wrote the Native Commissioner, Matopos, in January 1898, 'I can report that everything is absolutely quiet in this district.'[2] – the image of the Matopos as dangerous persisted for decades. As late as 1924 the Native Commissioners of Matabeleland were asked to predict the shape that any African resistance might take. Inevitably they imagined a repetition of 1896. The Mzingwane Commissioner thought that 'concentrations would take place in the Matopo hills' and that his Africans would 'group under one of the Matobo district chiefs'; the Bulilima-Mangwe Commissioner thought that 'the foothills of the Matopos' would be the 'storm-centre'; the Gwanda Commissioner believed that 'the Matobo Hills' would provide a refuge for those 'imbued with tribal pride' in his district. The Native Commissioner, Matobo, himself predicted that the leaders of any rising would be three *indunas* in the southern foothills of the Matopos, one of them being the aging but still formidable Mtuwane, 'the ablest leader in the district'. Close to him in the south-eastern hills lived 'the head-priest of the Mlimo ... and it is at a hill here (the Siluywi Hill on Gwandavale Farm) that the oracle is nowadays consulted and periodical gatherings assembled.' If the object were 'sheer rebellion or murder' the head priest 'would be employed by the ringleaders to communicate and spread the movement', and the 'storm centre in this district would therefore be the northern portion of Wenlock Block, which extends into the Matopo Hills.'[3]

There is no doubt that for Rhodes himself the danger of the Matopos outweighed all

---

[1] Native Commissioner, Bubi to Chief Native Commissioner, Bulawayo, 4 February 1898, NB 6/5/2/1; Native Commissioner, Tegwani to Chief Native Commissioner, Bulawayo, 10 July 1899; Native Commissioner, Belingwe 8 November 1899, NB 1/1/8; H. M. Hole to Chief Native Commissioner, Bulawayo, 25 May 1904, NB 3/2/1; Native Commissioner, Insiza to Chief Native Commissioner, Bulawayo, 8 January 1906, NB 3/2/2.

[2] Monthly report, Matopos, January 1898, NBE 1/1/1.

[3] Reports by Native Commissioners, Matabeleland, March, April, May 1924, S 728/6A/5.

the other visions he had of them – as a place to be buried in, as a place for recreation, as a place for agricultural experiment. He shared the anxieties of the leading Ndebele 'loyalists' when they told the Acting Chief Native Commissioner in February 1898 that

> they could not understand why the Government allowed any Matabele Indunas to live in the hills, that they [must] come out and live in the open. They felt convinced that there were Natives in the Matobo who would still like to rebel.[4]

In one way or another Rhodes was determined to defuse the menace of the Matopos. But how was this to be done?

Rhodes toyed with several different strategies. The Matopos might be secured by settling reliable black allies in them; or they might be made safer by persuading the 'Ndebele' to come out of the hills into 'the open'; or they might be pacified by meeting the grievances of their inhabitants. Rhodes tried all three of these strategies.

Settling the Matopos

We have already seen how Rhodes encouraged missionaries to settle in the hills so that they could build up groups of African Christians responsive both to development and discipline. He also sought to introduce African settlers who were already Christians and farmers. However impressed Rhodes was by the loneliness and the grandeur of the Matopos, his motives in the late 1890s were not at all conservationist. Instead, he sought to bring reliable African agriculturalists and cattle holders into the hills as a counter-balance to the rebellious Ndebele. If his plans had succeeded, much of the Matopos would have been given over to exploitation by a Christian progressive peasantry and the modern history of the hills would have been a very different one.

Rhodes sought for such loyal black settlers south of the Limpopo. In June 1897 the dissident Tswana chief, Raditladi, 'unable to live at peace with Chief Mphoeng', asked permission to migrate to Rhodesia. He was offered land in the Matopos. This offer was vetoed by High Commissioner Milner, who thought 'we should hesitate before assigning to Raditladi a position of great natural strength, as he seems to be of a somewhat insubordinate disposition.'[5] In May 1898, however, a larger-scale scheme was launched, with Rhodes's backing, to import 'loyal and progressive' M'fengu from the Cape. During the 1896 fighting most of the really dangerous operations in the Matopos had been carried out by 'Cape Boys', some of whom had been rewarded with grants of land. Rhodes now planned to make use of Cape loyalists to secure the peace.

M'fengu representatives were promised three 'reserves', one in the Matopos:

> Each man guarantees to work at least three months every year [and] ... after thirty-six months labour gets individual title to five morgen land as in Glen Grey Act.... No traders allowed within Reserves. Cattle will be conveyed Bulawayo at lowest obtainable rate.... This was

---

[4] Meeting between the Assistant Chief Native Commissioner and Induna Gambo's people, 11 February 1898, NB 6/5/1/1.

[5] High Commissioner, Cape Town to Acting Administrator, 14 September 1897, NB 1/1/5.

suggested by Mr Rhodes as good opportunity restock country with cattle. If natives called upon to defend country they are obliged to respond.[6]

The intention was to locate 10,000 M'fengu in Southern Rhodesia, some 4,000 of them in the Matopos, and thus to establish in the hills intensive farming by an individually tenured peasantry. Later in 1898 the Chief Native Commissioner, Matabeleland, toured the Matopos 'with some Fingo chiefs to look at this part of the country'.[7]

The M'fengu delegation were not enthusiastic either about the general terms offered them or about the Matopos as a site for entrepreneurial agriculture. But the Rhodesian administration persisted. In July 1899 the Chief Native Commissioner, Matabeleland, told gatherings of *indunas* that unless their young men came out to work for the whites either M'fengu or some other black South African immigrants would be established in the Matopos.[8] Nor were these idle threats. In addition to ideas of Tswana or M'fengu immigration, there were also plans to settle 800 Sotho families in the hills.[9]

None of these schemes were realised. Their only effect was to bring 'friendly' and 'rebel' *indunas* together in joint suspicion and protest. In November 1898 most of the *indunas* attended a secret meeting with a Bulawayo white lawyer 'to discuss that the Government were about to introduce a large number of Fingoes into the country and that the latter were to occupy the lands now inhabited by their people.' They planned to raise funds so that they could send delegates to appeal to the Queen in England against the introduction of the M'fengu, and at the same time to ask for the restoration of the Ndebele monarchy.[10] The search for black Christian allies from South Africa had merely made insecurity worse in the Matopos and contributed powerfully to rumours of another insurrection. Rhodes had to concentrate on his other strategies of pacification.

Bringing the Ndebele into the Open

When Rhodes held his series of *indabas* with the Matopos leaders in 1896 and 1897 he was watched with great suspicion by British military commanders and white settlers alike. They demanded nothing less than the unconditional surrender of the Ndebele and that was what Rhodes told them he had obtained. On the Ndebele side, however, it seemed as if Rhodes had himself asked for peace talks. At the least Ndebele oral tradition recalls deadlock between black and whites; at the most it recalls white desperation for the end of violence. The Ndebele, recalled old Mafimba Ncube in 1981,

were going to be victorious. The Europeans had no airforce at that time, the gun was useless

---

[6] Cable from 'Charter', Cape Town to Acting Administrator, 31 May 1898, NB 1/1/4.
[7] Chief Native Commissioner's address to Inungu *indaba*, 31 July 1899, NB 6/5/1/1.
[8] Chief Native Commissioner, addresses to Inungu and Tegwani *indabas*, 19 and 31 July 1899, NB 6/5/1/1.
[9] Native Commissioner, Fort Usher to Chief Native Commissioner, Matabeleland, 6 October 1898, NB 1/1/5.
[10] Native Commissioner, Malema to Chief Native Commissioner, Matabeleland, 23 November 1898, NBE 7/1/1.

when the people were lying between the rocks. They were both going to starve. How could the Europeans have settled? Rhodes then intervened, carrying a stick and saying 'Gentlemen, come home and plough for the children'.

According to Chief Wasi Ndiweni, interviewed in the same year, 'Rhodes pleaded with the Ndebele because the whites were starving.'[11]

The truth lies somewhere between these extremes. In order to end the fighting and to get the *impis* out of the Matopos, Rhodes *did* negotiate with the Ndebele leaders, but the promises he made them were not written down. This idiom of oracy created great difficulties later on when Africans were trying to use Rhodes's promises to fight eviction from the Matopos. 'Your petitioners have been unable to find any contemporary written record to support their contention', African protesters were forced to admit in 1948, though they went on to insist that 'no man would have asked an honoured man like the late Cecil Rhodes to make his promise in writing. It would have been a shameful thing to distrust a big man like him.'[12] Yet the promises were, nevertheless, taken very seriously at the time – not only by the Ndebele, but also by Rhodes himself and by the officials of the Native Department. Our best evidence for what Rhodes pledged comes from these officials. As we shall see, they believed that Rhodes made three sets of promises. First, he gave undertakings to large numbers of influential individuals that their particular interests would be protected. Second, he promised all those who came out of the hills 'into the open' that they and their descendants would enjoy secure occupation of the flat land. Third, he promised the largely Banyubi population which remained in the Matopos that it, too, should remain undisturbed. Taken together, these pledges amounted to a land settlement for central Matabeleland.

The correspondence of the Chief Native Commissioner, Matabeleland, is full of evidence of Rhodes's interventions on behalf of particular Ndebele notables. 'Can you spare a wagon to help the induna Mazwi to move out of the Matopo Hills, as recommended by the Rt. Hon. C. J. Rhodes?' wrote the Acting Chief Native Commissioner to the Assistant Controller in July 1897. 'Herewith letter from the Rt. Hon. C. J. Rhodes', he wrote again on 7 August. 'Can you help him to carry out his wish by providing the wagon [to] assist the mother of Lobengula's third son to move from Thabas Induna to his [Rhodes's] farm ?'[13] In the same month Rhodes asked the Deputy Administrator as a matter of urgency to send relief grain to Bozongwana Khumalo, 'a very big Dance and Impi doctor ... and a man of much influence under Lobengula', who was now settled on Rhodes's land but who had no food.[14] Once Mazwi had moved out of the hills and on to Rhodes's land he was given further support. In

[11] Interview by Mark Ncube with Mafimba Ncube, Intabazinduna, 9 October 1981, AOH/2; interview by Mark Ncube with Wasi Ndiweni, 8 December 1981, AOH/8, National Archives, Bulawayo.
[12] Petition to the Governor of Southern Rhodesia from the occupants of the National Park, November 1948; evidence of Sipambaniso Manyoba to the Commission of Inquiry into the Matopos National Park, 19 March 1949, S 1561/46.
[13] Acting Chief Native Commissioner to Assistant Controller, 26 July and 7 August 1897, NB 1/1/1/.
[14] Acting Chief Native Commissioner, Matabeleland to Secretary, Deputy Administrator, 19 August 1897, NB 1/1/1.

January 1898 the Native Commissioner, Matopos, reported that although Mazwi 'has no followers now', Rhodes had promised him £2 a month.[15]

Other important men were promised a variety of special privileges. In July 1898, for instance, the District Commissioner, Malema, reported the death of *Induna* Babayan, who had also been living on Rhodes's lands. Babayan had enjoyed the privilege of reporting directly to the Chief Native Commissioner without having to resort to the Native Commissioner of the district, 'a privilege conferred on Babaiyana individually and personally.'[16] Others who came out of the hills were given special permission to keep their guns or their cattle. And many of the 'rebel' commanders were appointed as salaried *indunas*.

Rhodes's close associate, and the man who came to administer the Rhodes-Matopos Estate, J. G. McDonald, has left a vivid account of the undertakings made to two particularly important Ndebele leaders, Faku Ndiweni and Hole Khumalo. Faku had been a key 'friendly' during the 1896 fighting; Hole had been a 'rebel' commander at the Inungu battle, which the whites regarded as the most serious engagement of the war.[17] I shall use the careers of the two men in this chapter to illustrate what happened to the promises of Rhodes.

But first to McDonald's account of Rhodes's dealings with the two:

> An occasional visitor [in late 1896] was Faku, a loyal chief who controlled a very large following. Both he and his men had been of much assistance during the rebellion, and it had been Rhodes' intention to give him ample reward ... 'I wished to see you, Mr Rhodes', said Faku, 'to talk to you of important matters. I am a very old man and have seen much fighting. I was old enough to guard cattle when Mzilikazi conquered this country, and I fought in many a battle with him, and afterwards with Lobengula.... Three years ago, on his death, I gave my allegiance to your Queen and I have kept my promise, but I am not happy about my people – many of them no longer have any land they can call their own, and it is only you ... who can help us. My people must have land to graze their cattle and grow their crops on. There will never be lasting peace till this is assured.' 'Have no fear, Faku', replied Rhodes. 'I promise you it will be put right. Ample land will be set aside for the whole of your nation, and I will buy all the land surrounding your kraal and also that surrounding the kraals of Lobengula's relatives which has been disposed of by the Government. None of you will be dispossessed. I pledge my word to you over this.'[18]

[15] Monthly Report, Matopos, January 1898, NBE 1/1/1.
[16] Native Commissioner, Malema to Chief Native Commissioner, Matabeleland, 26 July 1898, NBE 7/1/1.
[17] Faku was the son of Mabuyana Ndiweni, who lived ten miles south-west of Bulawayo but controlled territory stretching south of the Matopos as far as Kezi. Faku had usurped the chiefship and the control of his father's cattle from the rightful heir, Tala. He threw in his lot with the whites after the 1893 war and again in 1896, when many of his disaffected people joined the 'rebels'. Hole, son of Mkoti Khumalo, joined Dhliso, Nkonkobela and Mabela at Inungu, 'one of the hardest fights of the whole war.' Julian Cobbing, 'The Ndebele under the Khumalos', doctoral thesis, Lancaster, 1976, pp. 78, 108, 389, 427.
[18] J. G. McDonald, *Rhodes. A Life*, London, 1927, pp. 269–70. McDonald's account has to be taken with a large pinch of salt. This conversation is said to have taken place on Faku's death-bed, though the old man out-lived Rhodes himself and did not die until May 1904. Moreover, by the time he published his book McDonald knew perfectly well that Faku's people, led by his son and heir, Nyangazonke, had in effect been dispossessed of the land promised them by Rhodes.

As for Hole, McDonald portrays him as the most intransigent of rebels, retreating into the Matopos 'with the intention of fighting in guerrilla fashion'. Rhodes then said: 'We must go and camp alongside his kraal in amongst the hills and tire him out.' This they did, and at last Hole agreed to talk with Rhodes, opening his eyes to hitherto unsuspected Ndebele grievances. Hole was given 'assurances', and Rhodes told the Administrator of 'all the arrangements he had made with Holi and others, which he made it clear had to be adhered to.'[19]

Now, it was relatively easy for Rhodes to ensure that various important favours were extended to Faku and Hole. Thus the administration upheld Faku's shaky claim to personal ownership of 'tribal cattle'. 'Permission was granted to him personally by Mr Rhodes to continue to hold them and to kraal and graze them all over the unalienated lands of the district.'[20] In April 1904 the Native Commissioner, Matobo, discovered that Faku possessed a modern rifle in addition to the shotgun for which he had a permit: 'Faku represented to me that the rifle was retained by him by special permission of Mr Rhodes.... I think Faku should be allowed to keep this gun.'[21] Hole, who was 'strongly averse to submission to chief Faku', and who withdrew deep into the south-eastern Matopos, was himself recognised as an *induna* in 1897, 'though it places a premium on rebellion'.[22] But what was much more difficult was to fulfil Rhodes's promise of 'ample land' to Faku and the other leaders of the 'collaborator belt', or to find land to tempt Hole and other 'rebels' out of the hills.[23]

The Search for Land

Rhodes gave undertakings not only to Faku and Hole but also to the participants in the *indabas* generally, that if they came out of the hills they would have secure tenure of the land. The Native Commissioner, Malema, writing in June 1897 about 'the vital question of the future – the location of the natives', spelt out the difficulties in ensuring this:

> The whole country, practically speaking, has been cut up and sold to private individuals. The terms under which it has been so sold are such that the buyers have the legal right to demand the instant removal of every native residing on it, and they constantly owe the peaceful occupation of their lands, which they at present continue to enjoy, to the doubtful clemency of the European owner. It would, I believe, be impossible, at any rate until the whole nation has been thoroughly and decisively beaten, to enforce their occupation of the two tracts of country set apart as and for native locations [the Shangani and Gwaai Reserves in the far north].[24]

[19] J. G. McDonald, *Rhodes. A Life*, London, 1927, pp. 273–4.
[20] Chief Native Commissioner, Matabeleland to Secretary, Administrator, 2 March and 10 August 1922, N 3/4/5.
[21] Native Commissioner, Matobo to Chief Native Commissioner, Matabeleland, 23 April 1904, NBE 1/1/4.
[22] Monthly reports, Malema, January and April 1897, NBE 1/1/1.
[23] The 'collaborator belt' included men like Jozana, Maphisa and Nyameni, as well as Faku. These men lived north of the Matopos on land which had passed into white ownership and from which they might at any moment be evicted.
[24] Quarterly report, Malema, 30 June 1987, NBE 7/1/1.

Given that the peoples of the Matopos had not been 'thoroughly and decisively beaten', where could land be found on which they might be secure?

Rhodes found two answers. North of the Matopos he himself bought a great stretch of land on which to settle 'rebels' and 'friendlies', Faku among them. South of the Matopos lay the so-called *mapani* veld, which had not yet been taken up by more than two or three white landowners,[25] and into which the occupants of the hills might be encouraged to move, Hole among them. These expedients worked up until Rhodes's death in March 1902. After that, however, neither belt of land proved to be secure. White tenants on Rhodes's land began to evict Africans, and a veritable trek of white farmers arrived in the *mapani* veld in 1908 to take over the land. Rhodes's promises turned out not to have been worth much, after all.

Rhodes as Feudal Lord

Between 1893 and 1895 the British South Africa Company had disposed of all the land north of the Matopos to individual whites or to syndicates. The Company made some hesitant efforts to discover 'at what prices farms could be obtainable' from landowners between Bulawayo and the hills, but either the owners would not sell or the Company could not afford to buy.[26] If Rhodes wanted land in this belt he would have to buy it himself.

In fact he already owned one farm in the area – Westacre Creek, which he had bought in October 1895 and planned to develop through plans for irrigated farming. Now he set out to buy land adjacent to Westacre. In 1897 he bought from the Rhodesian Exploration and Development Company the very large Sauerdale Estate. In 1898 he bought from Harry Huntley the three farms Lonsdale, Lucydale and Hazelside.[27] On this belt of land – which became the Rhodes-Matopos Estate – he began to settle both 'friendlies' and 'rebels'. The land was Rhodes's own private property and the whole settlement operation was carried out in a characteristically unofficial way with the help of two of the young white fortune-hunters whom Rhodes enjoyed patronising.

A later settler account describes part of the process:

> In 1893 Mr Rhodes advised two young men in South Africa, Harry Huntley and Percy Ross, to seek their fortunes in Matabeleland. He told them to contact Dr Sauer and in June 1894 they found themselves the original tenants of Sauerdale. In the meantime, Mr Rhodes who was in London instructed these young men to look out for ground for him. They bought Westacre.... After the surrender of the Matabele during the rebellion, at Mr Rhodes's request, Mr Huntley took up residence on the farms Lonsdale and Lucydale to assist during

---

[25] In October 1901 the Native Commissioner, Matobo 'held a meeting between the landlord and tenants of Alalie farm on the Ovi River in the *mapani* veld. An agreement, based on the usual conditions was entered into, the rent agreed upon being 10/- per year.' Monthly report, Matobo, October 1901, NBE 1/1/2.

[26] Native Commissioner, Malema to Chief Native Commissioner, Matabeleland, 14 February 1897, NBE 7/1/1.

[27] Sauer and Huntley had both told the Native Commissioner, Malema, that they were not prepared to sell.

the surrender of the natives. When Mr Rhodes said goodbye to him on his setting out on his undertaking, he said 'They will probably kill you. I shall be very sorry but I wish you to do this to bring confidence to the natives'. Huntley was successful in this task and took the surrender of a large number of Matabele.... At the final meeting to arrange the newly won peace Huntley acted as interpreter.... As emblems of peace, Mr Rhodes distributed white sheep and blankets and informed the chiefs that he had purchased the Rhodes Matopos Estates, over 95,000 acres in extent.[28]

Now Rhodes had his land, he used it not only to attract the Matopos 'rebel' chiefs and to reward 'friendlies' but also to offer a haven to especially prominent Ndebele from other areas – to members of the Ndebele royal family, to Ndebele religious leaders, to Lobengula's queens. By so doing he was trying to live up to the promises he had made at the first Matopos *indabas* and also to neutralise the various elements in Ndebele society by grouping them all together in a monitored tension. For a brief period there gathered on his farms an extraordinary concentration of Ndebele notables and their followers, to many of whom, as we have seen, Rhodes had given individual pledges.

It is plain that the idiom of oral undertaking came naturally to Rhodes as part of a greatly relished patriarchal role. Rhodes saw himself partly as Highland chief and partly as ducal landowner. After all, these new networks of dependence and patronage were being constructed on *his* land rather than that of the state. The *Chronicle*, reporting an *indaba* held on 24 June 1897, described how:

> coming to speak to the indunas individually Mr Rhodes's manner underwent a startling change. It assumed a boyish exuberance and aspect of pleasure, which was immensely gratifying to the indunas personally known to him.... There was a suggestion conveyed to each of the circumstances under which they had last met.[29]

On 5 July 1897 Rhodes held another *indaba*, attended only by the chiefs and people of the Matopos. He 'undertook to let the Matabele, both rebel and friendly, occupy his farms ... on a permanent basis ... and after that *indaba* the Matabele settled on Mr Rhodes's farm.'[30] He also laid on a great feudal feast.

This made a great impression throughout Matabeleland. Early in 1898 the acting Chief Native Commissioner was travelling in the south-west among the 'loyalist' *indunas* of Bulilima-Mangwe. These complained of:

> the feast that Mr Rhodes gave the Rebels on his Estate (Sauerdale) in July last. They felt this very much, for they thought it had some political significance and that they were quite despised by the whites. I explained to them that the affair which they had referred to was absolutely a private affair, that Mr Rhodes in his private capacity as landlord had called his tenantry together for a sort of house-warming on the occasion of his buying the estate.[31]

Not surprisingly, the Bulalima *indunas* were not 'fully satisfied' with the explanation

---

[28] Petal Coghlan Chennells, 'Genesis', n.d., Ashton papers. Historical Reference Collection, Bulawayo.
[29] *Chronicle*, 26 June 1897.
[30] Advocate P. Lloyd's address to the Matopo National Park Commission, 16 March 1949, S 1561/46.
[31] Acting Chief Native Commissioner, Matabeleland to Secretary, Deputy Administrator, 17 February 1898, N 6/5/1/1.

that Rhodes was acting only as a private landlord. But Rhodes himself enjoyed the role enormously.

He took the view that his relations with his 'tenantry' were quite outside the routine provisions of Southern Rhodesian law. The Native Commissioner, Malema, Charles Stuart, handed down to his family a story which makes the point. Rhodes 'periodically visited his Matopo farms' and on one occasion invited Stuart to dinner 'at the Huts'. Rhodes asked Stuart what fine he would impose as Magistrate if 'I gave my boy a tot of gin.' 'The fine is £400, Mr Rhodes', said Stuart. Next day there was an *indaba*, at which Stuart interpreted. 'Half way through the "pow-wow" an elderly Native hobbled up, and seating himself opposite Rhodes, cupped his hands over his eyes the better to gaze on the great man.' It was Faku, who at eighty had walked six miles to attend the meeting:

> Rhodes swung round to his manager. 'Here get me a tumbler of gin'. The manager brought it and handed it to Rhodes. 'Now Stuart, if it is going to cost me £400, Mr Faku is going to have his glass of gin', and he stepped forward to Faku, handed him the liquor and made him drink it.[32]

Now, of course, usually Rhodes was not in Matabeleland nor on his estate. Like any other great absentee landlord he needed managers. He had two to hand in Harry Huntley and Percy Ross, the young men through whom he had acquired Sauerdale and whom he had used to facilitate 'rebel' surrender. He went on using them to bring the Ndebele out of the hills. Thus we find Percy Ross writing to the Chief Native Commissioner in August 1897 to tell him that Rhodes had 'promised one of the Queens a Government wagon to fetch her things ... and bring them as far as Sauerdale, where Mr Rhodes has given her a place to live.' Rhodes 'was most anxious that she should come to Sauerdale to live.'[33] And once the Ndebele *indunas* and their people had come out of the hills, Rhodes used Ross and Huntley to manage his 'tenantry'.

In fine feudal style he rewarded them by granting sub-leases and grazing rights on his land. In July 1901, for instance, he leased grazing rights over the whole of Sauerdale to Huntley, together with 'authority over certain native kraals on the farm.' Huntley was delegated 'the full control over all natives residing in the kraals of M'Tjan, M'Bantewa, N'Tambu, Fungu and Malonga situated on Sauerdale Block', and he undertook 'the full administration, supervision and discipline of the various natives and native kraals.'[34] In 1949 the commissioners who were examining the complaints of the Matopos residents and their claim that Rhodes had promised the Ndebele perpetual tenure on his land found that the leases Rhodes had given to Huntley and Ross were incompatible with any such undertaking. No such incompatibility was apparent to Rhodes. Huntley was not granted his lease as a farmer but as a manager. He did *not* have the right to collect rents, nor to demand labour, and he had to observe the various

---

[32] P. A. Stuart, 'My Matabeleland Experiences', *NADA*, 1942, p. 66. There is an obvious mythic element in this story since it shows Charles Stuart having to introduce Faku to Rhodes.

[33] P. H. Ross to Chief Native Commissioner, Matabeleland, 28 August 1897, NB 1/1/1.

[34] Agreement of 15 July 1901, enclosed in Director of Agriculture to Chief Native Commissioner, 30 October 1920, G 1/7/3/2.

undertakings given by Rhodes to individuals, like Mafungu, one of Lobengula's queens. Ross occupied and grazed Lucydale with similar managerial responsibilities, 'without any written agreements but on an undertaking with Mr Rhodes that he may remain undisturbed there for life.'[35] Neither man farmed. Both ran cattle in among the stock of the African 'tenantry' and acted as sub-chiefs to Rhodes's Highland chieftain. To begin with no-one had many cattle – even Faku had emerged from war and rinderpest with only five hundred – and there was no clash over the grazing.

Land, Labour and the Rise of Capitalist Farming

So far Rhodes's arrangements for his lands were 'traditional' rather than 'modern'. But with his propensity to seek many different advantages at the same time, he wanted to do much more with his estate than only to settle 'rebels' and 'friendlies' on it or to reward his managers with leases. He planned, as we have seen, to set up an arboretum. And while he was willing to set aside a large part of his land for African occupation supervised by white managers, he wanted to promote ambitious and exemplary capitalist farming on other parts of it, and particularly on Westacre farm. In September 1900 Native Commissioner Stuart recorded an almost total lack of white agricultural enterprise in his district:

> The oasis in the desert is Westacre farm, the property of Mr Cecil Rhodes. Here what money, enterprise and energy will do has been done to turn the bare waste to profitable account. A large vegetable garden flourishes; hundreds of acres have been fenced in.... Huge tracts have been ploughed up and sown; areas have been paddocked up for the thousand head of cattle.... The Dam which is nearing completion will cost £20,000 or £30,000.[36]

Once again – and not surprisingly – the 1949 commissioners assumed that this vigorous development was incompatible with occupation rights for Africans. Yet once again Rhodes did not feel any inconsistency. It had never been his intention that African rights of occupation on his land should be unconditional. If the main problem for blacks after 1896 was land, the main problem for whites was labour. Rhodes intended to resolve both problems in one arrangement.

Of course, Africans living on Westacre – as Faku himself did – had to evacuate the area of the 'enormous dam' and the irrigation channels that ran from it; they would have to vacate the 'huge tracts ... ploughed up and sown'; they would have to move their cattle away from the paddocks. If they were privileged, like Faku, they were given compensation for loss of the land. But even if they were not privileged they were given land elsewhere on the estate rather than evicted. After all, Rhodes's planned developments needed many African labourers. In mid-1899 Stuart remarked on the 'very large numbers' required for the labour-intensive construction of the dam, work on which had begun as early as September 1897. Work on the dam, noted Stuart's

---

[35] Director of Agriculture to Treasurer, 26 September 1917, G 1/7/1/2.
[36] Quarterly Report, Malema, 30 September 1900, NBE 7/1/2.

Assistant Commissioner in December 1899, 'is principally done by men carrying clay with scoops. All day this goes on and at the end of a day's labour about 2,100 loads of clay have been placed on the embankment.'[37] When the dam had been completed there were the irrigation channels to build, and after that, it was assumed, there would be rapid capitalist development on Westacre which would generate a great deal of employment.

Hence Rhodes envisaged one section of his estate on which there would be capitalist farming; another section on which would be set up an arboretum and park facilities for the white population of Bulawayo; and the greater part to be set aside for fairly intensive African settlement, gardens and grazing land under the supervision of white lessees. The labour for the developed part of the estate would come from the undeveloped; capitalism would coexist with 'tribalism' and 'feudalism'. Thus in the lease made by Rhodes to Huntley in July 1901 it was laid down that:

> The Proprietor reserves to himself the right during the term of this Agreement to demand from any natives resident in such area four months labour at any time during each and every year ... and the Occupier binds himself to exercise the authority hereby delegated to him and to take the necessary steps to compel such natives to render to the Proprietor from time to time such labour.[38]

We are now close to being able to understand what it was that Rhodes promised the Matopos *indunas* at the crucial *indaba* of 5 July 1897 so far as his own land was concerned. The Native Department reports at the time tantalisingly failed to spell out what the promise amounted to, though they made very clear the patriarchal nature of the proceedings:

> The Right Honourable C. J. Rhodes invited to his farm the Indunas and all the natives living in and around his ground on the out-skirts of the Matobo Hills for a talk and a feast. This call was responded to with great alacrity and the natives all enjoyed themselves to such good purpose that 200 sheep, various head of horned cattle and diverse refreshments and innumerable presents disappeared as by magic. Here those present renewed their vows of allegiance.[39]

The *Chronicle*'s report described how Rhodes had invited 'rebel' chiefs to come out of the hills and settle on his estate and how 'the majority said that they wished nothing better than to live on his farms.' There was rapid movement on to the land. As Sir Lewis Michell later recalled, Rhodes drove him 'to his huts in the Matopos' on 14 August 1897, and explained to him en route 'that he had settled 4,000 natives on the estate, including old Babyan and several witch-doctors and other dangerous characters, recently in rebellion. In almost every second hut there was a chief.'[40]

But the *Chronicle* also made it clear that there was more to the 5 July 1987 *indaba* than feasting and vows of allegiance. The paper's editorial remarked that 'the Matabele are flocking to Mr Rhodes's farms and soon we shall have the results of the system

[37] Quarterly Report, Assistant Commissioner, Malema, 30 December 1899, NBE 7/1/2.
[38] Agreement of 15 July 1901, G 1/7/3/2.
[39] Acting Chief Native Commissioner to Secretary, Deputy Administrator, 29 November 1897, NB 1/1/2.
[40] Lewis Michell, *The Life of the Rt. Hon. C. J. Rhodes, 1853–1902*, Edward Arnold, London, 1910.

which he is experimenting with. It will be a guide to other landowners and should tranquillise the natives.'[41]

The details of this experimental system have to be pieced together. In October 1901 Rhodes's representative at the estates, J. G. McDonald – whom we have seen above recording so unconditional a promise to Faku of ample land – spelt out what some of the conditions were. 'In lieu of paying rent Mr Rhodes has decided that all natives living on his block of farms ... shall work for three months in each year upon his farms.'[42] In itself this sounds like a mere labour tenancy agreement of the sort that later became common. But it was more than that. Routine labour agreements gave no guarantees of long-term occupation and included clauses allowing a landowner to give notice of eviction even if labour had been supplied satisfactorily. But Africans on Sauerdale were promised that they and their descendants could remain there in perpetuity provided the young men came out for paid labour. Moreover, they had an undertaking that control of their social life would be left to their chiefs. Further, they were promised protection not only from eviction from Sauerdale but also from random displacement within that estate. As the Chief Native Commissioner, Matabeleland, wrote in April 1903:

> The late Mr Rhodes made a promise to the natives residing there that, provided they complied with the conditions of their tenancy, they would not be disturbed. Any lands that might be required by him would be compensated for and other lands given them.[43]

Rhodes's experimental system, then, amounted to an attempt to combine regular labour supply to whites with long-term land security for blacks. It was not adopted by any other landowner nor, as we shall see, did it last long even on the Rhodes-Matopos Estates. But even as late as 1918 the ineffable McDonald, who by that time had done much to undermine it, spelt out the original intention:

> It may be that I omitted to inform you on the transfer of the Rhodes Estates to the Government [he wrote to the Director of Agriculture, Eric Nobbs] that the late Mr Rhodes promised that all natives who held rights on his Estates would be protected as long as they behaved themselves, and given sufficient land to provide crops for their families and for a reasonable number of cattle. In particular, special promises were made to one or two doubtful characters.... Some of these have died, but their families are still on the Estate and occasionally remind me of Mr Rhodes's promise. A considerable number of the 1896 rebels were also given land on condition they laid down their arms ... and there they have remained and fulfilled their promises satisfactorily.[44]

During the brief time between the July 1897 agreement and Rhodes's death, while his oral undertakings were fresh in his mind, the 'experiment' worked. No-one was evicted from the estate. A list of Africans on private lands in Matobo district drawn up in March 1904 showed that there were still 4,390 living on the Rhodes-Matopos Estate.[45]

---

[41] *Chronicle*, 6 July 1897.
[42] J. G. McDonald to Chief Native Commissioner, Matabeleland, 23 October 1901, NB 1/1/15.
[43] Chief Commissioner, Matabeleland to Charles Coghlan, 28 April 1903, NB 1/1/19.
[44] J. G. McDonald to Eric Nobbs, 27 August 1918, G 1/7/3/2.
[45] List of Africans on private land, March 1904, NBE 1/1/3.

African Understandings of the July 1897 Indaba

Yet if Rhodes believed that all his purposes could be successfully combined, his intentions were regularly misread – or read in their own way – by the Africans who lived on his land. The *indunas* who came to live on Sauerdale and Rhodes's other farms found it no easier than the 'friendlies' of Bulalima to distinguish between Rhodes as landlord and Rhodes as embodiment of the colonial state. Nor did they see themselves primarily as tenants. Rhodes was 'the government', and they were the leaders and spokesman of their people. In their eyes the offer of security was merely part of what they remembered as Rhodes's wider undertaking during the *indabas* of 1896 that the Ndebele would be able to return to their lands 'in the open'. There had then been no question of unconditional surrender and the *indunas* expected the conditions to be met. They constantly reminded the administration of these larger promises. At an *indaba* at Government House, Bulawayo, on 15 November 1897, for example:

> the Indunas said that if Mr Rhodes had been present they would remind him of [a] thing he had promised in the Matobo, viz., that Native Reserves would be formed, where Natives could live without fear of being made to move each year. In reply His Honour assured the Indunas that ... the Government had not forgotten Mr Rhodes's promise.[46]

Moreover, if Rhodes's tenants saw Rhodes in his patriarchal mode, so too did all the peoples of central Matabeleland. The Native Department constantly invoked his name in their dealings with Ndebele *indunas*. 'He knew and they knew', the Chief Native Commissioner told an *indaba* at Inungu, threatening them with an importation of M'fengu, 'that Mr Rhodes could be very angry, he was not a man who waited but a man who took action at once. He would say, "If I cannot get labour out of these people I will soon get some from elsewhere".'[47] Not only Rhodes's relations with his tenantry but the whole administration of Africans in Matabeleland was profoundly personalised. Its ethos was summed up after Rhodes's death when the Chief Native Commissioner told Ndebele chiefs at an *indaba* at Fort Usher in the Matopos that he wanted them 'to think today of that Great White Chief who is now sleeping in the hills yonder. Many of you will remember that at the last indaba in the hills he entrusted your welfare to my care.'[48]

So the occupants of Rhodes's land did not feel much different from the rest of the Ndebele and Banyubi. So far as the *indunas* on Sauerdale were concerned the main significance of their concentration there in the late 1890s was that it allowed them to coordinate political action. The intermingling of 'rebels' and 'friendlies', the presence of a chief in almost every second hut, allowed the rapid emergence of joint protest, as in November 1898 when most of the *indunas* on Sauerdale were involved in the move-ment to petition against the settlement of M'fengu and for the re-establishment of the

---

[46] Acting Chief Native Commissioner, Matabeleland, to Secretary, Deputy Administrator, 29 November 1897, NB 1/1/2.
[47] Proceedings of the Inungu *indaba*, 31 July 1899, NB 6/5/1/1.
[48] Chief Native Commissioner, Matabeleland, address, 24 February 1904, NB 3/1/1.

Ndebele monarchy. These were not men primarily concerned with the details of a tenancy agreement. In particular they were not men who took seriously Rhodes's demand for labour. What they heard was his promise of security. The call for labour they regarded as no more than the usual moral injunctions of colonial administrators.

Rhodes himself, indeed, regarded labour as much in moral as in economic terms. In November 1897, before much labour was needed for the dam and other development projects, he wrote to McDonald: 'I am glad you got cows at Sauerdale. Please insist on butter being made daily and some sent to you and Sauer. The whole thing is to make people work all day and not loaf around the huts.'[49] But this was disingenuous. Ndebele men were quite prepared to work. The real question was when, for whom and at what remuneration. The young men did not wish to give labour to Rhodes's agricultural operations during the time of clearing, planting or harvesting in their own gardens, surplus produce from which could be marketed in Bulawayo; they did not wish to work at any time for a wage which was always lower than they could obtain on the 'free' labour market; many of them particularly disliked the strenuous and dangerous work on Westacre dam.

Hence, although Rhodes liked to think of his lands as a state within a state, free from the petty regulations administered by the Native Department, his managers came increasingly to depend on the Native Commissioners to spell out and enforce the labour agreement. As the construction of the dam began to require more and more workers in late 1899, the Native Commissioner recorded the tensions between African agricultural activity and this labour demand. In October he was busy rounding up workers for the dam. He found that 'the natives are sowing everywhere.... A considerable number of young men were found idling at the kraals upon Mr Rhodes's farms and when asked why they were not at work at the dam they replied they had returned to plant. This is a very lame excuse.'[50]

He decided that he must call 'those headmen who reside on Mr Rhodes's block' together 'so that we may convince the natives that not only the contractors but Mr Rhodes and also the Government are concerned in the question' and to insist that 'only those natives reside rent free who do a fair share of work and that the rest must be prepared to leave the estate.'[51] A meeting was held on 7 November and, in the presence of McDonald and Ross, Stuart spelt out the conditions: 'every native fit for work (excluding kraal heads) who had not this year done 3 months work on the Estate must report for duty at once'; those who *had* done three months work would get tickets of exemption from Ross; any men away at paid work outside the estate must return at once and 'proceed to the dam on arrival'. Any headman who failed to report defaulters would 'be given notice at once to quit the Estate – before next ploughing season.' The whole elaborate scheme was to be enforced by the Native Commissioner's Messengers who were to patrol the kraals. Stuart was careful to record the exact words of his injunctions to the headmen:

[49] Cecil Rhodes to J. G. McDonald, 7 November 1897, MA 2/1/1.
[50] Monthly report, Malema, October 1899, NBE 7/1/2.
[51] Charles Stuart to P. Ross and H. Huntley, 2 November 1899, NBE 7/1/2.

Mr Rhodes told the indunas long ago that in lieu of rent he expected every young man to turn out for three months in the year ... and I am now to impress upon you most solemnly that every kraal which does not turn out all its young men ... will be removed from Mr Rhodes's Estate. It is no excuse that the boys will not obey your orders or that they go to work elsewhere.... The rains are coming on and Mr Rhodes will not be pleased with you if the work is not finished before they set in. You are now receiving no idle warning.[52]

In the event this ultimatum was not rigorously enforced. The dam contractors much preferred 'voluntary' labour to the sullen young men of Sauerdale, and much to Stuart's anger actually turned them away when they reluctantly reported for work. When the contractors *did* accept men from Rhodes's land they did not feel able to enforce the demand for a full three months' labour. They explained to Stuart that 'forced operations 3 months right off ... if compelled would cause a dislike for the work.' Stuart fumed at such 'wanton disregard to the main and fundamental provision of a carefully worked out scheme' and complained that the affair had made him 'inconsistent and childish in the eyes of the natives. But what can be done?'[53]

In fact there was little that could be done in the face of dogged African resistance. In October 1899 war had broken out between Britain and the Boer Republics and this made the Rhodesian administration especially nervous of a possible African uprising.[54] Detectives were sent into the hills to see whether the Mwali priests were advising rebellion and reported that at the shrine near Mtuwane's, Mwali had 'from the interior of a cave, counselled his worshippers to take no other part in the fighting but to secrete themselves in the hills if called upon to help.'[55] Native Commissioners feared that Africans would flood back into the Matopos after all the trouble that had been taken to persuade them to come out. There were special worries that the 'friendlies' might have been alienated over matters of land and labour. In February 1900 there were even rumours that old Faku and his people were seriously disaffected. Stuart thought they were unlikely to give trouble – 'they each have large herds of cattle, goats and sheep'. Faku was the pioneer in the district in the use of the plough. But he admitted that 'the natives feel that they are being harassed' over labour, by employers, government and the Native Labour Bureau. Those who lived on Rhodes's estate, who were protected from Labour Bureau recruiters, and in Stuart's view enjoyed conditions 'the most lenient which, so far as I know, exist', 'even on this basis would not voluntarily report themselves for work at the Dam.' In the atmosphere of early 1900 there could be no question of evicting Faku and his men from Sauerdale.[56]

A similar pattern of resistance repeated itself at the opening of the rainy season in September 1900. At the approach of Stuart's Messengers, men fled from the kraals, where they were working on their gardens.[57] It was difficult to maintain a work force of

[52] Stuart to McDonald, 7 November 1899, NBE 7/1/2.
[53] Stuart to G. H. Laidman, 28 January 1900, NBE 7/1/2.
[54] For a discussion of these anxieties see Arthur Keppel-Jones, *Rhodes and Rhodesia. The White Conquest of Zimbabwe, 1884–1902*, McGill-Queen's University Press, Kingston and Montreal, 1983, pp. 601–3.
[55] Quarterly report, Matopos, 31 March 1900, NBE 1/1/1.
[56] Stuart to Chief Native Commissioner, Matabeleland, 26 February and 5 March 1900, NBE 7/1/1.
[57] Stuart to Messrs Halse Bros, 26 September 1900, NBE 7/1/1.

80 men at the dam throughout the year. In March 1901 prosecutions for desertion from the dam site were brought against men under *indunas* Jozana, Faku, Nyameni, Maphisa, Mwapa and Maqina and fines of up to £3 imposed.[58] By this time the dam contractors had abandoned their own earlier scruples and were sending out their 'policemen' to raid for labour, who even combed nearby mission schools for youths from Rhodes's estates.[59] In response those residents living close to the dam attacked and wounded haulage oxen belonging to the contractors. It was not suprising that the Native Commissioner was obliged to summon headmen in November 1901 and again in June 1902 to explain yet once more the terms of Rhodes's 'promise'.[60]

This, then, was the situation at Rhodes's death, which Stuart believed that 'the natives of the Matopos' felt 'more keenly than those of any other part of the country, chiefly by reason of the fact that Mr Rhodes had come into contact more frequently with these natives [who] realise that they have lost a valuable friend.'[61] Reluctant as they were to turn out for work at the dam, men under all the *indunas* on the estate, both 'friendlies' and 'rebels', helped build the road to World's View for the carriage of Rhodes's body to his grave. The *indunas* themselves attended the burial ceremony on 10 April 1902 and gave their dead landlord the royal salute.[62] They thus reasserted their role in the colonial 'moral economy' and claimed their part in the myth of Rhodes as 'the Great White Chief'. They were able to do this with all the more enthusiasm because they had managed to interpret the promises of 15 July 1897 in their terms rather than his.

And for a while it seemed as though the dead hero could offer more protection than the living seeker of labour had done. A month after Rhodes's death old Faku was able to discomfort a new lessee on the Rhodes-Matopos Estate, C. J. Webb, by an appeal to the immortal memory. Webb cared nothing for patriarchal oral undertakings and gave Faku notice to abandon gardens on Lonsdale farm which he wished himself to enclose. Faku at once appealed to the Native Commissioner, H. M. Jackson, who in turned appealed to the Chief Native Commissioner – 'it would be both unwise and unjust to deprive Faku of any lands given to him by Mr Rhodes.'[63] The Chief Native Commissioner asked McDonald to lay down the unwritten law to Webb, and McDonald obliged with a remarkable letter which it is hard to imagine being written to any other white settler farmer on any other estate in Southern Rhodesia:

> I was surprised to hear that you had been endeavouring to take some of Faku's lands inside the 250 acres you have on lease from Mr Rhodes. This cannot be done unless you plough up other lands acceptable to Faku, or compensate him. This Chief was almost the only loyal native in the 1896 rebellion, and Mr Rhodes promised that none of his lands should be interfered with, unless he were either compensated or fresh ones ploughed up for him if he

[58] Entry for 25 March 1901 in Criminal and Civil Record Book, Fort Usher, D 4/25/1.
[59] H. M. Jackson to Walter Halse, 26 June 1901, NB 3/1/1.
[60] Rex ve Hlola, preparatory examination, 29 April 1901, D 3/26/1; monthly report, Matobo/Malema, November 1901, NBE 1/1/2; June 1902, NBE 1/1/3.
[61] Quarterly report, Matobo, 30 June 1902, NBE 1/1/3.
[62] Native Commissioner, Matobo to Road Department, 1 April 1902, NBE 1/1/3.
[63] H. M. Jackson to Chief Native Commissioner, Matabeleland, 9 May 1902, NB 1/1/9.

preferred it. Please bear this in mind and do not stir up dissatisfaction, else you will jeopardise your lease.[64]

Coming out of the Hills into the Mapani Veld

Meanwhile to the south of the Matopos thousands of Africans had been moving out of the hills into the *mapani* veld. They did so on the strength of Rhodes's general promise that those who came out into the open would be undisturbed on their land but without any of the detailed conditions which applied to the Rhodes-Matopos Estate. The land in the *mapani* had been surveyed and demarcated into farms but the great majority had not been allocated or occupied; the uncultivated soil was at first fertile, and there was ample grazing and water in the rivers which ran south from the hills. There had been little settlement in the *mapani* prior to 1893, but Faku's authority had extended into the area and its potentiality for grazing and hunting was well known to the *indunas* of the Matopos. In May 1897 the Native Commissioner, Matopos, reported that there were no resident white farmers in the *mapani* but that 'large game was found' there and there was 'continued hunting by the natives.'[65]

Hole was the first significant immigrant into the *mapani*. In early 1897 Native Commissioner Stuart was reporting that Hole and his followers – the only 'rebels' in his district – stood 'aloof, ever on the defensive in view of any encroachment on their liberties'. Hole's uncle, Umbiko, had rebelled against Lobengula and the king had refused to recognise the 'nephew of the late leader of the rebellion.' Hole had served with the *Imbizo* regiment and had married the king's favourite daughter, Famona. But he had only come to control his 'tribe' after the death of Lobengula and just before the 1896 uprising. He seemed the quintessential 'rebel' and Stuart found his manner 'insolently ironic'. He wanted to move Hole and his followers out of the hills but could not bring them north 'until land-owners have agreed to waive those of their rights which made a settlement possible.'[66]

Hole had been given assurances by Rhodes, however; he was recognised as an *induna*; he was allowed to keep his cattle; and in mid-1897 he moved out of the hills into more open grazing country. In September Stuart reported that:

> Hole's tribe consists almost entirely of Kalangas [Banyubis] who live in the rugged valley through which the Malema flows. He himself, however, resides away in what is called the Mopani veldt, some 25 miles south of this office, where he leads an unhealthy and isolated existence.[67]

Stuart did not trust Hole in his new home on the surveyed but unallocated Lana farm.

[64] J. G. McDonald to C. J. Webb, 20 May 1903, NBE 1/1/3.

[65] Native Commissioner, Matopos to Chief Native Commissioner, 8 May 1897, NBE 1/1/1.

[66] Monthly report, Malema, April, June 1897; Native Commissioner, Malema to Chief Native Commissioner, 7 September 1987, NBE 7/1/1.

[67] Half-yearly report, September 30 1897, NBE 7/1/1. Hole was contrasted to Faku, 'infinitely the most able man' among the six 'friendly' *indunas*, whose 'wealth in cattle adds to his influence.'

He followed him up, 'forcibly arrested him' and took him to the Chief Native Commissioner in Bulawayo; early in 1898 he prosecuted Hole for concealing guns, 'most of which were carried at the Nungu fight with Role himself in command.' But gradually Hole – a satisfied man with his salary and with ample grazing for his rapidly increasing herds – became an ally rather than an enemy. By October 1898 he was 'now quite a pleasant man to work with'; in August 1899 he was helping recruit labour for the mines from his 'tribe'; and in 1900 it was thought very important to keep Hole loyal in view of the South African war.[68]

For some time Hole was not followed south by many other people from the Matopos. The Annual Report, Matopos, for the year ending March 1900 commented that: 'There are large tracts of uninhabited desert country in the West and South West of the district covered with mapani trees. The Matopo range is the only part that can be said to be well populated.'[69] But soon an exodus from the hills southwards began. By June 1900 it was being reported that some of 'the late rebel faction' now lived 'out of the hills on the southern portion of the district'.[70] By May 1901 nothing less than 'a general exodus from the hill country' was reported, due to the depredations of baboons and locusts. But there were pull factors as well as push factors. In June 1901 'exceptionally good crops' were achieved in the virgin *mapani* soils by contrast with poor harvests in the over-farmed Matopos – 'the natives are continuing to leave the hills.'

Thereafter there were regular references to the movement south 'into the hitherto sparsely inhabited mapani veldt'. The monthly report, Matobo, for June 1902 summed up:

> The people continue to desert the hills for the mapani veldt. Various reasons are given for their removal, chiefly the depredation of baboons and the fact that the light sandy loam of the hills is exhausted.... The true reason is, I think, to be found in the fact that the soil in the mapani veldt is far better and richer.... I saw particularly good harvests on the banks of the Shashani, Ove and Malema rivers. This large and fertile tract of country to the south of the hills has always remained uninhabited until the European occupation of the country, apparently because it has always been open to the attack of tribes from the south ... I anticipate that there will soon be a large population stretching down to the larger tributaries of the Crocodile.[71]

This southwards expansion had very different effects from the movement on to Rhodes's lands. It was a movement away from Bulawayo with its lawyers – though Hole was involved in the protest movement of November 1898 – and its markets for crops. It was also a movement away from missionary influence. The *mapani* veld has always been traversed by pilgrims coming from the south to Njelele, and now the new settlers continued to rely on the Mwali shrine. It was from the *mapani* that Frances Davidson of the Brethren in Christ intruded into a Mwali cave and that the African Christians who accompanied her were threatened with death when droughts ensued. This

---

[68] Monthly report, Malema, September 1897; Native Commissioner, Malema to Chief Native Commissioner, 24 April 1898; monthly report, October 1898, NBE 7/1/1.
[69] Annual Report, Matopos, 31 March 1900, NBE 1/1/1.
[70] Quarterly report, Malema, 30 June 1899, NBE 7/1/2.
[71] Monthly report, June 1902, NBE 1/1/3.

traditionalist and prosperous African community was not harassed for labour or asked for rent.[72]

The Collapse of Rhodes's Promise North of the Matopos

Not long after Rhodes's death the fine balance of interests on his land began to collapse. In October 1902 a new tenant, S. R. Browning, gave Faku notice to move from part of Lonsdale, since he wished to enclose and farm the land commercially. This time, Native Commissioner Jackson showed some unease. No rebuke was administered to Browning. He was a new kind of white tenant, not on the land in order to administer Africans but in order to exploit and develop it. Ross and Huntley could coexist with African usages of the land but now Jackson saw the fundamental conflict inherent in Rhodes's multiple ambitions for his land:

> Mr Browning naturally claims that having obtained the lease of this land he is entitled to the entire use of it and that the natives must give up their gardens after reaping.... The natives state that the land has been tilled by them for generations and that Mr Rhodes allowed them to continue in their occupation of the land. That if forced to give up these gardens and break up fresh land they have no guarantee that they may not be dismissed next year, and so on ad infinitum.[73]

Jackson hoped that protection could be given to Faku's people yet admitted that 'I doubt if the natives have any legal rights but rely on the generous treatment they would have received from Mr Rhodes in such a case.'[74] Jackson here articulated the passage from oral patriarchy to colonial capitalist contract, and foreshadowed the coming white success in frustrating in their turn Rhodes's own intentions. Where Africans had once managed to achieve security of tenure without offering labour, white lessees now managed to assert their right to evict even if labour were provided.

In vain the Chief Native Commissioner tried to establish a new basis for African

---

[72] The Brethren in Christ persisted in the *mapani* however. In June 1903 Frances Davidson led a 'tour of exploration' through the hills 'and south for a long distance'. 'Very few natives were seen on the journey through the hills but in this rich, open plain of the south there were numerous kraals.' There was no missionary among them but Hole, 'a rich and prominent native', received them kindly. Mapani Mission was founded under Ndhlalambi in August 1904. After the 1908 occupation of the *mapani* by white farmers, Davidson applied for the grant of Holi farm as a mission station on which a white missionary would be based. 'One of the best openings for our work is in the "Mapani" land', and a mission farm would allow Christians to 'settle and be under the control of the Mission.' The application was turned down and the farm alienated to none other than C. J. Webb. But the Brethren evangelists continued their work. On a visit in 1910 Davidson found the evangelist at Mapani 'spirit-filled' and preaching 'powerful sermons'; a large brick church had been erected; there was 'a most precious waiting on the Lord ... many soul-stirring prayers and testimonies.... The Lord had been pouring out His Spirit upon some of them in a marvellous manner.' Frances Davidson to Civil Commissioner, 2 September 1908, L 2/1/24; Davidson, *South and South Central Africa*, Brethren Publishing House, Elgin, 1915.

[73] Native Commissioner, Matobo/Malema to Chief Native Commissioner, Matabeleland, 13 March 1903, NBE 1/1/3.

[74] H. M. Jackson to Chief Native Commissioner, Matabeleland, 22 April 1903, NB 1/1/19.

rights on the Rhodes Matopos Estate, asking Rhodes's executors to 'arrive at some definite arrangement as to the rights of Native tenants on the Estate.'[75] The Trustees declined, preferring an *ad hoc* payment to Faku to any written statement of contract which might have legal force. Jackson thought the compensation inadequate and feared Faku might soon be moved from his new lands. But he was forced to conclude in September 1903 that 'the granting of compensation is purely an act of grace.' Now that Rhodes was dead, commitment to the word of the Founder had been replaced by the 'grace' of the Trustees. It turned out to be an inadequate protection.

Faku was now growing old. Negotiations on his behalf were carried on in 1903 by his son and heir, Nyangazonke. Nyangazonke made it clear that 'compensation is a secondary consideration. What they wish for mainly is to be allocated lands which they may break up and cultivate without fear of deprivation in the future.'[76] No such guarantee could be given. Faku died on 3 May 1904. In July Nyangazonke was appointed to succeed him. But by then his people were already on the move away from the area they had occupied for so long. On 22 July 1904 Jackson reported that Faku's subjects were leaving to occupy 'formerly uninhabited land to the south, along the Shashani river.'[77] Nyangazonke set himself up in the *mapani* veld close to his father's old enemy, Hole.

This movement took place with the encouragement of the Native Department. As H. M. Jackson reported in March 1907:

> the movements from the hills are principally directed [to] a large block of unoccupied Government farms. The whole country south of the hills is known as *mapani* and the greater part of this country being government farms we have allowed them to locate themselves there under the supervision of the chiefs.

'Hundreds of kraals' had moved south.[78] Many came from Rhodes's land. As well as Nyangazonke, other large cattle owners moved south. One was the *induna* Maqina, whose people had gone so far as to kill cattle on farms north of the Matopos 'to force the Company owning the farms to discontinue farming operations, which necessarily clash with their interests.'[79] Failing to dislodge farmers and landowners north of the hills, Maqina's people went into the *mapani*. By January 1908 Jackson reported that 'all the Government farms to the south of the Matopo are occupied by natives from the Matopo Hills; the farm Kezi is occupied by the chief Maqina, the farm Lana by the chief Hole, and the farm Dope by chief Nyangazonke.' Between them the three chiefs owned over 10,000 cattle, many of them grazing in the *mapani* and others scattered among their people in the hills.[80]

Meanwhile the ordeal of the Africans who remained on Rhodes's estates intensified. The Westacre dam proved to be wrongly sited for productive cereal agriculture. The

[75] Chief Native Commissioner, Matabeleland, to Charles Coghlan, 28 April 1903, NB 1/1/19.
[76] Jackson to Chief Native Commissioner, Matabeleland, 14 September 1903, NBE 1/1/3.
[77] Jackson to Chief Native Commissioner, Matabeleland, 22 July 1904, NB 3/1/2.
[78] Jackson to Chief Native Commissioner, 11 March 1907, NB 3/1/2.
[79] Monthly report, Matopos, December 1901, NBE 1/1/2.
[80] H. M. Jackson to Chief Native Commissioner, 23 January 1908, LB 2/1/14/5.

Trustees decided to concentrate on cattle ranching and dairying rather than on cereal production. Meanwhile African herds were recovering from the ravages of rinderpest, confiscation and war. The new emphasis placed Estate cattle and African herds in direct competition. Even once Nyangazonke and Maqina's cattle had departed, the Trustees concluded that they could not tolerate the unchecked growth of African herds.

In August 1907 McDonald wrote to the Chief Native Commissioner to make an announcement that marked a key departure from the pledges of Cecil Rhodes:

> As you are aware, in accordance with a promise made by the late Mr Rhodes, the natives residing on the Sauerdale Estate have never been charged any rents since it became his property. I have discovered, however, that the majority of the natives now living on the property are not the original Matabele at all, and in many cases aliens.... I notice that the natives are well off in the matter of cattle ... and that they do not carry out the condition laid down by Mr Rhodes, namely that they should give a certain amount of labour each year to the Estate tenants.

McDonald therefore announced that the Trustees would levy rents from 1 September 1907, £1 per year for 'Matabeles' and £2 a year for others, unless they could produce a certificate from one of the white lessees testifying that they had worked for them.[81]

McDonald claimed that these arrangements were a minimal change from Rhodes's system. In fact the change was fundamental. For one thing it introduced for the first time an ethnic test, replacing Rhodes's inclusive promise to 'the Matebele' as a total society with discrimination between 'real' Ndebele and others. Moreover, it transformed the relationship between the African residents and the white lessees. Whereas both had previously been dependent on the word of Cecil Rhodes, the new relationship was for the first time to be embodied in written contract. On 15 February several chiefs and 116 other headmen and elders signed a formal labour and rental agreement. This provided for three months labour from 'Matabele' and four months from the rest; or for rent in lieu of such labour. Africans would lose all rights of residence 'in the event of bringing cattle onto the said land without the permission of the landlord,' or if cattle disease was not reported. Crucially, the agreement allowed for eviction if the landlord chose to refuse rent as compensation for labour and even if labour were offered:

> The African residents shall be entitled to continue cultivating the land ... and to run and depasture their livestock ... provided that the Landlord shall have the right at any time by giving twelve months notice ... to take possession of the land.[82]

In 1911 these eviction provisions were exploited on a large scale. The manager of the Estate farm, Hull, evicted 100 African families with 350 cattle and 2,000 sheep and goats. Hull also concentrated those allowed to remain 'on one section of the property', so that 'their cattle do not mix and stray with the farm stock'.[83] The other white lessees

[81] J. G. McDonald to Chief Native Commissioner, 12 August 1907, N 3/1/12.
[82] Draft agreement between J. G. McDonald and Native Headmen acting for the African residents of Sauerdale, Lucydale, Lonsdale, Hazelside, Westacre, World's View, 31 August 1907, N 3/1/12; completed agreement, 15 February 1908, NBE 3/1/1.
[83] Annual Report, Rhodes-Matopos Estates, NBE 3/1/1.

also began to turn Africans off their lands. What had happened was that Africans on the Rhodes-Matopos Estates had lost any special privileges. Rhodes's promise had become forgotten by almost all whites, even by the Native Department. When it was called to mind it seemed in the new age of colonial contract to be a self-evident absurdity. Rhodes had given leases to Europeans: therefore he must have intended those Europeans to possess full legal rights over Africans on their land. Rhodes had planned the commercial development of the Estate; therefore he could not have intended to tolerate the coexistence of an African pastoral economy.

When in 1917 the Southern Rhodesian government undertook a series of inquiries into the Rhodes-Matopos Estates with a view to taking them over from the Trustees, its investigator Eric Nobbs had nothing to say about African rights. He *did* say that the old, sloppy, oral era of patronage ought to be done away with – but by this he meant only leases to whites:

> Leases in the past were given on very nominal terms to various persons more or less closely connected with Mr Rhodes and on grounds of sentiment. There no longer exists occasion for this.... In future no leases shall be granted except on rent-paying footing.[84]

Nobbs stressed that 'we must take care not to interfere with the privileges of tenants in respect of natives on their farms', but by this he certainly did not manifest any concern for African rights. He meant that European lessees should continue to enjoy their rights to either rent or labour and must not be deprived of them by a government intervention to remove Africans from the land. Nobbs himself, who was so romantic about the Matopos and thought African kraals added to their picturesque antiquity, thought that all Africans *should* be removed from an estate so close to the corruptions of Bulawayo. But this would have to be done 'without interfering with the vested interests' of the white lessees. African residence on the Estate had become dependent on the whims of their white landlords.[85]

It was hardly surprising that when McDonald belatedly remembered in August 1918 to tell Nobbs about Rhodes's original promise no-one in government took him seriously. The Native Department had abandoned any attempt to guarantee the pledge. When he was appealed to, the Superintendent of Natives, Bulawayo, felt that neither 'rebels' nor 'friendlies' required 'special consideration at this late hour of the day', and pointed out that it was also late in the day to try to protect African residential rights when Hull and others had 'the power under their leases to give notice to whatever tenants to quit [and] exercised this right in an almost wholesale manner.'[86] Those lessees who had once been given the responsibility to manage Rhodes's experiment, now joined in the evictions. In January 1923 Percy Ross wrote to the Native Commissioner, Matobo:

[84] Report by Director of Agriculture, 26 September 1917, G 1/7/1/2.
[85] Nobbs to Native Commissioner, Matobo, 15 November 1917; Nobbs to W. E. Dowsett, 25 October 1917, G 1/7/3/2.
[86] Superintendent of Natives, Bulawayo to Chief Native Commissioner, 22 November 1918, cited by Hugh Ashton in his *ms* report on the Matopos National Park, Ashton papers, Historical Reference Library, Bulawayo.

I should be glad if you would kindly send one of your Police Messengers to warn certain kraals off Lucydale.... I gave these Natives notice to leave 15 months ago but did not enforce it as they were practically starving.... You might mention to the natives that the farm is small and therefore I require all the grazing and lands to my own use and that they have been here many years and that they have not been charged any rent, which I expect the ordinary Native will appreciate in these hard times.[87]

There was nothing left of Rhodes's pledge of secure tenure of ample land.

The Collapse of the Land Security of Africans in the Mapani

By 1923 it was much too late for anyone to follow the example of Nyangazonke and Maqina and to flee from the Rhodes Matopos Estates to the *mapani* veld. The *mapani* area had been occupied in October 1908 by an expedition led by the Acting Manager, Estates, Bulawayo. A decision that the government-owned farms in the *mapani* should be actively marketed to European settlers had been taken at the end of 1907 in view of 'the urgent need of giving some impetus to land settlement in Matabeleland'. From the beginning the Land Settlement Department took a very aggressive line on the African population already on the land.

The Natives already have their Reserves, which are some of the picked land of the country. They now appear to let these lie idle for a rainy day and to play havoc with the ground intended for European occupation. Apart from this it appears highly undesirable to establish independent Native communities in the midst of what are meant eventually to be European settlements.[88]

The Native Department was consulted but in the face of this aggressive incursion H. M. Jackson could do no more than to urge that since Hole had been in the area for the past ten years Lana farm should be 'reserved' for his occupation. The Chief Native Commissioner added Kezi and Dope farms, in the hope of securing them for Nyangazonke and Maqina. He had no success. 'Reservation is an extreme step' minuted the Administrator, 'to be resorted to only in very special cases.' It was determined that all the *mapani* farms be made available for purchase and all were advertised.[89]

Remarkably, at this last gasp, an effective appeal was made to the promises of Rhodes. The Chief Native Commissioner made strong representations that Rhodes had promised security to those who came out of the hills. If they could not live on the *mapani* farms, then a Reserve should be created not too far from the Matopos. Equally remarkably, his appeal worked. On 24 October 1908 the Accountant wrote to him:

With reference to your interview on the subject of the natives at present squatting on land in

[87] Ross to Native Commissioner, Matobo, 20 January 1923, NBE 2/1/1.
[88] Director, Land Settlement to Acting Commercial Representative, Bulawayo, 10 July 1908, S 211/25.
[89] H. M. Jackson to Chief Native Commissioner, Matabeleland, 23 January 1908; Chief Native Commissioner to Secretary, Lands, 7 February 1908; Administrator, memorandum on Secretary, Estates to Secretary, Administration, 17 September 1908; cable Charter to Native, 21 October 1908, LB 2/1/14/5; De Laessoe to William George, 29 July 1908, LB 1/3/1.

the Matoppo District which has been leased under Permit of Occupation to Europeans, I am directed to inform you that in view of Mr Rhodes's promise, the Company is willing to agree to your selecting in conjunction with Mr de Laessoe, approximately 18,000 morgen of land to accomodate the natives who may wish to remove from the adjoining farms [Kezi, Dope and Lana].[90]

It was even agreed that in order 'that such a change of habitat should not be too radical it was desired that such Reserve should not be too far distant; and also such a locality chosen the character of which the natives to move into might be cognizant of.'[91]

After much negotiation, the area of what is now Tshatshani Communal Land, southwest of the three farms, was set aside as a Reserve, the first in the Matobo district. The Land Settlement Department was grudging, demanding that compensation be given from land already set aside for Africans. For this they were rebuked by the Administrator in January 1909, in another reference to the undertakings given to the Africans of the Matopos:

If the circumstances attending the settlement of natives on the Matopo farms in 1897 are carefully examined, it may be held that the farms which they have recently been removed from were actually assigned to them for occupation and that the British South Africa Company in recovering possession of these farms for European occupation has actually received compensation for the other land now set apart for natives in the Matobo District.[92]

Before the boundaries of the new Reserve had been determined, the Acting Manager, Estates, Bulawayo, set off for the *mapani* with the Chief Native Commissioner, Matabeleland, the Native Commissioner, Matobo, and the intending white settlers of the land. On 29 October they met the African residents at 'Holi Station'. The Chief Native Commissioner put the best face on things:

As time went on this Mapani veld gradually filled up. There has been a great influx, not only from the Hills but also from all parts of the District. The majority of you were preceded by certain European farmers, amongst them Mr Leith and Mr Lees.... Mr Jackson reported to me from time to time that you were gradually moving down here [and] spoke favourably of your relations with these farmers.... I was very pleased to hear this and I saw no reason why you should not be allowed to take up your abode here, as I knew it was the intention of the British South Africa Company to divide the country up into farms and dispose of the land to Europeans. Now this has been done ... and latterly you have seen a number of settlers occupying the farms.... There is no reason why you should not continue to reside here ... but there may be a few instances where it is possible that owing to the land being required by the landlord ... we should give you an outlet and I have obtained a piece of land for those people who are unable to come to arrangements with settlers.[93]

Privately, the Chief Native Commissioner was much less sanguine. He was aware that there had been rumours of unrest as soon as Hole and the other *indunas* were called on to enter rental agreements with the new owners. 'They do not like it', wrote the

[90] Accountant to Chief Native Commissioner, Matabeleland, 24 October 1908, A 3/18/39/15.
[91] Draft Memorandum, 1909, A 3/18/39/19.
[92] Secretary, Administrator to Director, Land Settlement, 5 January 1909, A 3/18/39/15.
[93] 'Proceedings of a Meeting held at Holi Station on the 29th October 1908', LB 2/1/14/5.

Native Commissioner, Matobo, 'and they do not understand why the Matopo people in the hills should go scot free.'[94] On 2 November 1908 the Chief Native Commissioner wrote to the Secretary, Administrator to stress that the *mapani* had 'become very thickly populated'; that people had come in from the hills and that

> many natives who formerly lived on the Rhodes Estates and whose lands were required by the farmers there, left and took up their abode in this portion.... Among them were Chief Nyangazonke and Chief Maqina. They and their people appear to be very much concerned at the prospect of having large numbers of farmers settling here, as they feared they would again have to forefeit their land.

Hole was determined to move away and Nyangazonke and Maqina were likely to do so also. But there was no mention of 'assegais nor even of resistance in any form'.[95]

Deep resentment was felt by Africans in the *mapani*, and was compounded when for the first time the British South Africa Company began to demand rents for those living on unalienated lands. 'Landlords are in no greater favour here', commented the Native Commissioner in 1908, 'than they are reputed to be in the Emerald Isle.' The Matobo Annual Report for 1909 recorded:

> Horned cattle have done exceptionally well. Natives have an eye for a shapely beast and will obtain the services of a good bull if it can be had free of charge.... An increasing number of oxen for draught purposes are broken in yearly. [But] considerable dissatisfaction has been caused, especially among stock owners, at the amount of land alienated to European farmers, which has necessitated the removal of a number of kraals to unalienated land and reserves. Those who have cultivated at will for years and allowed their cattle to roam at will all over the country without let or hindrance, find it hard to conform to the restrictions placed on them by white settlers, who are now rapidly acquiring land in localities never before owned by Europeans.[96]

There was not yet the same response from tenants as in the Emerald Isle. Resistance was economic rather than violent. Nyangazonke and Maqina both used some of their cattle to buy farms of their own. After contemplating moving away altogether into the far south, Hole retired into the new Shashani Reserve.[97] From these bases, their cattle overran the whole *mapani* and competed with those of the new settlers. In 1914 Native Commissioner Elliott of Matobo asserted that Maqina, Hole and Nyangazonke between them owned more than 10,000 head; no more than 1,200 were owned by anyone else in

---

[94] Native Commissioner, Matobo to Chief Native Commissioner, Matabeleland, 25 September 1908, NB 3/1/9.

[95] Chief Native Commissioner to Secretary, Administrator, 2 November 1908, LB 2/1/14/5.

[96] Annual Reports, Matobo, 1908 and 1909, NB 6/1/9 and 10.

[97] In a report of 1914 Hole is shown as in the Shashani Reserve; he died late in 1915; in 1918 his son and successor, Nzula, was still in the Reserve where by now he possessed 10,000 cattle, S 728/64/4. Maqina bought 'Kapeni' farm in 1923, NBE 2/1/1. Nyangazonke bought the 7,528 acres of 'Stutterlingen' farm for £3000; his successor, Sinti, was living there in 1924, N 3/4/5; S.605; S 728/6A/5. Robin Palmer, in his Appendix 11 which lists farms owned by Africans in 1925, includes one 'George Nyangazonke, probably an Ndebele,' owner of Stutterlingen, Palmer, *Land and Racial Domination in Rhodesia*, Heinemann, London, 1977, p. 281. Nyangazonke himself died in 1919. He was succeeded by his son Tapi, who was deposed in 1922 for 'misconduct' in selling off 'tribal cattle' for personal use. Presumably Nyangazonke was retained by Sinti as a chiefly and family name.

the district, and the three chiefs took steps to prevent any of their people acquiring too many. The cattle were 'more or less distributed throughout the district', thereby giving the three chiefs enormous influence. But the bulk of their herds grazed in the *mapani*. 'There is a tendency among Europeans to push Natives off their farms. The cattle are at the bottom of it.'[98] In 1915 one of the white settlers, G. C. C. Montgomery of Lions Park Farm, gave vivid if erratic testimony to the vigour of Hole's herd. Three thousand of these cattle, Montgomery complained, had overrun his farm on their route to the Semokwe River:

> If we keep them away in the day time they steal the water at night.... The native cattle always brake thru these farms to get to the water. A native will always creep in between white people if allowed. A native is mearly a baboon in one way. Whenever he see long grass he want to pick there and spoil the veldt for white people.[99]

From the point of view of Matopos *indunas* now in the *mapani*, it was the white people who always 'crept in'.

Rhodes's Promises in the Matopos Hills

At one stage in the clearing of the hills, almost all those who had lived outside the Matopos before 1896 had come out of them into the open. The Assistant Native Commissioner, Umlugulu reported in June 1901 that

> those who went in the Matopo Hills during the Rebellion and remained there after it are now leaving the Hills. The old inhabitants born in the Hills do not wish to move. They evidently have the best part of the Hills suitable for cultivation.[100]

But soon these overwhelmingly Banyubi hillmen were joined once more by immigrants from the flat land, bringing their cattle back with them.

Many of Hole's and Nyangazonke's people responded to the arrival of white farmers in the *mapani* by going back into the Matopos. The allegiance of the residents of Whitewaters in the western Matopos, for instance, was divided between the two chiefs, and many of the cattle grazing there belonged to them. Sometimes, indeed, drought in the Shashani Reserve – an increasingly frequent phenomenon – resulted in *all* the cattle being sent to the 'unsurveyed Matopo Hills'.[101] In the same way, many of the people evicted from the Rhodes-Matopos Estate went back into the hills. Thus Kubulo, a follower of Babayan, had lived on what became Rhodes's land in Lobengula's time, had

---

[98] Evidence of F. G. Eliott, 8 July 1914, ZAD 3/1/1.
[99] G. C. C. Montgomery to Secretary, Reserves Commission, 14 May and 6 June 1915, ZAD 3/2/2. The Native Commissioner, Bulalima Mangwe commented on 11 June 1915 that Hole's cattle seem to overrun the whole country from the Shashani to the Semokwe.'
[100] Quarterly report, Umlugulu, June 1901, NBE 7/2/1, vol. 3.
[101] In 1922 Nyangazonke's son and successor, Tapi, who was himself living on a farm in the *mapani*, 'went round all the kraals in Whitewaters' to raise cattle for his expenses, N 3/4/5. In 1912 all the rivers in the Shashani ran dry and 8,000 head of stock were moved into the Matopos, monthly report, Chief Native Commissioner, March 1912, NB 6/4/13.

fought against the whites in the 1893 war and the 1896 rising (during which he had gone into the Matopos), and had been present at the 1896 and 1897 *indabas* and at the funeral of Rhodes. He returned to his ancestral lands on the Rhodes-Matopos Estate, worked for Huntley for three years and was then allowed to go to work on the mines:

> I lived for many years on that farm after I came back from the mine and it happened that it became the farm of one Mr Mitchell and then he moved me and I went to the Matopos. I objected although I did not go to the Native Commissioner to say so.

Kubulo ended up in Wenlock under Mtuwane.

Tuta, on the other hand, ended up in Whitewaters. He had been born at what became the site of the dam at Westacre. He had heard Rhodes say 'that he would be buried amongst us – we black people', and that 'we were to build our kraals and surround the place where he would be buried'. Rhodes had also assured them that 'those people who were on his farms were going to remain occupying his farms.' He lived there for many years until Native Messenger Ngungu came and said, 'We should leave the area because there were white people coming from Salisbury who were going to occupy that farm.... All of us left. No kraals were left.' Ngungu told them 'that we should go to our country in the hills', so he went to Whitewaters.[102]

These men, and many others, carried Rhodes's promises with them when they fell back into the Matopos. The promises had been betrayed both to the north and the south of the hills, but within them they might yet be honoured. So Rhodes's pledges came to be attached in oral memory to the Matopos especially. As Tuta put it:

> Mr Rhodes said that even if he died outside the Colony he wished to be buried among the African people in the Matopos.... I was present when Mr Rhodes mentioned to four chiefs that he wished them to care for his grave and remain in the vicinity. The chiefs were Mapisa, Hole, Faku and Dhliso. The Dutch people were to have the Kezi area, the Europeans the Bulawayo area, the Indians the outskirts of Bulawayo ... and we were given the Matopo Hills.[103]

Though most official reports of Rhodes's promises focussed on the flat lands north and south of the hills, there is some confirmation that he had also given undertakings to the inhabitants of the Matopos themselves. One such piece of evidence comes, oddly enough, from the main protagonist for white settlement in Matobo, De Laessoe, Acting Estates Manager in Bulawayo. In a memorandum on 'Native Reserves in Matabeleland' written in May 1909, De Laessoe included 'No. 3 Matopo Hills'. He explained that 'this area is reserved on a verbal promise of the late Mr Rhodes, that the natives there should not be disturbed. Most of the natives have, however, left there.... Except as a grazing area the tract is not of great value. Strategically it is, however, of some significance, being an impregnable stronghold. It should be decided once for all, whether it is to be regarded as a Native Reserve, and proclaimed as such.'[104]

In the end, as we have seen, the eastern Matopos was declared as a Reserve by the

---

[102] Evidence of Kubulo and Tuta, 17 March 1949, S 1651/46.

[103] Affadavit of Tuta, 18 August 1948, S 1516/46.

[104] 'Native Reserves in Matabeleland', 5 May 1909, L 2/2/117/10. In August 1908 the Chief Native Commissioner had reminded H. M. Jackson of 'Mr Rhodes' wish viz that the Matopo Hills should be reserved from pegging of farms'. L 2/2/117/32.

1915 Commission and the remainder was proclaimed a National Park in 1926. Immediately after the 1897 *indabas*, however, there had been attempts to create a Reserve to cover most of the hills and the adjacent areas and thus to give statutory effect to Rhodes's promises. At the end of 1897 proposals for Reserves in Matabeleland were prepared to be forwarded to the High Commissioner in Cape Town and from him to the Secretary of State for the Colonies in London. Two Reserves were proposed for the Matopos area. One was 'Sauerdale Reserve' but this turned out to have been due to an official taking Rhodes's benevolent intentions too seriously and it was quickly dropped. The other was a 'Reserve proposed to be made in the Matoppos' and this was approved by all concerned in Southern Rhodesia and South Africa and recommended to the Secretary of State for the Colonies early in 1898. The Colonial Secretary rejected the proposal, however, presumably on strategic grounds.[105] Thereafter, for a little while, the 'Matopos Reserve' maintained a ghostly identity. 'I have heard', wrote the Assistant Native Commissioner, Umlugulu, in July 1898, 'that there is a large Reserve in the Matopos Hills but I have not been officially advised as to its area.' 'Neither Mr Thomas or myself have been informed of the exact whereabouts of the Matopos Native Reserve', the Native Commissioner, Matopos, told the Chief Native Commissioner, 'but I know from a conversation with you that one exists.'[106]

The ghost of a formally proclaimed Native Reserve in the Matopos as a whole faded away, to be replaced by the much vaguer 'reservation' against alienation of land in the hills. As more and more Africans returned to the Matopos with their cattle their status remained totally ambiguous, both during the 'reservation' period and after the promulgation of the National Park in 1926. By the 1920s – as the eviction screw tightened on the Rhodes-Matopos Estate and the white farmers entrenched themselves in the *mapani* veld – the inhabitants of the hills alone retained their 'independence', free of rent and largely free from interference. But outside the Matopos Reserve in the eastern hills there was no legal base to this *de facto* autonomy. When times changed and the state began to intervene in the western Matopos – destocking, depopulating, banning hunting and the cultivation of the *vleis* – there was nothing to fall back on but the promises of Rhodes. It remained to be seen how effective an appeal to them was going to be.

[105] Under Secretary, Administrator to Secretary, Deputy Administrator, 20 April 1898, NB 1/1/4; Joseph Chamberlain to Sir Alfred Milner, 4 March 1898, ZAD 2/1/1.

[106] Assistant Native Commissioner, Umlugulu to Native Commissioner, Fort Usher, 25 July 1898, NBE 7/2/1; Native Commissioner, Matopos to Chief Native Commissioner, Matabaleland, 31 July 1898, NBE 1/1/1.

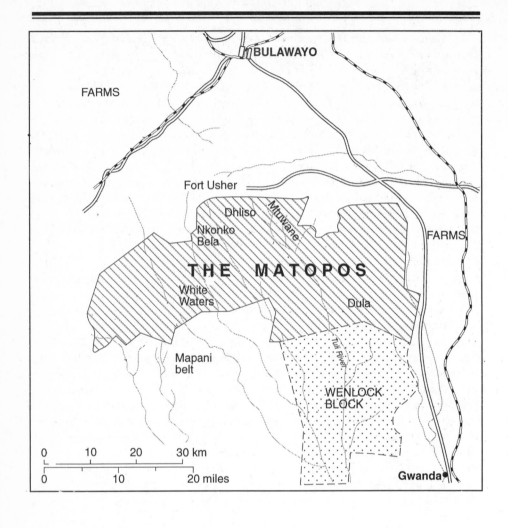

Map 2   Situation of the Nqameni chiefs, Mtuwane, Dhliso and Nkonkobela, before they began their movement south to the Mapani belt and to Wenlock.

4

Asserting Identity in the Matopos

Chiefship & Ethnicity in Wenlock 1897–1950

Early colonial administrators tended to present a complex ethnic picture of the Matopos area. They saw the 'indigenous' Banyubi people of the hills as very much non-Ndebele – 'the most ignorant and cowardly natives I have seen', wrote the Assistant Native Commissioner, Umlugulu, in March 1900, 'almost the whole population being a very poor class of the MaHoli'.[1] But, as H. M. Jackson reported, if 'the bulk of the people are of the Banyubi hill tribe occupying the rugged Matopos range ... the subsidised *indunas* are Matabele.'[2] Moreover, the people between the Matopos and Bulawayo, including those on Rhodes's farms, were regarded as Ndebele, 'essentially a fighting race'. To the south of the hills lived Sotho, Venda and other peoples.[3] The Native Commissioner, Matobo, calculated that in May 1901 the whole district contained some 25,000 Africans:

> Almost two-thirds of that population are represented by natives of the Abanyubi race, a branch of the Amakalanga, the remainder being Matabile, Uteshabi and other tribes. The prevailing dialect is Matabile, the majority of the natives being able to speak it fairly fluently.[4]

These ethnic distinctions were regarded as important; a man's ethnicity was entered in his registration certificate; and administrators provided copious information about the great difference between Banyubi and Ndebele marriage customs, agricultural methods, religious belief, etc.

There is indeed evidence that different sorts of 'non-Ndebele' who lived in the hills

---

[1] Assistant Native Commissioner, Umlugulu to Native Commissioner, Matopo-Mawabeni, 10 March 1900, NBE 7/2/1, vol. 3.

[2] Monthly report, Matopo-Mawabeni, June 1899, NBE 1/1/1.

[3] Chief Native Commissioner's Annual Report, Matabeleland Province, 31 March 1898, NB 6/1/1. The C.N.C., Matabeleland, added an account of the 'caste' system. There were three 'well recognised types of natives' – the zantsi or 'Zulu' aristocrats; the enhla, or 'Basuto' subjects of Mzilikazi, many of whom had settled south of the hills 'before the Matabele invasion and still keep their own customs and laws', and the holi, 'or slave, an original inhabitant of the country', including the 'Aba-Nyubi, a Makalaka race living in the Matopos.'

[4] Annual Report, April 1903, Matobo, NB 6/1/3.

99

in the mid-1890s felt not only different from but actively hostile towards their Ndebele overlords. Many Shona-speakers, captured in Ndebele raids before 1893 and placed under Ndebele *indunas* in or around the Matopos, now took the opportunity to escape. In June 1897, for instance, it was reported that

> a great many *Amahole* who were placed under either Hluguniso or Dhliso have left 'Egubeni' for their original homeland, 'Ebuswina', near Victoria. They have no intention of returning. It appears that all the *Amahole* in the Matopo Hills are desirous of seeking pastures new.[5]

There is also evidence of Banyubi commemorations of Ndebele brutality. Frances Davidson of the Brethren in Christ recorded a Banyubi threshing dance in the north-eastern Matopos:

> The two sides placed opposite each other ... each being armed with his threshing stick, they performed a mimic battle with the grain lying on the rock between the two lines of battle, each one alternately driving the other before it, and at the same time beating the grain with their sticks. They also sang their war song, of how the Matabele overcame them and impaled them alive, and of the dire vengeance they would inflict in return. The whole was exceedingly heathenish but not uninteresting.[6]

Charles Stuart reported from Malema in November 1897 that the Banyubi had tried to take advantage of the fall of the Ndebele state to break free from 'the *Ndunas* appointed over them'.[7]

Yet the story of the next decades was the evolution of a composite Ndebele identity which included all the peoples of the Matopos. This was a response to the turmoil of the 1890s, which had thrown so many different people together, and the evictions of the twentieth century which continued to mix people up; it was an effect of administrative 'reform' and missionary teaching; and it was an ideology of protest against the breaking of the promises of Rhodes.

I have written in various publications about how officials and missionaries responded to cultural confusion by 'inventing' an Ndebele ethnicity. Before 1893, I have argued, the Ndebele state was manifestly a 'machine for multi-ethnic assimilation of peoples.... There were not [any] ethnic "Ndebele" but rather a conglomeration of peoples who were members of the Ndebele state and *their* identity was very much open to question after 1893 and 1896 when the Ndebele state was destroyed.'[8] After 1896, the Native Department officials did not wish to reconstruct the Ndebele state. Instead they tried to hold the societies of central Matabeleland together by constructing an 'Ndebele' ethnicity on the Zulu model. Men like Charles Stuart, Native Commissioner for Malema – himself from Natal – found 'a state of anarchy in which the old vital and essential laws and customs were either forgotten or swept away', with a resulting collapse of chiefly,

---

[5] Assistant Native Commissioner, Umlugulu, to Chief Native Commissioner, 8 June 1897, NBE 7/2/1.

[6] H. Frances Davidson, *South and South Central Africa*, Brethren Publishing House, Elgin, 1915, p. 205.

[7] Monthly report, Malema, November 1897, NB 6/4/1. Stuart added that immediately after the 1896 risings 'it was with difficulty that effect could be given to orders delivered through' the *indunas*. However, 'they now, perhaps for the first time, see that the country is in the impregnable possession of the White People', with the result that Ndebele *indunas* appointed by the whites were able to exercise authority.

[8] Terence Ranger, *The Invention of Tribalism in Zimbabwe*, Mambo, Gweru, 1985, pp. 5–6.

patriarchal and husbandly authority. Stuart believed that the inhabitants of Malema district:

> be they regarded from a moral, a physical or an intellectual standpoint are infinitely inferior to the Zulu, the race from which they have sprung. They consist of heterogenous, isolated groups of hybrid birth of the most degraded caste.... There seems to be little doubt that most of the old Zulu laws and customs were observed at the time of Mzilikazi; that a great many became obsolete during Lobengula's reign; and finally that scarcely one worthy of mention is generally and strictly adhered to in practice at the moment.[9]

Stuart's solution, and that of many other Native Commissioners, was to teach the 'Ndebele' how to be 'Ndebele' by enforcing 'Zulu' laws. (By contrast with the pre-colonial Ndebele state, the Zulu kingdom *was* based on an imagined ethnicity.) In 1898 a commission was established, on which Stuart served together with W. E. Thomas of Bulalima-Mangwe, to 'draft a code of native laws for the administration of the natives of Matabeleland'. In Malema old Faku was fined 'for failing to be present at Bulawayo when the Native Code was being drafted.'[10]

But Thomas and Stuart sat for nine days with other senior Ndebele chiefs; the two Native Commissioners thought the Natal Code of 1891 'exactly adapted to the natives of this province' and had it intepreted clause by clause to the *indunas*. 'The unanimous desire of the assembled chiefs was that a complete revival of these laws and customs would be most gladly welcomed', reported the Chief Native Commissioner. The proposed code of law, Stuart thought, 'would be of extreme use in the resuscitation of what, now, cannot be otherwise described than as a nation more or less without customs.'[11]

In the event, a formal Code of Native Law was not adopted – Southern Rhodesia's was not an Indirect Rule administration. But the idea of 'reviving' the Ndebele on a Zulu model exercised a pervasive influence. Administrators enforced payment of bride price, or *lobola* – which they thought characteristic of Nguni societies – and discouraged bride service on the Banyubi model. *Indunas* and their courts were entrusted to enforce marriage law so that the domestic questions of the Banyubi, Kalanga and other groups were determined in Sindebele before an Ndebele *induna*. Missionaries used Sindebele – or more often Zulu – as the language of church and school. So successful did whites feel they had been in producing an Ndebele ethnicity that the population of the Matopos – which originally had been regarded as so eminently non-Ndebele – provided most of the field data for the first anthropological study of 'Kin, Caste and Nation Among the Rhodesian Ndebele'.[12]

Since I published in 1985 my first account of this white 'invention' of Ndebele

---

[9] *Ibid.*, p. 8, citing quarterly report, Malema, 30 September 1898, NBE 7/1/1.

[10] Monthly reports, Bulalima and Malema, September and October 1898, NB 6/4/2.

[11] *Ibid.*, p. 9, citing draft letter of Chief Native Commissioner, Matabeleland to Secretary, Native Affairs, September 1908, NB 3/14/4; quarterly report, Malema, 30 September 1898, NBE 7/1/1.

[12] A. J. B. Hughes, *Kin, Caste and Nation Among the Rhodesian Ndebele*, Rhodes-Livingstone Papers, 25, Manchester University Press, 1956. Hughes drew on studies of the Shangani Reserve and 'the Matopos area', though he knew that in the Matopos 'the inhabitants are mostly descended from the Shona-speakers who were here before the Ndebele arrived.' Nevertheless, most of the diagrams and photographs in his study relate to the Matopos.

ethnicity, I have sought to supplement it with studies of the imagination of Ndebele identity by Africans, without which, of course, no merely European constructs could have had much effect.[13] I have discussed at some length the influence of the African cultural nationalist intellectuals of Bulawayo in the 1930s and 1940s, but have not yet been able to trace in detail the development of Ndebele identity in the rural areas. This book provides both the opportunity and the necessity to do so.

The compelled movements of the 1890s and the first decades of the twentieth century – into the Matopos, out of the Matopos, and for many people back into the Matopos again – meant constant changes of location, environment and community. Many people started off before 1893 under one of Lobengula's *indunas*, served under a different military commander in the Matopos in 1896, found themselves under a Rhodesian government-appointed chief as they came out 'into the open' in 1897, and then were allocated to yet another *induna* as they were evicted in the twentieth century. Men who had served in regiments before 1893 found themselves working to produce an agricultural surplus after 1897 and were then called upon to work in the mines, towns and ranches. Women were first called upon to work with their men during the brief peasant option and then to take on almost all responsibility for both farming and cattle management as labour migration became dominant. Some men and women left the rural areas for Bulawayo and others for the mine compounds. Some acquired Christian literacy. These profound upheavals challenged not only cultural but also political, gender, class and generational identities.[14]

These challenges called for much imagination to be invested by Africans in order to articulate new definitions of community. As John Lonsdale has argued for the 'Kikuyu', so too for the 'Ndebele' imagining ethnicity was not a matter of producing a single, homogeneous set of values and assumptions. It was a matter of defining the boundaries of debate about class, gender and generation.[15] This meant that many different imaginations of Ndebele identity were developed – by *Zansi* aristocrats and by *Holi* commoners; by old and by young; by Christian intellectuals and by rural adherents to Mwali. That these were all imaginations of *Ndebele* identity – rather than Banyubi or Kalanga – was due above all to the political imperative. Ways had to be found of

---

[13] For example, Terence Ranger, 'The Invention of Tradition Revisited', in Terence Ranger and Olufemi Vaughan, eds, *Legitimacy and the State in Twentieth Century Africa*, Macmillan, London, 1993; Terence Ranger, 'African Identities: Ethnicity, Nationality and History. The Case of Matabeleland, 1893–1993', in Joachim Heidrich, ed., *Changing Identities. The Transformation of Asian and African Identities Under Colonialism*, Centre for Modern Oriental Studies, Berlin, 1994.

[14] During my research for this book I worked through the complete criminal case records for Matobo and Gwanda districts from the 1890s to 1950. These amply document the social upheavals of colonialism in central and southern Matabeleland. I have used some of them in 'Tales of the Wild West: Gold-Diggers and Rustlers in South-West Zimbabwe, 1898–1940', *South African Historical Journal*, 28, 1993. I used others in 'Murder, Rape and Witchcraft: Criminal Court Data for Gender Relations in Colonial Matabeleland', Gender in Empire and Commonwealth Seminar, Institute of Commonwealth Studies, London, 23 March 1995.

[15] John Lonsdale, 'The Moral Economy of Mau Mau: Wealth, Poverty and Civic Virtue in Kikuyu Political Thought', in Bruce Berman and John Lonsdale, *Unhappy Valley. Book Two: Violence and Ethnicity*, James Currey, London, 1992.

making claims upon the whites, and, when that failed, of combining against them. Political identity was necessarily 'Ndebele' since the whites had made war on the Ndebele state, had made peace with the Ndebele *indunas*, and had made promises of land to all the Ndebele. In this chapter and the next I shall show how Ndebele identities were appealed to and imagined in the context of the struggle for the land by two of the Matopos populations – the *Nqameni* of Wenlock, and the peoples of the National Park.

The Nqameni *Chiefs of Wenlock*

One focus for Ndebele identity was the chieftainship. After 1896 the Rhodesian administration tried to break direct connections between the colonial system and the Ndebele kingdom. It sought to fragment large regimental or regional units; it sought to replace pre-colonial *indunas* by new men; it emphasised the novel basis of chiefly authority and prosperity. Nevertheless, despite all these endeavours, some *indunas* retained an imaginative connection with the Ndebele state, controlled significant followings and enjoyed legitimacy and authority in the eyes of their people. They were able to combine these with control of wealth in cattle. They used cattle both to bind together 'tribesmen' and also to make connections with modernising stock keepers and African traders. The sons of some *indunas* obtained advanced mission education and were in touch with Bulawayo cultural nationalist intellectuals. Such men looked both back and forward, and around them an Ndebele ethnic identity could be imagined.

These generalisations are illustrated, I think, by the story of the *Nqameni* chiefs of Wenlock. In fact the very juxtaposition of these two categories of identity – *Nqameni* and Wenlock – is expressive in itself of the contradictions and ambiguities of colonial chiefship. The *Nqameni* were descendants of one of the most famous and long-established of pre-colonial Ndebele regiments; Wenlock was a name romantically imported from rural Shropshire and given to a vast ranch. There was little historical or geographical logic in the association. Before 1896 the *Nqameni* had lived along the north-central edges of the Matopos; Wenlock lies south-east of the hills, where hardly any Ndebele-speakers had lived in the nineteenth century, and certainly none who could claim any membership of the historic core of the Ndebele state. Even the term 'the *Nqameni* chiefs' requires explanation. In the nineteenth century there had been one *induna* of *Nqameni*, not three or four as there came to be under colonial rule. These ambiguities rose to their height with the appointment of Chief Sigombe Mathema in 1948 and his successive roles as progressive reformer and traditionalist nationalist. To tell this story I need first to introduce the *Nqameni*; then to introduce Wenlock; and finally, in a subsequent chapter, recount the dramatic career of Sigombe Mathema.

The Nqameni

The *Nqama* identity went back to the time before the establishment of the Ndebele state in western Zimbabwe. The *Nqama* regiment, under the command of Mpateni Mathema, entered the new country with Mzilikazi. It settled in the heartland of the new state, north of the Matopos, and developed from a regiment into a chieftancy, with

Somhlolo Mathema, confidant and son-in-law of Mzilikazi, as its *induna*. North of the Matopos the chieftancy incorporated numbers of the conquered people and during Lobengula's reign two *Nqameni* men were sent south of the Matopos to bring Sotho and Kalanga groups under the authority of the kingdom. The *Nqameni* were, in short, at the core of the history of the Ndebele state.[16]

They were also at the heart of resistance to the imposition of European rule. In the 1890s the *Nqameni* lived along and just inside the central northern fringes of the Matopos mountains under the chiefship of Dhliso Mathema, son of Somhlolo. Dhliso took the *Nqameni* into the uprising of 1896; they were first active north of the hills and then fell back into the fastnesses of the Matopos, where with the other 'rebels' they fought the white army to a standstill. Dhliso and the other *Nqameni* spokesmen were present at the *indabas* with Cecil Rhodes which brought the Matopos fighting to an end. Dhliso was made a salaried *induna* in 1897. The *Nqameni*, then, had helped conquer the country; helped create the state and helped integrate people of different ethnicities into it; helped defend the state; and maintained their regimental honour when the state was overthrown. Julian Cobbing writes of the twentieth-century *Nqameni* – 'descendants living under the traditional line of Mathema chiefs' – as a prime example of the 'fully matured chieftaincies which existed as concepts providing group identity' under colonialism.[17]

Matters were not, however, quite as straightforward as this. For one thing, after May 1905 the *Nqameni* were not under the 'traditional line of Mathema chiefs'; nor were they all in one bloc, but broken up into a number of chieftaincies and scattered over three administrative districts. It became a matter of hot controversy who had the right to appeal to the *Nqama* tradition. For another thing, the nature of the authority of the *Nqameni* chiefs changed, as did the basis of their prestige. All this happened as the result of the working out of the contradictory tendencies in the early Rhodesian administration – the desire of the local Native Commissioners to have effective African sub-prefects interacting with the determination of the Chief Native Commissioner, Matabeleland, to break up and weaken the old regimental chieftaincies.

After the 1896 *indabas* Dhliso was recognised as 'the head *Induna*' of the Matopos district at a salary of £5 a month. None of the other *Nqameni* war commanders were recognised and the people of the chieftancy stayed where they were, along the northern edges of the Matopos. As the two Native Commissioners at Fort Usher and Malema set about constructing a colonial 'native society', they agreed that everything depended on the quality of their chiefs. Characteristically drawing upon the example of Zululand, Stuart of Malema argued that it would be easy to erect a strongly centralised and effective system, whereby commands would flow from the Chief Native Commissioner to his field-officers and from them to the African sub-prefects. 'The *indunas* of every country ... hold the key to the whole position.' The recognised *indunas* should be given more responsibility and more remuneration; they should be allowed to hold both civil

---

[16] J. R. Cobbing, 'The Ndebele Under the Khumalos, 1820–1896', doctoral thesis, University of Lancaster, 1976, pp. 75, 128; entry for *Nqameni*, 16 December 1947, PER 5, District Administrator's Office, Gwanda.
[17] Cobbing, 'The Ndebele', p. 94.

and criminal courts and to collect court fees: 'A poverty-stricken Induna cannot command the respect of his following.'[18]

Such a policy might have led to the *Nqameni* under Dhliso playing much the same role under Rhodesian rule as they had under the Ndebele kings. The trouble was that Dhliso was not prepared to play the Rhodesian game. He did not want to be involved in collecting tax, sending out labour and confiscating guns. He soon gave 'cause for censure by his inactivity and irresponsibility.'[19] 'Dhliso seems to have little or no control over his people', complained the Native Commissioner, Matopos, as early as January 1897. Thus, if there were to be strong and useful *Nqameni* chiefs they would have to be found elsewhere. The Native Commissioner looked about for other 'men of influence'.[20]

Ironically, he found them in three *Nqameni* men who had come to the forefront because of their activity during the 1896 fighting. One was Hluganiso, who had been active in the fighting in the eastern Matopos, and who lived on the headwaters of the Mtshabezi River close to where the Brethren in Christ set up their Matopo Mission. He was appointed *induna* with a subsidy of £2 a year in March 1897; a year later he was said to have a large following; he welcomed the arrival of the Brethren, telling his followers: 'They are not like other white people. They have come to teach you and to do your children good.' In 1900 he accepted a mission school at this kraal, but as for 'the white man's religion he would have none of it for himself.' Frances Davidson thought him 'a rank heathen, greedy and superstitious, and a lover of wives and beer.' The administration, however, found him 'a good and efficient government servant.'[21]

The second *Nqameni* leader to impress the administration was Nkonkobela Khumalo, a nephew of Lobengula and head of the *Ehlalini* sub-section of the *Nqama* chieftaincy. Nkonkobela had emerged as one of the most successful Ndebele military commanders in the Matopos. The third was Mtuwane Dlodlo, brother of Lobengula's favourite queen, Losegeyi, but neither a chief nor a sub-chief before the 1896 rising. As we have seen, Mtuwane was believed by both blacks and whites to have a special connection with the Mwali shrines. For this reason, the Native Commissioner, Matopos, was particularly anxious to make him a salaried *induna*. Nkonkobela and Mtuwane were also appointed *indunas* in March 1897.

On 8 May the Native Commissioner took Dhliso, Nkonkobela and Mtuwane into Bulawayo to see the Administrator. Dhliso's salary was reduced from £5 to £3; Nkonkobela and Mtuwane were confirmed as *indunas* at a monthly salary of £2. 'These two chiefs were men of importance and considerable influence during the last

[18] Native Commissioner, Malema, quarterly report, 30 June 1897, NBE 7/1/1.
[19] Report on subsidised chiefs, 1903, NBE 1/1/3.
[20] Monthly report, Matopos, January 1987, NBE 1/1/1.
[21] Annual report, Matopo-Mawabeni, March 1898, NB 6/1/1; list of subsidised chiefs, 1903, NB 1/1/19; report on subsidised chiefs, 1903, NBE 3/1/1; Native Commissioner, Matobo to Superintendent of Natives, Bulawayo, 28 September 1914, N 3/4/1-2; the diary of the Native Commissioner, Matopos, on 2 May 1899 includes a map which shows the situation of Hluganiso and the other *Nqameni* chiefs, Hluganiso being the easternmost. Frances Davidson, *South and South Central Africa*, Brethren Publishing House, Elgin, 1915, pp. 51, 55, 77, 110.

rebellion', wrote the Native Commissioner, 'Mtuwani being the Mlimo's appointed Induna over all the forces of the Matopos. Both men have worked fairly well.' In March 1898 he was more enthusiastic. Dhliso 'prefers drinking kaffir beer to looking after his people', but Mtuwane was 'a good man' and administering many of the *Nqameni*, while Nkonkobela had 'a lot of people under him, absolute control of his followers and is a fine straight-forward man.' Administratively, then, the fragmentation of the *Nqameni* was working well, but the Native Commissioner added: 'The proud race, intead of being a compact quantity, is broken up under petty chiefs.'[22]

In fact it was this effect of the multiplication of *Nqameni* chiefs which commended itself to the Chief Native Commissioner, Matabeleland, Herbert Taylor. Taylor was determined that any illusion of continued Ndebele political authority should be brutally dispelled. In July and August 1899 he held a series of *indabas* in which he spelt out the new realities. 'They might as well understand', he told the *indunas*, 'that this is a white man's country and that the white man's object was to get the gold out of the land. They should understand finally that there will never be another native King in this country.'[23] More than this, Taylor was determined to break up any surviving large chieftaincy units. 'At present there is absolutely no cohesion among the natives', he boasted in March 1901, 'each little tribe is, as it were, opposed to the other. A certain amount of jealousy has been fostered by me as I am of the opinion it is the most politic form of governing the Natives.'[24]

Hence Taylor was happy to play the four *Nqameni* chiefs off against each other. He was also happy to appoint men as *indunas* whose traditional claims to inherit office were weak or non-existent. So when Nkonkobela died, he was succeeded by his brother, Zikali, who laboured 'under the disability of not being the successor *de jure*'; when Zikali became so unpopular that he had to be deposed, he was succeeded by his younger brother, Ndaniso Khumalo, who suffered the same disability but was kept in office despite the attainment of manhood by Nkonkobela's son and heir.[25] When Dhliso died in May 1905 his *indunaship* was allowed to lapse despite the existence of a legitimate heir. Ndaniso became senior Chief 'and appears to have absorbed the *Nqameni*' of Dhliso. In short, the recognised *indunas* owed their office to the administration rather than to tradition.

Similarly, Taylor was determined that *indunas* should owe their prosperity as well as their authority to the new order rather than to the old. In 1900 there was lively debate within the Native Department in Matabeleland about the ownership of so-called 'royal cattle', now that the monarchy had been overthrown and the colonial state had withdrawn any claims upon them. The Matopos Native Commissioners, true to their commitment to administration through the *indunas*, put the question to their chiefs. In the western Matopos the chiefs declared that 'the Induna of a community [was] the rightful custodian of King's cattle'; the Native Commissioner added that 'should such

[22] Half-yearly report, Matopos, June 1897, NBE 1/1/1; Annual report, Matopos, March 1898, NB 6/1/1.
[23] *Indaba* at Tegwani, 19 July 1899, NB 6/5/1/1. The Matopos chiefs were told the same thing.
[24] Chief Native Commissioner, Matabeleland to Secretary, Bulawayo, 14 March 1901, NB 2/1/1.
[25] Report on subsidised chiefs, 1903, NBE 1/1/3.

cattle be declared to belong to the Office of the Induna, the dignity and sphere of usefulness of such an office would be materially increased.' In the eastern Matopos, it was asserted that the cattle were 'the constructive possession of a region, or tribe, or corporation', such as the *Nqameni*.[26]

But Taylor repudiated this idea of collective property attached in trust to the office of *induna*. It was interesting, he wrote, to hear these traditionalist views but government should not be:

> entirely guided by the laws and customs prevailing under barbarous as opposed to white man's rule.... In my opinion the ownership of cattle and the rights thereto must commence from the time when the present Government took over the country. [The present allocation of cattle] was virtually the inception of a new order ... under white rule, and all cattle held in possession under the authority of the Government must in the natural course be handed down in due hereditary succession.

Immediately thereafter he decided a Matopos cattle dispute by proclaiming that 'the Government of today does not recognise tribal cattle in any way but looks for an individual owner.'[27]

This sort of judgement favoured the *indunas* as invididuals rather than as trustees *ex officio*. Many of them were well placed to emerge as the 'individual owners' the government was looking for. Many of the *indunas* built up very large herds, including Hluganiso and Ndaniso, but once again it was clear that they owed these to the colonial rather than to the traditional system.

In these ways the *Nqameni* were fragmented and their relationship to their *indunas* was transformed. And at the same time they were losing their land. In January 1898 Chief Native Commissioner Taylor, touring the northern Matopos, met with Hluganiso, Nkonkobela and Mtuwane – Dhliso was away in Bulawayo – and tried to encourage them to come out of the hills onto 'the Flats'. The three chiefs firmly replied that 'their lands were on the edge of the Matopos and they had always had good crops from them and they did not care to leave them.'[28] But whatever the *Nqameni* cared to do, within five years they had scattered far from these lands. In 1903 a list of the locations of subsidised *indunas* was drawn up to help Native Commissioners find their chiefs. Dhliso Mathema was then still in the northern Matopos with 262 able-bodied male *Nqameni*. So was Hluganiso with 289 male followers. But Zikali with 217 male followers was already south of the Matopos in the *mapani* veld; Mtuwane with 47 men was at Sizeze in what was to become the southern part of Wenlock, south-east of the hills.[29] Already, then, the *Nqameni* had become divided into two blocks, one north and the other south of the Matopos. When Ndaniso succeeded Zikali he moved with his people into Wenlock. After Dhliso's death in 1905 and the decision to overlook his son,

---

[26] Native Commissioner, Matopos, 2 October 1900; Native Commissioner, Malema, 12 October 1900, NB 1/1/1.

[27] Chief Native Commissioner, Matabeleland to Solicitor-General, 16 October 1900; decision in the case of Nkumzana and Ntola, NB 1/1/1.

[28] Meeting with Nkonkobela and Mtuwani, 17 January 1898, NB 6/5/1/1–2.

[29] Location of subsidised chiefs, 1903, NB 1/1/19.

only Hluganiso remained as *induna* for the *Nqameni* in the north. Gradually, and in a piecemeal way, they began to filter southwards. These movements were largely involuntary. They were the result of the alienation of land in the northern Matopos; the competition for the scarce grazing of the Matopos between white and black herds; and a desire to escape from close administration.

The results were unsatisfactory to both black and white. After 1908, as we have seen, white landowners began to take up farms and ranches south of the Matopos. At an *indaba* in April 1915 between the Administrator and the chiefs of southern Matabeleland, Ndaniso and Mtuwane bitterly complained of their insecurity. 'We live in the grass and cannot erect permanent abodes', protested Mtuwane. Ndaniso

> regretted that His Honour found before him the representatives of a broken people, full of grievances. They had no land on which they could permanently live. They occupied farms on insecure tenure and so were continually changing their habitations.

In the same year all Africans living on Matobo Block in the northern hills, where Hluganiso had his kraal, were given notice to quit, and another southward trek began.[30] Hluganiso himself ended up in Wenlock; many of his followers were scattered in the *mapani*.

At an *indaba* in April 1919 Ndaniso and Mtuwane petitioned against newly declared administrative boundaries which had placed Wenlock and their own immediate followers in Gwanda district, while leaving the bulk of the *Nqameni* in Matobo. They asked that 'the former Nqameni Regiment' be reunited.[31] Now joined with Hluganiso, they repeated their desire in October 1925, by which time they and 2,000 of the *Nqameni* were on Wenlock and in Gwanda, while some 7,500 remained in Matobo.[32]

Meanwhile, as we have also seen, the Native Department and Rhodesian Military Intelligence were unhappy about the *Nqameni* chiefs having escaped into the remoteness of Wenlock. In their regular assessments of the danger of rebellion, the three *indunas* featured as danger men. Hluganiso was 'looked upon as the head chief. He has a big say and is very rich in cattle'. Ndaniso with his 2,000 cattle was a man of wealth and influence; he could 'be termed the local advisor to the other Indunas.' Mtuwane was 'not a nice character. Tied a woman to a post in 1896 and threw her into a pool and drowned her.' His continued connection with the Mwali cult worried them most, and Wenlock was thought likely to be the storm centre of any future rebellion. In April 1924 the Native Commissioner, Matobo, thought that Ndaniso and Mtuwane 'would probably be leaders of any uprising'; they would take the *Nqameni* back into the Matopos and it would be 1896 all over again. By this time Hluganiso, though still described as one of the biggest chiefs, was 'very old and almost blind'.[33]

---

[30] Annual Report, Matobo, 1915, N 9/1/18.
[31] *Indabas* of 5 April 1915 and 8 April 1919, N 9/5/3.
[32] Native Commissioner, Matobo, to Superintendent of Natives, Bulawayo, 20 March 1924 and 8 October 1925, S 138/204. The Native Commissioner endorsed the chiefs' appeal, remarking that if Wenlock was cut off from Matobo district the chiefs would either have to move into Matobo and hence lose 'their homes and closest adherents', or stay in Wenlock and lose 'their present chiefships and stipends.'
[33] Military Intelligence Assessments, 1914 to 1924, AT 1/2/1/11/1; Native Commissioner, Matobo, to Superintendent of Natives, Bulawayo, 2 April 1924, S 728/6A/5.

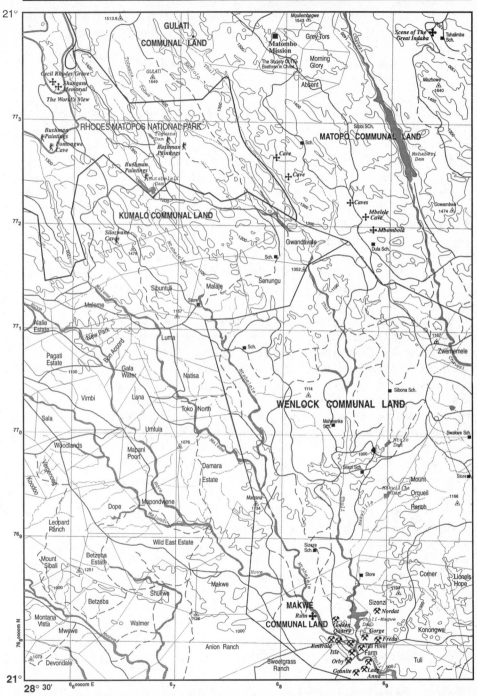

Map 3   Wenlock in relation to the Matopo Communal Land and the Dula Shrine to its north, to Mtshabazi Mission to its east, and to the mines in the south.

By the mid-1920s, then, *indunas* Ndaniso, Mtuwane and Hluganiso were busy trying to save something of the corporate *Nqameni* identity. Meanwhile, so long as these survivors of the Ndebele state and of the 1896 fighting were still alive and in authority, the administration feared an all too effective return to pre-colonial days.

Wenlock

These, then, were the *Nqameni*, and we have shown how many of them arrived in Wenlock. But what *was* Wenlock? As we shall see, the answer to this question was just as important to the politics of the area as were the problems of *Nqameni* identity.

The simplest answer is that Wenlock was a receptacle: a large, more or less empty stretch of land into which the displaced peoples and herds of the northern Matopos could flow. This stretch began in the south-eastern foothills of the Matopos, 'extremely broken granite country', where communities of Banyubi cultivators had lived for generations and where the influence of the Mwali shrines of the eastern hills was very strong. These Banyubi people continued to live in northern Wenlock, recognising the authority of the *Nqameni* chiefs. Wenlock ranch then ran south for many miles, into areas which had been very thinly populated in the nineteenth century, though there were small groups of Kalanga and Sotho living there.[34] When the movement south by the *Nqameni* and the other peoples of the northern Matopos began around 1900 this 'empty' land – like the *mapani* veld to the west of it – seemed like a refuge. It attracted the *Nqameni* and smaller numbers of other immigrants who, like the Banyubi, Kalanga and Sotho, had to be absorbed into the chieftaincies and the *Nqama* identity.

Unlike the Matopos themselves, where considerations of security resulted in much official and police attention, Wenlock was rarely patrolled and barely administered. It was part of the responsibility of the Native Commissioner at Fort Usher – exactly where the *Nqameni* had once lived – but he constantly complained that it was too far away to police. Moreover, when the migrants from the north first arrived in Wenlock it seemed as though it was not owned by anybody. There were no whites living on the land as farmers or ranchers, though in its southern third there were many gold prospectors and peggers. Hence 'the Africans occupied the land on a communal basis as a tribe living under a Chief and not as labour tenants who had come to the land to work for the farmers on it.'[35]

However, another answer to the question is that 'Wenlock' was shorthand for a cluster of alienated farms – Wenlock Block itself, Zemele, Sheet and Blanket. These farms, in fact, had been alienated 'at a very early date', though there was no sign of it when the *Nqameni* and other immigrants arrived. Clearly, however, *indunas* Ndaniso, Mtuwane and Hluganiso, and their people, were going to have to adjust themselves to a subsequent assertion of white ownership of the land and to whatever patterns of exploitation the white owners decided to adopt. For a long time this turned out to be very different from what happened in the *mapani* veld. Wenlock was not occupied by resident whites who wanted to grow crops and run cattle on the land. It belonged

[34] 'Land Husbandry: Gwanda District', November 1857, S 2808/1/10.
[35] John Gann's Memorandum to the Committee of Inquiry into Wenlock, April 1961, S 2823/13.

instead to a series of huge investment companies, the most important being Amalgamated Properties, and thereafter the London and Rhodesia Land Company's subsidiary, the Rhodesia Exploration and Development Company. These companies employed an old 'Matabele hand', A. G. S. Richardson, to manage the land for them. He was in charge for some forty years. During that time he developed his own very particular system of management.

In January 1907 the Rhodesian Land Owners and Farmers' Association complained that Africans were 'indiscriminately squatting' on Wenlock. This was an ominously early settler assertion that Wenlock should be part of a 'white' area. But in 1907 there was no danger that Africans would be evicted from Wenlock. Their presence there was too valuable to the company which owned it. As the Native Commissioner, Matobo, explained:

> I do not think there is a tenant [on Wenlock] who did not settle there by way of 'indiscriminate squatting'. The land is simply part of a gigantic 'kaffir farming' scheme. I do not think that Wenlock Block is visited by a European representative of the Company more than once a year. No farming is carried on, but the rent is annually collected. Every additional indiscriminate squatting increases the sole apparent source of revenue of the estate.[36]

By 1912 'native rents' for Sheet, Wenlock and Zemele amounted to some £880 a year. In that year Richardson provided a portrait of Wenlock Block. It amounted to some 126,992 acres, running 23 miles south by some 12 miles in width; its northern two-thirds lay in granite country, the southern third lay in 'gold-belt country', which was 'traversed by several roads and tracks used by wood-cutters.' There was good timber throughout the Block; 'a good-sized native population, mostly cattle-owners', who had developed along the Tuli River 'a long succession of native gardens, dug in good red sands. In ordinary seasons they grow good crops of kafir corn, rapoko, inyauti, groundnuts, beans, etc.' All grazing was sweet and 'the native stock I saw were all fat and sleek, and these herds have already "tamed" large tracts of country and tramped out the coarser herbage.' The Susannah, Sabiwa and Blanket mines lay immediately to the south-east of the estate and provided markets for African produce. Mtshabezi mission lay just to the east of northern Wenlock and offered schooling.[37] The *Nqameni* flourished in this environment. By 1933 there were some 2,400 Africans and 16,640 African-owned cattle on Wenlock.

As we have seen, the African tenants of the Rhodes Matopos Estates and the African settlers in the *mapani* veld deeply resented the breach of the promises made to them. Faced with the demands of white farmers, in the end they either left or were evicted. By contrast Wenlock had never formed part of the land 'protected' by the promises of Rhodes. The companies which owned it were the very epitome of irresponsible and exploitative capitalism, putting nothing into the land and merely extracting rent from it. Yet ironically, the regime of Richardson came to seem like a golden age for the *Nqameni*. Freed from the bureaucratic obligations of Native Commissioners, Richardson spent his year itinerating slowly round the estates he managed, pitching camp,

---

[36] Native Commissioner, Matobo, to Chief Native Commissioner, 24 January 1907, NB 3/1/8.
[37] Report by A. G. S. Richardson, 11 June 1912, S 2823/13.

collecting rent and tax, and chatting to the old men in his excellent Zulu. His regime was seen as an ideal patriarchy and he was nicknamed 'Eyes of the People', *Nkosi Mehlkazulu*. After his death Wenlock elders produced heart-felt eulogies to him. They developed their own moral economy myth in which Richardson played the role filled by Rhodes in other parts of the Matopos. Richardson had been the first Native Commissioner of the Matopos and Gwanda prior to the 1896 risings. During them he had been instrumental in making the contacts with led to the peace *indabas*. The Wenlock myth saw him as the saviour not only of the *Nqameni* but of the Ndebele nation.

When Richardson died in 1943 various local intellectuals wrote eulogies of him. One was Isaac Xiba Nkomo, a Protestant proto-nationalist, whose letters frequently figure in the *Bantu Mirror*. Nkomo's eulogy, 'Nkosi Richardson. The Lover of the Ndebele Nation', argues that Richardson saved the Ndebele from a terrible fate. In 1896, as the Ndebele fell back into the Matopos, 'men like F. C. Selous, Johan Colenbrander were now becoming trigger-happy to shoot us. But behind it all was a white man who was not happy. He set himself quietly to bring peace between the two opposing sides.' It was a misnomer, argued Nkomo, to call Cecil Rhodes 'the separator of the fighting bulls', since 'he was the principal bull which was fighting'. Richardson much better deserved the name. 'He so loved the Amandebele nation that he saved it from committing suicide to itself.'

Thereafter Richardson was the father of his people.

> He was an assuming aristocracy and a benevolent master. The African was required by *Nkosi Mehlkazulu* [to pay] a rent of £2 a year and could keep as many stock as he can acquire and plough as much lands as he was able to. Instead of disdaining his wards he came down to their level and treated them as human beings. He spoke Sindebele fluently.... He was an axle around which revolved the hub. He permitted schools and churches to be built on the lands.'

Nkomo finished by listing all those who had gone on to achieve distinction from these Wenlock schools.[38]

The Nqameni in Wenlock

Nkomo's eulogy struck a fine balance between tradition and modernity. This was appropriate to the sort of society that developed in Wenlock. Much that was valued in Wenlock was consciously 'traditional'; but at the same time Wenlock spokesmen saw their area as wealthy and progressive. The chiefs themselves, especially Mtuwane's successor, Matole, and Sigombe Mathema who became the sole *induna* in Wenlock in 1948, combined traditional claims to legitimacy with progressive claims to self-development.

The regimental identity itself was, of course, 'traditional'. So were the grounds on

---

[38] This and other eulogies are kept in the family scrapbook in the possession of Richardson's daughter, Stella Coulson, Esigodini. Another, entitled 'A Tribute by African People' claims that Richardson was 'respected and loved by all his tenants ... We are profoundly distressed, darkness envelops us. We are a scattered Nation without a leader, or one who will plead our cause ... We are as a fish accustomed to swimming in deep waters and now cast on dry land, where the sun will scorch us.' There were acutely practical reasons for this hyperbole as we shall see.

which the *indunas* claimed the Banyubi, Kalanga and Sotho residents of Wenlock as part – if a subordinate part – of their community. These went back to the reign of Lobengula when men from the *Nqameni* had been sent south of the Matopos to bring Sotho and Kalanga groups under the royal authority. Such ties might well have been cast off with the collapse of the Ndebele state, and no doubt would havè been had the *Nqameni* chiefs remained living north of the Matopos. In the event it was to the advantage of many non-Ndebele to associate themselves with a prestigious traditional identity which might have the clout to preserve the Wenlock way of life. Banyubi, Kalanga and Sotho in Wenlock itself were assimilated into the chieftaincies and numbers of the Kalanga groups in the Matopo Reserve, directly north of Wenlock, also petitioned to come under the control of the *Nqama* chiefs.

Wenlock was also a focus of endeavours to restore the Ndebele monarchy. The sole surviving son of Mzilikazi, Nyanda, who had been born in 1843 on the land which became Rhodes's farm of Westacre, now lived in Wenlock 'on the fringe of the main Matopo Hills.' He became the natural focus of commemorative celebrations of the monarchy.[39] Moreover, the *Nqameni* chiefs were members of the royalist party. Mtuwane had been constantly supportive of and in touch with the successive claimants to the kingship. When he died in 1927 he was succeeded by his eldest son, Matole, who lived at Sizeze in southern Wenlock.[40] Matole inherited his father's 'ownership' of Dula shrine, just north of Wenlock. He also continued the family support for the kingship. In the 1930s he was in trouble with the administration for his part in collecting cattle for the sons of Lobengula.

Chief Ndaniso in a sense went one better. He was selected to play Lobengula in a Gaumont British film about Cecil Rhodes and in 1935 was taken to England to take part in studio scenes. There he greeted King George – 'our heaven and our earth' – with the Ndebele royal salute. His hosts took care to impress him with various aspects of British superiority. He visited the War Museum to see 'all your terrible ways of killing' and was properly impressed: 'None could escape them, not by hiding at the back of caves, nor burrowing underground nor by getting below the water.' At Madame Tussauds he felt 'how far we are behind because we have no records of our past rulers and famous men.' But he also gave an interview to Marjorie Perham which fascinatingly reveals the persistence of his own sense of the past and of the landscape of the Matopos, both revitalised by the filming.

'We lived in the Matoppo hills. My father [Mhlahlo] was a brave man and a hero.' Ndaniso himself tended the royal herds as they ranged north and east; he was in the *Mcijo* regiment and raided across the Zambezi. During the 1893 war 'I was in the Matoppos and had not recovered from smallpox'. After the victory of the whites

> we were treated like slaves.... We thought it best to fight and die rather than bear it.... So many of our cattle were branded and taken away from us; we had no property, nothing we

[39] *Bantu Mirror*, 25 May 1946, reporting Nyanda's death.
[40] Native Commissioner, Matobo to Superintendent of Natives, Matabeleland, 10 October; 28 October; 5 December 1927, S 1561/10, 1915-36, Vol. IX, 1927–8. Mtuwani's surviving brother lived at Inyati in Bubi district; Matole and two other sons lived in Wenlock with 26 kraals.

could call our own.... I fought in the rebellion.... I remember a fight in the Matoppos when we charged the white men.... The place where we have been making the film is the very place where [my] cousins were killed.

Ndaniso had been reluctant to take part in the film but in the end it recharged his memory:

I was nervous all the time because there was a great deal of jealousy and it was thought I might be called on to be a successor to Lobengula. But the people were told that it was merely a play and no trickery. It was very well done; when the warriors came with their head-dresses and shields the old times came back into my mind.[41]

In 1930 the Native Commissioner, Gwanda, was instructed to create a Native Board for his district. He demurred on the grounds that the Ndebele of Wenlock had nothing in common with the Sotho chiefs in the south and 'an unfortunate and somewhat difficult situation may arise'. The Chief Native Commissioner, was 'not at all impressed' by this argument and insisted that a Board meeting be held. So on 5 February 1932 one was held, attended by Ndaniso, Matole, Hluganiso's son and also by the Sotho chiefs, with headmen and other representatives. The Native Commissioner's fears were realised.

After a general discussion of brideprice, the Wenlock members raised the question of 'the arrest and trial of Rhodes Lobengula', son of Njube and grandson of Lobengula himself. Rhodes had been seeking to collect 'royal' cattle so as to make a claim to the paramountcy. The administration charged him with extortion. The *Nqama* delegates now asked that the 'people could be informed whether it was the people who said that Rhodes had no claim to King's cattle or whether this was a matter on which the Government had decided.' It was certainly a matter that greatly concerned the Wenlock *indunas*, especially Matole, but was of no interest to the Sotho chiefs.[42]

Wisely, the Wenlock *indunas* left it to local members of the Matabeleland Home Society, especially Mawogelana, the Wenlock Chairman, to raise the question of Rhodes Lobengula at the Board meeting. But the traditionalism of the *Nqameni* chiefs and the presence of Nyanda made Wenlock a natural stronghold of the Society. Nyanda, at over a hundred years old, was the central figure of the Society's great pilgrimage to Mzilikazi's grave in the eastern Matopos in December 1945, where he 'communed with the spirits of the departed', sang 'an old war song' and ceremonially returned the late king's sword to the tomb.[43] In May 1946, when the old prince died, the Society held an elaborate funeral at his Wenlock home.[44] As we shall see, Matole was particularly closely involved with the Matabeleland Home Society.

Wenlock was a great place, then, for the invocation of Ndebele 'tradition'. But it was

[41] J. W. Posselt and M. Perham, 'The Story of Ndansi Kumalo of the Matabele Tribe, Southern Rhodesia', in M. Perham, *Ten Africans*, London, 1936, pp. 63–79.

[42] Native Commissioner, Gwanda to Superintendent of Natives, Bulawayo, 15 December 1930; Chief Native Commissioner to Superintendent of Natives, Bulawayo, 5 January 1931; report on a meeting of the Native Board, 5 February 1932, S 456. 493/37.

[43] 'Pilgrimage to Ntumbane, King Mzilikazi's Grave', 16 December 1945, S 2584/4251.

[44] *Bantu Mirror*, 25 May 1946.

also a self-consciously progressive place. During the long Richardson years in which men could plough as much land and graze as much cattle as they were able, numbers of prosperous African farmers and of stock keepers breeding selectively for the market developed in Wenlock. So also did African craftsmen. The area lay between two Brethren in Christ mission centres, the Matopo Mission to the north and Mtshabezi Mission to the east. A network of schools was spread out between the two centres, some of them deliberately sited close to a Mwali priest or shrine. The Brethren put great emphasis on 'industrial education', at Matopos for boys and at Mtshabezi for girls. Their approach was much praised by Native Commissioners and School Inspectors. 'The work is proved by its results', wrote W. R. Benzies, Native Commissioner, Matobo, about the Brethren's schools in 1931.

> Minds which have been controlled by fear and the extreme emotions of witchcraft, superstition and ancestral spirit-worship, cannot descend contentedly to simple Christianity. The way of descent is over the hill of manual labour and physical action. This should be more widely recognised by religious bodies.[45]

This was an approach which was eventually to lead to much hostility towards missionary education in Wenlock. But in the short run it had concrete results. 'At the two Mission stations industries are acquired, both by boys and girls', wrote the Native Commissioner, Matobo, in 1920. 'Quite a number have, for instance, become fairly capable bricklayers, stonemasons, rough carpenters, etc.' The Mtshabezi school inspection report in 1923 recorded 'excellent work' in laundry, knitting, sewing, dress-making, dairying, mat-making, basket-weaving, vegetable gardening and field tillage. There were 80 acres of crops and five of fruit and vegetables. It was no accident that Wenlock was to be the site of the first Women's Clubs in rural Matebeleland. Able Wenlock boys went to the Matopos Mission, and the academically most successful then went to the London Missionary Society school at Inyati.[46]

Becoming a teacher was one way forward; so also was becoming a trader and store-keeper. Men often began as the first and ended up as the second. Wenlock traders could begin in Gwanda town, just to the south-east of the Block, and later open stores in Wenlock itself. These teachers, farmers and traders developed into a group which prided itself on its Christianity and commitment to progress. They also prided themselves on their Ndebele identity.

One family in particular stood out among them. Reverend Nyamazana Dube became one of the few senior African leaders in the Brethren in Christ church. He was consecrated Overseer in 1921 and ordained in 1944. For very many years Nyamazana was based at Mtshabezi and he became a key figure at both 'traditional' and 'progressive' ceremonies. In May 1946, for instance, he said prayers at the Matabele Home Society's funeral service for old Nyanda; in June 1948 he opened a 'Pre-Harvest Meeting' in Wenlock at which the advantages of 'co-operation', new methods of farming and the marketing of hides were strongly urged.[47]

---

[45] Annual report, Matobo, 1931, S 235/509.
[46] Annual report, Matobo, 1920, N 9/1/23; inspection report, Mtshabezi, 5 July 1923, N 9/5/8.
[47] *Bantu Mirror*, 25 May 1946 and 5 June 1948.

11 Daniel Dube

But it was his son Daniel who became the best-known of Wenlock's progressives. He had been sent to Inyati for teacher training and returned to teach at Mtshabezi and to live on the mission. He was no submissive mission boy but rather a self-confident representative of a Christian second generation. At Inyati he took part in the famous strike of 1934. At Mtshabezi he was a constant critic of the missionaries. An informant who knew Daniel well told me:

> They say that sons of clergy often react against the church and Daniel did. He was a very outspoken man and sharply critical of the missionaries as landlords and hypocrites. He noticed that though they preached brotherhood they sat away from Africans in church and that they first took communion themselves before giving the cup to Africans. He used to attend the annual Brethren conventions and raise hell.[48]

Daniel's widow, Anna, whose own father had been a London Missionary Society minister, remembers that the Brethren seemed by contrast very narrow and puritanical.

[48] Interview with M. Sidile, Bulawayo, 8 August 1990.

They didn't like our customs. There was no dancing here at Mtshabezi. We could sing, but never move our bodies. When Daniel and I were married at Hope Fountain with wedding ring and veil the Brethren Bishop told us we were trying to copy Europeans. And they did not want to give Africans advanced education. But if they did anything wrong Daniel would tell them.[49]

Daniel's relations with the missionaries reached breaking point over their interference in his personal life. A handsome man, he was suspected of an affair with one of the mission teachers; an American missionary tried to use this as a way of cutting Daniel down to size; extraordinarily for a mission teacher at that time, Daniel took the man to court and won damages for slander.[50] The American went back to the United States. Daniel set off for Bulawayo to make his fortune. Soon he was appointed as Chief Inspector of Hides for the Rhodesian Hide and Produce Company. In this capacity he worked closely with Native Commissioners and Agricultural Demonstrators and became the leading advocate of modern farming methods. He was a protagonist of women's education – 'the greater number of the African people, living in the country districts, remain in utter ignorance of the fact that if many women were so educated as to take up work among their own African people out in the country conditions would not be what they are now'. He sought to shame Africans into self-development:

I have often read in the African press many letters written opposing the Government policy for Africans. As an African I have found out that such criticisms are alright to make, but what has to be remembered by the writers is what they themselves are doing to help the progress of the country.... What then has the African to say as he has so far done nothing as a nation to help himself. In fact he ought to be ashamed.[51]

We may well ask what this articulate moderniser had in common with old Ndaniso and his traditionalist memories. One answer is that both were supporters of the Matabeleland Home Society. An odd little item in the *Bantu Mirror* of 21 April 1945 (the first but certainly not the last item to be carried about Daniel Dube) makes this clear. 'On my way', wrote one Gula Mdlazika, 'I met with Mr Daniel Dube of Bulawayo. Towards the end of a short conversation, he drew my attention to the existence of a society formed by ama-Ndebele people, of which he was a member. He said that membership of this society is restricted to ama-Ndebele nationals only.' Mdlazika told Daniel that 'this is another way of keeping ourselves divided' and that there should be a Southern Rhodesia Non-European Unity Conference. Daniel was unmoved.

Here we reach an important point about the imagination of identity in Wenlock. The *indunas* kept the legitimating memories of the Ndebele state and the *Nqameni* regiment alive. But it was modernising intellectuals who based Ndebele *ethnicity* on these memories. It was they who debated language and culture. And it was they who articulated a specific Ndebele right to autonomous development. For the old chiefs and

[49] Interview with Anna Dube, Mtshabezi, 15 August 1990.
[50] *Bantu Mirror*, 21 January 1952; *African Weekly*, 21 April 1952.
[51] I quote from Daniel's letters published in the *Bantu Mirror* on 19 January 1946 and 17 June 1948. Many stories in the paper record his work as Hides Inspector.

the traditionalist elders, Richardson's Wenlock represented the best of all available worlds, though they still hankered after the freedom of pre-colonial days. Daniel Dube and the other progressives wanted Wenlock to change but they wanted this to be done through *Nqameni* self-help rather than through administrative direction or missionary benevolence. Daniel founded the *Sofasihamba* society in order to bring this to pass. He also tried to modernise chiefship in order to realise his dream of prosperous Ndebele autonomy.

And in the complex combinations which constituted Ndebele consciousness in Wenlock in the 1940s, Matole Dlodlo, the chief, rivalled Daniel Dube the new man. As we have seen, Matole supported the Ndebele royal family as stoutly as his father Mtuwane had done; he maintained his connections with the Dula shrine. But he was also a moderniser. He had connections with the Bulawayo cultural nationalists and with Wenlock's progressive elite. Like Daniel, he tried to bring all this together through the Matabeleland Home Society, which in itself was as much modernising as it was traditionalist.

Matole was 'a leading member of the Matabeleland Home Society', reported the Native Commissioner, Gwanda, 'a bad influence among his people.'[52] Matole would certainly have disputed this hotly. His idea of the Society's role in Wenlock was that it should aid in the 'modernisation' of the *Nqameni*.

The Society's aspirations come out very clearly in a report in the *Bantu Mirror* for 27 December 1947. (Wenlock progressives made constant and effective use of the *Mirror*'s columns.) The report was submitted by the Society's branch assistant secretary, Sima Maduma. It described a meeting held at Matole Dlodlo's kraal and attended by a hundred people.

The branch chairman, Mawogelana Kumalo, who had filled that role for at least fifteen years, addressed the crowd:

> We come under this tree at the chief's kraal every now and then to discuss programmes regarding our stay at Wenlock Block and sometimes to deal with criminals. But above all we come to create ... the spirit of cooperation.

The modernising cooperative spirit was symbolised on this occasion by the recent purchase of a Matabeleland Home Society bus. This was 'commissioned' by the branch secretary:

> We congratulate the Matabeleland Home Society on their new baby bus ... Before Almighty God, our Chief Matole Dlodlo, the chairman of this branch of the Association, and this congregation, We dedicate this little bus to this road: Bulawayo to Gwanda Reserve via Old Fort Usher, Chief Ndaniso's kraal, Chief Matole's, through Wenlock to Tuli Store, Gobatema Mission and Gwanda Native Reserve.

The bus was thus linking all the constituent parts of the new 'Ndebele' political consciousness: Bulawayo, the Matopos, the *Nqameni* chiefs, the Wenlock storekeepers.

But the secretary went on to link old and new in a wider rhetorical flourish:

[52] Native Commissioner, Gwanda to Provincial Native Commissioner, Bulawayo, 29 April 1949, S 2827/4/1.

We members of the Society pray God to grant us the cooperation our forefathers had before 1893, to build ourselves into a strong nation.... We pray that our motor bus will be a strong foundation, so that we who are standing before our Chief will build many strong houses on it, of education, civilisation and Christianity. We wish our children, who come behind, will be better educated and civilised, far from witchcraft, and the blood of superiority and inferiority, [and] will continue from where we have laid the foundation already.... Let us fight to destroy amongst the Matabele nation pride, jealousy, lies, variance, wrath, hatred, witchcraft, strife, sedition, heresy, envy, emotions and drunkenness.

It was a lot to ride upon a bus! But in his own speech Matole added even more, attacking in addition 'bad suspicion, cheating, laziness and disobedience.' 'Unless we insist on more love', he added, 'I am afraid this motor bus will be a fowl's nest, and you will hide your faces in shame.' But the main thrust of his speech was more positive. He declared himself a strong supporter of 'education in books.... We need 100 per cent of our boys and girls to go through secondary training.' Above all, 'we should not sit still and cry to Government to do everything for us.... This motor bus is the first miracle performed by the Matabeleland Home Society in my area. I appreciate it very much.'[53]

Rhetorically, at least, tradition and modernity had been brought together in this programme to restore 'the co-operation our forefathers had before 1893' by means of the development of higher education, communications and Christianity. It was a programme that might well have won the support of Wenlock's white administrators – save for one thing. By 1947 the *Nqameni* chiefs, the Matabeleland Home Society, Daniel Dube and his *Sofasihamba*, were all in opposition to the colonial state over the question of ownership and use of land.

The struggle for land in Wenlock

Nqameni contentment with the Richardson regime on Wenlock had been undercut ever since 1912 by fear that they might be evicted from it. The 1912 report, while emphasising the financial return from African rents, also found that there were real commercial possibilities. In the Tuli Valley 'a few hundred acres of arable land, conveniently situated, could be obtained, though of course the natives would have to be turned off to make room.' There were 18,000 acres of 'as good grazing as is to be found in Rhodesia', and 'a hundred thousand cords of firewood waiting for the axe.' Richardson concluded that a profitable ranch could be run on Wenlock and that 'plenty of native labour would be available'. But he pointed out that return from rents was double what 'a white farmer would probably offer to lease it.' The Company would have to decide whether to invest capital in a serious ranching scheme or to continue 'kaffir-farming'.[54]

What happened was that the successive companies who owned Wenlock attempted to do both. A Lonrho subsidiary, the Rhodesia Exploration and Development Company,

[53] 'Matabeleland Home Society Buys a Bus', *Bantu Mirror*, 27 December 1947. The reference to 'the blood of superiority and inferiority' concerns the so-called caste structure, and expresses the desire for all distinctions of *Zansi*, *Enhla* and *Holi* to be sublimated in a common Ndebele identity. This was one of the implications of Ndebele consciousness as ethnicity.

[54] Report by A. G. S. Richardson, 11 June 1912, S 2823/13.

carried out a 'certain amount of ranching and farming activities' up to 1928, and these involved removals of African settlers and demands upon the *indunas* to supply labour. It was these developments that led to Ndaniso and Mtuwane's bitter protests at the 1915 *indaba*. Ndaniso remained embittered even after 1928. The Company might at any time change its policy again; moreover, the Rhodesian state was itself now intervening in African farming and ranching with the Cattle Levy and the Maize Control Acts, both of which were designed to subsidise white agriculture at the expense of black. At a Native Board meeting in June 1934 Ndaniso protested about the implications of the Cattle Levy on cattle-owners who dipped their beasts on private land.[55] The next year, talking to Perham in England in 1935, he described how:

> We slowly bred up our herds again. Then we were told that we were on private land. We are on land where the rainfall is scanty. Things will not grow well. In our time we could pick our own country, but now all the best land has been taken by the white people. We get hardly any price for our cattle.... If we have crops to spare we get very little for them.[56]

In 1928 the London and Rhodesia Land Company ceased ranching activities and became once again totally dependent on rents. Richardson's laisser-faire regime continued. But the underlying legal and political situation was being transformed. The Land Apportionment Act of 1930 made 'kaffir farming' illegal. The only Africans who could legally reside on 'white' land, such as Wenlock (or the farms in the *mapani*), were those on labour agreements. Admittedly, a period of grace was given in Matabeleland since the immediate eviction of rent-paying tenants from huge areas of the province would precipitate a massive social and political crisis. It was laid down in the Act, therefore, that rental agreements might continue until October 1936.

In September 1933 the Native Commissioner, Gwanda, who was now administratively responsible for Wenlock, expressed his anxiety over the fact that in three years' time 'the major portion of the native population in this district' would have to move. He was particularly anxious about Wenlock, 'occupied by Chiefs Ndaniso, Matole and numbers of their people', 2,400 of them with 16,640 cattle. Wenlock was 'now given over entirely to native occupation' but its owners were 'aware it will cease to be a revenue producing asset' in 1936. The Native Commissioner thought that the government should buy the land. Indeed, in January 1935 the Company offered Wenlock to the state for £40,000. The 1930s were not the time for large-scale state expenditure, however, and the purchase fell through. The crisis was instead averted by further postponements of the implementation of Land Apportionment, which was in the end suspended for the duration of the Second World War so as to avert 'unrest'.[57]

So the old system continued right up to Richardson's death in 1943. But by that time both the economic and political situation had changed radically. The war-time boom in farming and ranching showed no sign of slackening; the white electorate was

---

[55] Gwanda Native Board meeting, 15 June 1934, S 1542/N2.

[56] J. W. Posselt and M. Perham, 'The Story of Ndansi Kumalo', pp. 72–8.

[57] Native Commissioner, Gwanda, to Superintendent of Natives, Bulawayo, 18 September 1933; Superintendent of Natives, Bulawayo to Chief Native Commissioner, 11 January 1935, AT 1/2/1/11/1.

demanding the full implementation of the Land Apportionment Act; government was imbued with a new determination to intervene in African agriculture and cattle holding and to protect the environment. The inhabitants of Wenlock – and of the whole Matopos – came under pressure from all sides. Investment companies began to think that it would be more profitable to exploit their lands directly and began to give notice to their tenants; European political pressure made it very difficult for the Native Department to offer paternalist protection. In any case, even on the Reserves and on Crown Land the government itself was now intervening to commandeer labour.

In 1945 the Rhodesia Company 'sought to commence ranching operations again [and] an approach seems to have been made to the Government to move the Africans.'[58] The crisis which had for so long been developing under the surface of the old regime in Wenlock now burst into the open. Chiefs and people were horrified and indignant. So too was the Native Department:

> There is considerable unrest, bitterness and ill-feeling consequent upon the removal of natives from European farms [ran one official comment on the actions of the Rhodesia Company]. The fault, of course, lies principally with that Company which 'kaffir farmed' for forty odd years, without regard to the ravaged soil on the one hand and without regard to the future resettlement of the natives when the time came for it to sell out.... The present choice is between moving to the hated 'amgusu' veld [in the Shangani Reserve in northern Matabeleland], staying on as labour tenants, or living an urban life ... The ground is ripe for the seeds of malcontent.[59]

For Wenlock, at least, there turned out to be a fourth choice. In 1946 the government at last bought the land from the Rhodesia Company. But although administrators throughout the Matopos hoped that the purchase 'might ease the position', in fact it did little to improve matters.

The Nqameni under government control

For one thing, the Matopos administrators had been hoping to find some space for the many people *they* now had to evict. The Native Commissioner, Matobo, for example, hoped to send those to be evicted from the Matopos National Park to join their old neighbours in Wenlock; the Native Commissioner, Essexvale, hoped to reduce population and stock in the Matopos Reserve by sending them south into Wenlock. And in fact there *were* some movements into Wenlock, in many cases of *Nqameni*. However, as the Native Commissioner, Gwanda, complained: 'The recent acquisition of Wenlock Block has not relieved the position to any extent as this land is already heavily populated.' There was a 'growing sense of unrest and despondency'.[60]

Moreover, the *Nqameni* of Wenlock were unhappy with government control. Even after the purchase of the land, government had not made up its mind what to do with it. It remained quite unclear whether there would in fact be long-term security of

---

[58] John Gann's Memorandum to the Commission of Inquiry into Wenlock, April 1961, S 2823/13.
[59] Annual Report, Essexvale, 1946, S 2827/4/1.
[60] Annual Reports, Essexvale, Matobo, Gwanda, 1946.

tenure for Africans, and if so whether the whole area would be allocated to the *Nqameni* or whether the gold-bearing zone would be excluded. Moreover, there was unprecedented interference with *Nqameni* stock raising and cultivation. After so many years of Richardson's laisser-faire, the people of Wenlock were quite unused to such intervention. It began with the compelled recruitment of so-called Food Production labour, conscripting men from Wenlock to work on European maize farms. It continued with enforced conservation and agricultural rules; with schemes for centralisation and destocking. The people of Wenlock, having moved there in the first instance to escape from white interference, did all they could to resist. By 1947 the Native Commissioner, Gwanda, was reporting on the baleful 'influence of a few malcontents' in Wenlock. By 1948 it had become 'the difficult Wenlock Block', with its 'openly disaffected peoples', and with two chiefs in Ndaniso and Matole who 'made no pretence of being either progressive or cooperative.'[61]

But what were the two chiefs to do about all these threats to their people? They could, of course, take advantage of the established form of the *indaba*. Thus on 16 October 1945, when the Chief Native Commissioner met with chiefs and headmen, the two Wenlock chiefs were the most outspoken in their complaints. They both protested against Food Production conscription. Matole alleged that 'the men sent to work are harshly treated'; Ndaniso pointed out that absence of male labour undercut food production in Wenlock – 'Is it possible for a wife to buy a plough or inspan oxen to grow monkey nuts?'[62]

But there were other possibilities too. One lay in an appeal to the past and for this Ndaniso was obviously the man. Others lay in collaboration with new forces and here Matole was active. But one cannot really make a sharp distinction because it was these new forces which were now mobilising the appeals to the past and especially to Ndebele identity and rights.

In 1946 Bulawayo lawyers were collecting evidence on behalf of all the peoples of the Matopos in order to combat eviction from the whole of the Greater Matopos area. They were particularly interested in the promises of Cecil Rhodes. Clearly Ndaniso – 'an outstanding Chief in his day, now suffering from extreme old age' – would be a key witness.[63] On 3 November 1946 white lawyers from Bulawayo drove out to Ndaniso's kraal. Ndaniso was 'the only Chief living who attended Rhodes' meeting'; his testimony was critical.

So once again the old *Nqameni* chief recalled the events of 1896 and 1897 in the Matopos. At that time he had been a warrior in the *Mcijo* regiment; early in 1897 he had accompanied his elder brother, Nkonkobela, to an *indaba* on Rhodes's farm to the north of the hills. 'I was present and he gave us some sheep'. Dhliso was also there. In his testimony Ndaniso spoke not only for the *Nqameni*, who in the main had remained on their own land in the northern Matopos before going south to Wenlock, but also for

---

[61] Annual Reports, Gwanda, 1947 and 1948, S 2827/4/1.

[62] Chief Native Commissioner's *indaba* with Chiefs and Headmen, 16 October 1945, S 1542.C6.

[63] 'Notes regarding the *Nqameni* section', 16 December 1947, PER 5, District Administrator's office, Gwanda.

all those who had accepted Rhodes's invitation to come out 'in the open':

> Rhodes congratulated us and said 'Your country, the whole of Rhodesia, now belongs to Great Britain. Your kraals will be in the hills, as you are used to baboons. Your King will be the baboons. You will inhabit all the land between the Bulawayo-Plumtree and the Bulawayo-West Nicholson lines, that is south of a line drawn from the source of the Khami through Fort Usher to the Mzingwane.' We would pay nothing. We would never be disturbed. He took some of us on forced labour to work on the dam near the Experimental Farm and on the mines. We received payments [but] he had not warned us before that he would take us for labour.

So people moved away from Rhodes's land into the zone 'promised' to them. 'I, Ndaniso, have lived here since the Rebellion when cattle died, after which we bought some cattle with the money we had earned.'[64]

In a sort of historical paradox Ndaniso insisted that Rhodes had promised the Matopos rent-free as a home specifically for the Ndebele, most of whom had not lived there before 1896. But this kind of historical memory made an Ndebele identity essential to the fight against eviction in the Matopos and against interference in Wenlock. Ndaniso died on 27 June 1948 before he could appear before the Commission of Inquiry into the Matopos National Park. But even in death the old chief was still central to the new appeal to the past. The *Bantu Mirror* of 17 July reported his funeral in Wenlock which was attended not only by his own people but by a large contingent from Bulawayo. These visitors were officers and members of the Matabeleland Home Society. Master of Ceremonies was the executive secretary of the Society, Sipambaniso Manyoba Kumalo, who in fact had guided the lawyers to Ndaniso's kraal eight months earlier and acted as intepreter while the old *induna* gave his testimony.

Under the energetic direction of Sipambaniso Manyoba – born in Bulawayo to aristocratic Ndebele of the royal clan, and in the late 1940s simultaneously star footballer, Bulawayo trade union leader, executive member of the Bantu Congress and doyen of the Bulawayo African elite – the Matabeleland Home Society was taking up the land grievances of the Ndebele. Its inventions of new 'traditional' ceremonies – like the pilgrimage to Mzilikazi's grave in the Matopos and the funerals of princes and chiefs – were linked with Matabeleland's rural grievances.

The Society sought to correct Rhodes's spiritual displacement of the Ndebele king, while at the same time appealing to the promises of Rhodes himself. The President of the Society, C. S. Hlabangana, told the pilgrims at Mzilikazi's grave at Entumbane on 16 December 1946 that:

> thirty years ago the Matabele people spoke of Ntumbane in hushed tones, in whispers ... because the Matabele [feared] to display and advertise their deeper feelings [but now] both races have confidence in each other. Here in the Matopos fate has provided a resting place for two champions of freedom – C. J. Rhodes, who believed that the greatest amount of freedom was possible only under the British rule, and King Mzilikazi who sought that freedom which was denied him under the rule of Chaka.... We settled [here] to be free.

[64] 'Alleged Promises Made by Mr Rhodes to the Matabele', in Native Commissioner, Gwanda, to Provincial Native Commissioner, Matabeleland, 21 January 1947, *ibid.*

In his own speech Sipambaniso admitted that 'this place is a sacred place ... According to Native customs we should not be here, but we are here to do work which is very important.' This was no less than to turn the grave into the African equivalent of Rhodes's tomb. Sipambaniso quoted Rhodes to the effect that 'in these hills is a great King and Founder of the Matabele Nation'. And he proclaimed at this solemn moment of the rededication of the Ndebele nation to its King that 'we are aware that Rhodes bought land to be used by African Chiefs.'[65]

At the same time Sipambaniso linked the Society with the interests of urban Sindebele speakers. He was a leading actor in the Bulawayo General Strike of April 1948. The Society now stood unequivocally for the interests of urban 'new men', many of whom unlike Sipambaniso himself were 'Ndebele' only in the widest sense of that term. For them the claim to Ndebele identity was a way of demanding superior status in Bulawayo, just as in the rural areas it was a way of asserting a right to the land. The Society's notion of 'tradition', and its claim to speak for the Ndebele, were derided by many Ndebele *indunas*. But this was not so in Wenlock. Ndaniso allowed himself to be used by the Society. Matole, as we have seen, played a much more active role.

Now, in the late 1940s, Matole brought the Wenlock branch of the Matabeleland Home Society into collaboration with Daniel Dube's *Sofasihamba* self-help organisation. 'The Matabeleland Home Society was a town organisation', says Mark Dokotela Ncube, nationalist pioneer and master farmer in north Wenlock. 'Sofasihamba was a local organisation. But the Wenlock branch of the Matabele Home Society co-operated with Sofasihamba to fight eviction.'[66]

Sofasihamba was an expression of *Nqameni* solidarity. It brought together traditionalists and progressives, members of the Matabeleland Home Society Wenlock branch and non-members. Its inspiration was Daniel Dube, the second generation modernising Christian. Its chairman was Sigombe Mathema, a junior member of the Mathema line which had led the *Nqameni* in the nineteenth century, and a wealthy cattle-owner who was managing his herd on commercial lines. On its committee were officers of the Matabeleland Home Society like Sima Maduna, agricultural entrepreneurs like Mark Dokotela Ncube, young Turks like Johnson Sigodo Dube, a fiery orator who was Daniel Dube's main rival for the political soul of Wenlock, and who was to become the local leader of the mass nationalist parties of the late 1950s. And there was Chief Matole Dlodlo. Wenlock labour migrants in Bulawayo came out at weekends by bus or bicycle to attend *Sofasihamba* meetings and to make financial contributions. Wenlock men working in South Africa sent donations.[67] In 1948 the Native Commissioner, Gwanda, reported that in 'the area openly showing disaffection,

---

[65] 'Pilgrimage to Ntumbane', 16 December 1945, S 2584/4251. At this stage the Matebeleland Home Society was not seeking to displace Rhodes as tutelary deity of the Matopos by Mzilikazi but only to give them equal status. Rhodes and Mzilikazi jointly represented the Ndebele right to the Matopos and to autonomy.

[66] Interview with Mark Dokotela Ncube, Wenlock, 30 August 1990.

[67] Interviews with M. Sidile, Bulawayo, 8 August 1990; Anna Dube, Mtshabezi, 15 August 1990; Mark Dokotela Ncube, Wenlock, 30 August 1990.

Wenlock Block, the people are largely swayed by the *Sofasihamba* (We die if we go) Society.'[68]

As its name suggests, *Sofasihamba* was primarily concerned with the insecurity of tenure in Wenlock. This was an issue on which even such an admirer of progressive government policies as Daniel Dube felt very deeply. As Inspector of Hides he had been working in the sandy and malarial Nkayi and Lupane districts in northern Matabeleland into which thousands of Africans were being evicted. On 27 September 1948 a letter from Daniel appeared in the *Bantu Mirror* under the heading 'Defended the Colony. Now Being Shifted'. He wrote:

> The Africans joined the European war which they fought and won.... We were told that they were defending their country. Has the African any country? I now meet him daily carrying his goods leaving the same ground he fought for. Who is coming to occupy that ground now? Did the African defend Lupani to where I often meet them going? We have spent large sums of money for the homes we are now quitting and large sums of money have been paid for rent and dipping fees.... No European can adequately represent Africans.... Only an African who has himself felt the pinch of what it is to be African, can fully represent his fellow men.

It was an issue which brought everyone together to contest any threat of eviction from Wenlock. *Sofasihamba* meetings were strategy sessions, seeking to work out how best to make the administration proclaim Wenlock as a Native Area. The Society raised funds and opened a bank account in Bulawayo in order to be able to brief lawyers. With the backing of Matole it offered a formidable challenge to the administration.

Matole was certainly more than merely a passive patron of this opposition. During 1948 the administration bumped up against his counter-authority at every turn. In the interests of gaining control over Wenlock cultivation, the Native Commissioner and the Land Development Officer forbade anyone to open up new gardens or to move on to new land without their permission. Hundreds of people ignored these orders, so remote from the days of Richardson. When they were prosecuted they testified that 'Chief Matole told me I could cut new lands. He said there was a law about not cutting new lands but that I could cut new lands.'[69] Matole himself told the court that in one such case 'I allowed him to move in. Before this new law was made I used to allow people to move in on my permission.'[70] The cases had to be dismissed. In these cases Matole was merely continuing to exercise chiefly authority. In others he was reasserting long-lapsed rights. He began to hear criminal cases, pass sentences and impose fines, all without informing the Native Commissioner.

Ndaniso was dead. Now the administration took steps to deal with Matole. In December 1948 he was prosecuted for illegally extracting fines. 'He was convicted, and in view of his bad record, he was suspended as functioning as a chief and an application was made for his suspension.'[71] On 14 April 1949 Matole was told in front of a large meeting of his followers and other 'elders of Wenlock Block' that the Governor had

---

[68] Annual Report, Gwanda, 1948.

[69] Rex v Mabuso, 3 December 1948, S 2836/85/1948.

[70] Rex v Simanda, 4 December 1948, *ibid.*

[71] Quarterly Report, Gwanda, December 1948, S 2827/4/1.

approved his dismissal. He was given twelve months' notice to leave Wenlock altogether. His followers 'appeared to be very dissatisfied and protested against his removal from Wenlock.'[72]

In July 1949 the Chief Native Commissioner received a petition from 'The People of Wenlock Block, Gwanda District, and Some People of the Matopo National Park', the inclusion of the latter demonstrating that Matole's fate had become an issue for the peoples of the Matopos as whole. It protested against Matole's dismissal. This petition – or two sentences from it – has become well known as an expression of rural attitudes to the state. The sentences run: 'Sir, as far as we are concerned we hate everything in force. We appreciate with pleasure everything free will.' I used them myself as the opening text for *Peasant Consciousness and Guerrilla War*. They have been put into the mouths of archetypal peasant elders in Colleen Crawford Cousins's splendid cartoon history of the land struggle in Zimbabwe.[73]

And the body of the petition certainly documents rural passive resistance, with its constant refrain of 'we refused'. 'In the year 1946', it begins, 'our Native Commissioner, Mr Holl, told the people of Wenlock to move to Dibulashaba giving reasons that the Rhodesia Co-operation Farm did not want the people to remain there any long. We humbly but strongly refused.' In 1948 they 'refused destocking continuing because we felt ... that livestock is a black man's bank.' They tried to refuse Food Production Labour but conscription was enforced – so 'the young men ran away to Joburg.'

But the petition was not just a peasant manifesto. It was also about the *Nqameni* and about chiefship and Matole's exercise of it. 'The Chief is the Government servant for his African people. We therefore feel that if any judgement was passed on the Chief people should be told. Under the British rule should a person be condemn to some judgement and not be given a chance to answer? We feel the Chief is ours tribally. We should work together in times of trouble.' If Matole had offended, he had done so only in the interests of his people against those of inhumane bureaucracy:

> In 1947 diptheria took over and spread so rapidly throughout our area and not less than ten people died in a few days. Our Chief immediately reported the matter to the Native Commissioner who sent an opposite reply, saying he would come and count the cattle instead of helping stop the disease among the people. Then the Chief wrote a protesting letter complaining that the NC should take steps to stop the disease first, and then talk about beasts next. We fail to understand if Chief Matole was wrong.

And if Matole 'was accused because he allowed some men to open up his lands', well this too was the role of a chief. It surely could not be the job of the Land Development Officer – 'we did not know that he had come to carry out the Chief's duties.' Matole had been a true *induna*; his people were lost without him. 'We ask you, sir, to restore his Chieftanship back to him for us.'[74]

The Native Department could not just dismiss this petition out of hand. As the

[72] Annual Report, Gwanda, 1949, *ibid.*
[73] Colleen Crawford Cousins, *A Hundred Furrows. The Land Struggle in Zimbabwe*, Harare, 1991, p. 19.
[74] Petition from 'The People of Wenlock Block', 23 July 1949, S 1542 C6.

Chief Native Commissioner explained, the issue was complicated by 'our lack of knowledge as to the future of Wenlock Block'. It was not possible to defuse the situation by giving any assurances of security of tenure. For fear of unrest he decided not to ask the Governor to expel Matole.[75]

Sigombe Mathema and the Nqameni Reunited

By the end of 1948, then, the structure of 'traditional' authority erected under early colonialism was in complete disarray. There was no living heir of Dhliso; Ndaniso was dead; although Matole had living brothers, it was clear that his people would refuse to recognise any of them as *induna* in his stead. When J. M. C. Cramer arrived to take up the post of Native Commissioner in November 1949 he found 'a very disturbing anti-European feeling among the *Nqama* and agitators were very active. There was no Chief.'[76]

It was a terrible moment for the people of Wenlock. They were still in danger of losing their land, and if they did so then they would have to scatter. There was no chance any longer of their being able to fall back into the Matopos, from which thousands of families were being evicted. The *Nqameni* might be broken up and placed under other chiefs in distant places. As the people of Wenlock remember it today they were saved by the appearance of a chief.

One of the last acts of Cramer's predecessor, N. C. McLeod, had been to make a bold proposal for resolving the problem of Wenlock. It needed a chief – and his candidate was none other than Sigombe Mathema, Chairman of *Sofasihamba*! Sigombe was 'a man wealthy in cattle and agricultural produce, elderly, wise, of very great personal standing and strength of character.' In short, he was already the unofficial leader of the people of Wenlock. The administration should now back this popularity. After all,

> the Chief's political importance will be considerable; he lives near the disaffected people in Matopos Reserve and Matopo National Park and ... his people also are disaffected and disloyal to the Government.... What loyalty the people have to the Government will be severely strained by destocking. A strong, reasonable and intelligent Chief, whose loyalty to the Government can be won over, is essential to good government in this area.

Admittedly, Sigombe was not 'the traditional candidate', not descending directly from any of the previous *indunas* and having brothers older than himself. But the people would accept him. He should be the only chief. 'He will assume the responsibility for all the inhabitants of Wenlock and will face the task of welding all factions (followers of Matole, Ndaniso and Udhliso) into one tribe.'[77]

Immediately Cramer arrived in Wenlock he threw his weight behind this proposal. Cramer was an unusual man. He was impressed by Wenlock's large number of entrepreneurs and intellectuals, and by their creation of *Sofasihamba*. If only they could be

---

[75] Chief Native Commissioner to Provincial Native Commissioner, 20 May and 13 September 1949, *ibid.*

[76] Statement by J. M. C. Cramer, 2 December 1960, S 2823/13.

[77] Native Commissioner, Gwanda, to Provincial Native Commissioners, 17 September 1949, PER 5, District Administrator's Office, Gwanda.

given guarantees of security on the land, he believed, they would switch from opposition to collaboration for the development of Wenlock. The *Nqameni* could then become a bulwark against the spread of disaffection, not only in Wenlock but in the Matopos generally.

> The political situation that is developing among the natives of Matabeleland, and in this and Matobo Districts particularly, calls for Chiefs of character.... The Chiefs are under constant pressure by their people to throw in their lot with the agitators ... while the major question of lack of security on the land remains unresolved. These men will find it extremely difficult to resist this pressure much longer.

It was no longer a matter of finding the 'right' tribal chief. What were needed now were 'enlightened leaders, whose leadership tactfully directed by the Administration might defeat the mere agitator.'[78]

The Native Department accepted Cramer's recommendations. In January 1950 he was able to report that representatives of all the people in Wenlock and from the *Nqama* section of the Matopos Reserve had unanimously chosen Sigombe. He would represent 1,121 taxpayers.[79]

Sigombe's elevation was accompanied by some inspired inventions of tradition, which combined the glorious past and the progressive present of the *Nqameni* and by extension of the Ndebele in general. Despite Cramer's warning that he was not the 'traditional' candidate, the *Bantu Mirror* carried a story entitled '*Inqama* People Nominate New Chief. Tribal Elders Recall Matabele History.' Sigombe had been chosen by precedents out of 'scarcely remembered Matabele history'; he was the choice of 'specially selected people' entrusted with the duty of nomination. Ndaniso had been survived by ten sons, but the elders had disclosed that Sigombe had been the old man's preferred choice. Sigombe's own elder brothers declared 'that they had no objection to his nomination since they regarded him as their father'.

But the installation ceremony allowed for statements of the progressive as well as the traditional legitimacy of the new chief. Daniel Dube gave an oration on 'behalf of the young folks':

> We have a very high regard for Mathema. He is the Chairman of our society known as Sofa-sihamba. In this capacity he has proved to be a good and true leader.... Mathema, we look upon you as a father. We expect every assistance and cooperation from you. We shall be very disappointed to find that you have a class of AmaHole and AmaNguni.

Daniel was here appealing to a wide definition of *Nqama* identity rather than a narrow glorification of the founding aristocracy.[80]

There is no doubt, then, that Sigombe was chosen, installed and perceived as a new kind of chief – as the ally of the modernisers, ready for an experiment in local self-help. But there was a paradox in the Native Commissioner's insistence that one of the new things he had to do was to weld 'all factions (followers of Matole, Ndaniso and Udhliso) into one tribe.' After all they *had* been one community under Dhliso before the early

[78] J. W. C. Cramer to Provincial Native Commissioner, 16 November 1949, *ibid*.
[79] Native Commissioner, Gwanda, to Provincial Native Commissioner, 19 January 1950, *ibid*.
[80] *Bantu Mirror*, 11 February and 8 July 1950.

colonial fragmentation of the *Nqameni*. No matter that Sigombe was overriding Ndaniso's ten sons, taking precedence over his own brothers, helping to extinguish the claims of the Dlodlos. In a very real sense he *was* the traditional candidate, since he brought all the *Nqameni* together again. As we shall see, Sigombe began his chieftaincy with the rhetoric of modernisation. He ended it by appealing to his responsibility to unite all the *Nqameni* wherever they might be. In the name of progress he supported Daniel Dube's projects of autonomous development. In the name of tradition he gave his chiefly blessing – and transmitted the heritage of the Ndebele past – to the nationalist movement. Ndebele ethnicity as it had developed in Wenlock was flexible enough to nourish both.

5

Identity & Opposition in the National Park

1926–49

The *Nqameni* solution to the problem of identity could not work in the Matopo hills themselves. The population there was too varied; there was too strong a legacy from a past in which the Banyubi had not been fully incorporated into Ndebele society; no single regimental tradition predominated among the rest of the inhabitants. Indeed, in 1918 the Native Commissioner, Fort Usher, went so far as to think that Ndebele identity would lapse altogether:

> No chief has a particular tribe under his control, but the people under each chief are a conglomeration of different tribes. Nor do natives who come under a particular chief live in one part of the section. The Ndebele population live for the most part in the open country known as 'Maqaqene' (i.e. the little round hills) embracing all that portion of the section to the north of the Matopo Hills. They are beginning to lose their identity as a race by inter-marrying.... In the course of time this process will be completed and the Kalanga tribes will be found to have absorbed their conquerors.[1]

Later officials realised that an Ndebele political identity, at any rate, had not disappeared. But their reports emphasised ethnic heterogeneity. Here, for example, is a report on the Matopos Reserve in the eastern hills:

> Prior to the occupation the Reserve was apparently occupied by isolated kraals of Banyubi and of Batshabi and Bavenda 'doctors' imported by the Mandebele. [It was also] used as grazing by neighbouring Ndebele groups, notably the Ihlahlanhlele [Mhlahlandlela] stationed at Fort Usher. Two agricultural systems were followed, one by the local tribes and the other by the Mandebele. The local tribes were in the habit of planting on ridges and separating crops, individual ownership of cattle was not uncommon. Ndebele agriculture was confined to one main food crop (kaffir corn) grown on the flat.

When Sindebele speakers began to move into the eastern Matopos as a result of the evictions from land all round the hills, people of the *Mhlahlandlela* came in, but so also

[1] Security report, Fort Usher, 1918, S 728/64/4.

130

did some *Nqameni*, some *Matshetse* from Essexvale, together with people from many other regimental groupings.[2]

From 1943, the chief of the Matopos Reserve, Bafana, was

> not a descendant of the traditional Mate clan of the Mhlahlandlela.... After the deposition of Bavayi by the Government, the remaining members of the Mate family declined to take the chieftainship because they feared that witchcraft would kill them. (None of the Mate chiefs lived very long).

Among the headmen were men whose authority had nothing to do with *Mhlahlandlela* overlordship. Some were Banyubi descendants of autonomous pre-colonial chiefs; the Banyubi headman Sar..son Nkala of the Bezha area derived his legitimacy from his role in the Mwali cult.

> In this community is one of the temples of Mlimo. Naturally the chief figure is the custodian of the temple, but the contact between him and the people is the *mlisa* [headman]. It is he who arranges the traditional *U ku yebula inxosa*. Pilgrims flock from all over the country to petition Mlimo for rain.[3]

Although it was remarked that 'the Abenyube have to a large extent intermarried with the Amandebele' and that 'Sindebele is spoken' it was also noted that 'Nyubi customs have remained.' It was all very different from the hegemony of the *Nqameni* chiefs in Wenlock.[4]

Certainly some *indunas* had great influence in other parts of the Matopos, the most prominent being Nzula, son of the 'rebel' Hole, many of whose cattle were lent out to kraals in the western hills and who had many followers in Whitewaters. Nzula – 'educated, wealthy and of high social standing as being the son of Famona, Lobengula's favourite daughter, and of Hole, the late famous rebel chief whose father was one of the King's big indunas' – was himself a passionate antiquarian, ceaselessly researching into and writing about the Ndebele past.[5] But if the people of the Matopos were going to proclaim an Ndebele identity – as indeed they came to do – it had to be reached by a different route than this. Their route turned out to be largely political. To defend their right to the hills they chose to invoke Rhodes's promises to 'the Ndebele' rather than the centuries of Banyubi occupation. They relied on the Matabeleland Home Society to assist them. And they appealed to what its President, Cephas Hlabangana, called 'the God of David Livingstone, of John White, of David Carnegie, of Bowen Rees, of Baleni Gumbo, one of the earliest converts', rather than to Mwali as the Creator of the Matopos. In short, the political identity of the Matopos up to 1950 was made by the

---

[2] Provincial Agricultural, Conservation and Extension officer, Matopos, to Provincial Native Commissioner, 1 October 1956, Box 100356. Residents drawn on in compiling the conservation report on Matopo Reserve came from Beitbridge, Gwanda, Fort Usher, Gokwe and other districts.

[3] The shrine concerned was Dzilo.

[4] Delineation report, Matopo Tribal Trust Land: the Bafana chieftainship; the Mbetshi community; the Samson community; A. D. Elliott, February/March 1964. By contrast the 'Interim Report on the Wenlock TTL, Gwanda' of 25 June 1964 recorded that most residents were *Nqameni*.

[5] Security report, Fort Usher, 2 April 1924, S 728/6A/5.

Christian progressives of Whitewaters and the Matopos Mission rather than by Ndebele *indunas* or Mwali priests.

Nevertheless, there was much in common between protest in the Matopos Hills and in Wenlock. In both places the main leader was a second-generation Christian rebel – in Wenlock Daniel Dube, in the Matopos Nqabe Tshuma. In both places the main thrust of opposition came from a local association – in Wenlock from *Sofasihamba*, in the Matopos from *Sofasonke*.[6]

Out of the Mapani and into the Hills

At the end of Chapter 3 we left the African occupants of the *mapani* veld in retreat from and in competition with the incoming European settlers. Over the next 30 years the European victory became complete. This was not because of the efficiency of capitalist agriculture. In fact the farms south of the Matopos became a by-word for inefficiency and debt.

An instructive case study is that of Holi farm – once grazing land for Chief Hole's herds and then the target of the Brethren's application for a mission farm. Hole's people and cattle were moved off, so that by 1913 there were no 'taxable natives' on the land. The Brethren's application had also been turned down on the grounds that Holi could become a profitable capitalist enterprise. In August 1908 it was leased to one W. S. George, a Scot from Aberdeen, for £14 6s 4d a year. George had the greatest difficulty in using Holi for farming. 'The land was boulder strewn and heavily covered with bush', he complained in 1914, 'as is the whole of the adjacent land'. He planned to plant lucerne under irrigation; it cost him £6 an acre to remove stones and to manure the land; the return fell 'far short of the cost of seed and tillage alone.' Between 1910 and 1914 there were three seasons of drought and the crops had 'been an absolute failure.' Forty of his cattle died and 90 had to be sold at a loss. There was no point in planting maize – 'this is cattle country only.'[7] 'The occupation effected does not appear to have been very progressive', remarked the Assistant Director of Land Settlement.

George was still on the land in 1928 when he wrote to the Director of Land Settlement that

> owing to three years drought, plus heavy losses of cattle, I am unable to reduce my liability for quit rent.... For 4 years I have not sold a bag of produce.... I am losing heavily cows calving and the survivors are in such a condition that even given good veld they will take two or three months to reach a condition in which they can be milked.

---

[6] There was a *Sofasonke* squatter movement in Johannesburg which has hitherto been better known than the Matopos association. After extensive inquiry, however, I am convinced that the latter does not derive its name from the former. Even labour migrants to South Africa, who supported the Matopos *Sofasonke* by sending contributions from their wages, denied any connection with the Johannesburg movement. I have concluded that the term *Sofasonke* was widely available to speakers of Sindebele or Zulu as a statement of defiance and resistance.

[7] W. S. George, Holi to Director, Land Settlement, 2 March 1914, S 456/132/52A.

By 1932 he was seven years in debt and in 1934 he told the Secretary, Lands, that 'for four years in order not to become hopelessly involved, I have been living on practically a· kaffir standard.'[8] Another settler, F. J. R. Peel, took Lana, Luma and Umfula farms, in the same block as Holi. But he did no better as a developer. In May 1919 he was reported as 'simply using Luma as a base for his cattle trading and collecting rents from the natives.'[9]

Moreover, many of the *mapani* farms were taken up by Afrikaners – 'in no way an asset to the district', wrote a Land Inspector in October 1939:

> they have no capital with which to farm. They refuse to pay their natives a fair wage. They continually break the game laws and some of their number have been convicted of selling arms to natives. Their standard of living is deplorable and the Government for the most part has to feed and educate their children.[10]

These Afrikaners attracted the severe eye of Charles Murray even before the Africans of the Matopos fell under his condemnation. Murray believed that almost all white land use south of the Matopos, and Afrikaner land use in particular, was hopelessly under-capitalised and inefficient. Land units were much too small in what was 'essentially ranching country'. The Senior Inspector of Land, F. Gillward, agreed with him. Writing of farmers like Du Preez of Undza and Malala farms, and of his fellow Afrikaners, Lotter and Herbst, Gillward condemned their uncommercial attitude to their herds and their 'tribal' attachment to kin, almost as if he was writing about the previous African occupants:

> To this type of South African Dutch farmer the herd of cattle represents a savings bank, to be drawn upon only when other sources of revenue fail.... These South African Dutch settlers are still imbued with the herd instinct which impels them to foregather in closely settled areas. You will find then that each and every one will always find accommodation for the 'poor relation' whether he be brother, uncle or fifty-second cousin. These 'leeches' or 'bywoners' invariably aspire to ownership in cattle, which like their owners, enjoy the free hospitality of the farms.[11]

What was needed, he thought, was 'radical change, uprooting sections of the [white] population which have taken root in these pastoral areas. Under authoritarian form of Government, these changes would be brought about in the twinkling of an eye.' In settler Rhodesia, however, one could uproot blacks but not whites. These inefficient farmers remained on the land. As late as 1949 the National Park Ranger, Grobler, reported that 'the farms adjoining the Park seem to be occupied by people who have been there for about 30 years and I cannot see any improvement that they have made to their farms. I don't know if they are not interested in farming or if they are dis-appointed with that part of the country. They have done no improvements. They have not even put a pig-sty down or a cattle kraal.... Government should do something to improve their farming methods, otherwise it will be quite impossible to teach the

[8] 'W. S. George, Holi, Matobo', S 456/665/30.
[9] H. T. Wood to Director, Land Settlement, 10 May 1919, S 456/132/52A.
[10] J. W. S. Cobban, Report on Babuli farm, 31 October 1939, S 2111/25.
[11] F. Gillward to Under Secretary, Department of Lands, n.d. but after 1933, S 2111/25.

Natives because they will just tell me what the next door farmer is doing.'[12]

In fact, it was partly because of the similarity in land use that the *mapani* whites clashed so sharply with the Africans of the area. Both groups were running great herds of 'scrub' cattle, which constantly clashed for grazing and water. By the 1930s these contests were being regularly resolved in favour of the white herds. In October 1931 *Induna* Maqina's successor, who had inherited many cattle, complained bitterly that 'the present Reserves [Shashani and Semokwe] were inadequate ... They are over-shadowed and hemmed in by farms owned by Europeans, who impounded their stock.'[13]

Despite the inefficiency and rapacity of the *mapani* whites, the Native Department had abandoned any reference to the promises of Rhodes. It stopped trying to defend Africans in the belt south of the hills. In June 1931 the Chief Native Commissioner met the chiefs and headmen of Matobo district:

> I have heard your complaint about the inadequacy of the land assigned to you [he told them]. There is no record of Mr Rhodes having promised to divide the land between the white people and the black people, except in the manner in which it has been done. You have your Reserves.[14]

In December 1935 the Native Commissioner, Matobo, asserted that

> the Matopos South Central Area should be cleared of natives, as they are a continual source of annoyance to the farmers. The National Park should remain as at present.... The whole area south of the Antelope-Gwanda road should, if possible, be reserved as a Native Area.[15]

By 1938 the Native Commissioner could report 'slow and steady progress ... a large block of Alienated and Crown lands south of the hills is being slowly cleared of its inhabitants.' Next year he recorded

> the wholesale ejection of natives from Crown Lands on alienation.... Large blocks of land have been cleared of squatters. South of the National Park the following farms were evacuated during 1939: Maleme, Sibuntuli, Luma, Lana, Pagati and Sala.[16]

Gradually the Native Commissioner's vision took shape – a belt of white land in the *mapani*, with Africans pushed either south into Shashani and Semokwe Reserves, or north into the National Park. In the mid-1930s Nyangazonke's successor, Sinti, abandoned Stutterlingen farm and took all his people south 'from the Matopos to Kezi'.[17] Hole's successor, Nzula, eventually went the other way, and took many of his following

---

[12] Evidence of J. H. Grobler, 22 March 1949, S 1561/46.

[13] Minutes of Native Board, Shashani, 14 October 1931, S 1542/NZ.G.

[14] Notes for Chief Native Commissioner's meeting with Chiefs and Headmen, Fort Usher, 15 June 1931. S 1542/N2. The idea of the promises of Rhodes, however, was still not entirely dead. In Mzingwane in May 1931 'the Natives appear to have convinced themselves that Mr Rhodes did make them a promise' and the Native Commissioner thought that some sort of gesture would have to be made to them.

[15] Native Commissioner, Matobo, to Superintendent of Natives, Bulawayo, 16 December 1935, AT 1/2/1/11/2.

[16] Annual Reports, Matobo, 1938 and 1939.

[17] District Administrator to Under Secretary, Development, Matabeleland South, 17 December 1981, PER 5/CHK, District Administrator's Office, Kezi.

and cattle back into the western Matopos. During the late 1930s and 1940s the hills began to fill up again with people and stock. The Native Department itself settled families there in 1924 and 1934. Meanwhile, the flow of people from the Rhodes-Matopos Estate into the hills accelerated. The great operation of bringing Africans out into the open and on to the flat, which Rhodes had taken so seriously, was being reversed.

Official Visions of the Matopo National Park between the Wars

While the hills were filling up with people and stock, official images of them were changing. The Native Department, the Forestry Department, the Prime Minister's office and the newly created Natural Resources Board all came to be preoccupied with the threat posed by these people and their herds to the Matopos environment. It was now land rather than people which needed to be protected in its primal state.

In the 1920s and 1930s most whites continued to regard the Matopos as wild and remote. But so far as the Native Department was concerned, it had become the remoteness not of romance but of backwardness. In 1920 the Native Commissioner, Matobo, recorded that 'the majority of the Natives live in the Reserves and in the unalienated Matopos rent-free'. The erection of seven dipping tanks in the 'fastnesses of the Matopo Hills' exercised, he thought, 'a most wholesome influence over tribes who have hitherto pursued an existence far too remote from the movement of progress and the outside world to be healthy for them.'[18] The admiration which earlier Native Commissioners had expressed for Banyubi agriculture had long vanished. 'Science has not yet come to regard the Hill country as arable', wrote Native Commissioner Benzies in 1931. 'Only most careful study and observation and extensive work could make more productive those sandy sloping soils carelessly littered between the Hills by nature.'[19] And to the Superintendent of Natives in Bulawayo he developed this view:

> Natives are allowed to reside in the National Park (unsurveyed Matopo Hills) free.... They overstock and their methods of agriculture are most destructive to pasture lands: they cultivate large areas for a few years without any attempt at fertilisation, the impoverished land is then left fallow and fresh ground is broken up and so the process of exhausting the fertility of the soil goes on.[20]

The Native Department's solution to remoteness, backwardness and erosion was to 'regularise' the position of the Western Matopos. The area should be made a Native Reserve not so much to protect its residents, but in order that there could be effective intervention in their lives. 'There are no less than 44,800 located in the National Park', wrote the Native Commissioner, Matobo in 1934. 'The future of the Area requires defining. Virtually, it is at present a Reserve, and it would ease the position considerably

[18] Annual Report, Matobo, 1920, N 9/1/23.
[19] Annual Report, Matobo, 1931, S 235/506.
[20] Native Commissioner, Matobo, to Superintendent of Natives, Matabeleland, 27 November 1931, S 1542/N2.

if it were possible to declare the region as such.' In 1938 he returned to the charge. There should be a coherent plan of water conservation in the Matopos, but 'the unsatisfactory status of the National Park again needs accentuation. Under the present conditions ... it is still nobody's baby when funds are required for its development.' The whole area should be made a Reserve so that centralisation, survey, destocking and other measures could be applied to it.[21]

Other official agencies did not favour the idea of a Reserve but were equally concerned with what they saw as agrarian 'backwardness' and land spoilation. In default of any National Parks legislation, administrative structure or funds, the so-called National Park was up to 1940 under the Forestry Department, 'not in connection with forestry at all', as the Chief Conservator of Forests told the 1949 Commission of Inquiry, but because his department found itself in charge of 'all game reserves':

> The Matopos National Park, as declared in 1926, was proclaimed a Game Reserve in 1930, and as we had taken over Wankie Game Reserve we assumed that we also had to take over control of the Matopos National Park. All through our association with the Matopos National Park was nominal only.... We never had any forestry or game reserve officers attached to the area.[22]

No large game had been reported in the hills at the end of the nineteenth century and there was little to conserve in the 1930s. The abundant woodlands were under no threat. Moreover, in 1930 the official attitude to the 'very large area' of the western Matopos was still that 'the Aboriginal Natives living in this area should be left undisturbed as far as possible in their natural condition.' When the Chief Forest Officer 'proposed very elaborate regulations dealing with it as a Game Reserve, which were so obviously impossible if the Natives were to remain, the question was dropped.' The Department was instructed that 'the area could not be dealt with as Game Reserve in view of the Native population, but the Forest Officer at Matopos was to exercise supervision over the destruction of timber by Natives.'[23]

The Forestry Department, while in practice completely ineffective, found the situation humiliating. It soon sought to advance the theory that National Parks should in principle be free of human occupation. The western Matopos 'should either be a National Park or a Native Reserve' but could not be both.

In January 1935 the Chief Forestry Officer proposed a scheme of partition. 42,000 acres around Rhodes's grave should be reserved 'for the true purposes of a National Park' and should be cleared completely of Africans; the remainder could be a Reserve.[24]

This time there was no more official talk about picturesque aborigines lending charm to a primal landscape. Prime Minister Huggins thought, indeed, that 'it might be advisable to remove the Natives from a larger area than the 42,000 acres proposed' so as to 'prevent the continuance of damage to the timber and pasturage.'[25] But though

[21] Annual Reports, Matobo, 1934 and 1938, S 235/512 and 516.
[22] Evidence of E. J. Kelly Edwards, 21 March 1949, S 1651/46.
[23] Secretary, Prime Minister to Prime Minister, 26 October 1933, S 482/386/39.
[24] Chief Forestry Officer to Acting Secretary, Agriculture and Lands, 28 January 1935, BE 8/3/2/1.
[25] Private Secretary, Prime Minister to Secretary, Agriculture and Lands, 4 December 1934, S 482/539/39.

official attitudes to the Matopos had thus changed very significantly, the scheme foundered for lack of funds; the Native Department insisted that if people were to be displaced from the western hills they had to be resettled on farms in the *mapani* bought by government; a hard-up cabinet decided that the idea be abandoned. Huggins made it clear, however, that the area should not be proclaimed as a Reserve:

> The Prime Minister considers that there are certain objections to giving the Natives living in the Matopo National Park any definite assurances that they will at no time in the future be evicted. That would have the effect of tying the hands of future Governments.[26]

In 1938 the Forestry Department tried again 'to get an area representative of the Matopos reserved for true National Park purposes', and in 1940 agreed with the Native Department that 17,000 acres should be thus set aside. But 'because of the international situation the matter was shelved'.[27]

Meanwhile, developments were taking place which ultimately were to lead to the setting up of a formal National Parks authority with a commitment to a depopulated Matopos. In November 1933 Southern Rhodesia signed the London Convention, undertaking to establish National Parks, and in a subsequent schedule to the Convention listed the Matopos along with the Victoria Falls, Kazama Pan, Gono-re-zhou and Wankie. The London Convention defined a National Park as an area 'set aside for the propagation, protection and preservation of objects of aesthetic, biological, pre-historical, archaeological or other scientific interest.' Under the influence of international conservationism, romance was giving way to science. In 1939 the McIlwaine Commission, appointed to report on the preservation of natural resources, drew attention to the evidence of rapid destruction of fauna and flora, and to the importance of the North American model in which 'every activity of the [National Parks] service is subordinate to the duties imposed upon it to faithfully preserve the parks for posterity in essentially their natural state.'[28]

The Natural Resources Act and the Natural Resources Board emerged as a result of the Commission's report. But there was still no National Park legislation and ironically it was doubtful whether the Matopos National Park area came under the provisions of the Natural Resources Act. Despite the growing hostility to their way of life from Native Department, Forestry, central government and the rising conservationist lobby, the peoples of the western Matopos lived through the 1930s in blissful ignorance of the various abortive schemes to discipline or displace them. When Agricultural Demonstrators finally got into the Park in the early 1940s 'they tried but they cannot succeed. They get scared of the Park Natives.'[29] While Africans were being harried all around them, the inhabitants of the hills stood aloof, living in what a hostile observer was later to call 'a state within a state', occupying a little pocket of time and space between two European ideologies of conservation, two white myths of the Matopos.

---

[26] *Ibid.*

[27] Evidence of J. Kelly Edwards, 21 March 1949, S 1561/46.

[28] 'National Parks and other Places of Scenic or Other Attractions', 14 January 1947, S 1194/1608/1/1.

[29] Evidence of Park Ranger, J. H. Grobler, 22 March 1949, S 1561.

Life in the Matopos to the 1940s

Yet this apparent 'isolation' and conservatism was misleading. Official views of the hills were mistaken in many ways. African agricultural and pastoral methods in the Matopos were not the product of mere traditionalism. They were a response to contemporary needs. Nor were the hill communities cut off from ideas and experiences outside them. They might have been reluctantly 'left to themselves' by whites, but they were in constant and fruitful interaction with other Africans.

The Matopo Reserve, set up in the eastern hills in 1917, admirably illustrates these generalisations. In 1917 the Native Commissioner, Matobo, reported that 'the Natives of the new Matobo Reserve have not yet fallen into line [over dipping], but in a scattered community of small owners this is a matter of time and patience.'[30] But time and patience had little effect upon the scattered communities of the eastern Matopos. When the area had been proposed as a Reserve in 1915 the guardian of the British South African Company's commercial interests, Assistant Director of Land Settlement Frank Inskipp, had responded with cheerful cynicism: 'As the area in question, which is practically a conglomeration of *kopjes* with very small cultivable valleys in between, is infested with baboons and is only traversable by pack animals, I see no objection to this.'[31]

In fact the Matopo Reserve developed a very effective intensive 'market garden' agriculture based on the exploitation of *vleis* and valley bottoms.[32] This agriculture was 'traditional' in that its practitioners observed the ritual ecological rules of the Mwali shrines which clustered in the Reserve; it was 'modern' in that market gardening aimed to sell its products in Bulawayo. By breaking all the rules of colonial agricultural science, peasant farmers in Matopo Reserve enjoyed a success which infuriated and confounded the experts, whose inquiries regularly revealed this 'stony' and 'barren' land to enjoy a higher family income than most African rural areas. The inhabitants of the Reserve were ready to accept advice about commercial crops from Agricultural Demonstrators – in 1932 one was described as 'doing extraordinarily good work in that difficult, hilly, granite country'. But they were not prepared to accept interference or instructions to fence *vleis* and stop farming valley bottoms, which would have undercut the whole basis of their production system. In 1934 the Matopo Reserve Demonstrator was said to lack control, 'but he has a difficult group to contend with.'[33]

[30] Annual Report, Matobo, 1917, N 9/1/20.

[31] Quoted in Robin Palmer, *Land and Racial Domination in Rhodesia*, Heinemann, London, 1977, p. 117.

[32] In the 1924 Annual Report it was noted that already 'a good many grow vegetables for the market'. In 1925 the Native Commissioner of the adjoining Mzingwane district recorded that 'natives whose lands are near the river go in for market gardening, irrigate their lands and sell their produce in Bulawayo.'

[33] Annual Reports, Matobo, 1932 and 1934. On 10 September 1988 Mark Ncube and I had a group interview with some 30 men and women gathered at Kumbudzi clinic in Matopo Communal Area. They explained to us that they observed shrine rules for 'traditional' crops and 'the rules of the government' for new crops, like hybrid maize. The *Isitunywa* messenger takes seeds from his area to the *Wosana* who in turn goes to a shrine. The shrine blesses the seeds of food crops but not those of cash crops like sunflower, tomatoes, cotton. But on the cultivation of *vleis* and wet places they follow the rules of the shrine entirely and ignore those of the government.

Moreover, there was constant interaction between the Matopo Reserve and Bula-wayo; cultivators took their vegetables to town in scotch carts; where wage seekers were concerned, the 'best labour gravitates to Bulawayo'; at weekends scores of town workers cycled out or caught buses into the hills. 'One is apt to wonder, when watching a queue of anything up to fifty native cyclists streaming back to town in the early hours of a Monday morning', wrote the Native Commissioner in 1938, 'mostly bathed in perspira-tion and exuding surplus beer, how they can possibly find it worth while.'[34] It was these men – and many women who also moved between the Reserve and Bulawayo – who kept the eastern Matopos elders and resident cultivators in touch with Bulawayo politics.

One of them was Nduna Ncube, who lived with his mother on Absent farm, close to Matopo Mission. In 1930, when he was 20, he went to work in Bulawayo. To this day he remembers the excitement of those times. 'I used to go to ICU [Industrial and Commercial Workers Union] meetings. I didn't become a member but I did like it. I liked it very much.' He greatly admired Masotsha Ndhlovu, the ICU's militant leader, 'an outstanding man, ready to go to England to see the queen to demand our land back.' He took part in boxing, singing, dancing and cycling. He learnt songs adapted from South African National Congress texts – 'What is the work of Congress ? We are paying tax for huts, dogs, scotch-cart wheels. Our country has been taken from us because we have no representative in Parliament.' He still says that 'South Africa was where the wisdom came from'. He took private studies up to Standard Four; he read Marcus Garvey and Booker. T. Washington. In June 1937 he married a girl from Wenlock. Then in 1939 he 'went home for ploughing, thinking I would be better off there.'[35]

Another eastern Matopos labour migrant, who worked in Bulawayo in the 1940s, was the young radical firebrand, Influenza Sibanda, better known as Frazer Gibson, whose home was also on Absent Farm. Born during the influenza epidemic in 1919 Sibanda learnt about the heroic Ndebele past from his father, who had fought in 1896 and had attended the *indabas*. He worked in Bulawayo first as a messenger at the magistrate's court and then in the archetypal Matopo Reserve activity of vegetable seller.[36] He was deeply involved in township politics – 'Gibson Fraser is my young man', claimed Masotsha Ndhlovu[37] – but he was always ready to take up and organise a grievance in the eastern Matopos.

Meanwhile, teachers at the Matopo Mission itself became increasingly outspoken and ready to voice local suspicion of the state. One of them, James Chatagwe, ultimately gave voice to the rooted eastern Matopos repudiation of state intervention in their methods of production:

> I want to draw the attention of the African people to the often repeated allegation that they cause soil erosion. My recent surveys and observations have landed me at a clear conclusion that the people who cause soil erosion are the so-called demonstrators who are taught to preserve and fight against soil erosion. I have seen many fields where demonstrators work and all the field areas are being destroyed by erosion. They teach people to plough when some of

[34] Annual Report, Matobo, 1938, S 235/516.
[35] Interview with Nduna Ncube, Bulawayo, 15 July 1988.
[36] Evidence of Frazer Gibson Sibanda, 22 March 1949, S 1561/46.
[37] Interview between Tom Wodeskzi and Masotsha Ndhlovu, Bulawayo, 10 September 1981, AOH/69.

them have no fields of their own to prove they are better soil masters. I would suggest that all the demonstrators be taken to the Sahara or Kalahari deserts to improve those as they are taught to improve soil.[38]

All in all, then, the Matopos Reserve was a baffling place for officials. It possessed a thriving market gardening system based on rules totally opposite to those propagated by the state; its cultivators responded to the edicts of the rock shrines rather than those of the Demonstrator. The people of the Reserve would not accept any of the institutions urged upon them by the state. In 1948 the more cooperative members of the Shashani and Semokwe Reserves Native Council decided to set up a sub-committee 'to hold a meeting with Chief Bafana, headmen and other influential persons in the Matopo Reserve in order (1) to find out why the inhabitants of the Matopo Reserve were not keen on forming a Native Council and (2) if they were able to persuade them to form a Council, to discuss the possibility of the Council in the Matopo Reserve amalgamating with the Matobo South Native Council to form a District Council. Council members expressed their concern at the backwardness and conservatism of the inhabitants of the Matopo Reserve.' The Assistant Chief Native Commissioner was 'particularly pleased' about this initiative which he hoped would bring the 'difficult' Matopo Reserve into line. But at the next Matobo South Council meeting it had to be reported that 'this visit failed to materialise, although transport had been arranged. The reasons given were that members were not prepared to go to the Matopo Reserve to be laughed and scoffed at [and] that it was felt that the Council did not want to associate itself in any way with the attitude that had been taken up by the inhabitants of the Matopo Reserve and the National Park.'[39]

As this Council minute suggests, the peoples of the National Park were just as unco-operative. Like the people of the Matopos Reserve, the residents of the western Matopos were in touch both with 'tradition' and 'modernity'. This was particularly the case for the 'wild' area of Whitewaters, from which came the leaders of the Matopos in the 1940s.

Just as the market gardening of Matopo Reserve observed the rules of production laid down by its local Mwali shrines, so the people of Whitewaters were very aware of their closeness to the senior shrine of Njelele. Progressive Christian plough users observed traditional rituals:

> Even when people ploughed their fields, they wouldn't just go to their field and eat. There was a process where ijambo would be organised, for young children. Ijambo was an exercise which was meant to control the birds from eating the crops when they are ready.... You would go and eat by the river there, where there was an old man called Mbedzi. He would organise the medicines for the young people to do what needed what to be done.... Whitewaters holds the ancestral beliefs. There are people there we would not like removed.... They know the secrets and ceremonies of the rains, the diseases, the disunity, and all those things. Because once the people went to the shrines and reported about disunity or disease it stopped immediately.[40]

[38] *Bantu Mirror*, 17 May 1952.

[39] Minutes of General Meeting of Matobo South Native Council, 14 and 28 May 1948; Assistant Chief Native Commissioner to Provincial Native Commissioner, 24 June 1948; Minutes of the Matobo South Native Council, 16 November 1948, S 2797/2445.

[40] Interview with Thenjiwe Lesabe, 24 August 1988

The Njelele priests deplored the white occupation of the *mapani* veld farms: 'To mark the end of a year, a lion went past. That was Mambo's spirit. But today since there are farms where can the lion pass ?'[41] Nevertheless, the flow of pilgrims from the south continued, linking the south-western Matopos to a wider world. Even some of the white farmers in the *mapani* sent gifts to Njelele for rain.[42] And Whitewaters Christians approached the shrine. Japhet Ngwenya, who came to be headmaster of the Seventh Day Adventist school at Njelele, told me about his time as a schoolboy in Njelele and Whitewaters in the late 1940s and early 1950s. Japhet was born at Njelele, south-west of Whitewaters. Around Njelele:

> the major thing was growing crops. You know when you look at Njelele, if you are far away from that place, you would think it is all hills, but there are open places where people have ploughed fields, where they cultivated crops. I grew up there and we had good harvests.

Naturally the Ngwenya family observed the Mwali productive rituals. Japhet's father was a staunch Seventh Day Adventist but before his conversion in the early 1940s 'he took quite an interest in the shrine. At times my father whenever they had some traditional festivals there he actually went there.' Japhet began his schooling in the SDA schools at Njelele and Halale but then transferred to Whitewaters school which offered Standard Three.[43] He stayed there for four years – 'when I was living in Whitewaters we went around quite freely. I remember we were hunting on those hills without any problems at all.' But in 1948 this Christian boy went with his traditionalist grandfather, Mabiza, to the rain ceremonies at Njelele, where Mayabu Ndlovu was priest:

> I actually led a black ox there with my grandfather, which was going to be slaughtered there. We went up that hill and at that place everybody was there, even people from down Dula area they were up there, and people from all over Matopo. Well, we spent the whole day there and it was in the evening when we left. There was rain.[44]

The old network of shrines subsidiary to Njelele continued to function. In the 1940s Denge Sibindi was a messenger for one of these shrines in Whitewaters, the Mashakambayo cave. Whitewaters emissaries went there first for rain, engaging in a

---

[41] Interview with Sitwanyana Ncube, Mguza, 28 July 1988.

[42] I. G. Cockcroft, later Native Commissioner and author of a special report on the Mwali shrines, was a farmer's child at Kezi between 1909 and 1922. 'I frequently heard of Njelele and the rain-making ceremonies. During September to November of each year many elders from various parts traversed our farm en route to Njelele', and on their return admitted that they had heard the Voice 'advising the times of planting.' In 1924 he went with one of the *mapani* veld farmers, Leslie of Duta, to the Njelele shrine, entered the cave, and inspected the offerings. When he returned again in 1968, and once more entered the cave, he found no offerings. He was told that the Voice had ceased because of 'interference by curious Europeans'. Cockcroft, 'The Mlimo (Mwari) Cult', *NADA*, 10, 1972.

[43] The Seventh Day Adventist school at Njelele was approved by the government in November 1934, S.605.

[44] Interview with Japhet Ngwenya, Tshatshani School, 30 August 1988; for an oral account of a visit to Njelele in 1945, see interview between Mark Ncube and Dima Bhebhe, Pelendaba, 18 April 1983. 'If there was outbreak of birds they went there and brought a special smoke for the birds. They would vanish from the fields.'

ritual hunt of wild pigs in the hills, and only going to Njelele shrine at the time of the great rain ceremonies in October.[45]

Yet despite the continued relevance of the Njelele shrine to local production and to the regional movement of pilgrims, there was a sense in the 1940s that the shrines had nothing to offer in organising the people to resist white intervention and threats of eviction. Moreover, by this time the Voice was no longer heard at Njelele. Denge Sibindi – who hopes that now colonialism is over the Voice will return – says that in the late 1940s 'people should have resorted to the shrine' to seek divine aid against eviction. 'But they didn't and so Mwali couldn't help'. Japhet Ngwenya explained:

> What people were saying really was that the traditional God at Njelele had left, long left. Since he had left there was no more Voice there.... You know, nobody really paid much attention to that shrine in relation to the political movement.... People meant politics. Rain ceremonies were still performed but we went straight to politics.[46]

The same balance is struck in white reports from 1948 and 1949. In November 1948 the *Chronicle* carried a story under the heading 'Floods, Warn the Oracles From the Matopos'. This described how

> this year, because of the late rains, more attention than usual has been paid to appeasing the weather prophets. White-haired, goatee-bearded old men, who are sticklers for tradition, have been trekking from their kraals to the sacred hills, and rain dances have been taking place near Njelele.

The 'weather prophets' reportedly told 'Africans paying homage to them' that there would be very heavy rains in January which would flood valleys. But the Native Commissioner, Matobo, while noting such ecological activities, insisted that 'the Mlimo has not pronounced his attitude to the affair of the National Park.'[47]

In the late 1940s the peoples of Whitewaters, Njelele and the rest of the Matopos had to replace the now silent Voice of Mwali with a live voice of political leadership. Even Denge Sibindi was a member of *Sofasonke* whose inspiration came from the Whitewaters 'modernisers'.

In the 1930s and early 1940s the area had not followed the example of the Matopo Reserve and developed market gardening – 'Whitewaters had plenty of water: a very good place', remembers one of its residents. 'At the time we stopped there we had no intention of making vegetables, but now – we would be rich!' There was no store. But everyone kept cattle; rice and maize were grown – 'in Whitewaters there was plenty of water; growing crops was as easy as anything; one could harvest all year round';[48] the school under a male teacher evangelist and two women teachers attracted students from

---

[45] Interview with Denge Sibindi, Whitewaters, Kumalo, 26 July 1988.

[46] *Ibid.*

[47] *Chronicle*, 26 November 1949; Annual Report, Matobo, 1948. If one were to judge simply from the Annual Reports, the ecological influence of the Mwali shrines had revived in the 1940s. In 1935, 1936, 1938 and 1939 the reports stressed 'no activies on the part of the Mlimo' despite droughts. In 1947, 1948 and 1949, however, pilgrimages and ecological advice are recorded.

[48] Interview with Zephaniah Moyo, Bulawayo, 14 July 1988; interview with Benjamin Nyathi, 6 September 1988.

a wide area; and Whitewaters lay on a major communications route.[49]

The main road south to the *mapani* farms, to the Antelope Mine, to Kezi and the Shashani and Semokwe Reserves passed through Whitewaters. By the early 1940s there were frequent bus services. The main entrepreneur was Richard Makoni, 'the African who conducts the bus service between Bulawayo and Antelope Mine.' Makoni ran three buses every Wednesday and five on Saturdays; an Indian businessman ran one on Wednesday and another on Saturday. Makoni charged 6 shillings to Antelope and 5/6d to Kezi, but despite this his buses were in great demand. When petrol rationing cut them back in 1944 it was reported that 'nowadays many pupils walk from Bulawayo to Kezi'. Whitewaters was a key stop on the southern route – indeed in November 1948 the Matobo South Native Council complained that 'operators, especially at week-ends, [dropped] all passengers at Whitewaters, returning to Bulawayo to pick up a second load before returning to Antelope.'[50]

Many sorts of people travelled by these buses: students, traders, women – the patriarchs of southern Matobo protested in both 1944 and 1951 that 'young girls and women were drifting into town without the permission and away from the control of their parents and guardians ... on a native bus disappearing into town.'[51] Increasingly the buses carried politicians out from Bulawayo to Whitewaters or from Whitewaters into Bulawayo. It was little wonder that Whitewaters became the communications hub of the hills.

Some Whitewaters residents travelled further afield. Many men went to South Africa, a few for education and many for work. They underwent a political education and came back with radical ideas. As early as 1927 there was a strike of 'a gang of road party natives on the Matopo-Antelope road' that ran through Whitewaters. Inquiry brought to light evidence that

> an organisation existed in one part of the district for disseminating propaganda of an industrial nature. About 5 months ago a certain native of the district who had returned from Johannesburg was found to have been in communication with the Industrial and Commercial Workers Union in the Union and was holding meetings.

Meetings were attended 'either by native foreigners or indigenous natives who had worked in the Union.'[52] These attitudes to road gang work and other compulsory labour continued through the 1930s and 1940s.

Business interests were as lively in southern Matobo as 'worker consciousness'. Just as in Wenlock, there grew up a cluster of storekeepers and other local entrepreneurs. These interacted with school teachers and African ministers of religion but also with chiefs. In the 1940s, indeed, there was great pressure from chiefs and Native Councils

[49] Interview with Benjamin Nyathi, Njube, 6 September 1988. Nyathi was born in Whitwaters in 1918, went to school there and lived there until 1942.

[50] Matobo South Native Council meeting, 12 July 1944; Inspector, Native Education, Matabeleland Circuit to Director of Native Education, 27 September 1944; Council meeting, 16 November 1948, S 2797/2445. Bus services were a regular preoccupation of the Council which wanted more buses, operated by more African entrepreneurs, than the licensing authorities were prepared to allow.

[51] Meetings of Matobo South Native Council, 12 December 1944; 4 January 1951, *ibid.*

[52] Annual Report, Matobo, 1927, S 235/505.

to reserve store sites in southern Matobo to Africans. 'The time was coming when all Natives could not farm [and] other avenues of work should be opened up,' it was asserted in October 1946. 'It was only right that all trading sites should be reserved for Africans'. The Native Commissioner, arguing in September 1947 that an African monopoly was not yet possible, nevertheless claimed that 'since his arrival many Natives had been granted trading licences.' Led by chief Sinti, successor of Faku and Nyangazonke, the Matobo South Native Council formally resolved that only Africans should be granted sites, and when in January 1950 it looked as if a store was to be erected by a European trading company, Sinti 'attempted to make derogatory remarks about Europeans and Asiatics'.[53]

Thus there arose a 'connection' of modernisers in the Matopos and south of them – teachers, labour migrants, bus-owners, store-keepers, linked with headmen and chiefs. Two men in particular came to represent this combination of interests in Whitewaters and to link it with the rest of the Matopos and with Bulawayo. One was the *Zansi* chief, Nzula; the other was the Sotho commoner, Nqabe Tshuma.

The careers of Chief Nzula and Nqabe Tshuma

Nzula had been sent to South Africa as long ago as 1910 when his cattle-rich father, Hole, had enrolled him at Lovedale, where Tshekedi Khama was a fellow pupil. *Induna* Maqina's son, Sinda, went to Lovedale at the same time; *Induna* Nyangazonke's son, Tapi, went in 1913. These *mapani* veld chiefs were by far the richest Africans of their day and they began to spend lavishly. In 1910 'two chiefs are to be seen disporting themselves in wagonettes and carts drawn by horses'.[54] When Nzula and Tapi returned from Lovedale, they soon surpassed this modest display. Tapi bought cars and suits and led 'a life of monstrous prodigality and dissipation' in the eyes of the Native Department. Nzula 'alienated 1,000 head of cattle, bought car after car, innumerable motor-cycles. At the present moment [March 1922] he sports a four-in-hand, and has recently purchased a sword and scabbard and khaki uniform with Field Cap and Sam Browne belt.'[55] This naive display was soon curbed. Tapi was deposed for mis-using 'tribal resources'; Nzula was severely warned. Abandoning Chief Native Commisssioner Taylor's insistence on private ownership of cattle, the Native Department told Nzula that he was expected to act as a 'traditional' chief – it being 'well known, by Zulu, i.e. Matabele custom' that cattle 'cannot be dealt with as if they were the personal and absolute property of the chief. He holds them in trust to "govern with".'[56]

Nzula's extravagance did not attract such condemnation from his people. In the mid-1920s a Security report characterised him as 'a terrible spend-thrift' but also as 'a

[53] Meetings of Matobo South Native Council, 23 October 1946; 13 September 1947; 14 and 28 May 1948; 24 June 1948; 24 February 1950, S 2797/2445.
[54] Annual Report, Matobo, 1910, NB 6/1/11.
[55] Native Commissioner, Matobo, to Superintendent of Natives, Bulawayo, 2 March 1922, N 3/4/5.
[56] *Ibid.*

strong character, well educated, has a firm hold, keeps excellent order.'[57] But he was not satisfied to play the role allocated to him by the Native Department. He soon stopped attending the Matobo South Native Council. Increasingly this frustrated chief, prohibited from disposing of his cattle and with little opportunity to use his education, put his energies into the Matabeleland Home Society. In some ways Nzula was the archetypal Society member – descended from great figures of Ndebele history, yet with connections and sympathies with the educated urban cultural nationalists. 'He wasn't a speaker but he was a big writer', remembers Thenjiwe Lesabe. 'Books about the Amandebele, history of Mzilikazi, and tradition in general. They were never published.'[58] This intellectual chief certainly had no objections to the Matabeleland Home Society's fascination with and up-datings of Ndebele ceremonial.

During the 1940s, by which time he was resident in Whitewaters, he attended many of the Society's great invented traditionalist rituals, most of them staged in the Matopos. Together with *Induna* Bafana of Matopo Reserve, with Sipambaniso Manyoba's father, and with the teacher and praisesinger Ginyilitshe Hlabangana, he was a pall-bearer at the funeral of Lobengula's son, Nguboyenja, on 21 June 1944. At the Society's initiative the prince was buried at Entumbane, the site of Mzilikazi's grave in the eastern hills. The ceremony was a typical blend of ancient and modern. There was a Guard of Honour provided by African boy scouts, the Pathfinders. There was a religious service performed by Anglican clergy, black and white. Leaders of the African Methodist Episcopal Church had a place of honour. The ceremony was attended by the acting Provincial Native Commissioner and the Native Commissioner, Matobo. Ginyilitshe recited praises 'in a controlled but passionate voice'. As the coffin 'was lowered into the grave three Matabele queens, the widows of King Lobengula, knelt down sobbing quietly and Sidojiwe, the only surviving son of Lobengula, stood at the head of the grave holding an assegai with its head pointing down.'

Sipambaniso Manyoba Kumalo himself made the occasion into another bid to rewrite the symbolism of the Matopos:

> The piece of ground where the Chief is being buried is associated with sacred memories of the past and we trust that the Government will set this area aside as a burial place for the descendants of Lobengula and for other Africans who deserve well of their country.

The echoes of Rhodes's will were quite deliberate. As the *Bantu Mirror* commented in its editorial:

> Those European leaders who deserve well of their country are laid to rest at the World's View, in the Matopos, with Cecil John Rhodes.... The request that is to be made on behalf of Africans, if accepted, will make Entumbane Hill to Africans what the World's View is to Europeans, a national shrine.

This was the Matabeleland Home Society at its imaginative height, bringing together all the elements of central Matabeleland's elite and basking in temporary official

---

[57] Security Report, Matobo, n.d., S 728/6A/4.

[58] Interview with Thenjiwe Lesabe, Bulawayo, 24 August 1988. Mrs Lesabe's maternal grandmother, with whom she stayed in Whitewaters, was a cousin of Nzula.

approval, seeking to embellish the myth of the special relationship between the Ndebele and Cecil Rhodes. As Ginyilitshe put it: 'When we saw the European coming to our country long ago, they looked warlike, but we have discovered many good things they have done for us', like inventing the idea of a national shrine.[59] Nzula's daughter, Violet, later became guardian of Mzilikazi's spirit at Entumbane.[60]

Nzula was thus important in linking Whitewaters to the imaginers of Ndebele identity in Bulawayo. He also made connections with the Wenlock alliance of tradition and modernity. He attended Sigombe Mathema's installation as chief of the *inqameni* in 1950 and was the next speaker after Daniel Dube, whose sentiments he warmly endorsed. Yet, for all this, Nzula could not play the role taken by Sigombe – or even by Matole – in Wenlock. Ndebele chieftaincy was not enough in itself to focus identity or provide leadership in the Matopos. In Whitewaters, and in the Matopos as a whole, the more important role was played by the Sotho commoner Nqabe Tshuma.

Nqabe owed his prominence not to breeding but to character and Christianity. He was born in the early 1890s, son of Xhosa Tshuma, a member of the *Isiziba* regiment, who fought against the whites in 1896 and attended the *indabas* with Rhodes. Xhosa Tshuma's forbears were Sotho. The family lived north of the Matopos, either on or close to what became the Rhodes Matopos Estates, and Xhosa acknowledged the authority of *Induna* Mapisa who was one of the chiefs who came out of the Matopos to reside there. His four sons – Nqabe, the eldest, and his brothers David, Sampson and Sidakwa – went to the London Missionary Society school in Figtree. 'The Tshumas were very hard working people', remembers S. M. Ncube of Hope Fountain, 'a very leading family.' David became carpenter and store owner; Sidakwa was a lay preacher both in Figtree and Whitewaters; Sampson became a headmaster. He was famous for his lavish houses, first a brick house at Whitewaters and then the headmaster's house at Gohole school, a house as fine as any in the western suburbs of Bulawayo and with a door imported all the way from Umtali. 'I want people to see I've got money', he used to say. These improvers arrived in Whitewaters in 1923 when the family was evicted from its ancestral land. They then transferred their loyalty from *induna* Mapisa to Nzula.[61]

Thenjiwe Lesabe, who went to Whitewaters when she was eight years old to stay with her grandmother and to attend the school there, remembers both the community and her neighbour, the middle-aged Nqabe of the 1940s:

[59] *Bantu Mirror*, 1 July 1944.

[60] In this capacity she became involved in 1982 in the strange case of the Bulawayo dentist, Frank Bertrand, who approached her in order 'to try to obtain the state of Matabeleland by using spiritual methods.' Bertrand wanted an independent Matabeleland stretching as far 'as the Indian Ocean. This was the extent of the old kingdom of the Rozwis.' Violet 'favoured federal government but not violence.' This was invented Ndebele tradition at its most extraordinary. *Chronicle*, 9, 17, 19, 20 March 1982.

[61] I construct this picture of the Tshuma family from interviews with Nduna Ncube, 13 July 1988; Dazana Ncube, 13 July 1988; Zephaniah Moyo, 14 July 1988; Nduna Ncube, 15 July 1988; J.R.Danisa, 15 July 1988; Obadiah Mlilo, 3 August 1988; S.M.Ncube, 3 August 1988; Sidakwa Tshuma, 6 September 1988; Benjamin Nyathi, 6 September 1988. Nqabe himself at various times suggested that his father had lived all his life at Whitewaters, or that he had moved from close to Mzilikazi's grave, but I take these as symbolic statements and have chosen the testimony of his brother and his widow.

It was a very progressive, organised community.... You can still identify my group that grew up in that place at that time by our behaviour. Moral behaviour, hard work. Because in that area, really, I never heard of thieves, I never saw so many illegitimate children as I see now ... Nqabe's first wife had died and left him with two children. He stayed for many years without marrying. He was more committed to the education of his children, to hard farming and to the interest and welfare of the people of Whitewaters, because the setters wanted to remove them to different places.... He had come from a Christian family and in terms of civilisation of those days his home background was very much that of the elite of the time. The Christians of the time. Because they had houses with whitewash, outside and inside, they had windows, they had wire gauze for mosquitoes and things.... They were very much involved in gardening. Then he took a second wife. He really had hidden qualities, Nqabe. He didn't talk much, Nqabe. Nqabe, you can describe him if you look at Churchill's pictures, you've never seen him smile. Nqabe was like that.... Talked very little but very hard-working. He was not a material man. He was not interested in his own profit.[62]

So far, so sober. But Mrs Lesabe prefaces this account of the dedicated, industrious Nqabe with the words: 'He was a very cheeky man.' Like Daniel Dube, Nqabe was a Christian but a dissident Christian. Before settling down with his children in White-waters he had a past of radical activity, just as he was to have a future. The late Reverend Joshua Danisa, who knew Whitewaters and Nqabe well, gave me this account of him:

Nqabe was a very strong nationalist. He had been to Johannesburg and got this influence. Other people were afraid to oppose. But with Nqabe, anything that was proposed he would at once oppose it. He was very good at raising oppositions.... He was very strongly London Missionary Society. He was not very educated. He went to work in Johannesburg for a short time. Then when he came back he went to Inyati as a student, though he was a full-grown man. He was the cause of the trouble at Inyati when there was a strike over food that caused a lot of problems. He was expelled and that was the end of his education. After that he stayed in Whitewaters as a farmer.[63]

Danisa's account is amply confirmed by both oral and archival sources. During his stay in Johannesburg in the late 1920s Nqabe became a member both of the National Congress and the Industrial and Commercial Workers Union. 'He wasn't afraid to speak out', recalled the late Obadiah Mlilo. 'He believed that this was a British colony.'[64] On his return to Rhodesia, Nqabe was recruited as a teacher at Hope Fountain and sent to Inyati school for teacher training. There he spoke out, leading both the strike of 1931 and the bigger outbreak of 1932. Reverend W. G. Brown ran Inyati with a heavy hand – 'We could not help likening Inyati to the growth of a successful slave plantation in the United States', wrote one of the other missionaries sent to report on the situation, 'with the big house of the owner gradually dominating the whole position'.[65]

Faced with protest coordinated by Nqabe – a man among boys – Brown called in the police and Native Department officials, and there were skirmishes and injuries. On 5 April 1932 the Superintendent of Natives, Bulawayo, arrived at Inyati to investigate –

---

[62] Interview with Thenjiwe Lesabe, 24 August 1988.
[63] Interview with J. R. Danisa, 15 July 1988.
[64] Interview with Obadiah Mlilo, Mpopoma, 3 August 1988.
[65] A. J. Haile to A. M. Chirgwin, 24 April 1932, LMS, South Africa, 1932–3, SOAS.

'This has become an obsession with Mr Brown', he wrote. 'Discipline, discipline and still discipline. What a Regimental Sergeant Major he would have made!' The Superintendent of Natives went to the church, where the 'boys' were assembled and called on them to speak. There was a nervous silence, broken by a confident Nqabe. Describing Brown's threats to thrash them, and the arrival of police with sjamboks, Nqabe told how they had scattered into the bush. But then 'we said to ourselves "Let us go into the Church; if we are to be thrashed, it is better to be thrashed in the Church than hurt on the hills".'[66]

The Inyati strike lost Nqabe his teacher's post but made him famous throughout the London Missionary Society connection. He came to be thought of as a Voice, as a quiet man ready to speak out. My informants spoke of him in terms of this paradox. Nqabe was short – 'he was not a big man but his action made him a big man. He was a real leader of the community like Nkomo is today'; 'He was just a commoner but they chose him because of his ability. He was the spokesman of the whole community.'[67] Nqabe's organisation, *Sofasonke*, one informant told me, meant 'We'll die together' or 'What Nqabe says we'll follow it to the end.'[68] Nqabe believed in the promises of Rhodes – 'he believed that this was a British colony.' He was ready to work with the Matabeleland Home Society. But his experience took him beyond Nzula's political horizons. He was able to make connections with more radical forces; with Masotsha Ndhlovu, once of the ICU and now of the African Voice Association. He was able to think of identity in terms much wider than a regimental community. Though a Sotho, surrounded by Banyubi, and close to the still-functioning shrines of Mwali, he conceived of the Matopos identity as Ndebele:

Tshuma was not from the Nguni group [the late Obadiah Mlilo told me] but Sofasonke did not have ethnicity in mind when they claimed to be Ndebele. They saw themselves as a group of people living together, not divided by ethnicity. The word Ndebele is a difficult one, since to make up the Ndebele you need not only Nguni, but Kalanga, Banyubi, everything. With the people in the National Park the question of tribe did not come in at all. It would have been divisive for one to say he was Banyubi and another to say he was Nguni. They were one community.[69]

As the Native Commissioner, Matobo, put it in his report on the year 1948, 'with the approval of a large number native Nqabe Tshuma has become their accredited representative in spite of the fact that they look to Nzula as their chief.'[70] Even the *inqameni* of Wenlock looked to Nqabe when the going really got rough. The July 1949 petition of protest against the deposition of chief Matole, quoted in Chapter 4, came from 'The People of Wenlock Block, Gwanda District and Some People of the Matopo National Park, Nqabe Xosa, Chairman and Organising Secretary'; was written in

---

[66] Superintendent of Natives, Bulawayo to Chief Native Commissioner, 30 May 1932, *ibid.* Predictably enough the next 'boy' bold enough to speak was Daniel Dube from Wenlock.

[67] Interview with Nduna Ncube, Bulawayo, 15 July 1988; interview with Jacob Minindwa Moyo, Numbane, Gulati, 21 July 1988.

[68] Interview with Benjamin Nyathi, 6 September 1988.

[69] Interview with Obadiah Mlilo, Mpopoma, 3 August 1988.

[70] Annual Report, Matobo, 1948, S 1563.

Nqabe's hand; and addressed as from Whitewaters school. Its recurrent phrase, 'We refused', accurately reflected the temper of Wenlock, but it also came straight from the heart of a man who 'was very good at raising oppositions.'[71]

The Official Onslaught on the Matopos

What I have been describing in this chapter and the last has been a double process: ethnic simplification taking place simultaneously with social differentiation. People in Wenlock and throughout the Matopos came to regard themselves primarily as 'Ndebele' rather than as belonging to a whole series of smaller identities. This 'Ndebele' identity, moreover, transcended and ideally abolished caste distinctions between *zansi*, *enhla* and *holi*. An imagined community was coming into existence. At the same time, however, fresh differences of status and attitudes arose: between chiefs who owned thousands of cattle and families without any cattle at all; between agriculturalists who followed only the rules of Mwali and the aspirant peasant modernisers, with their enthusiasm for the guidance of agricultural demonstrators; between the great majority of the illiterate and the literate teachers and clerks; between the storekeepers and bus owners and the unskilled labourers; between the majority of women, who spent their time in domestic, agricultural and pastoral labour in the Matopos and the very many men who lived for some of the time in urban centres in Rhodesia and South Africa. Class or generation or gender conflict might well have come to replace linguistic, cultural, 'ethnic' conflict. Indeed, there is plenty of evidence from the Matopos, as elsewhere in Matabeleland in the 1930s and 1940s, of acute tensions between the generations, or of violent disputes between men and women over changing gender divisions of labour. And, as we shall see, class tensions emerged sharply in the later 1950s and early 1960s.[72]

In the 1940s, however, these disparate interests were brought together by a common threat. The threat to their very possession of the land, the threat of depopulation and destocking, united the spokesmen of the Matopo Reserve (who wanted to send demonstrators to the Sahara) with the leaders of *Sofasihamba* in Wenlock (who wanted to follow official guidance on the road to agrarian prosperity). It united the cattle-rich and the cattle-poor. No African interest in the Matopos stood to gain from official policy in the 1940s or could be bought off as a 'loyalist' group, as had happened even in the 1890s. There were certainly differences in the degree of opposition. Some were prepared to move if offered enough reasonable land elsewhere; others were determined to hold on to the Matopos at almost any cost. Some, like Daniel Dube of *Sofasihamba*, longed to work with the state if only it was prepared to accept the relative autonomy of African modernisers; others, like Nqabe Tshuma of *Sofasonke*, were determined to

---

[71] The petition is in S 1542 C6. The Chief Native Commissioner's response to it – a predictable refusal of the demand to reinstate Matole – was sent to Nqabe on 13 September 1949. In February 1950 the Acting Native Commissioner, Matobo, recommended 'the deposition of Chief Nzula and the eventual absorption of his following by Chiefs Bafana and Mako.'

[72] For gender tensions see Terence Ranger, 'Murder, Rape and Witchcraft: Criminal Court Data for Gender Relations in Colonial Matabeleland', Institute of Commonwealth Studies, London, February 1994.

'refuse' and 'object' to whatever the state proposed. Some prominent men, like chief Nzula, preferred to lead (if at all) from the back; others, like Nqabe Tshuma, were prepared to lead from way out in front. As the contest became more bitter, so the radicals gained more support and the moderates began to count the cost.

But at least a leadership was in place by the 1940s which could respond in one way or another to white attacks on the people of the Matopos. And from the mid-1940s the whole of the Matopos came under intense pressure. This was partly because the Land Apportionment Act was at last to be fully implemented, and there was much lobbying by newly successful settler farming interests to ensure that this was done. It was partly because the Natural Resources Board and other conservationists were calling for action about erosion and the danger to water resources. And it was partly because new ideas about National Parks required the depopulation of the western Matopos. These factors in combination affected every part of the hills.

In Wenlock, as we have seen, the *inqameni* were first told to quit by a company and were then left in uncertainty after government bought the land. North of Wenlock in the Matopo Reserve there was increasing official interference with the market-gardening economy. In 1944 there was an attempt to reallocate arable land in the Reserve. At 'a well-attended meeting' at chief Bafana's kraal the scheme was explained to a resentful African audience. 'The Africans complained that 6 acres for man and wife would not be sufficient to grow their grain requirements.'[73] In January 1946 the Acting Agriculturalist, Bulawayo Circle, told the people of the Reserve that 'indiscriminate ploughing, cutting and burning of good timber' must cease, and 'this shifting agriculture must stop without delay.' He 'personally ordered three or four lands to be stopped immediately and instructed the Agricultural Supervisor to report to the LDO if ploughing continued here.' Ploughing nevertheless continued with permission from the Native Commissioner, since the people had to be allowed to live.[74]

Indeed, as government conservation schemes developed over the next ten years, both officials and the residents of the Reserve concluded that their implementation was totally inconsistent with the continued functioning of African society there:

> By far the greater portion of this area is totally unsuited to agricultural activities [wrote the Provincial Native Commissioner] and in practice it would be impossible to grant farming rights.... To grant rights would in effect be tantamount to condoning practices which are anathema to good conservationists. In brief, the inhabitants are perforce cultivating the only land that is capable of cultivation since solid rock cannot be tilled and yet the land that is being put under the plough should be preserved and not utilised.[75]

The Native Commissioner, Matobo, urged that 'while the population [of the Matopo

[73] Land Development Officer to Native Agriculturalist, Bulawayo, 6 September 1944, S 2386/3959.
[74] Acting Agriculturalist, Bulawayo Circle, to Acting Provincial Native Commissioner, Bulawayo, 10 January 1946, S 160 SC44/46. In his annual report for 1948 the Native Commissioner, Matobo, reported that in the Matopo Reserve 'there is an actual antagonism towards the Agricultural Demonstrators' because of 'the limitation of the size of the lands and the prohibition of the cultivation of sponges.' S 1563.
[75] Provincial Native Commissioner to Assistant Secretary, Administration, 7 October 1955, 'Matopo Reserve', Box 100356.

Reserve] remains any conservation work would be a complete waste of effort. In fact proper conservation measures there would render the area untenable by the present population.' The conclusion he drew was not that conservation should be abandoned but that the population should be removed, despite the protection given to them by Reserve status.[76]

Meanwhile, cattle could be destocked, but this too was vigorously opposed. In 1946

a large protest was held by Natives from the Matopo Reserve prior to the culling. Some advocated direct disobedience to the Regulations.... Eventually after much discussion the meeting agreed that compliance was the correct course, but that a strong protest should be registered. Many Natives are still suspicious and allege that there is plenty of land available for settlement, and that the real trouble lies in the fact that the Europeans are allowed too much country for ranching purposes.[77]

Thereafter the people of the Matopo Reserve resisted both destocking and the fencing of *vleis* and felt profoundly insecure as rumours spread that they might themselves be removed. The Reserve came to be described in official reports as 'difficult' and 'disaffected'; its spokesmen became militant supports of *Sofasonke*. Late in 1949 the Provincial Native Commissioner travelled through the area in a jeep – 'no other type of vehicle could negotiate the roads'. He noted that 'these Natives have proved hostile to demonstrators and advice. It will be necessary to deal sternly with these people as soon as machinery is ready.'[78]

At the same time, the residents on Absent farm, which lay between the Reserve and Matopo Mission and which had been thought secure for African occupation, were told that they were on private land and must leave it at once. Notice to quit was first given in 1943 and some residents left then; others refused to go. In November 1947 the Native Commissioner called people together to tell them to move and this injunction was repeated in March 1948. But urbanised radicals like Nduna Ncube and Frazer Gibson Sibanda were determined to resist. As Sibanda later testified, he remained on the land 'without anybody's authority because I felt that the country was part of the country which was promised to the natives by Mr Rhodes. I would not go even if that signature were bearing two stamps – one from here and one from England.' He was arrested and sent to prison.[79] Intelligence analysts reported that:

Certain minor upsets occurred in the Matobo District during September 1948. Several natives who refused to leave a farm on which they had been living were dealt with by the Native Commissioner. The excuse that the land had been given to them and their parents by Cecil Rhodes was again brought to the fore. Monies are being collected by certain members of the Matabeleland Home Society in order to employ legal assistance in connection with any further instances of being ordered to move their homes.[80]

The Absent activists were regular visitors to Whitewaters and to *Sofasonke* rallies.

[76] Native Commissioner, Matobo to Provincial Native Commissioner, 26 October 1955, *ibid*.
[77] Annual Report, Matobo, 1946.
[78] Quarterly Report, 30 September 1949, Provincial Native Commissioner, Bulawayo, S 1618.
[79] Evidence of Frazer Gibson Sibanda, 22 March 1949, S 1561/46.
[80] Quarterly Intelligence Review, 30 November 1948, S 482/517.

The last African tenants were now evicted from the Rhodes Matopos Estate by Charles Murray – 'they used the place essentially for beer drinks for Bulawayo', he claimed. 'They had colossal nests.' By the mid-1940s the Experimental Farm run by Murray covered 45,000 acres of the Estate; 85,000 acres was in the hands of white tenants.[81] Further south, the long exercise of expelling Africans from the *mapani* veld was reaching a climax. All the hitherto unalienated Crown Land south of the Matopos, reported the Native Commissioner in 1948, had now been sold to whites. At the moment these lands were 'fully occupied by natives and stock and these farms are required by Europeans who already own the land. These natives will have to be moved soon.'[82]

But what really brought Nqabe Tshuma into the fray, caused the formation of *Sofasonke*, and thus enabled the coordination of the whole Matopos protest, was the threat to the National Park itself. In the mid-1940s the long official paralysis over the western Matopos came to an end and the period of active intervention began. As we have seen these official incursions were the end result of many forces and had been long in the making. But in the eyes of the people of the Matopos they were the work of one man, Charles Murray of the Matopos Government Experimental Station. 'We objected, sir, because Mr Murray came', said one *Sofasonke* activist in 1949. 'Is Mr Murray going to close all these European farms that have been like that [eroded] by things that God causes to come? Is he going to do that?' And another protested that 'someone we did not know was initiating these things. That was Mr Murray.... Had Mr Murray not existed we would not have been here today.'[83]

We have seen in Chapter 2 that Murray represented the self-confidence of the new agricultural and ecological expert. We have seen that his calculations of the 'carrying capacity' of land underlay the evictions of many African populations and the destocking of their herds. As manager of the Rhodes Matopos Estates he evicted many Africans.

It was this self-confident man who determined the fate of the African occupants of the National Park. In 1940 the Forestry Department relinquished its oversight to Murray, 'who had always shown himself extremely keen on National Park matters, [and] was able to exercise a certain supervision, which we, as a Department, had never been able to do.'[84] In 1944 the Irrigation Department were made formally responsible for the Park but they continued to work through Murray, as the man 'on the spot'. So empowered, he set out to draw up a scheme for the reclamation of the land. The Park was to be divided into five sections, each of which would in turn be 'rehabilitated' over a period of five years. This rehabilitation would involve drastic reduction of both human and cattle populations; demarcation and reallocation of arable lands; the construction of conservation works and the building of dams, using labour from the very Africans who were going to be displaced. At the beginning of 1945 J. H. Grobler was appointed as the first Ranger of the National Park and Murray at once ordered him to carry out a detailed survey and to begin the allocation of land. The charmed isolation

---

[81] Evidence of Charles Murray, 21 March 1949, S 1561/46.

[82] Annual Report, Matobo, 1948, S 1563. The Native Commissioner added that no land was available for the resettlement of these families.

[83] Evidence of Kutjekaya, 18 March 1949; evidence of Tshoko, 16 March 1949, S 1651/46.

[84] Evidence of E. J. Kelly Edwards, 21 March 1949, S 1561/46.

in which the African inhabitants of the western Matopos had lived was coming to an end. The first section marked out for rehabilitation was Whitewaters.

In January 1946 Grobler and Murray jointly signed the survey report and the set of accompanying recommendations. The 1,952 African families resident in the Park were to be reduced to 403; only 73 families out of 337 were to remain in Whitewaters; cattle were to be destocked to 4,030; cultivation of *vleis* and sponges was to be prohibited; all arable land was to be protected by conservation works; scenic roads, dams, rest-camps and hotels were to be constructed.[85]

Murray's report became the benchmark of the new conservationist movement in Rhodesia. Indeed others outdid him in their severity. J. Savory of the Irrigation Department thought him too lenient, since his scheme envisaged the cultivation of all possible land which had not been fenced off, a level of exploitation which would 'preclude the proper development of a National Park.' Savory urged that only 200 families be allowed to remain with 2,000 head of cattle, all their male heads being employed full-time in essential National Park work:

> This area is a National Park and not a Native Area. There is no precedent that I know of for populating and stocking a National Park to its full capacity and then trying to develop it as a facility for the whole population of the country.... This would be impossible.[86]

The Chairman of the local National Parks Committee, R. H. N. Smithers, Director of the National Museum in Bulawayo, also suggested the figure of 200 families, though in a last-ditch attempt to have both his scientific cake and his romantic one he thought the 200 could best be deployed picturesquely: 'We would like to see Natives living in the National Park as they did before the arrival of the European.... It would be very nice to see them in their pristine condition.'[87]

But the general tenor of official reports was by now very different and reflected a different sense of history. In April 1947, a month after *all* families in the National Park had been given notice to quit, the Under Secretary, Lands, wrote to justify removing people from the hills down into the fly-infested low veld:

> Many natives are accustomed to living on high veld, among mountains or hills (such as Eastern Districts and Matoppo National Park).... It must not be forgotten, however, that the Natives are, historically speaking, new arrivals in the country and that most of the tribes entered from [regions where] conditions are hotter, while the Matabele came up from Zululand, and there is no reason why they should not acclimatise themselves to the warmer areas of the Colony in the way that they have acclimatised themselves to the cooler areas.[88]

African Opposition in the Matopos

Whitewaters was the chosen battleground for the policy of 'rehabilitation' – and for eviction into 'warmer areas'. It was selected as the first section to be redeemed; Grobler

[85] J. Savory to Chairman, Matopos Commission of Inquiry, 15 March 1949, S 1541/46.
[86] *Ibid.*
[87] Evidence of R. H. N. Smithers, 22 and 23 March 1949, S 1561/46.
[88] Under Secretary, Lands to Secretary, Agriculture and Lands, 3 April 1947, S 1194/190/1.

himself lived there; due to the motor road it was visited by many other officials. Because of this, the only detail given of social and environmental change by those who urged the clearing of the Matopos was their account of what had happened in White-waters. District Commissioner D. G. Lewis, for example, noted the 'enormous number of women [who] have kraals of their own' in Whitewaters, 'which was not the case years ago.' These were 'women who live separately from their husbands, unmarried women, divorcees or wives of absent husbands.' Women will not figure in my account as officers of *Sofasonke* but we must think of the great crowds which gathered for rallies at Whitewaters as partly female.[89]

These 'grass widows' were said to attract large numbers of non-residents to beer drinks every weekend. Not many of these women owned cattle of their own. But cattle had increased in Whitewaters. Dip Supervisor F. J. Heros found 146 holders of dipping books there in 1933; by 1949 there were 96 new book holders. It was hard to tell how many of the cattle belonged to chief Nzula and had been lent out by him, but it was clear that there were many independent cattle owners, some holding as many as 80 head.[90] Grobler found it almost impossible to demarcate six-acre blocks of arable land, as called for in Murray's plan, because fields in Whitewaters were scattered all over the area in plots ranging from half an acre to two acres. Whitewaters was thought of as 'untraditional' – because of all the women kraal heads, and the spread of individual cattle owners. It was thought of as endangering the environment because of the increase in cattle and the cultivation of *vleis*. Yet it was admitted that cattle were not dying of poverty; that 'widows' in Whitewaters were able to maintain themselves; that rich crops were grown.

Murray's arrival in Whitewaters not only brought two different sets of assumptions about society and environment into conflict; it also brought the two great figures of the struggle for the Matopos face to face. Nqabe Tshuma at once 'objected'; under his leadership the Whitewaters community refused to supply any labour or to collaborate in any way; through his formation of *Sofasonke* all the peoples of the hills were brought together; first the Matabeleland Home Society and then the African Voice Association were drawn from Bulawayo to great rallies in the hills. All this had two effects. Immediately, it greatly delayed the implementation of Murray's plan. Refusal of labour and collaboration meant that hardly any of the 'rehabilitation' work could be carried out; by 1949 hardly anything had been done to reallocate land, protect *vleis*, destock or depopulate in Whitewaters, and nothing at all in the other four sections. The publicity given to *Sofasonke* focused the attention of all Matabeleland and seemed to symbolise the general opposition to eviction and destocking; the government had to pay serious attention to the issue and to concede a full Commission of Inquiry in 1949. In the longer term it both politicised and ultimately divided the population of the Matopos and in this way laid the foundations for the rise of nationalism in the hills.

We can trace the successful resistance of Whitewaters largely in the words of the

---

[89] Evidence of D. G. Lewis, 21 March 1949, S 1561/46.
[90] Evidence of F. J. Heros, 22 March 1949, *ibid*. The overall National Park figures showed that there had been an increase from 590 owners in 1933 to 1,121 owners in 1949.

protagonists. The first tactic was to ignore all orders given to them. Grobler began his work in 1945, travelling around with one of the Demonstrators. As Murray put it later, the people of Whitewaters were:

> as backward but more difficult than cultivators in other parts of the country. During 1945 when the Ranger was going round on survey he had this Demonstrator with him and he spoke to them and I think in 99 out of every 100 cases they deliberately refused to move anywhere.[91]

Grobler himself described how he 'tried to stop them' cultivating the *vleis* – 'they have not taken any notice, though.' He asked the Native Commissioner to reinforce his instructions. The Commissioner 'told them that they should not plough in the vleis as they damaged the water supply and also about cutting trees. Shrubs they could cut but not big trees.' Yet 'it can still be noticed that they are still cutting trees about 6 feet from the ground and that they still plough vleis.'[92]

The next tactic was to refuse to supply labour for the planned work on roads, dams, and reclamation of *dongas*. All this work had to be done by 'hand labour or by ditchers and oxen.' Hundreds of men were needed but by the beginning of 1946 only 20 had turned out to work 'from the whole Park'. Murray was later asked whether it would not have been 'wiser to ask for labour after you had decided who would be moved out and asked for the labour from those who were willing to do it? Isn't it somewhat unjust to ask people who are going to be moved out in any case to provide labour in an area where they will receive no benefit from it?' No, replied Murray, this was 'a deliberate, straightforward refusal to work.' It was unprecedented; the Ranger and the Native Commissioner had approached the chiefs and headmen in the ordinary way; such an approach had never failed before. But in 1945 and the following four years there was an almost total boycott:

> With the exception of a small amount of road making ... and one or two dams [said Murray in 1949] nothing has been done. It has not been possible to move any of the inhabitants or to move their lands to more suitable areas and it was not possible to do any of the protection work because no labour was available.[93]

In October 1945 the first of a series of confrontational meetings took place in White-waters. The people were told that they were now under Murray's jurisdiction rather than that of the Native Commissioner; they were given formal notice to leave; they were instructed to pay their dipping fees to Murray before they left. In Nqabe Tshuma's account:

> The Native Commissioner said: 'Today I want to outline the conditions under which you live in the Matopos. The Matopos were not meant for Africans but for the white people. There are too many people and too many cattle and the result of this is that we will have to send many people away. I want to give out conditions to those who remain behind. They must dig dams and dig dips. You will get a new attendant from Mr Murray. He will bring six Demonstrators. You will no longer plough the swamps. There will be forced labour and you will have to destock cattle.'

[91] Evidence of Charles Murray, 21 March 1949, S 1561/46.
[92] Evidence of J. H. Grobler, 22 March 1949, *ibid.*
[93] Evidence of Charles Murray, *ibid.*

We replied: 'This is the first time we hear of this and we are surprised, because we have been living here under the impression that we were given this place by C. J. Rhodes. If we leave here this shows that we have no future in our own country. We find that we are unable to carry out your instructions, and we will not build up the dams and we will no longer prepare the roads.'[94]

From this moment on the resistance of Whitewaters was explicit rather than implicit and Nqabe was the unchallenged spokesman of the people. In May 1946 the Native Commissioner sent to chief Nzula a demand for 200 labourers. He also told the chief and headmen: 'You are too many. People will have to be sent away'. In Nqabe's words: 'We objected to this conscription and asked for a week within which to present our case to the Native Commissioner.' A week later another meeting was held at Whitewaters. The Native Commissioner told them that 'the only people who could stay here were those who would agree to be conscripted.' Cattle would have to be destocked:

> We objected to this, as we do not like to sell our cattle without reason, as they are our living. We were also told that we could not plough in the valleys but only on the hills. Before this time we could plough wherever we liked. We told the Native Commissioner that we objected to all the foregoing proposals as the land had been given us by Rhodes.[95]

On 1 July 1946 the Chief Native Commissioner arrived in Whitewaters, determined to break this unprecedented defiance. He combined firmness with a concession calculated to divide the opposition. Those families who could prove continuous residence from pre-colonial times could stay. But government was determined 'to remove all the squatters who had infiltrated into the Park'; these were to leave by August 1947. It was up to the 'indigenous' inhabitants to provide lists of who fell into each category. Those who stayed would have 'to enter into labour agreements by which they would give a certain number of months work per annum at current wages to enable us to carry out the necessary soil and conservation in the Park.' Anyone who did not provide labour would have to leave, and 'if none of them would play they could all go as there are thousands of other indigenous Natives who would be only too pleased to enter the Park and conform to the provisions of Government Notice No.45 of 1946.'[96]

Nqabe's reponse remained defiant. 'We refused. We failed to obey the orders because we were forced to go on dam construction work and it was forced labour.... They had made an intimation that we were going to leave the area which we considered was ours.' He told the Chief Native Commissioner:

> We feared that the dams to be constructed would ultimately be taken over by the Government as had happened in the case of the dipping tanks, and that in any case we did not see the necessity for dams as there was plenty of water. We told the Chief Native Commissioner that we were still not prepared to agree and proposed to send a deputation to the Governor.[97]

In fact, the administration was bluffing. In July 1946 no land had been made available for the resettlement of people from the Park; the August 1947 deadline was soon

---

[94] Evidence of Nqabe Tshuma, 16 March 1949, *ibid*.
[95] Affidavit by Nqabe Tshuma, 8 November 1948, S 1561/46.
[96] Secretary for Native Affairs to Webb, Low and Barry, 28 November 1947, S 1561/46.
[97] Nqabe's affadavit, November 1948; evidence of Nqabe, 16 March 1949, *ibid*.

extended to August 1948, and then to August 1949. Moreover, the Native Department's legal powers to destock and evict were very doubtful. They had relied on the customary submission and did not know how to handle defiance. Still, after the Chief Native Commissioner's visit Nqabe realised that it was now necessary to organise and to extend opposition. This was why he created *Sofasonke*.

Organisation was required locally, to prevent anyone from claiming to be an 'indigenous inhabitant' and denouncing others as 'squatters'. It was required to extend the resistance from Whitewaters to the Matopos generally. It was also required in order to raise funds so that lawyers could be engaged. In addition, a Matopos organisation was needed so that it could deal on equal terms with the Matabeleland Home Society or the African Voice Association. By September 1946 *Sofasonke* was able to engage Bulwayo solicitors Webb, Low and Barry to represent them. An official minute summarised the instructions which *Sofasonke* gave to the lawyers:

> The Natives declared that the late Rt. Hon. Cecil Rhodes had promised them in 1897 at one of the 'Peace Indabas' following the Rebellion, security of tenure in the area which is now known as the Matopo National Park. They further declared that they had already been removed from land originally occupied by them in the area consequent upon its alienation by the Government to certain Europeans, and they had therefore withdrawn to the Matopo Hills, also forming part of this area.... The Native Commissioner informed them that other land would be made available to those to be removed and they would be selected from among the more recent arrivals in the hills, so that the original inhabitants would be disturbed as little as possible. They were not satisfied and replied that they were all tribal followers of the original Chiefs to whom Rhodes made this promise.[98]

On 28 September Webb, Low and Barry wrote the first of a long series of letters to the administration, complaining that the Park residents 'have been accustomed to a peaceful and undisturbed possession' but were now 'labouring under a pronounced sense of insecurity and unrest.'[99]

Oral testimonies allow us to reconstruct the character of *Sofasonke*. It is remembered as very much a Whitewaters affair. 'They met at Nqabe's home in most cases', says Thenjiwe Lesabe,

> or else under a tree. There was a big tree there. This *Sofasonke* was not organised by the ICU or the African Voice. This was purely by Nqabe. On Wenlock there was *Sofasihamba*, but all those were offsprings of *Sofasonke*. Because that was the founder organsation, *Sofasonke*. It spread all over the whole Matopo area. It meant, 'We will die together, come what may, we will stand together, come what may', and for sure they did.

In its heyday people came to Whitewaters from all over the hills. Nduna Ncube of Absent, in the north-east Matopos, recalls that 'the will of the people' was expressed by *Sofasonke*. 'Oh! I loved *Sofasonke*.... The Chairman was Nqabe Tshuma. Then came committee members: Malila Nyathi, Nkhutshwa Mgutshini, then Sileni Moyo, then there was Mbejana Nyoni, a headman, and Japhet Moyo, the interpreter.' Some of

---

[98] Memorandum, Secretary for Native Affairs, 8 January 1949, *ibid*.
[99] Webb, Low and Barry to Native Commissioner, Matobo, 28 and 29 September 1946, *ibid*.

these committee members represented the people of the Matobo Block or of other areas outside Whitewaters. *Sofasonke* 'proved a force for resistance. It was at the forefront as it seemed to enlighten the people. It became a general word.' The leaders of *Sofasihamba* – Johnson Sigodo Dube, Mawogelana Kumalo and Sigombe Mathema himself – came to Whitewaters for the great *Sofasonke* rallies.[100]

The urban-based organisations, like the Matabeleland Home Society and the African Voice, were called in by *Sofasonke*. 'Rural people would organise a meeting', recalls Patrick Makoni, bus entrepreneur and President of the African Voice, 'and ask us to go, so we were drawn into the country. People would use taxis, buses, anything to get to these meetings.' Matopos informants told us that 'we worked together' with these other organisations, but 'we didn't join because we were already under *Sofasonke*.' Sipambaniso Manyoba of the Matabeleland Home Society or Benjamin Burombo of the African Voice advised on strategy, collected evidence and contacted lawyers. *Sofasonke* raised the funds. 'It was almost everybody, every adult, every grown-up man, they came together.... They put money together, they sold a lot of their animals.' Jacob Mnindwa Moyo, whose father Mbejana was a headman on Matobo Block, 'taking over from those Mathemas', and a member of the *Sofasonke* executive, recalls that he was himself then working in South Africa. 'I used to pay the subscription of £1 a month. Nearly everybody used to contribute. It was sort of fees for the solicitor.'[101]

Sofasonke proclaimed an 'Ndebele' identity and insisted on the promises of Rhodes. But many of its firmest adherents were conscious of their pre-Ndebele identity, and stated their case against eviction in more traditional terms. Denge Sibindi, messenger to one of the sub-shrines of Njelele, was a member of *Sofasonke*, knew Nqabe very well, and expressed the association's case thus:

> Sofasonke demanded that we should not be evicted from this place because the hills are fruitful. Once it rains a bit everything sprouts. There are now no fruits, honey, etc. It might be because of the eviction of the people.[102]

This remarkable organisation was able to exert considerable pressure on the administration. The Matopos were not just another disaffected rural area. They were the ceremonial heart of the Rhodesian nation. Early in 1947 plans were being made for a Royal *Indaba* at Fort Usher, where the chiefs of Matabeleland would greet King George VI and Queen Elizabeth. The *indaba* became the subject of much controversy. The Matabeleland Home Society protested against the appointment of the Chief Native Commissioner to read an address of welcome on behalf of Africans; the Ndebele chiefs disliked their new uniforms – 'red and blue nightshirts' which 'made them look like Mahommedans'. There was barely muted disaffection:

> One old chief refused to meet the King looking like 'lo butcher boy' and wore his leopard skin over his 'robe'. He also saluted the King in the manner of his people which was a stout gesture

---

[100] Interviews with Thenjiwe Lesabe, 24 August 1988; Nduna Ncube, 15 July 1989; Mark Dokotela Ncube, 30 August 1990.

[101] Interviews with Patrick Makoni, 19 July 1989; Nduna Ncube, 15 July 1989; Japhet Ngwenya, 30 August 1988; Jacob Mnindwa Moyo, 21 July 1989.

[102] Interview with Denge Sibindi, Whitewaters, 26 July 1988.

of independent thought.... A great number of Chiefs protested very strongly against the Address.... The Matabele did not like to capsize the Address on the spot but felt that it was their duty to behave and show their loyalty, [but] it was an act of injustice for the Chief Native Commissioner to say that Africans had come to an agreement on the Address.[103]

In this strained atmosphere *Sofasonke* was able to extract a promise of negotiation from the Chief Native Commissioner, by reporting that 'there is some inclination among the affected dwellers in the National Park to ventilate their grievances on the occasion of the Royal Indaba.' Thereafter, when he proved resistant to *Sofasonke*'s request for a commission of inquiry, Webb, Low and Barry wrote in January 1948:

You will recollect that at your request our clients cooperated fully and loyally in regard to the visit of His Majesty the King and refrained from embarrassing the Government in any way at that time. They are at a loss to understand the lack of response to their spirit of cooperation. It has always been the wish of our clients to settle this matter by negotiation. This is still their wish but we are directed to inform you that any attempt to implement your directions will be met by immediate measures.[104]

In February 1948 the solicitors met with the Chief Native Commissioner and a new official proposal was made. This offered security of tenure to 'those who can prove residence in the area up to and including 1896 and their direct descendants' and also to all those 'who have been removed from the present Rhodes Estate farms to the National Park.' In return Webb, Low and Barry would seek to persuade their clients to enter into labour agreements. In April the lawyers met with *Sofasonke* to recommend these terms. In May a *Sofasonke* committee

advised us that the feeling of the vast majority of dwellers in this area is against the terms of settlement. They are, it would appear, quite prepared to take the matter to higher authority even against our advice.[105]

Even now that the royal visit was safely out of the way, and the solicitors won over to the Native Department's point of view, *Sofasonke* still had means of putting pressure on the Rhodesian administration. In April 1948 the general strike had taken place in Bulawayo; thereafter Benjamin Burombo's African Voice Association had turned its attention from the town to the grievances of the rural areas. Government were very worried for fear that Burombo would be able to take up the sensitive and symbolic issue of the Matopos. This meant that Nqabe could afford to strike more radical positions. During 1948 he extended the boycott on everything official by calling upon people in the Park not to accept smallpox inoculation; he called 'frequent meetings both general and of the "inner circle".' These meetings refused to supply any names for removal, and the Native Commissioner believed that 'the leaders are obviously hoping that *all* will remain and that there will be a State within a State.' Nqabe led the opposition to destocking:

Nqabe said they were overstocked and overpopulated because some of the Europeans have large farms and turn the natives off the land they have occupied for years.... There is a spirit

---

[103] *Bantu Mirror*, 29 March, 26 April, 3 May, 7 June 1947.

[104] Webb, Low and Barry to Sipambaniso Manyoba, 31 March 1947; Webb, Low and Barry to Secretary, Native Affairs, 13 January 1948, S 1561/46.

[105] Webb, Low and Barry to Chief Native Commissioner, 24 February and 7 May 1948, *ibid.*

of nationalism among these people and the situation calls for careful handling if the link between nationalism and communism is not to be found.[106]

In November 1948 Nqabe declared that he would accept no settlement save one that gave security of tenure to everyone; abandoned destocking; and ensured 'that we can plough where we like.'[107]

All this was infuriating for the Native Commissioner – 'the Natives on the National Park are temporarily untouchable', he complained. But it was doubtful whether he possessed legal authority because of the still uncertain status of the Park, and 'to give orders in regard to cultivation, especially to these people in their present mood, without being able to enforce them, would be foolish.' And then Nqabe turned the last screw and 'enlisted the help of Burombo.'

'During November 1948 matters worsened', ran the March 1949 quarterly intelligence review, 'and a mass meeting of Natives was called for by Burombo, a known professional agitator, on the 12th December in the Matopos.'[108] In fact the December 1948 meeting was addressed by Sipambaniso Manyoba and Nqabe himself, as well as by Burombo and Masotsha Ndlovu of the African Voice. It was attended by 'several thousands of Matabele, chiefly those residing in the Matopo Reserve and the Matopos National Park and the Matopo Crown Land.'[109] The *Chronicle* added that there were also speakers from Gwanda, Plumtree and the Fingo Location, one of whom

> reminded his listeners that both Cecil Rhodes and Mzilikazi were buried in this area and they felt they should be allowed to carry out the ideas both of them held for the development of the African people. Another speaker pointed out that it was because Cecil Rhodes had been respected as an honest man he had not been in danger of his life when he entered the Matopos for the Rebellion indaba. They could not understand why his word was not respected.[110]

But it was the speeches of Burombo and Masotsha Ndlovu which made the most impression. Dokotela Ncube, who was there with the *Sofasihamba* delegation from Wenlock, remembers to this day that

> Burombo told us about the quarrel between the squirrel and the mountain as to which was the most powerful. The mountain said I am so much larger than you. But the squirrel said, I can sit on top of you and you cannot sit on top of me. Ah, it was the beginning of nationalism.

Nduna Ncube, who was there from Absent Farm, remembers Burombo asking the meeting whether they knew his tribe. 'My ethnic group is African because I am black.'[111] The quarterly intelligence report reported Burombo as 'charging the Europeans and Indians with making use of the Africans to amass wealth and discarding the African to a life of poverty and misery.' Masotsha 'called on the Africans to wake up and fight for their rights.' It was heady stuff.[112]

---

[106] Annual Report, Matobo, 1948, S 1563.
[107] Affidavit by Nqabe, 8 November 1948, S 1561/46.
[108] Quarterly report, 12 March 1949, S 482/517.
[109] *Bantu Mirror*, 1 January 1949.
[110] *Chronicle*, 13 December 1948.
[111] Interviews with Nduna Ncube, 15 July 1989; Mark Dokotela Ncube, 30 August 1990.
[112] Quarterly report, 12 March 1949, S 482/517.

The main fruit of the gathering was a petition 'prepared and approved by the meeting' calling on the Governor 'to appoint a Commission to inquire into their dispute'. By this time, government was prepared to accept the need for a commission after all. This was because of the situation in Matabeleland as a whole. As the Native Commissioner, Matobo, urged: 'Politically the natives of this district cannot be ignored.' Webb, Low and Barry pointed out to the Chief Native Commissioner in an 'urgent' letter in August 1948, that

> the claims of the National Park dwellers appear to have become fairly widely known, at least in Matabeleland, and there have been indications of support for the cause from native dwellers in other areas. Our fear now is that if drastic eviction proceedings are taken open defiance may result and this may become widespread.[113]

In August the Native Department were still refusing to consider an inquiry. But the meeting of 12 December changed official minds and in January 1949 the lawyers were informed that a commission would be set up after all.

The thinking behind this change of mind is clearly set out in a Native Department memorandum of 8 January 1949:

> Burombo is a dangerous man and at this meeting there was no disguise of their defiance of authority in regard to their removal from the Matopo National Park. The situation is a most dangerous one, as there is not the least doubt that to effect their removal a considerable force prepared to protect itself would be necessary. This action can only be viewed with the utmost gravity as the Native population of Matabeleland, a large proportion of whom are without security of tenure of land themselves, is watching events in the Matopo National Park with the keenest interest. It is the considered opinion of this Department that the forcible eviction of these people will be met by open defiance amounting to rebellion, probably extending over the greater part of Matabeleland with repercussions the extent of which it is difficult to estimate.

The Matopos, with their unique symbolic significance and their unprecedented show of defiance, might become the focus of another uprising.

The memorandum took it for granted that people would have to be moved from the Matopos, but it also thought that *Sofasonke* had made some strong points. Indeed, it accepted much of the historical case based on an 'Ndebele' identity. 'These people have a natural affiliation with this area because it contains the burial places of Mzilikazi and Cecil Rhodes, and by reason of their long residence as a tribal entity.' There was no possibility of the people moving to Gwaai Reserve – the only land available at the time – two hundred miles distant, undeveloped 'and completely strange to this people'. They must be given land in Matobo district itself and this would have to be bought by government. 'It must be clearly emphasised', the memorandum concluded, perhaps a little late in the day, 'that we cannot continue to move the Natives of Matabeleland as one would pawns on a chess board without incurring the danger of serious disturbances.'[114]

[113] Webb, Low and Barry to Chief Native Commissioner, 2 August 1948, S 1561/46.
[114] 'Comments on the Petition from Natives of the Matopo National Park', Secretary for Native Affairs, 8 January 1949, S 1561/46.

6

The Movement to Mass Nationalism in the Matopos

1949–66

The National Park, 1949–52: Protest and Eviction

The Commission of Inquiry into the Matopos National Park began its hearings on 16 March 1949. It was awaited with high excitement and confidence by *Sofasonke*. On 10 March there was a large Voice meeting in Bulawayo, which was attended by chiefs from Manicaland as well as from Matabeleland. One of the chiefs was Nzula, who was accompanied by Nqabe Tshuma and five other *Sofasonke* activists. Burombo attacked evictions from 'white' land, particularly the threatened evictions from the Park, and said that if thousands of Africans came to the city to protest the traffic would be disrupted; the gaols would not hold them; and government would be forced to concede.[1] To give a foretaste of such mass demonstrations Burombo took the delegates on a march from the Location into Bulawayo, which is still remembered by *Sofasonke* supporters as a landmark in the development of national consciousness:

> We walked to the place in four lines. The whites were greatly concerned.... When we got to the Provincial Commissioner's office, sergeant Mkwananzi asked us our problem. We told him we wanted to talk to the whiteman. He replied that he could not see both the chiefs from Mashonaland and Matabeleland at one meeting. What should have happened is that the chiefs from Mashonaland came separate from those of Matabeleland. Then Burombo asked us: 'There is the problem, masses, what do you say? The white man wants to separate us'. We said we did not want to be separated at all. We wanted to see him as one group. Then he asked: 'Is it Burombo who says that?' We shouted that it was us and not Burombo. We left along Fort Street and turned into 3rd Avenue to Stanley Hall. We were singing 'Nkosi Sikelela Africa' all the way.[2]

When the Commission hearings began there were further demonstrations of *Sofasonke* enthusiasm, though this time emphasising an historic Ndebele rather than a

---

[1] CID Native Affairs Reports, Memorandum 35, 16 March 1949.
[2] Interview with Nduna Ncube, Bulawayo, 15 July 1989.

national identity. 'The High Court was crammed to the corridors yesterday', reported the *Chronicle*,

> by Matabele tribes-men from the hills, some in their black war bonnets and nodding white plumes, some in skins and tails. Among them were natives who were actually present at the Matopos 'indaba' and sons of the chiefs to whom Rhodes' promise was made.

Next day the paper described how

> white-haired, goatee-bearded old Matabele warriors, who had fought the British with Lobengula's impis in 1893 and again during the rebellion of 1896, tottered into the witness box of the Bulawayo High Court yesterday to give evidence of a promise made to them nearly 50 years ago.[3]

The old men in the gallery, and their juniors among the *Sofasonke* membership, listened intently as the story of the promises of Rhodes was recounted. The late Ndaniso's testimony was laid before the Commission; Nzula testified; Nqabe made a long deposition, claiming to have attended the *indabas* at which Rhodes made his promises, and appeared before the Commissioners twice; Sipambaniso Manyoba of the Matabele Home Society gave evidence; so did many *Sofasonke* activists. To the gallery their testimony seemed conclusive. One listener remembers that Nqabe was unshakeable:

> On the day of the Commission of Inquiry they asked him, 'You say Rhodes gave the land to your people! Where were you? Did you hear with your own ears?' They asked Ngungu Mnkandla whether boys of Nqabe's age were allowed to attend an indaba.... Then they asked Nqabe how he attended meetings of the elders. He replied saying, 'Because my father liked me and I was the first born.' They wanted to prove that he was a liar. But they failed to humiliate him. It was like he had come as a ... like when Joshua Nkomo came, as if he was god-given.

But best of all, this listener remembers, was a *Sofasonke* committee member, Nkhutshwa Mgutshini, who 'spoke until he cried tears.... They asked him who had told him about the Land Apportionment Act and all that and he replied that he had been taught by his suffering.'[4]

To this day old men in the hills remain convinced that African witnesses proved their case before the Commission, dismissing the lack of written evidence as beside the point. 'Even if Rhodes had written', says old Qazane Ncube, 'it would have been hidden. Do you think they would have told us? Our people were not yet educated. But when the issue went to court it was agreed that Rhodes had given that assurance.'[5] *Sofasonke* and its followers left Bulawayo certain that the Commission would find in their favour.

In fact the Commissioners' reactions were rather different. They *were* worried by the lack of written evidence. Asked to make a search of his records, the Chief Archivist

---

[3] *Chronicle*, 17 and 18 March 1949; *Bantu Mirror*, 19 March and 23 April 1949. The Commissioners themselves remarked in their final report that 'at least one hundred and fifty natives occupied seats in the Court, a further hundred or more standing in the passages.'

[4] Interview with Nduna Ncube, Bulawayo, 15 July 1988.

[5] Interview with Qazane Ncube, Nyombane, 13 July 1988.

came up with virtually nothing even though, as we have seen, there was plenty to be found. The Commissioners were left with the feeling that *some* promise had been made but they did not know what. Naturally enough, they thought it improbable that at the very moment he was so anxious to get Ndebele fighting men out of the hills Rhodes would have promised them secure tenure there. But they could find no evidence that Rhodes had promised security of tenure on the flat lands either. Leases survived which granted parts of Rhodes's own land to various whites, but no document set out African entitlements. The Commissioners did not believe that Nqabe had been present at the *indabas* or had first-hand evidence of what was said.

By contrast with the lack of documentation for the earlier period, the Commissioners were presented with a mass of data on the previous decade. Every step along the way of *Sofasonke*'s defiance was recorded; so too was every plan made by Charles Murray and other conservationists for the 'rescue' of the hills. And in the end this was what proved decisive. What the Commissioners took to be proven and incontestable science won out over unproven and doubtful oral history.

The victory of science was powerfully assisted by the attitude of *Sofasonke*'s counsel, Paddy Lloyd. During the Commission hearings, Nqabe and the others 'had their belief in the lawyer'; later they were told by a Native Commissioner that 'You people were wrong in choosing a lawyer. You should have explained yourself'.[6] Nqabe's eventual belief that Lloyd had been 'bought' by the government was certainly wrong. The record of the Commission shows that Lloyd fought hard for what he believed to be the best interests of his clients. But there is no doubt either that Lloyd fought for his own view of the matter rather than for the position of *Sofasonke*.

From the beginning the lawyers made it clear that they would not associate themselves with any *political* stance. Thus on March 11 *Sofasonke*'s solicitors, Webb, Low and Barry, met at the Chief Civil Commissioner's office to swear statements to lay before the Commission. Burombo appeared with the chiefs who had attended the Voice rally the previous day. All of them, including Chiefs Makoni and Mtasa of Manicaland, offered to swear statements on behalf of the people of the Matopos. The solicitors at once said that if Burombo interfered any further they would withdraw from the case.[7] On 14 March Burombo and Masotsha Ndlovu addressed another Voice meeting in Bulawayo, suggesting that the Commission should also inquire into destocking and forced labour as well as evictions. When the Commission began its hearings Lloyd dissociated himself from any connection with those who claimed to represent the people of the Matopos politically.[8]

By this Lloyd meant to save his clients from Burombo. But he also thought that *Sofasonke*'s own position was unreasonable and that it could not possibly be argued

---

[6] Interview with Jacob Mnindwa Moyo, Gulati, 21 July 1988.

[7] Native Affairs Memorandum 35, 16 March 1949.

[8] Statement by Lloyd, 21 March 1949, S 1561 46. Lloyd said that press reports that Burombo was seeking an inquiry were 'most unfortunate'; there was 'no connection' between Burombo and the legal representatives; and that he had himself been ignorant of any previous connection between Burombo and *Sofasonke*. The *Chronicle* for 21 March had reported that the chiefs had authorised Burombo to draw up a petition on land.

before the Commission with any chance of success. In his opening submission Lloyd noted that his clients wanted him to raise many issues which he thought were 'not relevant, but the Commissioners will realise the difficulty of impressing on the Native mind as to relevancy.' He added that he would state his clients' position on conservation 'because I act as a mouthpiece', but that he himself believed they were bound by the Natural Resources Act like everyone else.[9]

Indeed Lloyd's fundamental disagreement with *Sofasonke* lay in their contrasting visions of the landscape of the hills. *Sofasonke* argued that the Matopos could contain its present population of people and cattle; that its members were progressive farmers; and that the abundant water resources of the hills enabled them to be so. Lloyd's view was very different. He had a house close to the Matopos – 'a very beautiful, big house on quite a high rise'[10] – and often travelled through them. As he told the Commissioners in a written 'historical account':

> There can be little doubt when one stands back to take an impartial view of the matter that the Government fears as to the deterioration of natural resources in the area are fully justified. I have had an opportunity of visiting some parts of the area and have seen the deterioration of land which is proceeding apace. There can be no doubt unless this process is arrested by large-scale anti-erosion work that in the course of time the Consultants themselves will be faced with the necessity of leaving the area in large numbers in order to subsist.... Despite the assertion of Consultants that the water resources are adequate, in my view ... it is obvious that such water resources have deteriorated and will continue to do so.... Thus far I am in agreement with the experts and with Government policy in the matter.[11]

It was Lloyd himself who offered to the conservationist, Dr West, Pasture Research Officer at the Matopos Research Station, the proposition that ecology was 'a very exact [science] very recently developed'.[12] So in his closing address to the Commissioners Lloyd accepted that they would be guided by the opinion of the experts, 'based as it is on scientific knowledge and practice'. Despite this, his clients held that 'every man should have his holding'; that there was no need for destocking, nor for contours. Questioned by the Commissioners, Lloyd admitted what he thought was the illogicality of *Sofasonke*'s position. 'You are putting it to me on a logical and reasonable basis', he replied, 'but that is not always the basis on which I have to act. Reason, in these matters, comes naturally to us in dealing with them, but it is only sixty years since this country was occupied.... It is impossible to get certain of them to understand'. He then argued his own position – that official intervention had been too impatient; that the inhabitants of the hills had a cultural affinity with them; that those evicted should be resettled as close to the Matopos as possible. With excessive optimism he thought that

---

[9] Lloyd's opening address, 16 March 1949, S 1516 46.

[10] Interview with Japhet Ngwenya, Tshatshani School, 30 August 1988. According to Japhet, Lloyd was widely known to Africans in the Matopos by the name of his house.

[11] Annexure B, 'General Correspondence', S 1561 46. As early as 4 March 1947 Webb, Low and Barry had been prepared to 'concede that Government's fears as to the deterioration of natural resources in this area through overpopulation and overstocking are justified.'

[12] Cross-examination of Dr West, 18 March 1949, S 1561 46.

they would readily agree to the reduction of the number of families in the Park area and the removal of those the Commission recommended should be removed ... if the Commission could recommend that land should be given immediately south of the hills.[13]

The Commissioners reported on 16 May 1949. Broadly, they accepted Lloyd's position. They found that the Ndebele had not occupied the hills before 1893; they found no evidence that Rhodes had promised security either in the hills or on his own land; but it seemed 'that some sort of statement was made at one or more of the indabas which led the Natives to think that they and their heirs would be given security of tenure somewhere in or near their homes.' They did not endorse 'allegations of arbitrary action on the part of officials' but recommended the appointment of an Assistant Chief Native Commissioner since 'the problems of Matabeleland differ materially fron those of other parts of the country'. They found that the Park was badly eroded and much overpopulated both by humans and by stock.

They recommended that 500 families be allowed to remain in the National Park because of 'the attraction of long established families to this particular area.' A further 1,500 families would have to move. There should be legislation constituting a National Park and preserving 'places which are sacred to the Natives' as well as protecting natural resources and establishing tourist 'amenities'. The families remaining in the Park should be given security of tenure 'subject to their complying with the conditions of occupation' and should have written confirmation of this. Those to be removed should be settled on surveyed but currently unalienated farms in the Matopos foothills – Gwandavale, Shentsheli, Cliveden, Shama, Ove North, Famockwe, Mount Francis and Mavure; or on farms alienated but currently unoccupied – Mount Edgecombe, Alalie, Over South, Maleme, Manyoni, Sibuntuli, Malaje and Kozi. These should be bought by government. So too should Absent farm, which should be added to the Matopo Reserve, and the Matobo Block, which should be added to the area of the National Park. The remainder of those moved from the Park should be accommodated on Prospect ranch, south of Gwanda.[14]

Between May and 29 September 1949, when the Commission's findings were finally reported to the Matopos Africans, an uneasy peace reigned in the hills. The longer the delay, the more *Sofasonke* felt that it had won. But in fact the delay was caused by the government's attempts – and failures – to implement the detailed recommendations of the Commissioners for purchase of land. At the same time the advocates of a developed National Park were making their own plans.

Sofasonke's prestige soared as for five months there were no more eviction orders, destocking programmes, or forced mobilisations of labour. The Native Department was holding back and there was no sign of any effective National Parks authority.

A report in the *Bantu Mirror* in early September, however, gave notice of things to come. 'Matopos to Become Tourist Resort' it proclaimed: 'Almost completely in-accessible at present, Matopos will in a few years become an important name on the tourist map.... Drives will be constructed to link the most attractive features and rest

---

[13] Lloyd's closing address to the Commission, 23 March 1949, S 1561 46.
[14] Report of the Commission of Inquiry, 16 May 1949, S 1561 46.

huts will be provided.' It added reassuringly, and in the spirit of the old romantic conception of the Park, that 'no-one desires that the Natives should be removed altogether, for their picturesque thatched huts, their cattle and their crops add features of interest.'[15]

Meanwhile government had been considering the Commission's Report. It was presented to Cabinet on 2 June 1949 by the Minister of Native Affairs who recommended acceptance. Inquiries began about the farms recommended for purchase. In August it was reported that most of them were not for sale since their owners had plans for development. In the middle of August the Secretary of Native Affairs urged that an announcement soon be made.

> The Natives are anxiously awaiting the news of the result.... The matter is of some importance to the Native Administration, owing to the very restive attitude among Natives throughout the country.

The final decision should be announced by the Minister himself at a meeting in the Park. At the end of August a memorandum to the Governor reported that government had bought Prospect ranch on which 900 families could be settled; it had not bought the farms close to the Matopos, but was still seeking to buy Absent and Kozi which would be added to the Matopo Reserve. All this meant that Lloyd's pleas for land immediately south of the hills and the Commission's attempts to respond to them had failed. Those removed from the Park would have to travel to the arid flat lands of Prospect Ranch, and when Prospect was full they would have to go yet further afield, to the forests of Lupane or the deserts of Wankie in northern Matabeleland.[16]

A speech was drafted for the Minister of Native Affairs. It summarised the general findings of the Commission; emphasised that 'this land that you have been occupying is now a National Park and you really have no legal right to remain there'; but announced as a great concession that 500 families – 'the oldest inhabitants and their heirs' – might remain in the Park with security of tenure conditional on their observing conservation regulations. 'The Commission you asked for say the majority of you must move'. The Minister admitted that 'the Commission did, in fact, recommend that the Government should try to buy farms immediately south of and contiguous to the Park ... but it has been found that the owners will not sell.' Nine hundred families would therefore have to move to Prospect. Government was still trying to buy Absent farm. 'I rely on you to cooperate with the Native Commissioner in telling him which are the original inhabitants of this area'; otherwise 'he will just have to go into the area and choose five hundred without any regard as to who they are and how long they have been there.'[17]

The *Bantu Mirror* thought that the government had done 'what was humanly possible' and had acted 'very wisely' in allowing 500 families to remain. Most African urban politicians hastened to withdraw their support for any further protest by *Sofasonke*, advising it to accept the decision as final. But the *Chronicle*'s report was more

[15] *Bantu Mirror*, 3 September 1949.

[16] Memorandum to Cabinet, Minister of Native Affairs, 2 June 1949; Secretary, Native Affairs to Secretary, Cabinet, 8 August 1949; Secretary, Native Affairs to Minister, Native Affairs, 15 August 1949; Memorandum to Governor, 23 August 1949, 'Matopo National Park', P 3623, Box 35596, National Archives.

[17] Minister of Native Affairs' speech, 29 September 1949, *ibid*.

perceptive. The thousand Africans who heard the Minister's speech made 'no demonstration of any kind'. But they asked many questions of the Native Department officials present and also of their advocate, Lloyd. 'The Africans were evidently deeply disappointed and dissatisfied with the decision', concluded the *Chronicle*. 'But they listened in complete silence to the news that most of them must shortly pack their bags.'[18]

The silence was soon broken by many raised voices from the rocks. The government had badly mishandled the grievances of the inhabitants of Absent farm, which had been articulated so effectively by Frazer Gibson Sibanda. Having announced on 29 September that it was buying Absent it later had to admit that it had failed to do so. The *Sofasonke* activist and resident on Absent, Nduna Ncube, recalls that:

> We were very serious about this. We faced Mr Lewis, the Native Commissioner of that time. We told him, you are hating us, because were were given this and you are depriving it from us. Ah! he had it very thick.

Later the owner of Absent gave them notice of eviction. 'We refused to leave. Then he got us arrested for cutting trees at his farm, grass.... We told them that ever since we were born we have been doing that.'[19]

In the Park itself Nqabe at once began to collect money for a delegation to travel to appeal to the High Commissioner in South Africa or even to the King in Britain.[20] On 18 December 1949 a meeting was held at Whitewaters. Chief Nzula was present with headmen Gwezha and Bejini; Nqabe was there, with other *Sofasonke* officials; so, too, were 'their European legal advisers'. 'It was not understood why 500 people would be allowed to remain while 900 had to go.' Speakers 'insisted on being granted permission to interview His Majesty the King'. Lloyd told them that the King had no power to intervene, but 'eventually realised the futility of trying to instil reason in his hearers and informed them that he would have nothing more to do with them.'[21] The late Obadiah Mlilo attended this meeting as interpreter for Lloyd. In August 1988 he remembered the final breach between *Sofasonke* and its advocate:

> Lloyd argued that it was no use going ... Then they said, 'We see now that Advocate Lloyd has been bought by the other side'. Lloyd said, 'Very well if you think I have been bought, go to Greenfield, a very clever lawyer, and see what he will tell you.' Nqabe refused, saying Greenfield too had been bought. They said they would go to Britain themselves.[22]

Nqabe never got to Britain. *Sofasonke* now fell back on itself. Africans in the Park were urged neither to inform the Native Commissioner who the oldest inhabitants were, nor to accept orders of eviction, nor to carry out the conditions of their residence permits. For their part, Native Department officials 'aimed at defeating people like Burombo, Nqabe, and Mcutshwa who are dissuading natives from carrying out the declared policy of the Government'. The Native Commissioner drafted conservation

---

[18] *Bantu Mirror*, 8 October 1949; *Chronicle*, 30 September 1949.
[19] Interviews with Nduna Ncube, Bulawayo, 15 and 28 July 1988.
[20] Native Affairs Memorandum 41, 21 October 1949, S 482/517.
[21] Native Affairs Memo 43, 24 December 1949, S 482/517.
[22] Interview with O. Mlilo, Mpopoma, 3 August 1988.

regulations which laid down that cultivation should only take place 'in accordance with methods approved by the Land Development Officer' and that no-one should cultivate 'any natural springs nor vleis'. It would be a criminal offence for anyone to persuade a permit holder to ignore these conditions; it would also be a criminal offence to refuse to leave the Park when told to do so.[23] It was decided to bring criminal cases against *Sofasonke* leaders whenever it was possible to do so. Early in 1950 Frazer Gibson was successfully prosecuted for 'criminal defamation' of Native Commissioner Lewis over his handling of Absent.[24] Nqabe was living on borrowed time.

Early in April 1950 the CID reported that Nqabe was 'the leading agitator and stay-put disciple', alleging at the same time that he 'has a record of insanity'. The Acting Native Commissioner thought that people ready to move to Prospect were subject to 'continued rumours that they will be beaten up and their cattle killed'. He was convinced that Nqabe was behind it, and vowed to give the volunteers protection.[25] When on April 11 the first group of families chosen for involuntary removal were notified by the Native Commissioner that they must leave in July they flatly refused to go. The CID believed this was because of a meeting held in Whitewaters on 9 April at which Nqabe had addressed a hundred people, and Malila had read a letter from Burombo advising the people to ignore any notice to move. It was noted that Nqabe, 'leader of the rebels', had not yet been served notice to quit.[26]

On May 7 Nqabe held another meeting at Whitewaters where the matter was put to the vote. Forty people attended, half of them women. Twenty-five voted not to move and the rest abstained. Meanwhile other *Sofasonke* activists were sounding out opinion at cattle dips throughout the Park. There was a majority everywhere for defiance even though 25 volunteers left for Prospect on 25 May without interference. The Native Commissioner held many meetings at Nzula's, 'most of which have fallen flat.'[27]

The Chief was adopting his usual stance of passive resistance. Nzula was 'a quiet old man', remembers Japhet Ngwenya,

> very quiet.... He would say, 'Alright now, we have been told that we are moving from here and we are going somewhere else.' Just leave it like that and the people seemed to take it up on their own, without very much involving the old man. And yet at times you know he would make his feelings known clearly to the authorities. When people said no, they would come to him and say, 'Alright, now we are taking you and sending you to that place and your people will follow you', and he said, 'Alright, now you can't take me, I can't leave my people. If the people can leave this place, then I'll go.'[28]

On 21 July Nzula and Nqabe were summoned by the Native Commissioner to explain

[23] Native Commissioner, Matobo to Provincial Native Commissioner, 3 November 1949, 'Matobo National Park', Vol. 2, P 3623, Box 35596.

[24] Captain, Staff Officer, BSAP to Commissioner of Police, 7 February 1950 and minute by Chief Native Commissioner, *ibid.*

[25] Native Affairs Memo 45, 11 April 1950; Acting Native Commissioner, Matobo to Provincial Native Commissioner, 27 April 1950, P 3623.

[26] Native Affairs Memo 46, 4 May 1949.

[27] Native Affairs Memo 47, 31 May 1950.

[28] Interview with Japhet Ngwenya, Tshatshani School, 30 August 1988.

why the people ordered to leave were making no preparations to do so. Nzula asked why these particular people had been singled out for eviction. Two days later headman Bejani and some 90 of his followers attended a Matabeleland Home Society meeting at his kraal where it was resolved that 'we'll only go if *all* go.' Bejani went to the Native Commissioner and asked for a letter to permit him to take his protest to the Governor. He was refused and the police had to be called before he would leave the office.[29]

Faced with this opposition by chiefs, headmen and the leaders of *Sofasonke* – so different from Lloyd's prediction of collaboration – the Native Department was doubtful how to proceed. It was worried that it had no powers to evict until the Land Apportionment Act was amended. It decided that there should be no forceful eviction until then. The amendment was promulgated on 11 August and on 23 August the Chief Native Commissioner met with local officials to determine strategy. They noted that 43 families had moved to Prospect voluntarily but that a further 140 were refusing to go. The Native Commissioner reported that 100 men had come to tell him that they would not leave. 'They also refused to leave his office, but when later he told them of the powers which will be given him under the new Act, the deputation left'. The meeting agreed that the Native Commissioner should at once return to the Park and 'send for the selected men from each of the five areas who were to move this year' and give them three weeks' notice under the new Act.[30]

On 6 September the men were served with these notices; they refused. Nqabe came with 40 followers to tell the Native Commissioner that the people were prepared to meet force with force:

> We are under the Government and the Government can do whatever it likes with us. But we wish to let the Native Commissioner know that we don't want to see Africans amongst those who will come to evict us. If Africans join that group and come we shall fight them and kill them. It will be another rebellion as it was in 1896. But if Europeans alone will come to evict us we shall die like dumb sheep.[31]

On 4 October the Secretary for Native Affairs visited the Park, found that the notices to leave were being ignored, and instructed the Native Commissioner to prosecute 23 men under the amended Act. The Act as amended laid down that people could be evicted 14 days after notice had been given, and the Secretary had arranged for the police to act. The Act also provided that 'the owner' of the land could 'demolish the huts' after their occupants had been removed. Admittedly it was unclear in this case who 'owned' the National Park but he hoped that difficulty might be overcome.[32]

The machinery of repression was being assembled. On 11 October 17 men were due to appear in court for prosecution under the amended Act. They did not appear

[29] Native Affairs Memo 49, 21 July 1950; Memo 50, 23 August 1950.

[30] Minutes of a meeting on the National Park, 23 August 1950, P 3623, vol. 2.

[31] Native Commissioner's memo on meeting of 11 September 1950, *ibid*. Several other men spoke in addition to Nqabe. Mfazo complained that they were being evicted even although 'at the High Court, Bulawayo, we were told that the National Park belongs to us. Books of old times were consulted and disclosed that Cecil John Rhodes gave this land to the inhabitants in it today.'

[32] Secretary for Native Affairs to Secretary, Agriculture and Lands, 4 October 1950, *ibid*.

although their names were called. The police were sent out to fetch them and found the men standing quietly outside. Nqabe was among them, urging them to leave, and saying that 'he did not care about the police'. Nqabe was arrested – 'there was fighting. His clothes were torn as they tried to remove him from the crowd'.[33] The next week Nqabe appeared in court himself.

> When charged, Nqabe said all he knew was that he was chairman of an African organisation at Matobo and he was surprised that instead of making that charge against him he was being charged with urging the accused to evade arrest. He was only one of the people of Matobo and was among them as such.

But he was sentenced to ten weeks in prison.[34]

The administration hastened to take advantage of his absence. On 21 October the Chief Native Commissioner approved forced removal. Perhaps in view of Nqabe's warning, it was decided that only European police would be employed 'for actual eviction'. But the Police Commissioner pointed out that 'from a Police point of view it would be very difficult to evict the whole 76 families at once, and it is suggested that a few be evicted to start with, when it is hoped that others who have to move will follow peacefully.' Only a small number of unarmed Police would be used 'as it is agreed that force is apt to beget force.'[35] The carefully prepared operation was carried out in November. The recalcitrant men were carried off on lorries to Prospect. 'There is no doubt we had to act as we did', wrote the Chief Native Commissioner, 'unpleasant though it was.'[36]

The authorities felt that they had broken National Park resistance. In March 1951 the CID reported that 'Nqabe appears to have lost face since his term of imprisonment and is a much subdued man' and that the general attitude in the Park was much 'less truculent'.[37] Families on the 1951 list for removal – in which Nqabe himself was included – received a notice from the Native Commissioner: 'You have seen for yourselves from what was done last year that the Government intends that its order shall be carried out. Therefore I advise you to proceed to Prospect forthwith and obtain a site of your own choice.' But at this point Benjamin Burombo and the Voice Association intervened.

The Voice provided lawyers for Africans faced with removal from 'European' land in Filabusi and the courts found that the eviction orders were faulty. Yet another amendment to the Land Apportionment Act would be necessary before further forced removals could be carried out on any large scale. The 1951 Annual Report for Matobo recorded the consequences. It stated that 210 families had been moved from the National Park to Prospect and a further 313 families had been removed from Crown

---

[33] Interview with Nduna Ncube, 15 July 1989.

[34] *Bantu Mirror*, 21 October 1950; Native Affairs Memo 50, 23 August 1950 and 51, 20 October 1950.

[35] Chief Native Commissioner to Native Commissioner, 21 October 1950, P 3623, vol. 2.

[36] Assistant Native Commissioner, Matobo, to Native Commissioner, 21 October 1950; Compol to Dispol, Bulawayo, 22 October 1950; Assistant Chief Native Commissioner to Commissioner of Police, 26 October 1950; Chief Native Commissioner to Provincial Native Commissioner, 27 November 1950, *ibid.*

[37] Native Affairs Memo 53, 19 March 1951.

Lands in the Matopos to the forested and feverish Lupane district in northern Matabeleland. But 49 men 'who had been ordered to go refused and have been left for the time being.' These included Nqabe himself and 'most of the remaining agitators in the Park'. 'After the debacle at Filabusi' no action could be taken against these men. But once the Act had been amended again and 'the new regulations are water-tight ... we can move these agitators'. Everyone else would then cooperate; and the people already moved to Prospect would be freed from propaganda and agitation. The Voice had been holding meetings in the Matopo Reserve and the Park and Chief Nzula was 'a mere figurehead ... a pawn in the hands of various societies and agitators'. The Native Commissioner looked forward with relish to the restoration of order, the removal of the 'agitators', the collapse of the societies, and the deposition of Nzula.[38]

At the same time his report revealed the ambiguities of the whole process. Cultivators in the Park and the Matopo Reserve had been making increasing use of chemical fertilisers, which were effective in well-watered soils but useless in the arid lands to the south. 'One individual we had to evict from the Park to Prospect had over 30 bags of good white maize', while 'the maize crop in the south was a total failure'. There was abundant water to supply progressive agriculture in the hills and all that needed to be done was to fence sponges; the south, on the other hand, was entirely dependent on artificial water supplies. Africans in Matopo Reserve were building admirable brick houses by contrast once again to the shabby huts of the south. It was little wonder that there was reluctance and resistance as Christian progressives were moved out of the hills.[39]

It took a long time to perfect and pass the new amendment to the Land Apportionment Act. It was not until August 1952 that the authorities were ready to act on a large scale, though in October 1951 three kraal heads were evicted, 'while a small force of police stood by'. One of them was Nkutshwa, whose tearful eloquence had so impressed the African gallery at the Commission hearings.[40]

The long delay gave Nqabe time to recover his self-confidence and influence over the people. On 10 November 1951 he invited two lawyers from Bulawayo to a meeting at Prospect where he urged people to claim compensation for losses incurred during their eviction.[41] He worked closely with the Voice Association, whose prestige had greatly increased after the Filabusi success. In particular he took up the case of Nkutshwa and the others evicted in October 1951. In February 1952 the Voice made further representations to government through its legal representatives. It raised a wide range of issues, and added:

> Another instance is the case of some of the Matopo Park Natives. The Prime Minister will know the bitterness caused here. While conceding once again that in some cases such bitterness arose from blind reasoning, there are rumours that cause grave disquiet. At the urgent request of some of the Matopo natives, the Voice's legal advisers, Advocate Davies and Messrs Ben Baron and Partners, visited a new settlement on Prospect Farm in November

---

[38] Annual Report, Matobo, 1951.
[39] *Ibid.*
[40] Native Affairs Memo 59, 31 October 1951.
[41] Native Affairs Memo 60, 28 November 1951.

1951. The conditions were appalling and Mr Davies was greatly upset. The only water supply was a borehole which by dint of most arduous pumping gave a trickle of water equal to about half a gallon a minute. The well was dry; there was no thatching grass within miles; and the area was most isolated. It was stated that intransigent Africans had been forcibly moved together with their families, and their wives and young children and 'dumped' in the veld. The temper of the women-folk in particular was most dangerous.[42]

In the same month the Governor issued a proclamation under the new amendment to the Land Apportionment Act listing all those 'squatters' who were required to leave the National Park by 31 August. One of those listed was Nqabe.[43]

This time the government fully intended strong action against all those who did not observe the August deadline. But rather than suppressing opposition, the proclamation sparked further criticism. On 15 March the *Bantu Mirror* published a letter from the Christian progressive, James Chatagwe of Matopo Mission, attacking the proclamation as ungodly:

> When God created the land he did not say this is to be occupied by this man and not by that one ... The Bible says that the first shall be the last and the last the first.

Chatagwe followed this up with his critique of official conservation policy which I quoted above. He was influenced by conditions in the nearby Matopo Reserve, where 'traditional' intensive cultivation of the wetlands could produce abundant crops but where large-scale ploughing had destructive effects.

Nevertheless, his letter was at once taken up by an ecological 'expert', G. McNeilage, who was working in the Reserve and who thought that 'the only beings who could possibly share Chatagwe's views are those fellows with tails who live in the hills and bark their protest at civilisation.'[44]

Meanwhile plenty of protest was still being barked by human voices in the hills. On 13 July *Sofasonke* delegates met with delegates from Filabusi and Rhodesdale – the two other areas most threatened with evictions and in which the Voice was also active. Burombo took them to the meeting of the All African Convention, where urban African politics from many different associations and trade unions were meeting to seek to achieve a common mind of the proposed Central African Federation. The Convention participants were scandalised at the intrusion of rough rural politics into their deliberations and the delegates from *Sofasonke* and the other areas were ordered to leave. They gathered instead in the Bulawayo Location where Burombo addressed them both on 13 and 14 July. He told them that the Voice was making representations to government and that there would be no evictions for five years.[45] On 13 August Nqabe and Malila told a large meeting in the Park what Burombo had promised.[46]

In fact government intended no further delay. This time there was no question of an understated deployment of a few unarmed police, nor any expression of the fear that

---

[42] African Peoples Voice, Memorandum, 26 February 1952, RH 16/1/3/1.
[43] *Bantu Mirror*, 23 February 1952.
[44] *Bantu Mirror*, 7 June 1952.
[45] Native Affairs Memo 68, 13 July 1952.
[46] Native Affairs Memo 69, 28 August 1952.

violence might beget violence. Resistance was to be broken. CID reports and the Matobo Annual Report for 1952 described what happened. During the year 265 families had moved from the Park to Prospect and 150 off Crown Land to Lupane; a further 268 families had been given notice in the Park. By the end of August all cooperators had left, while 195 families had refused to go. On 3 September a strong force of police 'descended without warning on a number of kraals' in Filabusi, 'before the inhabitants could take any action. Resistance was negligble, the natives being somewhat over-whelmed by the force brought to evict them.'[47] On 19 September the police moved into the National Park, beginning with Whitewaters. They 'were able to take the ring-leaders by surprise and evict them that day.... Nqabe, the instigator of most of the trouble in the Park was the first to be evicted.' His close ally Malila was the second. The Police remained in the Park for a week picking up and evicting families outside Whitewaters.[48]

These forced evictions became legendary in the Matopos and in Prospect. Councillor Makaya Malila Nyathi of Gohole in Prospect remembers seeing his father and other men in Whitewaters seized by the Police, handcuffed and carried off in trucks. 'It was terrifying'. Nqabe's capture has been elaborated in oral memory:

> They could not find Nqabe so they waited until dark, then they rushed into his house and captured him. They put chains on him and sent him away, leaving his property behind.
>
> Everything was put into the lorry [says Nduna Ncube]. The head of the family would have been handcuffed and put in the truck first ... They collected the grains, destroyed the huts and tied the grass. You were dumped at the place of their choice. [Evictees] felt the pains that are felt by an orphan. It was like a child without a mother and a father.[49]

Chief Nzula was left behind, protesting that his people had been removed from him. 'He is a pawn in the hands of the agitators.... It is proposed to recommend his deposition', noted the Annual Report.

The immediate effect of the police swoop was to subdue protest. The Voice was discredited. The 500 families left in the Park, deprived of experienced leaders, were for some time reluctant to enter into any other political activity: 'Because people did not know what is politics at this time. They had seen people being moved away and some of them might fear they might get into trouble.'[50]

Nqabe and the others evicted to Prospect had plenty to do to settle themselves there. As the 1952 Annual Report boasted, even 'the agitators have been busy building kraals and making lands and have not been holding meetings'; Nqabe was 'keeping quiet at present.' In any case, he found himself amongst men who had had good experiences on the new land:

> Soon after those people had been evicted from the hills there, the next two years after they had settled down some of them were saying that they had no interest in going back because the harvest had been so good and their cattle were so good.[51]

[47] Native Affairs Memo 70, 30 September 1952.
[48] Annual Report, Matobo, 1952.
[49] Interview with Makaya Malila Nyathi, Gohole, 6 September 1988; Interview with D. A. Moyo, Gohole, 6 September 1988; Interview with Nduna Ncube, Bulawayo, 28 July 1988.
[50] Interview with Jacob Minindwa Moyo, Gulati, 21 July 1988.
[51] Interview with Japhet Ngwenya, Tsatshani School, 30 August 1988.

One of these men was Nqabe's brother, Sidakwe Tshuma, who told me in 1988: 'I was a master farmer and I wanted to leave the baboons. In Mbongolo (Prospect) whites used to come to see the improvements I had made.'[52]

Eviction and Nationalism

Yet, for all this, the evictions were at the root of much later nationalist activity. Nduna Ncube, who was evicted from Absent, says that nationalism 'did not come as a new movement. Remember, they already had been involved in resistance movements earlier'. People thought that nationalism 'would bring them freedom' and a return to the Matopos.[53] Matopos men and women who were evicted into the forests of northern Matabeleland arrived there in a mood of deep resentment. It was intensified by the conditions they found there. In January 1952 the Land Development Officer, Lupane, reported that the Matopos evictees did

> not appear to be reaping the benefit of this good rainy season [and] there is not much hope of them reaping anything like their requirements ... due to the virgin land they are using ... and secondly whole families have been down with fever, making work in the lands impossible.

Many were fleeing from the district for fear of malaria.[54] The Roman Catholic pioneer in Lupane, Father Odilo Weeger, told me that:

> When you talked to people they were bitter. They would say 'Rhodes promised us that we could stay in the Matopos. Now we have been moved among the mosquitoes, the tsetse and the midges and into the thickets'.

This bitterness gave an edge to their later nationalism.[55] Matopos evictees in Wankie strongly resisted any interference with their methods of cultivation or grazing, saying: 'You want to kill us and our cattle.... It's like being on the farms again. We were given this country to do what we like with'.[56]

Nor did passivity in Prospect long survive the first two seasons of good rain. At the September 1949 meeting in the National Park when government's decision was announced, Native Commissioner Lewis lavished praise on Prospect 'with its 22 fenced paddocks, lush grass, many bore-holes, electric pumps and automatically fed water storage tanks.' Africans were inheriting the sophisticated apparatus of a highly capitalised European ranch.[57] Prospect had in fact been run by the Congo Rhodesian

[52] Interview with Sidakwa Tshuma, Enkanini, Prospect, 6 September 1988. Sidakwa was then in his nineties; Nqabe himself died only in 1984, also in his nineties. My visit to the family was a disconcerting one. Nqabe's widow, Musa, refused to accept that he had ever been a militant or nationalist; Sidakwa was affronted that I had come to talk about Nqabe rather than about him. Although we were meeting in Enkanini, the place of resistance, both asserted that the name was a mere coincidence and had nothing to do with Nqabe's settlement there.

[53] Interview with Nduna Ncube, 28 July 1988.

[54] LDO, Lupane, Report for January 1952, S 160 AGR 4/7/51.

[55] Interview with Father Odilo, Mater Dei, Bulawayo, 7 January 1995.

[56] Annual Report, Wankie, 1959.

[57] Bulawayo Chronicle, 30 September 1949.

Ranching Company to supply beef to the Katanga mines.[58] By the time the land was sold to the Rhodesian government it was more or less grazed out. An inspection report made in May 1950 by experts from the Matopos Research station found that the 'area in which water was available to the previous owners' had been heavily overstocked; 'owing to mismanagement in the past considerable encroachment by non-edible thorn scrub has taken place'; 'the area in the vicinity of the Shangani River has been grossly mistreated. Erosion has set in'. In other parts of the ranch water supplies were inadequate.[59] And if Prospect had severe limitations as grazing land, it was little better for cultivation. When he gave evidence to the National Park Commission on 21 March 1949 Charles Murray had insisted that families evicted from the Matopos must be placed in areas where the annual rainfall was predictable and regular. The evictees should not be settled on Prospect. 'Even under good farming methods it is not an area where good crops can be produced. In my opinion all that low veld country is entirely unsuitable from a land use point of view for Native occupation'.[60]

There was, of course, a bitter irony here. The government was evicting families from the Park because Murray and the Matopos grazing experts had told them that the hills were being eroded. Now the only land available to resettle them was regarded by these experts as in an even more 'delicate state of balance'. Soon most Park evictees repented of any favourable first impressions:

> Because the place is dry, without rain, it soon turned out to be uninhabitable. They are no longer happy, because it is quite dry. There is no water. The bore-holes that were sunk there cannot solve the problem because they've just got hand-pumps on them.... You will find people walking to the borehole for more than eight miles.[61]

Discontent was intensified in Prospect because the first land allocations involved 'so many errors' that there had to be a completely new division of land, and the contours already built with much labour had to be ploughed up.[62]

In these circumstances the old *Sofasonke* leaders recovered their self-confidence and influence. Malila, his son remembers, always hated the Gohole area of Prospect on which he had been settled, and joined in turn the African National Congress, the National Democratic Party and the Zimbabwe African Peoples Union (ZAPU).[63] Nqabe ignored the views of his brother and returned to his policy of objection. For him there was an easy transition from *Sofasonke* to nationalism. In April 1958 the Provincial Native Commissioner wrote to the Secretary of Native Affairs. He reported that Nqabe was undermining the incumbent headman and chief on Prospect so that 'they can no longer exercise control'. Nqabe was demanding that Nzula be installed as chief. The PNC had considered trying to buy Nqabe off with the offer of a job but he was too old.

---

[58] For the earlier history of Prospect see files S 456/132/52 and AT 1/2/11/2.

[59] Report on Prospect Ranch by Animal Husbandry Officer and Pasture Research Officer, Matopos Research Station, 10 May 1950, S 160 LS 102/1/50.

[60] Evidence of Charles Murray, 21 March 1949, S 1561 46.

[61] Interview with Japhet Nwenya, Tshatshani, 30 August 1988.

[62] Annual Report, Matobo, 1958.

[63] Interview with Makaya Malila Nyathi, Gohole, 6 September 1988.

So he recommended that he be removed from Prospect just as he had earlier been removed from the National Park.[64]

In May 1958 Nqabe led a delegation from Prospect to Bulawayo where they were joined by Nzula and headman Bejani. Nqabe told the Provincial Native Administrator that people in Prospect had voted heavily to be transferred from Chief Dumezweni Ndiweni of Shashani Reserve back to Nzula, and that they 'were infuriated when they noticed that all new issues of Registration Certificates were under Chief Dumezweni's name'. Having made this traditionalist point, 'the deputation also interviewed Mr J. Z. Moyo, Assistant General Secretary of the Southern Rhodesia African National Congress and are eager to start a branch of Congress in their area.'[65] Nqabe and the others went back to Prospect and opened one of the first Congress branches in rural Matabeleland. While most districts in Matabeleland in 1958 reported no sign of Congress, in Matobo the ANC had 'obtained a firm footing' with branches in Prospect, Shashani and Semokwe.[66]

Nqabe thus passes out of documented history. He was not deported from Prospect and oral informants say that he joined the successor movements to Congress, lived through the guerrilla war of the 1970s and the dissident war of the 1980s, and died only in 1984. But in the late 1950s leadership was passing to another generation. By that time, too, the focal point of Matopos nationalism had moved back from the diaspora to the hills themselves.

Nationalism in the Hills

Many grievances remained both in the Matopo Reserve and in the National Park after the evictions of 1952. Partly because of the unique history, culture and agriculture of the hills, and partly because they were so close to Bulawayo, the Matopos became one of the hottest nationalist areas by the early 1960s.

No one had yet been evicted from the Matopo Reserve by 1952. But there was a constant threat that everybody would be. Flushed with their partial victory in the National Park, the conservationists pressed for the evacuation of all people and stock from the Reserve. If this was not to happen, they insisted, then the provisions of the Land Husbandry Act must be strictly enforced there. In practical reality neither could be done. Rights of occupancy in a Reserve were guaranteed under the constitution and could only be removed with the assent of Britain. And while the population of the Reserve could be maintained at a relatively comfortable standard of living by using the 'traditional' methods of wetland cultivation, the methods on which Land Husbandry was based were either irrelevant to the environment or impossible to implement without great reduction of population. Hence the inhabitants of the Reserve existed for more than a decade in great uncertainty, with perpetual rumours that one or other

---

[64] PNC to Secretary for Native Affairs, 26 April 1958, LAN/15/GEN, Box 100839.
[65] *Bantu Mirror*, 17 May 1958.
[66] Annual Report, Matobo, 1958.

drastic course would be taken against them. The government could neither act nor stop talking about acting. It was a situation ready-made for local activists, and in particular for Fraser Gibson Sibanda, the man who in his own person linked *Sofasonke* to the Voice and the Voice to Congress and its successors.

The pressure to depopulate the Reserve came mainly from the Natural Resources Board. From 1954 onwards the Board told government that unless all humans and stock were removed from the eastern Matopos the whole southern lowveld would be in peril; the Mzingwane, Tuli, Mtsheleti and Mtshabezi rivers, which all originated in the eastern Matopos sponges, would silt up; these sponges were 'the very source of the lifeblood (water) of major low veld areas.... Destroy that source and you ruin the low veldt'; government's policy of resettling Africans on low veld grasslands and developing a major cattle industry there would be doomed.[67] This millenarian scenario haunted official imagination until the Rhodesia Front's revolt against modernising experts dispelled it in 1964.

The Natural Resources Board used every available tactic to press their case. The original 1954 warning had been a private letter to the Minister of Native Affairs; this was followed up in August 1955 by another 'Dear Ben' letter from the Board's Chairman. This revealed a blithe disregard for the realities of Rhodesian politics. African resentment at their removal would be mollified if it was 'made clear to them that they were not "displaced persons" being removed by decree to the other end of the country' and that the intention was solely 'the future well being of their own kith and kin' in the low veld. Of course, they would have to be offered excellent land in return, and the Chairman thought this could be found on unalienated Crown land, most of which was better for African than for European use even if the Department of Lands seemed anxious to alienate it all to whites as quickly as possibly. Champion Ranch, for example, should be offered to Africans and not to 'yet another of our friends from the Union ... without any intention of engaging in serious ranching'.[68]

Impressed though they were by conservationist warnings, government knew that these proposals were impossible. 'We do not want to raise a political storm', warned the Under Secretary, Native Economic Development. Rhodesian whites already felt that 'the natives had been too generously treated over land' and would revolt against any proposal to settle Africans on 'white' land south of the Matopos, while 'for a survey team to walk into the Reserve may make the natives suspicious, particularly as it is bound to leak out that a suggestion has been made to depopulate the Reserve'.[69] The Natural Resources Board cheerfully responded to these demands for secrecy by featuring the Matopo Reserve in their published annual reports. These were naturally picked up by the African press. 'Matopo Reserve Tribesmen may have to shift', announced the *Daily News* on 9 August 1958, summarising the NRB's assertion that the Reserve's

---

[67] The citation is in fact from Provincial Native Commissioner Parker, writing to support the demand for depopulation made by the Chairman of the Natural Resources Board in August 1954. PNC to Assistant Secretary, Administration, 7 October 1955, S 2808/1/23.

[68] 'Dear Ben' from 'Gordon', 22 August 1955, *ibid.*

[69] Under Secretary, Native Economic Development to Provincial Native Commissioner, 25 January 1956, *ibid.*

'multitude of sponges' were gravely damaged, 'spelling the death of the Gwanda area and the eventual evacuation of the inhabitants.' On 9 July 1960 the *News* reported that according to a Natural Resources Board report at least 500 families were to be moved 'from the much discussed' Matopo Reserve. All this kept African suspicions well on the boil.

On their side white farmers south of the Reserve, basking in their recently achieved virtue as members of Intensive Conservancy Areas (ICAs), kept up the pressure on the Matopo Reserve. The old struggle between the black peasant farmers of the hills and the white ranchers to their south was renewed, with whites determined to make no concessions nor to yield land to what they stigmatised as destructive African cultivators. In October 1955 the Filabusi ICA complained about the devastation of the Diana's Pool area in the Matopo Reserve; the next month the Umzingwane ICA resolved that unless it could be protected properly by fencing, destocking and contours, the Reserve 'should be declared a National Park and the people and stock removed'. Patiently the Native Affairs officials explained that the inhabitants of the Reserve could not be compulsorily removed under the constitution and would not move voluntarily unless they were offered land which the whites were not prepared to give up. Without this, 'proper conservation measures there would render the area untenable by the present population because the arable area in the narrow valleys [would] become one large "sponge", useless for agriculture'; 'further destocking will cause a great deal of harship ... further contouring will greatly reduce arable land.'[70]

Government twisted and turned between the rocks and a hard place. Decisions to remove families were taken and then rescinded. In March 1957, the Minister ordered the removal of 1,000 families and the implementation of Land Husbandry with the remaining 450. Five hundred of the families to be evicted might, he thought, accept tenurial rights on residential stands in Sibomvu township in Mzingati Native Purchase Area from which they could commute to Bulawayo for work; the other 500 might be offered land in Nuanetsi or Beitbridge. No land designated as European was available.[71] The Provincial Native Commissioner, now M. Campbell, at once expressed 'serious regret':

> Natives have more than once in this Province called upon Administrative officials to prove to them that Native Reserves are in fact Native Reserves. Following mass movements from Crown Lands they began to think – suitably primed of course by agitators in the shape of the British African Peoples Voice Association – that the next movements would be from the Native Reserves.

He had always denied this; now Africans' worst fears were coming true. He was certain that no-one would accept township stands; he did not even wish to sound people out since this would cause 'suspicion and uneasiness'.[72] He was ordered, nevertheless, to inquire if people would accept plots in Sibomvu. Suspicion and uneasiness were thus created but the plan to evict 1,000 families fell away.

---

[70] Native Commissioner, Matobo to Provincial Native Commissioner, 26 October 1955; Provincial Agriculturalist to Director, Native Agriculture, 6 January 1956, S 2808/1/23.

[71] Under Secretary, Native Agriculture to Under Secretary, Native Lands, 4 March 1957, *ibid*.

[72] Provincial Native Commissioner to Secretary, Native Affairs, 22 March 1957, *ibid*.

In March 1958 Sir Edgar Whitehead brought the issue to his cabinet after yet another demand for depopulation by the Natural Resources Board. 'Considerable sympathy would be felt for the Africans', he feared. In April Whitehead ordered the Native Department to set on foot a survey of land within the Matopo Reserve itself which could be used to build a township to house 'landless families' there. 'Absolute silence in the field' was to be maintained about the purpose of this survey.[73] The survey was carried out, creating yet more alarm. But the township was never built. Then early in 1959 it was decided after all to try to apply Land Husbandry to the Reserve and an Assessment Committee met in September to make its recommendations. This concluded that at least 25 per cent of the population, some 500 families, would have to move before anything could be done. Chief Bafana destroyed his credit locally by signing these recommendations. But no attempt was ever made to carry them out.[74] In vain the Native Commissioner, Mzingwane, to whom responsibility for the Reserve had now been transferred, complained in October 1960 that 'subversive elements are favoured by delay' and called for 'a fully backed destocking policy'. A district survey of Mzingwane carried out in July 1962 found that the recommendations of the Assessment Committee had proved impossible to implement.[75]

All these interventions were vainly attempted despite the fact that successive investigations found that the Matopo Reserve was not, after all, in a state of crisis. In October 1956 a report by the Provincial Agriculturalist, the Conservation Officer and the Soil Conservation Officer, Matopos, found that 'the standard of agriculture is fairly high'. The majority used manure and rotated crops; there were 48 Master Farmers; many sold crops in Bulawayo and 648 had market gardens. The average annual income was £106, £59 of this coming from agriculture. They found a mixture of Banyubi short-hoe ridge cultivation and Ndebele long-hoe flat land cultivation, overlaid by the use of the plough.[76] When depopulation was ordered in March 1957 and Africans were offered township stands, the Provincial Native Commissioner drew an almost idyllic picture of the Reserve. He stressed that the inhabitants of the Reserves

> have their homes which they have built at no little cost over the years ... gardens, containing fruit trees, especially guavas, which are often sold. They are not huddled together ... there is space and freedom and an opportunity to help themselves to what nature provides. If I were similarly placed, I should certainly not exchange my lot for the doubtful privilege of becoming the owner of a stand in a Township.[77]

Even the Land Husbandry Assessment committee, with its two Nature Resources Board representatives, rather grudgingly found that 'the position in the Reserve is much better than it should be' and that there was much less erosion than expected, 'due

---

[73] Cabinet Minute, 4 March 1958; Under Secretary, Native Agriculture to Provincial Native Commissioner, 15 April 1958, *ibid.*

[74] The Assessment Committee's report is dated 29 September 1959, *ibid.*

[75] Native Commissioner, Mzingwane to Provincial Native Commissioner, 14 October 1960, *ibid.* District Survey, Mzingwane, 2 July 1962, Box 82725.

[76] Report, 1 October 1956, S 2808/1/23.

[77] Provincial Native Commissioner to Chief Native Commissioner, 25 April 1957, *ibid.*

to the tenacity of the sponges and the ability of the country to recover quickly'. 'The standard of agriculture is above average'. Predictably, they also found that the 'long-term effect will be serious'. Schedules to their report documented the capacity of hard workers to earn £209 a year off an acre of wet land, an acre of dry and quarter of an acre of orchard; 600 vegetable gardens averaged half an acre each; the men worked in these gardens while women tilled the dry land; 'all valleys have strong sponges'; 'there are many brick houses' and 'ample timber for domestic use'.[78] The Assistant Director of Native Agriculture summed up the message of all these reports: 'Contrary to previous opinion we are not dealing with an impoverished group of people'.[79]

It was left to the Rhodesia Front administration, however, to draw the obvious conclusion – in its own terms the economy of the Matopos Reserve was outstandingly successful. As it moved to policies of Community Development and self-help, the new regime found the Reserve an almost ideal example. In July 1964 W. H. H. Nicolle, acting secretary of Internal Affairs, writing to the Natural Resources Board, savagely criticised 'ultra experts and idealists' who had 'dived in on preconceived plans [to] debar the cultivation of sponges, river banks, etc.' In fact, 'the Matopo Tribal Trust Land has developed its own unique agricultural economy, which is based on small-scale vegetable gardening tied to the lucrative Bulawayo market.' Some cultivators earnt over £1,000 a year:

> There must be no forcing of the people to abandon their existing lands or reduce their stock holdings. What is required is a plan that will protect existing arable land and improve its production.

There was no need for an 'aggregation of numerous experts. All that is required is one good agriculture man.'[80] A chastened Board accepted this new emphasis.

Many positive discoveries were being made about the Matopo Reserve. A. D. Elliott's delineation report of the Bafana Community concluded that 'the concept of self-help is nothing new to them' and that

> market gardening has placed many people on a cash economy and this gives them a great advantage over most other subsistence level communities. Not only do they have the manpower and will, but they have a certain amount of cash. Conditions appear favourable for the introduction of local government.[81]

In 1969 the Primary Development Officer in charge of the Matopos Tribal Trust Land Reclamation Scheme was enthusiastic about the essential 'buffer' provided by cash cropping; thought that with more effective exploitation the wet lands could produce at least double the crop; and announced his discovery that 'the most refractory area in the district, that of Headman Mnindwa ... has had a grazing system in use for years. Certain valleys are reserved for bad seasons'.[82]

[78] Schedules to Assessment Committee Report, 29 September 1959, *ibid.*
[79] Assistant Director, Native Agriculture to Mr Davies, 11 October 1956, *ibid.*
[80] Acting Secretary, Internal Affairs to Secretary, Natural Resource Board, 15 July 1964, Box 100843.
[81] A. D. Elliott, Bafana Chiefship, 27 February 1964.
[82] Annual Report, Matopos TTL Reclamation Scheme, 1969, Box 100359.

The Rhodesia Front administration had come to a much more sensible assessment of the eastern Matopos than millenarian environmentalists either before or after them. But that did not mean that nationalist opposition, so stimulated by the blunders of conservationist intervention, was now going to come to an end. As Eliott remarked in March 1964, 'nearby Bulawayo is a stronghold of nationalistically inclined politicians who from time to time make their presence felt in the area. This may be an inhibiting factor' to Community Development.[83]

Throughout the interventionist period, officials had reported that 'the Natives in the Reserve are very suspicious about their future'.[84] Their suspicions were canalised by the leadership of two men, Mcutshwa Ndawana Sibanda, a resident of the Reserve, and Frazer Gibson Sibanda. Frazer Gibson was an office holder of *Sofasonke*, of the Voice and of the Bulawayo branch of the original Congress; he was a member of the Matabeleland Home Society; he was elected to Njube Township Advisory Board and in 1956 made use of something called the Mhlanhlandhlela Residents Association to attack Chief Bafana; by February 1958 he was organising secretary in Bulawayo for the revived African National Congress, was detained during the 1959 emergency and restricted to Gokwe; he emerged from restriction to become secretary of the National Democratic Party branch in the Matopos; he was a stalwart of ZAPU. In short, he was of those universal men characteristic of Bulawayo African politics. The *Home News* described him as a young man, anxious to assume leadership, stubborn and often incautious. He 'favours freedom of speech, freedom of association but not least freedom of beer consumption.'[85]

Mcutshwa and Frazer were prominent in manifestations of Matopo Reserve discontent. In 1952 the Native Commissioner, Matobo, reported that Frazer, 'who lives on an adjoining farm, tried to instigate passive resistance to destocking' by organising refusal to produce dipcards – 'a symptom of the times', thought the Commissioner, adding gloomily that 'destocking is something that will go on for years' and go on provoking opposition.[86] The CID added that Frazer had worked with Frank Mcutshwa, 'an agitator in the Reserve'.[87] In 1956 Frazer launched a campaign to depose Chief Bafana, who had discredited himself by appearing to agree to depopulation, and whom Frazer claimed 'had no backing from the African people in the Reserve'.[88] In August 1957 the *Bantu Mirror* reported that Frazer was now organising secretary of the Bulawayo branch, which was then all that remained of the original Bantu Congress. He had organised a branch in Njube township, would set up branches in the other townships, and then 'he will soon be exploring the reserves'.[89] Later in the month Frazer acted in another capacity – Secretary of the Voice for Matobo district – and called Voice delates from branches in seven other districts of Matabeleland to meet him

[83] Elliott, 'The Bafana Community', 5 March 1964.
[84] Provincial Native Commissioner to Secretary, Native Affairs, 4 October 1956, S 2808/1/3.
[85] *Home News*, 25 May 1957.
[86] Annual Report, Matobo, 1952.
[87] Native Affairs Memo 63, 31 January 1952.
[88] *Bantu Mirror*, 24 and 28 April 1956.
[89] *Bantu Mirror*, 8 August 1957. For the history of the Bantu Congress see Terence Ranger, *Are We Not Also Men?*, James Currey, London, 1996.

in the Matopos. He told them of his Congress activities and they said they would like him to visit the Reserves so that 'members may be converted to Congress'.[90] Congress was revived as a mass movement in September 1957; by February 1958 Frazer was proclaiming that 'Todd has gone! Africans should turn to Congress'.[91]

In March 1958 Frazer met Voice delegates from nine districts, including Matopo, who assured him that 'they were interested in forming Congress Branches.'[92] By the end of 1958 there was a Congress branch in the Matopo Reserve.[93] Hardly had it come into existence than Sir Edgar Whitehead banned Congress and detained many of its leaders. Frazer was among them. He was not released from Gokwe restriction area until April 1960, but he at once took part in setting up the National Democratic Party (NDP) branch in the Matopo Reserve. Nduna Ncube describes how people in the Reserve hated Messengers coming and docking the tails of beasts for subsequent culling. Contours were 'very painful because the best part of your field was cut'. Land Husbandry allocations were random and 'at times your field could be given to your neighbour'. Nduna joined the NDP branch – 'it was a continuation of the Park resistance'. The chairman was Mcutshwa; his secretary was Frazer Gibson.[94]

The NDP at once mobilised a mass campaign of defiance in the Reserve. Dip tanks were sabotaged; agricultural rules were ignored; and in 1961 there was a more or less complete boycott of tax payments. Together with the rest of the Matopos, the Reserve was by far the most turbulent area of southern Matabeleland, only rivalled in the north by Lupane and Nkayi districts, to which evictees from Matobo and Filabusi had been sent.[95] At the end of 1961 police and soldiers were deployed in the valleys and hills of the Reserve to enforce payment of tax and to round up NDP activists. This deployment of troops in the hills for the first time since 1897 was an omen. The sensible agrarian policies of the Rhodesia Front towards the eastern Matopos came too late. As we shall see, the area was destined to become a hub of guerrilla activity during the 1970s.

In the early 1960s, however, the National Park itself was even more strikingly a centre of radical nationalism. After the 1952 evictions Native Department theory was that the Park had been purged of all its agitators and that the families given permits to remain there would be contented and obedient. Things didn't turn out like that.

Sofasonke had been a mass movement rather than something got up by a few troublemakers. Those left behind shared the resentment of those forced to go. Moreover, the new nationalist parties threw up a younger leadership to replace older men like Nqabe. During the later 1950s some of those who had been away as labour migrants, and who had supported *Sofasonke* by sending subscriptions, came back home and assumed political leadership. They were familiar with the organisation and ideology of black politics in South Africa. Typical of such men was Jacob Mnindwa Moyo, son of Headman Mnindwa of Matobo Block, which was now integrated into the National Park.

[90] *Bantu Mirror*, 24 August 1957. Frazer added that birth-control was 'unChristian and politically futile'.
[91] *Bantu Mirror*, 22 February 1958.
[92] *Bantu Mirror*, 29 March 1958.
[93] Annual Report, Matobo, 1959.
[94] Interview with Nduna Ncube, 28 July 1988.
[95] Annual Report, Mzingwane, 1961.

Jacob had been a policeman in South Africa but was friendly with Mandela and other Congress leaders. He came back home in 1959; bought cattle with his South African savings and ran them in the eastern Park. He at once joined the revived African National Congress and, as we shall see, was active in the successor movements, the NDP and ZAPU. At first he found the National Park people reluctant to support nationalism. But this soon changed.[96]

It changed because of the multiple and increasing grievances of the National Park residents. They found themselves under a bewildering variety of pressures – from the Native Department, which was formally in charge of land allocation, conservation and destocking; from the National Park authority, which tried to redistribute population to fit with tourist flows and to restrict hunting so as to develop game; from the Natural Resources Board and the neighbouring ICAs, which kept up constant complaints about erosion. Many of the grievances of the National Park residents were the same as those of the Reserves of southern Matabeleland. But there was in addition a conflict over landscape, history and culture which added a peculiar bitterness to the nationalist confrontation with the state.

By the mid-1950s the conservationists were already demanding the eviction of all people and cattle from the Park despite the pledges given in 1949. In 1962 there was a sudden and unnegotiated partition of the extended Park area. The scenic core of the land became the National Park as we know it today; the rest of the area became Tribal Trust Lands. This meant the total removal of people from the core zone; the final destruction of the old Whitewaters community, school and church; and the creation in the new people-less Park of a re-invented Nature, complete with Game Reserve and Wilderness. The old political moral economy focused on the promises of Rhodes, which was already undermined by the 1952 evictions, now collapsed altogether. By the early 1960s Rhodes's Grave was under physical attack; Park staff at Maleme Rest Camp were taking up defensive positions in fireproof structures guarded by armed men and dogs; deliberately set fires were sweeping through the Park's grassland.

This confrontation took time to develop. It was many years before the National Parks authority made itself felt in the Matopos. Parks were one of the responsibilities assigned to the Federal Government in 1953 but there were prolonged negotations between the Federal and Territorial governments before the Southern Rhodesian National Parks Advisory Board was replaced by a Federal body in March 1958.[97] One of the difficulties with Federal control of Parks arose from African residence within them. The territorial governments were responsible for African administration. As a result, none of the Parks in Northern Rhodesia and Nyasaland were handed over to Federal control. In Southern Rhodesia the Matopos presented special problems since Federal pressure for a 'proper' National Park conflicted with the pledge of secure tenure given by the Territorial Minister in 1949. The Southern Rhodesian Native Department was left in charge of the African residents and of enforcing their conditions

[96] Interview with Jacob Mnindwa Moyo, Gulati, 21 July 1988.
[97] Annual Report of the National Parks Advisory Board, March 1955; Secretary, Home Affairs to Federal Attorney General, 8 January 1957, F 148 AGF/66/1.

of tenure.[98] It was not until 1959 that the Parks authorities deployed their own police in adequate numbers to enforce Park policies.

But conservationist lobbying about the Park had begun well before 1959. Initially L. H. Stewart, Director of National Parks, was 'greatly impressed with the potentialities' of the Matopos and noted that 'the Department was indeed fortunate in being able to take over a Park where so much development had been done in the way of dams and scenic roads'.[99] But it was not long before Stewart was declaring African occupation inconsistent with the proper development of the Park. In a memorandum of November 1955 he expressed his shock at the 'devastation' of this 'beautiful country', with 'signs of erosion' around the dams and silting of all the streams. If nothing effective was done, 'not only will the Park itself be ruined from an aesthetic point of view, but the land below will be severely affected.' National Parks were supposed to be 'shop windows of the State', but unless the conditions of the Matopos Park were improved 'the area should be closed to the public without delay'. He urged that 'steps be taken to remove all the natives living in the Park', and asked the Southern Rhodesian Natural Resources Board to support eviction. The Board, which was demanding the depopulation of the Matopos Reserve, obligingly added the National Park to their list.[100]

The Southern Rhodesian Secretary for Native Affairs thought that it was 'hardly conceivable that the Federal Government would press for the revocation of a Territorial Government promise to the Natives ... made before the land passed to the control of the Federal Government.'[101] Nevertheless, the idea of depopulation had been floated and soon the idea of partition surfaced. In January 1956 a member of the Parks Advisory Board, Kelly Edwards, proposed that 'a truly representative area of the Matopos' should be set aside for a Park and the rest ceded to the Native Department.[102] Thereafter one idea or the other was constantly being mooted. Partition was pushed by the Park Warden in May 1958 and discussed as a practical policy from November 1960 until its implementation in February 1962.[103]

Meanwhile, the conservationists had to make do with reshaping the Park while it was being occupied by Africans. To begin with they reiterated the old policy of scenic co-existence. 'A few of the better type of families would be permitted to settle alongside tourist routes', noted the Advisory Board in December 1952, 'and would be an added attraction'.[104] Even in October 1958, Senior Planning Officer, H. R. Hack thought that although 'some of the settlement in [Matobo Block and Gulati] lies adjacent to main tourist routes, with a few exceptions the dwellings and land are attractive and do not

[98] Director of National Parks, Memorandum, August 1959, F 121.G1.

[99] National Parks Advisory Board meeting, 4 December 1953, F 128 HAF 54/15/1; Annual Report, NP Advisory Board, March 1955, F 148 AGF 66/1.

[100] L. H. Stewart, Memorandum, 25 November 1955; Acting Secretary, NRB, to District Secretary, Bulawayo, 15 December 1955, F HAF 54/15/1, vol. 2.

[101] Memorandum, Secretary, Native Affairs, 28 February 1956, S 160 AGR 5/25/55.

[102] Meeting of the NP Advisory Board, 27 January 1956, F HAF 54/15/1, vol. 2.

[103] Director, National Parks to Federal National Parks Board, 5 May 1958, F HAF 54/15/1, vol. 1; meeting of Federal NP Board, 18 November 1960, F HAF 54/15/1, vol. 4.

[104] Meeting of the NP Advisory Board, 4 December 1953, F 128 HAF 54/15/1.

detract from the natural beauty of the countryside'. Hack thought it convenient, however, that the 'most picturesque' parts of the Park in the north and north-east were thinly settled. Only 'a few families' precluded the development of 'a natural game sanctuary'. In the central area of the Park a handful of families 'preclude enormous blocks of otherwise virgin veldt from being developed as natural game sanctuaries'. He thought that Badja plateau was particularly promising. There should be a 'readjustment' of settlement within the Park to clear these areas.[105] If his detailed recommendations were implemented, 'then a broad band of mainly waste land can be set aside as a complete sanctuary, a retreat for wild animals'; this would include 'all the main tourist routes and the main dams'.[106] 'The Park has been divided into occupied and game areas', noted the Warden's monthly report for October 1960, but 'the "putting over" of these game areas to the Africans had not yet been done.'[107]

Of course, Hack's 'virgin veldt' also included rain caves and other historically significant sites. The Park authorities, anxious to discover picturesque sites and paintings, found resident elders 'very reluctant to allow their caves to become known to Europeans and even refuse information to their sons who might divulge the whereabouts of the more secret places.'[108] The Park authorities were also anxious not only to develop fenced game sanctuaries but to develop game in the occupied areas of the Park. Africans were forbidden to kill baboons who were raiding their crops; killing a leopard which had been raiding cattle was regarded as a serious offence. 'The Park officials want game', wrote a perceptive conservationist in October 1960, '(even vermin like leopards and baboons) but no dogs. The Natives want no game (especially no baboons) but they want dogs.' He added that Africans wanted to 'develop' themselves and their surroundings but their farms and their 'improved houses are an eyesore to the Parks', which would tolerate at best only picturesque authenticity. Africans resented 'the continual presence of Europeans in their farming areas for recreational purposes.'[109]

For their part, the Park authorities frowned on modern brick houses but dressed up African employees 'traditionally':

> The custodian at Nswatugi Cave was issued with an Ndebele tribal uniform [it was reported in January 1960], as is the case at Silozwana, and has proved popular. Shields were made by an old man in Filabusi district, who is remarkable in his knowledge and pride of the Matabele nation.[110]

They 'discovered' picturesque specialists within the Park population itself.

> An old lady, Umede, who is perhaps the last of the *Ziwosana* (female rain dancers) in the National Park, called the pay her respects. She is a wonderful person, and wore her beads and feathered head-dress etc. and elected to dance a bit. She is of Venda extraction and was alive and nearby during the Rebellion of 1896.

---

[105] Senior Planning Officer, Conservation, to Director, 3 October 1958, Box 100356.
[106] H. R. Hack to Director of Conservation, 4 September 1959, F HAF 54/15/1, vol. 3.
[107] Monthly Report, 8 October 1960, F 121 G161, vol. 1.
[108] Annual Report, Federal NP Board, 31 March 1959, F 121.G1.
[109] District Secretary, Natural Resources, to Secretary, Natural Resources Board, 26 October 1960, Box 13336.
[110] Monthly Report, 12 January 1960, *ibid*.

But they were less lucky with Melusi, 'the foremost tribal dancer in the Park, when he threatened assault on a dam custodian and brought his uniform into disrepute.'[111]

The conservationists interfered with customary use of wet places, even at Njelele itself where the sponge was fenced off. 'Natives no doubt resent this fencing in of their winter grazing, but ... the sponge must come first.'[112] The people of Njelele cut the fence and drove their cattle on to the sponge.[113]

By 1960 the Park population were intensely resentful of all these pressures. There was constant demand that they destock, that they give labour for makings dams and roads, that they make contours. Prosecutions for hunting first meant that groups of men no longer went out with packs of dogs but one man with two or three, and then meant that hunting was done by moonlight. So-called 'bachelors' – the labour migrant sons of Park residents – were denied land. The Park even objected to the allocation of a two-acre plot to widows. Residents felt that the land was no longer their home but being used for white tourists or for wild animals. 'The Native Commissioner chases them, the Park officials chase them.... They resent being chased by all and sundry.'[114]

The monthly reports by the Park Warden from late 1959 to 1961 reveal relentless prosecutions for 'poaching', 'increased police patrols', heavier fines for failing to make contours or starting fires, warnings that expulsion from the Park would follow further breaches of the regulations. 'With the tightening up of hunting and coursing with dogs', noted the Warden on 12 April 1961, 'these people are at the mercy of baboons and wild pig.' He thought they wanted to escape. There were constant meetings of permit holders to discuss 'Park restrictions generally', from which dip tank attendants and other African officials were excluded:

> These people may do what little they can to try and get themselves removed to other land. It may seem illogical to them that they were asked to move in 1949 but did not want to due to their long association with the hills, and now they want to go ... they are unable to do so.[115]

In fact, of course, the residents did not want to go. They did want to obstruct and even to attack all those who were overriding 'their long association with the hills'. In 1960 Jacob Mnindwa Moyo became chair of the local NDP branch, with 'a very active young man', Timoti Ncube, as secretary. People 'were flocking in now.... They were not satisfied about these things.'

Moyo travelled on his motor scooter throughout the hills. 'In the Park people were beginning to resist, breaking the dips. Anything that government owned they used to destroy. There was underground organising.' In this nationalist period, the proclamation of Ndebele identity became a statement of unity rather than a claim to a military heritage or to a share in the promises of Rhodes:

> Ndebele has no tribe [says Moyo]. I'm also Banyubi you see, but now I'm Ndebele. My children don't know that. They don't know we're Banyubi, they think they are just Ndebele....

[111] Monthly reports, 12 January and 6 February 1960, *ibid.*
[112] Monthly report, 8 October 1960, *ibid.*
[113] Monthly report, 22 November 1960, *ibid.*
[114] District Secretary, NRB to Secretary, NRB, 26 October 1960, Box 13336.
[115] Monthly report, 12 April 1961.

If [Kalanga is taught in schools] you will find that people will start boasting 'I am a Kalanga' and so on. It's nice to teach Ndebele here. Because we are different tribes. If we started to drag one tribe here, one tribe there, if someone will come and teach Kalanga, I will start to teach Nyubi ... Ndebele is alright for everybody. Because no one will boast that I am Ndebele, we are all Ndebele, so no one will boast.

Associations like the Sons of Mzilikazi 'wanted the Ndebele to be on top of other tribes. If you are a Moyo you are not allowed to be there.' But in the NDP and ZAPU 'they became nationalist, everybody'.[116]

In 1961 the Park became a stronghold of the NDP. As the Annual Report recorded:

The first area to show signs of obvious acceptance of NDP beliefs was the Matopos National Park where the defection commenced as early as February 1961. In the Reserves the start was not so early.... The NDP has been very much more active in the Matopos National Park. It is nearer to Bulawayo and it is no great effort for party members to travel to and fro.

Young men returned from Bulawayo 'as able disciples of their messiah, Nkomo'; Nkomo himelf addressed many meetings in the Park. The Annual Report noted that 90 per cent of the Park residential permits had either been handed in to Nzula or were 'in ashes' as people affirmed their hereditary right to be on the land. Nzula himslef had 'ceased to trouble to deny his defection. He adopts an attitude of silence and hatred.' 'In the Park dip-tanks were filled in.'[117]

The Director of Parks, Stewart, drew a yet more alarmist picture. 'The African with his traditional way of living – in the end it was absolutely hopeless, we could not get it right.... There has been definite and deliberate resistance.'[118] Parks staff had been 'in a precarious position. They were threatened by some of the squatters.'[119] There were arson attempts on the Park offices and a bomb attack on Rhodes's Grave. There could have been no more spectacular way of repudiating the old political moral economy.[120]

On 13 December troops moved into the National Park and the Reserves to the south. Government announced that 'exercises would be conducted by the troops and police with the sole purpose of getting rid of the fear from which the inhabitants are suffering'; NDP leaders proclaimed that the people suffered fear at the sight of the soldiers. 'At the sound of a car the people in every kraal dash into the bush, And when the children see a policeman coming they have to raise the alarm so that elderly men should not dare come near the kraal'. NDP cards were demanded and burnt; there were shows of force. Whites were increasingly used to the tourist routes of the National Park. Now the press carried photographs of white squaddies back from forays into 'the primeval bush.... A jolly fine experience really.'[121]

The time seemed propitious to push through partition. In May 1961 the Parks

---

[116] Interview with Jacob Mindwa Moyo, Gulati, 21 July 1988.
[117] Annual Report, Matobo, 1961.
[118] *Chronicle*, 25 March 1962.
[119] *Chronicle*, 17 March 1962.
[120] E. H. Ashton, 'The Matopos. Socio-historical Survey', 2 January 1981. This valuable report, together with folders of supporting data, is now in the Historical Reference Library, Bulawayo.
[121] *Daily News*, 13, 20, 23 December 1961.

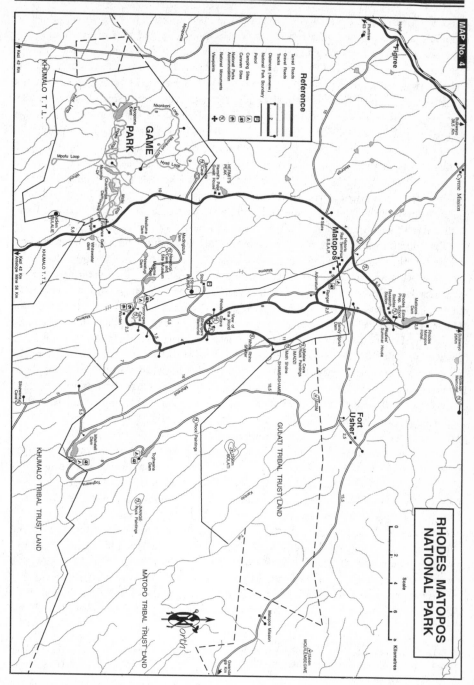

Map 4 The partitioned Park surrounded by Gulati, Matopo and Kumalo Trust Lands. The site of the old Whitewaters is indicated.

Advisory Board had decided that Federal and Territorial ministers should meet to negotiate a division, and that thereafter Nzula should be 'enlisted in persuading the African to co-operate'. In August the Board approved a detailed plan by which some 38 per cent of the land should be retained as a National Park, but containing 'all the existing dam sites and a number of hills and best tourist attractions'. The ban on the NDP and the deployment of troops rendered consultation with Africans more or less unnecessary. In February 1961 the ministers agreed. Partition was announced in a press statement of 21 March 1962. This stated that 107,645 acres would become a peopleless National Park; 152,300 acres to the east and south would become Gulati and Khumalo Native Areas. Eighty-five families would be evicted from the Park; a further 74 would be evicted from World's View and Hazelside, so that Rhodes's Grave would no longer be attended by resident Africans. These two farms, which up to this point had been administered by the Rhodes Matopos Estate, would become part of the National Park. The butterfly-shaped National Park of today was born.[122]

The announcement was met by a barrage of complaint from Rhodesian whites. Letters to the *Herald* attacked 'our weak-kneed government', and thought that since 'Parks in Rhodesia are not sacrosanct ... there is no reason why the western part of the Wankie Game Reserve should not be handed over to the bushmen who regularly hunt there.'[123] The Director of the Bulawayo Publicity Association wrote to the Secretary for Home Affairs to complain that the news would discourage tourists since 'it does not inspire confidence in the Government's efforts to prevent intimidation'. Members of parliament called it 'a breach of faith' to reduce 'national land'.[124] The *Chronicle* sought to strike a more balanced note: 'If we regard the huge area which has now been diminished as a sacred heritage over which brooded the spirit of the Founder, then of course we shall disturbed'. But wasn't the original Park 'a bit more than [the Park authorities] could chew?' Would government 'be justified in tying down a force of police to make sure Park regulations were observed?'[125]

It did not seem to occur to any white commentator that the Africans of the Matopos might also feel that they had been betrayed. But many of them had good reason to feel so. The 86 families evicted from the newly defined Park had been formally promised tenure there. Now they had either to squeeze in to Khumalo or Gulati or else go to Lupane. The partition was the end of the old Whitewaters community. 'By necessity', as the Advisory Board minutes for 18 August 1961 put it, 'the Whitewaters school, the Whitewaters dip tank and the Whitewaters sale pen' were included in the new Park and so were all demolished. The Advisory Board did not mention the famous Whitewaters church but that was demolished too. Mac Patridge, veteran London Mission Society missionary, remembered in 1988 how he used to go for holidays to Neville Jones's little cottage at Whitewaters; how he admired the 'beautiful little stone church', the old fig

122 Parks Advisory Board, meeting of 26 May 1961, F HAF 54/15/1, vol. 4; meeting of 18 August 1961, *ibid.*, vol. 5; press statement, 21 March 1962, Box 84272.
123 *Herald*, 21 March 1962.
124 Ashton folders.
125 *Chronicle*, 19 March 1962.

tree where *Sofasonke* meetings were held, and headmaster Timothy Chadi's rice fields. Now all were gone: 'Those vandals, the Southern Rhodesian Government, pulled down the church and added insult to injury by using the stones to build the gate into the Game Park.'[126] Hugh Ashton, interviewing in the Matopos in 1980 for his report on the Park, found 'great bitterness' at the destruction of 'the Elite' of Whitewaters.

Nor did the African residents to the east of the new Park feel any less bitter. The old Matobo Block was now part of Gulati. Jacob Moyo, who lived there and in 1962 was an office bearer in ZAPU, says that when the partition took place, 'we objected very strongly. We started to reject but it was real hard'. They objected because Land Husbandry now began to be implemented and 'the young people they are not allowed to have a place';

> there was also a destocking of cattle. Each person was supposed to have only five cattle. I went to prison for that for three months in 1962. I told them that this was not good work. Everybody refused to take these permits to sell cattle.

Moyo was jailed as 'spokesman for the people as well as District Chairman.'[127]

In particular the peoples of Gulati and Kumalo complained that the new Park contained all the dams on which they had laboured, and that they were cut off from water and grazing. The *Chronicle* of 23 April 1962, under the heading 'Matopos Africans Complain', reported that a delegation objected that all rivers and pools 'empty their water into the National Park' from which they were excluded. The complaints were persistent and continued after ZAPU had been banned. On 15 June 1963 the *Chronicle* reported that Jacob Moyo and Timoti Ncube were petitioning the Prime Minister 'that this move had left them with rivers that dried up in the winter and with poor grazing land.... They would ask for the abolition of the National Park.' Moyo had told Winston Field that 'we are starving because wild animals are being looked after.... These conditions whereby a wild animal is made to take the place of a human being were brought about by the Government without the knowledge of the inhabitants of the area.'

In July 1963 it was reported that Nzula would join another deputation, together with 'known agitators of this area', to demand that now the Federal government was coming to an end the Park should be abolished.[128]

In September 1963 an area report for Gulati and Kumalo summed the situation up:

> Strong resentment was caused and still exists today by the enforced settlement of 1949 ... Much resentment was felt by many of the farmers at this split, so although it removed many of the conditions they found so irksome, it also took away what they claimed was their land. All the dams built were included within the Park and they see the dams lying apparently unused when they claim their cattle are often short of water.... Farmers in this area are generally anti-Government. The people have a real fear of further enforced movements.

The local slogan was 'If the Government wants it, we don't.' It was widely believed that there were official intentions to expand the National Park again by allowing

[126] Interview with Mac Patridge, Hillside, 22 July 1988.
[127] Interview with Jacob Moyo, Gulati, 21 July 1988.
[128] Warden's Memorandum, 29 July 1963, F 128 TD 1079/1, vol. 3.

baboons to raid crops across its borders – 'farmers will be forced to move away from the boundaries and Government will take over the vacated areas, until all Africans have been driven from the TTLs [Tribal Trust Lands].'[129]

In short, the partition intensified confrontation rather than ending it. Jacob Moyo says that

> it was very hot in the ZAPU time. It's when women started to come in. We had very strong women. We had one lady called Mongwavi, she used to stay in Gwandavale. She was a very strong lady. We destroyed schools, churches, everything. Those people who were told they could not plough they came in and dug their fields and ploughed. They were breaking every law that comes in.[130]

Park records show their sense of emergency. It was noted in October 1982 that 'in the light of threats made and information received', the Maleme Camp was 'regarded as one of the highest security risks in the District'. A road was opened along the Maleme Valley to allow either for evacuation or for police reinforcements. At the end of the year the Park's Annual Report reported that 'the local inhabitants continue to agitate for further areas of the Park to be excised, and have shown their resentment by the destruction of fences, setting of veld fires and petrol bombing of the office.'[131]

The Commission for the Preservation of Natural and Historical Monuments tried to save Rhodes's Grave from any further attacks by urging that World's View be not incorporated in the new Park:

> It should not be taken over by the Department of Federal Parks because they as a Department are very unpopular with Africans owing to their policy of removing all Africans and cattle....World's View farm and its momuments and relics should be left in as natural a state as possible and families at present resident should be allowed to remain ... I should not like to see anything done which might antaogonise African opinion and lead to further damage to the monuments.[132]

But World's View *was* added to the Park; its African residents were evicted; and the grave's African guardians were dressed 'in authentic tribal costume.' In December 1962 Ranger Marshall, who was reponsible for the area, reported that 'since the attempted sabotage of Mr Rhodes's grave, it has been necessary to have guard duty there', which meant that there was no one to stop poaching or grass fires.[133]

Still, 'the repairs to the stonework and the plate on Mr Rhodes's grave have been carried out'. Gradually the policy of toughing things out, not ceding an inch to African demands to graze in the Park, and hoping that the ban on ZAPU and the restriction of its leaders would undermine resistance, seemed to be paying off. Animals were trucked into the new Game Park west of Whitewaters, three white rhino arriving in July 1963.

---

[129] Area Report, Khumalo and Gulati, September 1963, S 2827/1/9/.

[130] Interview with Jacob Moyo, 21 July 1988.

[131] Meeting of the Matopos sub-committee, 12 October 1962; Annual Report, 1962/3, F 128 TD 1079/1, vol. 2.

[132] Director, Historical Monuments Commission to Chairman, Rhodes Matopos Estate Advisory Board, 25 February 1963, Ashton folders.

[133] E. A. Marshall to District Secretary, NRB, 5 December 1962, Ashton folders.

12 Cyrene Mission chapel after a firebomb during the period of nationalist sabotage

By 1965 it appeared safe for white tourists to sample the delights of the peopleless Park without fear. An area without motor roads was created in the eastern part of the Park and it was noted in August 1967 that 'Africans will never be allowed back into the Wilderness Area'. There were some ambiguities in National Park findings now that people had been removed from the Park. Having so long blamed the people for erosion and silting, conservationists now wrote unapologetically about erosion 'due to climatic factors' and 'the natural phenomena of the silt and weed growth in Maleme Dam'.[134] But the greatest irony was that now they had got rid of the people, the Matopos Park authorities were able to celebrate its culture and history without cost by dressing up its employees in 'traditional' costume.

Private enterprise soon joined in the game. Tourists visiting the new Park could no longer see African life. So an 'Ndebele Village' was built on the Bulawayo/Matopos road:

> The village was named Mthethwa's kraal. It resembled a typical Ndebele village with its inhabitants carrying out daily duties as if they were in a real Ndebele village, all for the benefit of tourists … women grinding meal, others busy on beadwork, baskets, mats and many other crafts depicting African crafts as they were made by the tribesmen before the advent of the

[134] Conservation Officer, Matopos to Secretary, NRB, 2 July 1965; District Secretary to Secretary, NRB, 9 August 1967, F 128 TD 1079/1, vol. 2.

white man.... Tourists paid entrance fees just to see the setting of a typical Native village. Inside was a bone-thrower who told them their fortune. A young man carrying an assegai and a shield was gyrating on the side of the road to attract passers-by. His garb was that of a warrior of old. The whole scene was scintillating.[135]

Here were authentic traditionalists, without tourists having to see incongruous modernisers and improvers!

Once the new Park had been created and fitted out with rest camps and picnic areas and roads the white eye triumphed over the black in 'seeing' the Matopos. The revived school of Christian landscape painting at Cyrene Mission received a setback when ZAPU saboteurs set fire to the church. Meanwhile, white water colourists flourished; white poets drank in the silence of the peopleless hills. This was certainly a triumph over African nationalism. It remained to be seen whether it would survive the turn to armed violence and the coming of guerrilla war.

[135] *Chronicle*, 18 February 1986. In this piece Lewis Sibanda was flashing back 'to the late 1960s and early 1970s'.

7

Tradition &
Nationalism

Regiments,
Shrines
& Monuments

The Passage from Collaboration to Nationalist Resistance,
Wenlock, 1950–66

Wenlock entered the 1950s in a mood completely different from that of the embittered people of the National Park and the Matopos Reserve. Chief Sigombe Mathema had been installed as the candidate both of Native Commissioner Cramer and of *Sofasi-hamba*. Land Development Officer L. A. Thompson, who had faced so much opposition in Wenlock, nevertheless agreed with Cramer that its people were not intrinsically 'undisciplined and difficult'. If they were given secure tenure they would prove 'very useful material'.[1] Soon after Sigombe's installation the Land Apportionment Act amendments of 1950 redefined most of Wenlock as a Native Area. Cramer at once told Sigombe this news and the people became 'generally quiet'.[2] The conditions were now in place for collaborative improvement in Wenlock. While in the National Park the iron hand was being shown and Nqabe Tshuma was first jailed and then seized at his kraal, handcuffed, thrown into a truck and forcibly evicted, the velvet glove caressed Sigombe and Daniel Dube. Links between the *Nqameni* and the rest of the Matopos, between *Sofasihamba* and *Sofasonke*, were for a time severed.

Daniel Dube now came into his own. The self-help policies of *Sofasihamba* began to be implemented. Advised by Dube, Sigombe adopted an ambitious scheme for the improvement of Wenlock by its own people. Cattle were to be sold to pay for a bridge across the Tuli River, which divided Wenlock into two; yet more cattle were to be sold to pay for new schools and the addition of advanced classes at existing ones; Daniel's wife, Anna, was to set up the Sigombe Women's Club, the first African women's club in Matabeleland. Sigombe welcomed Agricultural Demonstrators, providing they were *Nqama*, and called on local agrarian innovators, like Mark Dokotela Ncube, for advice

[1] L. A. Thompson to Director of Native Agriculture, 20 January 1949, BE 8/3/2/1.
[2] Cramer's statement, 2 December 1960, S 2823/13.

195

and assistance with winter grazing. Sigombe and Daniel believed that by doing all this they could escape the sort of direct government intervention that was happening everywhere else in the Matopos. The culling of cattle to raise money for the bridge and for schools; Sigombe's stock improvement – these would make destocking needless.

Cramer gave them full support. He urged that the agency for self-development should be a properly constituted Council rather than the continuing mass meetings of *Sofasihamba*. By the end of 1952 he was able to report that 'a properly directed and active Council' was in place to manage the rehabilitation of Wenlock.

> Sufficient land has been allocated for the needs of a peasant community. The native population is generally free from political reaction. In such an atmosphere the machinations of political agitators and other self-seekers have little effect and they are given scant recognition.[3]

The next eighteen months saw the honeymoon period of collaboration, as money was collected for the bridge; the Sigombe Women's Club was set up; the Council met; and there was no destocking, forced labour or prosecution for breaches of the agricultural rules. The influence of the Matabeleland Home Society, whose organising genius, Sipambaniso, died in April 1952, withered away in Wenlock. *Sofasihamba* was fully behind the new policy. It was almost as if 'Home Rule' for the *Nqameni* had been achieved. In October 1953 Daniel Dube felt sufficiently self-confident as an African leader to announce that it was 'his intention to stand in the Federal elections'.[4]

Then in July 1954 Cramer was transferred to another district. Daniel Dube, now Secretary of the *Nqama* Council, bitterly lamented his going. The people were 'deeply wounded and heart-broken. They were worried that [their] schemes which had not yet been completed in Mr Cramer's time might not come to fruition.'[5] For a time, however, it seemed that the progressive alliance with the administration was continuing. The 1955 Annual Report of the Secretary for Native Affairs expressly singled out Chief Sigombe for his 'good and solid work'; the Gwanda Annual Report praised the completion of a 'high-level bridge' across the Tuli. In April 1956 Daniel Dube organised a festivity at the bridge, at which he laid on a demonstration of Wenlock's traditional modernity. There was 'tribal dancing by local Africans who dressed in warrior costume'; there was a competition for mission school choirs; Dube himself was Master of Ceremonies.[6] As late as June 1958 the bridge still figured as the centre-piece of Wenlock's public relations with the state. The Governor came to open it; he was hailed with the royal salute of *Bayete* by happy tribesmen; Sigombe declared his people 'highly honoured'.[7]

Yet the next reference to Wenlock in the *Bantu Mirror* revealed that the consensus between Chief, Council, the Wenlock progressives and the Native Commissioner had decisively broken down. Daniel Dube himself was quoted on 4 April 1959 to the effect that government had allowed inadequate powers to chiefs 'in such matters as the

[3] Annual Report, Gwanda, 1952.
[4] *Bantu Mirror*, 17 October 1953. In the event Daniel did not contest the elections.
[5] *Bantu Mirror*, 10 July 1954.
[6] *Bantu Mirror*, 21 April 1956.
[7] *Bantu Mirror*, 7 June 1958.

allocation of land and destocking which are all decided upon by Demonstrators', and on 29 August – when he was referred to as 'of *Sofasonke*' – he contended that 'because the chairmen of Reserve Councils are Native Commissioners the Councils have become ineffective and should die a natural death.' When Daniel Dube of all people was repudiating the Council it was obvious that a profound change had come over Wenlock politics. Other Wenlock progressives made equally disillusioned comments on the results of self-help. On 4 April 1959 another Dube – E. Dube, headmaster of Mayezane school in Wenlock – wrote to the *Mirror* to complain that 'Africans in rural areas for many years now have been putting up very beautiful school buildings', yet when they asked that higher standards should be taught in them they were told 'they cannot have the higher standards they wanted because the Government cannot pay for extra teachers. Missionaries are the same.'

In 1959, as it turned out, Wenlock was just on the verge of nationalist politics. Indeed, Sigombe was soon to become the nationalist chief *par excellence*. How are we to account for this second crucial transition in Wenlock's politics?

We cannot explain Wenlock's transition to nationalism by focusing upon 1959. The answers lie much deeper. There was an opposition to, or at least a reservation about, the policy of progressive collaboration even while it was being attempted and doubts about the Council from its inception. Wenlock had one major grievance throughout the 1950s; and two others which became more and more sharply felt. The standing grievance concerned land; the accentuating grievances concerned destocking and schooling. Taken together they reveal that Cramer's solution was doomed to failure. Just as the well-known case of Chief Mangwende, hailed as a developer but then deposed as a staunch supporter of Joshua Nkomo, had shown that the Rhodesian state could not work with progressive chiefs in Mashonaland, so the story of Chief Sigombe and Wenlock proved the same for Matabeleland. The hopes and abilities which had been invested in Wenlock's period of self-help now came to be entrusted to the emerging movements of nationalism.

The land grievance arose from the decisions made when Wenlock was declared a Native Area. The government's purchase of land in 1946 had amounted to 165,092 acres. In 1948, however, the Danziger Committee recommended that Sheet Farm and the 'gold belt' area be excluded from the area for African occupation. The Committee suggested that only 119,673 acres be set aside as Native Area. Exclusion from the southern zone meant that the *Nqama* were unable to water their cattle. But worse was to follow. During the parliamentary debate in 1950 on the amendments then proposed to the Land Apportionment Act, the Minister of Native Affairs announced his intention to reduce the Wenlock Native Area still further. Only 84,767 acres were now allocated – little more than half the 1946 purchase. The Minister admitted that the whole area was 'presently overpopulated' and that 'as we are only taking approximately half the area, certain movements would have to be made.'[8]

When Cramer told Sigombe in 1950 that a Native Area had now been securely established he also had to tell him about these exclusions. Cramer could only hope that Sigombe and Daniel Dube would accept his own good faith in being prepared to protest

---

[8] Memorandum, April 1961, S 2823/13.

against the decision and to lobby for more land. Certainly his Annual Reports were unequivocal in their condemnation. Indeed his report for 1951 reveals that even in the heyday of his collaboration with Sigombe the land issue was creating serious problems:

> Another error in legislation has occurred, as a result of which there is strong anti-European feeling which is being fanned by irresponsible people in Bulawayo with whom the local intelligensia are in constant touch.... On a declaration of good faith by the Government, these people would change their present attitude of resentment and hostility to one of co-operation.[9]

His 1952 report continued the attack, this time focusing on 5,500 acres of land 'vital to the well being of the people ... as affording access to water in the Mtshabezi River'. Cramer declared that:

> This situation should never have arisen in the first place and to permit it to continue because of blind observance of the Land Apportionment Act, regardless of human and economic factors, and thus cause further resentment unneccessarily, can only be described as crass stupidity. Most urgent representations have been made by this office ... but to no avail. The Government thus plays directly into the hands of the agitator.[10]

The land issue allowed radicals like Johnson Sigodo Dube to carry on their argument against reliance on the *Nqama* Council and collaboration with the state. For the time being, though, Sigombe made use of the avenues open to him. In 1951 he raised the land issue at the Chiefs Assembly. When the Council was formed the question was at once raised there. Cramer urged that some sort of concession by the state was crucial to the credibility of the Council system in Wenlock and in the 1953 Land Apportionment amendments the Native Area was extended to make a connection with the Mtshabezi River.[11] Cramer was later able to gain other concessions which brought the size of the Native Area up to the total 119,673 acres originally recommended by Danziger. Nevertheless, Sigombe and his supporters continued greatly to resent the exclusion of the rest of the land.

The issue flared to life again after Cramer had left Gwanda and after even Daniel Dube had lost faith in the conciliar system. Late in 1960 part of the excluded land was advertised for alienation as ranch land. There was an immediate agitation in Wenlock. *Sofasihamba* was dead, or existed only as a self-help ideology and the name of a store. The time of Daniel Dube's leadership was past. The Council was discredited. Sigombe now created new structures of opposition and action. He began to hold regular meetings at his kraal which were addressed both by his most trusted elders and by the firebrand, Johnson Sigodo, whose moment had now come. Johnson was on his way to prominence first in the NDP and then in ZAPU, but at this time he preserved an image of respectability in administrative eyes as a 'wealthy businessman'. He took the lead in collecting money with which to brief lawyers – £800 in all – and contacted Ben Baron in Bulawayo to represent the interests of the *Nqameni*.

The outcry and the legal representations were successful; the advertisement was withdrawn, much to the fury of local European farmers; an inquiry was promised into

---

[9] Annual Report, Gwanda, 1951.
[10] Annual Report, Gwanda, 1952.
[11] Cramer to Provincial Native Commissioner, 1 May 1953, S 2831/3/1.

'the land and cattle problem of the area'.[12] The Committee of Inquiry consisted of a white chairman and three officials together with two representatives of the *Nqameni*, Johnson Sigodo himself and Masoja Sibula Ndlovu, both of whom had been active in Wenlock politics for a long time, having attended Burombo's meeting at Whitewaters in December 1948. On 11 April 1961 Sigombe came to Gwanda for the Committee hearing, accompanied by some 70 of his followers. The chief was in a mood of high expectation. Perhaps it was still possible to extract something from the official system. But the day turned out to be a fiasco.

The lawyers sent a message to say that they could not appear because their fees had not yet been met; Sigombe was asked if he nevertheless wanted to present evidence or whether he would rather postpone; he asked if the two African Committee members could advise him and was told by the Chairman that they were supposed to be impartial and not party to the complaint. Sigombe withdrew and then returned and again asked the advice of Sigodo and Masoja Sibula. Under questioning from the white members, Sigodo admitted that he had raised funds and contacted lawyers. Thereupon the white members declared that the Committee was invalid and could no longer sit. At this point the lawyers phoned to say that they would appear after all; Sigodo offered to withdraw; Sigombe protested that to abandon the inquiry would be 'to the detriment of his people'. But it was all too late and the Committee broke up in confusion. It was a landmark day on Sigombe's road to nationalism.[13]

Belatedly the lawyers submitted a cogent memorandum, urging that

> the history of the Wenlock area is the history of the land problem in Southern Rhodesia.... The constant moves, the resulting insecurity of tenure and the inevitable limitation of stock have done much to put the inhabitants of the area in an un-cooperative frame of mind.

It made no sense to squeeze a large population into a smaller area and then destock:

> Under these circumstances the application of the Land Husbandry Act is merely providing dissatisfaction without any real benefit to the soil ... The reason for the persistent failure of Southern Rhodesia's land policies has been the policy of providing only just enough land for the existing African population and then an attempt or series of attempts are made to squeeze in the un-provided as they are ejected from the European areas.... The difficulties encountered by the Government in the Wenlock area are as much of its own making as those of 'evil doers'.[14]

It was one of the most perceptive comments on the Rhodesian land crisis but it came too late. So too did the eventual concessions made by the state. In March 1962 the land which had been advertised as a ranch was set aside for African settlement after all, becoming what is today Makwe Communal Land.[15] There had never really been a practical possibility of creating a thriving European ranching economy on Wenlock, but

---

[12] Cramer's statement to the 'Committee to Inquire into the Allocation of Wenlock Block for Native Occupation', 2 December 1960; protest by Gwanda Intensive Conservation Area against the withdrawal of the land from alienation, 14 April 1961, S 2823/13.

[13] European members of the Committee to Minister of Native Affairs, 11 April 1961, S 2823/13.

[14] Memorandum by counsel, 13 April 1961, S 2823/13.

[15] *Daily News*, 17 March 1962.

the belated recognition of this came only after a direct clash between the now nationalist *Nqameni* and the Rhodesian state.

This clash was exacerbated by resentment over cattle. During Cramer's time no attempt was made to destock. But in 1955 his successor, while still praising Sigombe for 'good and solid work', nevertheless noted that Wenlock was 'grossly over-stocked'. He applied for the Land Husbandry Act to be applied in order to achieve destocking.[16] In May 1956 an assessment committee recommended a greatly reduced number of stock. Destocking was to be achieved by early 1958 at which time grazing permits would be issued under the Act. 'The Chief and his people vigorously protested against the application of the Land Husbandry Act and particularly against the limitation of stock and lands. They felt that their economy was being undermined and that industry could not absorb the surplus population. The virus of opposition to the Land Husbandry Act spread from Wenlock southwards into the rest of Gwanda.'[17]

The 1956 Annual Report identified that year as the beginning of the struggle for Sigombe's mind between those who wished to cling to the conciliar system and those who wished for resistance – between Daniel Dube and Johnson Sigodo:

> Chief Sigombe's Nqama people, through a few vocal leaders, who seem to hold the chief in their sway, have protested vigorously against the findings of the assessment committee. Several acrimonious meetings have been held, deputations and petitions have been presented to the Provincial Native Commissioner.... Sigombe has had a very troubled year, being swayed by two contending elements ... unable to make up his mind whether to join those who oppose the application of the Land Husbandry Act or those who support it.[18]

For the moment, both factions combined to try to avoid destocking by claiming success for Wenlock's own self-help management of cattle. On 23 June 1956 the *Home News*, reflecting the Wenlock progressive line, praised Sigombe for giving ten of his own cattle towards the Tuli bridge, being guided in this, as the paper noted approvingly, by Daniel Dube of *Sofasikangele* store. In January 1957 the paper returned to the issue. Destocking was becoming intolerable – 'even the chiefs are literally crying'. It took the case of Sigombe, 'one of the few chiefs willing to reduce the stock of his area.... He effects his destocking in different ways' to meet the cost of the bridge and of schools:

> But strange to say, the Chief seems now to be given a hard time by the Native Department of Gwanda.... He has been told to get rid of surplus cattle within a comparatively short time.... Why should Chief Matema be treated in this unfair manner? What is the grievance against him?[19]

In 1958 the Governor opened the Tuli bridge and the Annual Report rejoiced in being able to claim that 'there was no whisper of African National Congress activity' in

---

[16] Annual Report, Gwanda, 1955.

[17] 'Land Husbandry Act. Gwanda District', November 1957, S 2808/1/10.

[18] Annual Report, Gwanda, 1956.

[19] The *Home News* for 4 May 1957 carried a report from a 'Wenlock Resident' noting that the Provincial Commissioner had visited Sigombe 'in connection with his refusal to have cattle counted in his area'. The correspondent asserted that stock in Wenlock were 'in very good condition'.

Wenlock. Yet Sigombe's opposition to Land Husbandry and to destocking remained absolute. 'Early in the year an attempt was made to issue grazing permits to one section of Wenlock. The meeting was boycotted however and it was decided to drop the matter temporarily.'[20] In 1959 the conciliar system collapsed and was abandoned even by Daniel Dube. By this time Sigombe had made his position plain in an episode still joyfully remembered in *Nqameni* myth. A white cattle inspector coming to the chief's kraal to mark cattle for culling was told: 'Here are my cattle and here is my assegai. Take one of the beasts and you get my assegai with it. Take all of them and I may as well use it on myself.' The white man went away, so it is said, and the people's cattle were saved.

However coloured this tale may be, there is no doubt that in mid-December 1959 Sigombe wrote a remarkable letter of protest to the Native Commissioner, which even more remarkably he copied to the press. It marked his final repudiation of the Cramer-style alliance:

> At my place, it seems as though I have always been at grips with the Native Commissioner, as though I am trying to defy the regulations of the Native Commissioner or the Government. This has been put by Native Commissioners of my place in succession. As chief I thought I had some powers of this area to enable the authorities to understand the people of that place.... Is it fair for the Native Commissioner to cut short their needs before consulting the chiefs for explanation? The reports I have sent as a chief to the Native Commissioner have always been met with oppositions.... I have been asking the Native Commissioner to let me do what I want with my and my peoples' cattle.... I have not been listened to. Truly speaking, during these days I have not yet seen any of my people who can live, educate children, clothe them, his wife and himself without cattle.

Sigombe ended with something close to nationalist sentiment:

> God provided all people with their different gifts in life. Black men were given, as their treasure, cattle to live on and whites were shown the wisdom of money ... What evils have Africans done that whites feel disturbed by their cattle? Are not Africans as important in the eyes of God as whites are?.... One European is given chances to buy for himself hundreds and hundreds of cattle at the expense of the African.... Is there any sense in that cattle have got to be for Europeans alone, and land also has been taken from the African by them?[21]

It was clear that the issue was about to be directly joined in Wenlock. In July 1960 the *Home News* reported that while Sigombe and his people knew 'only too well' that they 'cannot fight the government', they were 'adamant' against destocking. In the same month the *Bantu Mirror* reported the formation of a NDP branch in Gwanda.

Informants in Wenlock see the shifting political struggle there rather as the Native Commissioners saw it, as a struggle between two factions for the soul of Chief Sigombe. 'Daniel and Johnson Sigodo quarrelled', says Mark Doketela Ncube. 'They were at loggerheads over the chief. They had a tug of war over the chief and Johnson pulled him to his side.'[22]

---

[20] Annual Report, Gwanda, 1958.

[21] *Home News*, 9 January 1960. The English version of Sigombe's letter was written by his secretary, M. N. Dube.

[22] Interview with Mark Dokotela Ncube, North Wenlock, 30 August 1990.

Clearly personalities, and especially that of Sigombe, were very important, but other wider forces were at work. Wenlock and the *Nqameni* had intensive interaction with Bulawayo. In August 1990 I interviewed Mr M. Sidile in Bulawayo. Sidile is of mixed Kalanga and Venda origin; his family had lived on crown land in Matobo district and had been moved off it in 1953 and into north Wenlock, close to *Sofa* store. Sidile himself worked for the City Council in Bulawayo. Although he was not one of the *Nqameni*, nor even Ndebele in a narrow sense, he became chairman of the Wenlock 'home boys' committee in Bulawayo which organised receptions for Sigombe when the chief visited town. He can remember cycling from Bulawayo to Sigombe's kraal when the 'home boys' needed to make representations to him – about the inadequacies of the Bulawayo to Wenlock bus service, for example.[23] Gradually this constant interaction between the chief and Wenlock men in Bulawayo came to exercise a nationalist influence. Young Wenlock men became some of the most ardent nationalists in town. A significant example was the son of Daniel and Ann Dube, Ethan, who became a leading figure in the NDP and ZAPU Youth Leagues. As Wenlock became solidly nationalist in the early 1960s, Native Commissioners began to deplore the stream of urban 'agitators' who came out to Wenlock to 'intimidate'.

But the rise of nationalism in Wenlock was plainly not just a question of urban influences. Among the *Nqameni* the disillusionment with the old 'moral economy' myths, both of Rhodes and of Richardson, was particularly sharp. Nationalist leaders in Wenlock saw themselves not as backwoodsmen opposed to all change but as modernisers frustrated by colonial inequalities and rigidities. Above all, nationalist mobilisation in Wenlock was rapid from the second half of 1960 because of the previous existence there of a succession of organisations. *Sofasihamba*, the meetings which gave expressions to the wishes of what Johnson Sigodo variously called 'the people and their chief' or 'the chief and the community' – these opened up the way for nationalist mobilisation and all the more readily because Sigombe himself was at the heart of it.

Admittedly, nationalist influence at first spread slowly in Wenlock. The revived African National Congress (ANC) was formed in 1957 under Joshua Nkomo; through 1958 there was no sign of it in Wenlock; only at the beginning of 1959 did the agrarian entrepreneur, Mark Dokotela Ncube, busily draining his sponge in the foothills of the Matopos, become chairman of an ANC branch. He says that he took the step with Sigombe's approval but neither he nor the chief expected that within a few weeks of the formation of the branch a state of emergency would be declared and Congress banned. Much to his astonishment and alarm Mark Dokotela found himself a prisoner in Khami jail, along with seven branch officials from Gwanda town, and very many more radical men.[24] When he was released in May 1959 Dokotela's nationalist sympathies went 'underground'.[25]

For the remainder of 1959 there was no nationalist organisation so that Daniel Dube's expression of disillusion with the Council and Sigombe's proto-nationalist letter

[23] Interview with M. Sidile, Bulawayo, 8 August 1990.
[24] Annual Report, Gwanda, 1959.
[25] Interview with Mark Dokotela Ncube, north Wenlock, 30 August 1990.

of protest both took place in a political vacuum. The NDP, when it emerged in January 1960, was at first very much an urban phenomenon. But in the second half of 1960 it began to penetrate the rural areas and by that time Wenlock was ready for it. A key element in the spread of the NDP in southern Matabeleland seems to have been Joshua Nkomo's election as President of the NDP. The *Bantu Mirror* reported on 5 November 1960 that Nkomo's elevation had generated 'widespread approval and excitement' and cited a 'sympathiser of the NDP' in Gwanda town to the effect that there was 'an almost uncontrollable wave of excitement' in the district. 'The news is being flashed to the reserves near here where the party has established branches.'

In 1961 Wenlock really went NDP. A few days after the fiasco of the Wenlock Inquiry on 11 April, the *Bantu Mirror* reported that despite prohibitions on NDP meetings in the Reserves, the Gwanda branch was determined to 'get at the rural areas'. An NDP meeting in Gwanda town had attracted people from Wenlock and other reserves on foot and on bicycle and 'speakers were wildly cheered'.[26] On 24 May the *Daily News* reported that Joshua Nkomo himself had addressed a meeting of two thousand people in Gwanda town. Most of the audience came from the surrounding rural areas and they received Nkomo with 'thunderous cheers'. By November 1961 – and probably considerably earlier – Johnson Sigodo was himself chairman of the Gwanda district committee of the NDP.[27]

Official reports show that by this time Wenlock ranked with Matobo and Nkai as the nationalist trouble spots of Matabeleland. The 1961 Annual Report admitted that

> in Wenlock stock rights have still not been accepted by the people. Cases brought against a few of these people failed through a technicality in the Land Husbandry Act and the Proclamation of Wenlock. These have since been amended but further prosecutions have been avoided for political reasons.

Wenlock was alive with 'active opposition to the Land Husbandry Act'; there was 'illegal ploughing' and 'politically inspired resistance to follow up work'; fences which separated Wenlock from white farms and ranches were being cut. Sigombe was 'constantly under pressure' and the NDP had a 'strong following'. It had become essential to take 'a firm stand'.[28]

In December 1961 that firm stand was taken. The *Bantu Mirror* reported on 9 December the arrest of Gwanda NDP officials as part of the general swoop consequent on the banning of the party. Soldiers and police were deployed in Wenlock. As Nkomo complained on 30 December, 'the troops collect all the people on arrival at a kraal and ask them to produce their NDP cards. When they fail to do so the tribesmen are made to sit down and the troops fire into the ground just in front of the people.'[29]

On 19 December Chief Native Commissioner Morris paid a visit to what he hoped was the properly cowed Sigombe. He later described his address to Sigombe's people:

[26] *Bantu Mirror*, 22 April 1961.

[27] *Daily News*, 8 November 1961.

[28] Annual Report, Gwanda, 1961.

[29] *Bantu Mirror*, 30 December 1961. The Sindebele version of this report focuses especially on Gwanda district.

During the course of a long meeting I explained to the Chief and his people that there had been a great deal of undermining of Law and Order practice lately in reference to the Native Land Husbandry Act.... I told them that I felt sure that they were being misguided by the Chief and a few of his misguided advisers.... The time for talking was now finished, and I told the Chief and all his kraal heads who were present there that if they failed or refused to take possession of their [grazing] permits within 14 days it would be considered a continuance of the defiance and disregard of the Act.... We were quite serious and intended prosecuting.

Morris then spoke to Sigombe privately, telling him that he was personally responsible for the breakdown of law and order. He must now take out a grazing permit. Sigombe replied that 'his people could do as they pleased but that he was not going to take out a permit. He put his hands over his stomach and said "You are killing me".' Morris told him that his salary would be suspended as from 1 January 1962.[30] Sigombe at once responded to his suspension, writing to the Provincial Comissioner on 2 January 1962:

I must leave the chieftainship. I do not want my name to be known as chief. I do not want my name to be known on the grazing rights. Sir, it is surprising that the Government is killing all the people. The bridge was built out of cattle, also schools were built out of cattle. So all this work must be destroyed.... It is better I die with my own people. All is o.k. Get rid of me.... The law does not want the people to get lands but is allowed to go into the people's cattle.[31]

He took no steps to obtain a grazing permit.

He was at once arrested, together with his 'right-hand man', Headman Masole Nkala. 'What is upsetting the people very much', reported the *Daily News* on 13 January 1962, 'is the presence of police jeeps in the area shortly after the troops had been around before Christmas, terrorising the people.'[32] During the course of the pre-trial proceedings Sigombe was held in a cell overnight. 'I was put in a police cell. Anyone could relieve themselves in my presence', complained the chief at his trial on 19 January. He also declared that as chief he could not have taken a grazing permit until he was sure that all the people had agreed to it. But he was found guilty and fined £20.[33]

All this left Sigombe in a state of deep resentment. He complained that continued suspension of his salary was unlawful – 'I do not recognise Mr Morris' *bundu* court'. The Wenlock people wrote to rebuke the Native Commissioner for dishonouring their chief:

The people will not respect the chief and later they will not respect you and you will not be able to handle them ... and children will not even obey their parents and good conduct and behaviour will be lost. What a disaster.[34]

But as well as expressing this resounding statement of the patriarchal ethos, the *nqameni* were as ardently ZAPU as they had been NDP. Johnson Sigodo Dube was now the leading ZAPU official in the district. And in August the patriarchal and nationalist

[30] Regina versus Sigombe, 19 January 1962, Per 5, Gwanda Provincial Administrator's office.
[31] Sigombe to PNC, 2 January 1962, original in Sindebele, Per 5, Provincial Administrator's office, Gwanda.
[32] The *Bantu Mirror* of 20 January 1962, in a Sindebele report, said that most people in Wenlock were still refusing to take out permits or to dip cattle, despite Sigombe's arrest and the presence of troops and police.
[33] Regina versus Sigombe, 19 January 1962, Per 5, Gwanda.
[34] Letter from Wenlock Tribesmen to Native Commissioner, Gwanda, n.d. 1962, Per 5, Gwanda.

tendencies came together on the national stage. On 8 August 1962 Sigombe went to the Native Commissioner's office, Gwanda:

> I told him that I was still in the box.... I said that [since] I was not eating I'd not be expected to work for the Government. I was still closed in. I did not belong to the Government ... I told the Native Commissioner that I was finished with him and it was only the people that remained.[35]

He then went outside where Johnson Sigodo was waiting in the ZAPU car. They drove straight to Bulawayo where a huge ZAPU rally was to be addressed by Joshua Nkomo.

Nkomo's meeting of 8 August 1961 attracted 30,000 people. Nkomo called for a boycott of Rhodesian industrial goods. Then Sigombe was called on to bestow *Nqama* legitimacy:

> Chief Sigombe Matema of Wenlock, who was present by invitation, presented assegais, a knobkerrie, a shield, a feather head-gear and armbands of feathers to Mr Nkomo and said these things were very essential for him to have in his warrior fight for political rights.[36]

Interpreted by Ethan Dube, son of Daniel, Sigombe told Nkomo: 'No man fought without a weapon in the olden days. Take this shield which our forefathers used when they went to fight. And take this spear which our forefathers used to attack the enemy and this knobkerry they also used to finish the enemy off with.'[37] As the huge audience cheered, *Induna* Sigombe Mathema of the *Nqama* regiment invoked the days of Dhliso and Nkonkobela and Mtuwane and of the risings of 1896.

In the eyes of the administration the chief had changed from being their most reliable ally in Matabeleland to being one of their most dangerous opponents. The administration had hoped to use Ndebele identity against nationalism. Now Sigombe had put the aristocratic Ndebele military tradition at the service of the Kalanga/Ndebele Nkomo. When he had been made chief, Sigombe had been given the task of uniting all the *Nqameni*. Now this unity of progressives and traditionalists, literate and illiterate, Christians and non-Christians seemed threatening. The Native Commissioner set out to break down Wenlock solidarity.

He did this by backing school teachers and mission station elites against Sigombe. While storekeepers like Daniel Dube and Johnson Sigodo had been active in Wenlock politics and agrarian modernisers like Mark Dokotela Ncube had been nationalist pioneers, serving teachers were not allowed to participate in politics. In any case, a tension had arisen between the ambition of 'the Chief and people' to control education and the determination of the Brethren in Christ missionaries to continue to run their network of primary schools. One of the ambitions of *Sofasihamba* had been to raise funds to improve standards at schools. One of the disillusionments expressed in 1959 was that when the community built extra school buildings the use made of them remained firmly under mission control.

In the early 1960s there was a counter-attack against the 'interference' of 'the Chief

---

[35] Evidence of Sigombe, Regina versus Sigombe, 10 September 1962, Per 5, Gwanda.
[36] *Home News*, 9 August 1962.
[37] *Daily News*, 9 August 1992.

and people'. School committees were formed, largely consisting of opponents of Sigombe, some of these being partisans of the now extinct Dlodlo chieftaincy, others being mission loyalists. The Brethren in Christ missionaries were themselves acutely sensitive to any criticism of, or threat to, their monopoly. Even when Anna Dube, through the still respectable Sigombe Women's Club, and making representations to the United Federal Party's Build a Nation campaign, ventured in 1961 to criticise the inadequacies of educational provision in Wenlock, the missionaries asserted that the schools were their business and no-one else's. Anna maintained that higher education had once been unneccessary in the rural areas where the wealth of people had lain in land and cattle; now that both had been so sharply reduced and young people had lost cattle rights, the only hope lay in education for urban employment. By contrast the missionaries persisted with their ambition for a basic Christian education which would maintain rural solidarity.[38]

Native Commissioner Williams backed the new school committees against Sigombe and his supporters. The tension between the two groups dominated Wenlock's internal politics in 1963. The Wenlock tribesmen complained to the Native Commissioner that 'it is the duty of the chief to bring to you any matters that affect the people of Wenlock. If you will accept complaints from anybody on matters that affect the people, you will be making too many chiefs in the area.' Sigombe himself complained against the Sitezi school committee which was dominated by Dlodlo partisans: 'There is no peace at Inqama where I was made a chief by three branches. I want to restore order and peace in our own African laws.'[39] The chief's supporters complained that the teachers and the Native Commissioner were working together against him:

> Is it lawful for the Christian deacon to work with the Native Commissioner to do down the duties of the chief? The Bible Matthew 24 tells us that the Christians shall be betrayed by the un-christianised people. But why does a Christian deacon and Christian teachers betray the unchristianised chief and his people?[40]

The quarrel with the missionaries came to a head in February 1963 when the Brethren raised school fees. A great meeting was held at Sigombe's kraal, which was addressed by Johnson Sigodo Dube and others. The meeting decided that rather than pay the increased fees they would shut the schools down. On 30 March Sigombe sent two of his police 'to compel or induce children not to attend school ... and certain teachers not to open the schools.' I spoke to informants in Wenlock who still recall their boyish excitement when they were given an unexpected holiday by the arrival of the chief's policemen.

The administration decided to crack down. One of the policemen, Nemezi Ndlovu, was sentenced to six months in prison under the Law and Order Maintenance Act. Sigombe himself was prosecuted under the same Act on 14 October 1963. He was acquitted because no-one would give evidence against him and Ndlovu swore that he had not been given orders by the chief. The administration was relentless. On 8 January

---

[38] Anna Dube showed me her letter to the Build a Nation campaign at her home near Mtshabezi Mission; she herself told me of the mission response.

[39] Sigombe to Native Commisssioner, 4 July 1963, Per 5, Gwanda.

[40] 'Agenda' for meeting of 30 July 1963, *ibid.*

1964 Ndlovu was again on trial, this time on charges of perjury. He was given another six months. Sigombe was sentenced in Bulawayo on 30 January 1964 to a fine of £20.[41]

The fine was not the point, however. The administration now had the pretext it needed for deposing Sigombe. The Secretary for Internal Affairs visited Wenlock in early March and decided to act against the chief. 'The air in and around Bulawayo is very thick with rumours', noted the *Home News*,

> true or untrue, to the effect that Chief Matema Sigombe of Enqameni in Wenlock is facing possible dismissal. He seems to believe that his duty and responsibility lie in doing all in his power to help his followers through his wise leadership to be as happy and contented as possible. In doing this he has unfortunately made himself very unpopular with the Department of African Affairs who seem to like and prefer the sycophantic type of chiefs ... Chief Sigombe is a good leader, frank and outspoken by nature.

This was a nationalist accolade, the *Home News* now being edited from Gonakudzwinga, where its editor was detained with Joshua Nkomo.[42]

In the second week of March 1964 the new District Commissioner, Ferguson, told Sigombe that his deposition was being considered. But Ferguson thought it would be difficult to find a successor or anyone competent to act. Headman Damu was in jail for perjury; Headman Masole had a previous conviction; Sigombe's only son was blind and a cripple; 'there is no clear cut line of succession'; it was 'most difficult to find a line of approach to the people or even to find out who are the influential leaders or leaders of the people'. In any case it was widely said that the people 'will not accept any other chief while Sigombe is still alive.'[43]

Still defiant, and still very much chief of the people, Sigombe fired off a letter of protest against the missionaries:

> As you know I built the schools with my people by ourselves. The missionary just came to need fees from us. What worries me is the methods he uses in order for him to get school-fees. He allows my people like the teachers, church leaders, storemen to be leaders of the opposition, who of course go horrible and really hostile that I could hardly control.... N.B. What is there that ties the African education and the Gospel preachers from America? Can the African lose his education because of the Gospel of God?[44]

It was not until December 1964 that the Provincial Commissioner came to Wenlock, called the elders together and announced the deposition of Sigombe. Headman Masole 'expressed the feelings of the people and said they were now dead as people'. My informants say that they went on regarding Sigombe as chief. In Wenlock the Rhodesia Front policy of Communal Development and cooption of traditional institutions never stood a chance. The people stood behind their deposed chief and operated outside the structures of local government.

[41] This reconstruction is based on the Sigombe file in the Provincial Administrator's office, Gwanda.
[42] *Home News*, 7 March 1964.
[43] District Commissioner, Gwanda to Provincial Commissioner, Matabeleland South, 16 March 1964, Per 5, Gwanda.
[44] Sigombe to District Commissioner, Gwanda, 25 March 1964, *ibid.*

Meanwhile, during the time of contestation between Sigombe and the missionaries, Wenlock had become yet more intensely nationalist. When ZAPU was banned in September 1962 Johnson Sigodo became a regional councillor on its thinly veiled successor, the People's Caretaker Council. Ethan Dube began to prepare for sabotage. After Nkomo's leadership was challenged by the formation of the Zimbabwe African National Union (ZANU) as a rival party, the Gwanda nationalists made their views plain. ZANU, they said, was a 'hideous cancer'; Nkomo was 'the soul, will, spirit and personality of our divine cause'.[45] In February 1964 Johnson Sigodo was arrested. Thereafter Wenlock exploded into nationalist violence.

My informants vividly remembered the heroes of 1964:

> People were very, very ZAPU. The party had very well organised structures. People opposed government very strongly. Schools were burnt, the fences of commercial farms were cut. Very many people were arrested and tortured, like Sigotwana who under torture revealed the names of colleagues. Johnson Sigodo was already in detention at that time, so it was these other men who were arrested and put on trial. One was Maboroyi Ndlovu, the district chairman, who was alleged to have led people to cut the fences. He was severely tortured but he refused to identify any of those who followed him, claiming to have cut the fences all by himself. Because of this he was given the nickname of 'Shield of the People'.... One leader committed suicide in 1964; he was detained, tortured, released, heard the Land Rover coming again and hanged himself. This was Sinoti Kumalo, a firm NDP and ZAPU man and a great politiciser of the people. Another activist was Thomas Ncube or 'Tomo' who was arrested and sentenced to three years in Khami. After the repression of 1964 there was surface quiet but people very much remembered and supported these men. And they still took Sigombe to be their chief.[46]

By 1964 a remarkable nationalist solidarity had been built in Wenlock. Nationalism had significantly changed in the process, becoming much less Christian progressive and much more populist than it had been four years earlier. But Sigombe, patron of the progressives, had no difficulties with revived tradition. In 1966, when the administration were desperately trying to find a successor, threatening letters were sent from Bulawayo to all the possible candidates:

> We have kept a very keen eye on all your activities and you should not think you are not seen. Today we are taking steps against you and your family. We are advising you to collect corn and make beer, kill a black beast and speak to your ancestors to bid farewell to all your relations. Because on the day of our arrival you will not be able to bid farewell.[47]

In October 1966 the District Commissioner reported that Sigombe 'has been promised the post of Paramount Chief of Matabeleland South when the country goes to majority rule'.[48] *Nqameni* traditionalism had been placed squarely at the service of nationalism.

[45] *Home News*, 10 August 1963.
[46] Interview with Abraham Mabuto Moyo and Calvin Madlela, Bulawayo, 24 August 1990.
[47] District Commissioner, Gwanda to Provincial Commissioner, 25 August 1966, Per 5, Gwanda.
[48] District Commissioner, Gwanda to Provincial Commissioner, 19 October 1966, *ibid*.

Nationalism in the Matopos: Graves, Momuments and Shrines

It was not only Ndebele regimental military traditions which were placed at the service of nationalism. The symbolic and religious resources of the Matopos were also profoundly drawn upon. Even after the evictions from the Matopos, the Rhodesian government had continued to try to use their monuments in the old way. In June 1953, for instance, there was a 'National Pilgrimage to Rhodes's Grave', which involved the participation of the chiefs and of Ndaba Ncube, 'the original caretaker of the grave and one of those Natives who assisted at the burial'.[49] But after the creation of the peopleless Park and the eviction of all those who lived around Rhodes's Grave, there was a radical re-reading of the landscape of the Matopos. The National Park was re-imagined – and re-made – by the whites as wilderness. For nationalists this meant that it was all the more important to emphasise the great historical signs of the human history of the hills – its graves and monuments and shrines. But nationalist commemoration also involved many changes in the way these monuments were seen. Rhodes's grave and Mzilikazi's tomb at Entumbane had often been coupled together by Ndebele cultural nationalists. Now in radical nationalist rhetoric they were sharply separated. Rhodes's Grave became a sign of conquest and alienation. Entumbane became a symbol not only of Ndebele but also of African national independence. The Mwali shrines had often been seen as survivals of the pre-Ndebele past. In 1948 most people had regarded them as concerned only with rain rather than with politics. Now there were a series of historical re-imaginings. The shrines came to be thought of as an essential part of the Ndebele political order. They also came to be thought of as symbols of African ownership of the soil. The shrines both represented and gave legitimacy to the nationalist struggle to regain the land.

These new readings were partly the work of Bulawayo cultural nationalists, among whom Joshua Nkomo was by far the most important. They were also partly the work of the inhabitants of the Matopos themselves, whose commitment to the shrines and graves intensified as they were threatened with eviction and agrarian interference. Small-scale peasants, whose interests the shrines had always represented, now developed a counter-offensive against the Christian modernisers who had pioneered nationalism. A deeply rural nationalism developed which demanded loyalty to the Mwali rest-days and to the cult's ideologies of reciprocity between people and the environment. Finally, the new readings were the work of the shrine officials themselves as they developed the theocratic historiography of the cult to fit the new situation, or as they developed a scathing critique both of European 'development' and of the 'preservationist' ideology of the National Park.

Joshua Nkomo was himself a child of the Matobo district, and his family story repeats many of the themes of the preceding chapters of this book. As he writes in his autobiography, 'my parents were born when the country was still free'. They were Kalanga subjects of the Ndebele state. After the colonial conquest his father, Nyongolo,

---

[49] Native Commissioner, Gwanda to Provincial Native Commissioner, 22 April 1953, S 2831/3/1.

taught at the London Missionary Society school at Tshimale in the *mapani* veld. Nyongolo was sent to South Africa for three years of study. He returned to find that Tshimale was being closed down because white farmers had occupied the area. So the family moved to Bango school, 'a lovely place, in the high rainfall area of the Matopos foot-hills.' Chief Bango came from a leading Nyubi family, 'settled in the Matobo Hills area long before the arrival of Mzilikazi'. Nkomo remembered an idyllic childhood:

> The rivers Semukwe and Tshatshane flowed nearby from the Matopos, bringing year-round water for the people and the livestock. In this delightful place I was born. As children we swam in the pools and raced in little canoes. We snared small game.... There were steep slopes of water-polished granite, where we would slide on make-shift sledges.

But 'in due course the white people claimed it too for their own and once more we had to move on.' This time Nyongolo's family moved south of the *mapani*, first to Mbembeswana, 'dry, flat land, very bushy', then to Chief Malaba's area, and finally to Bidi in the Semokwe Reserve, where Nyongolo was dip supervisor.[50]

Joshua was educated in the mission school and his 'upbringing was strictly Christian'. Writing his autobiography in the 1980s he recalled, however, that 'I became much attracted to the traditional religion of our people' and stole away to take part in ancestral ceremonies. John Lonsdale has recently described the 'political theology' of another great nationalist culture-broker, Jomo Kenyatta, which emphasised the power of God – whether Kikuyu or Judaic – rather than the intercessory role of Christ.[51] In much the same way, Nkomo writes: 'The Christian word for God was translated as *uMlimu* in the Ndebele and *Mwali* in the Kalanga language. This God, it seemed to me, was the same whatever language was being used.'[52]

Nyongolo was a 'progressive' farmer, trading his surplus grain, owning a scotch cart, cattle, sheep, goats and donkeys. He also taught and preached. He was anxious that his son should gain practical skills, though until he was fifteen Joshua was needed to herd the family's thousand head of cattle. Then Joshua went north, to Tjolotjo Government Industrial School. After his training there he took a variety of jobs in Bulawayo, sometimes using his Kalanga when making lorry runs into Botswana; but mostly becoming part of the composite Ndebele identity of the city.

He saved up his wages until he was able to enrol at Adams College in South Africa. From there he went to the Jan Hofmeyer School of Social Work in Johannesburg, where he met Nelson Mandela and Seretse Khama. In 1948 he was back home in Bulawayo, one of its best educated and most travelled young men. Soon he was drawn into the ANC leadership.

Nkomo's travels had made him fascinated by identity. He rapidly became involved in exploring every level of his own. He became a leading member of the Kalanga

---

[50] Joshua Nkomo, *Nkomo. The Story of My Life*, Methuen, London, 1984, pp. 7–9. For the story of the successive evictions of the Bango people see Richard Werbner, *The Tears of the Dead*, Edinburgh, 1991, pp. 44 and 45.

[51] John Lonsdale, 'Kenyatta, God and Modernity', Public Lecture, Humboldt University colloquium, Berlin, October 1997.

[52] Joshua Nkomo, *Nkomo*, p. 13.

Culture Promotion Society and of the Matabeleland Home Society (MHS) as well as of Congress. His identity at home was Kalanga; in Bulawayo it was Ndebele; in Rhodesia as a whole it was nationalist. He believed in the possibility, indeed the desirability, of everyone possessing such a hierarchy of identities, each deep and valid and each enriching the other. Nkomo was a great synthesiser. In August 1950 he combined with a leading Shona moderniser, Jerry Vera, to announce their plans for a Society for the Preservation of African Culture. In London, they said, 'people respect their past'; so too should Africans. Nkomo 'spoke at length of people like Chaminuka, Mzilikazi and Mambo the Emperor', thus bringing together heroes of the Shona, Ndebele and Kalanga past:

> The aims of the Society are to encourage and collect all African folkstories, songs and dances; the erection of momuments to great Africans; the preservation and collection of African national costumes.[53]

In this syncretic vision Mzilikazi's grave at Entumbane was a national monument. Nkomo regularly went there to pay his respects to the Khumalo dead as a national rather than a 'tribal' gesture. His influence within the Matabele Home Society was radicalising its own view of the past. In November 1950 the Society refused to provide 'Matabele Tribal dancers' to participate in the Rhodes Centenary Exhibition, because 'so many families were unsettled [by eviction] and their joining in the merry-making on this occasion would be out of place.'[54]

Nkomo's quirky ally in the process of nationalist re-imagining, Charlton Ncgebetsha, took the implications of black 'unsettlement' a stage further. Rhodes's Grave at World's View, he wrote, 'was a place which has attracted kings, world statesmen and lesser mortals.' But 'there is something which should not be there at all. We mean the board with pictures on it showing how the Matabele of long gone by massacred, without mercy, white people in their frantic efforts to drive them back where they came from.' This board, with its subscription, 'There was no survivor', should be removed, Charlton warned. After all, all too many Africans thought of Rhodes as 'him who dispossessed them of their heritage' and admired 'their old heroes for butchering the white man'. This was a very long way from the old MHS idea of the graves of Rhodes and Mzilikazi as twin beacons lighting the Ndebele to freedom and progress.[55]

Nkomo's ideas were given much reinforcement by his visit to London in 1952. He found the city 'very grubby and not at all what you would expect of an imperial capital'. But if the British were not all that impressive in their modernity, they were remarkable for their traditionalism:

> We went to Westminister Abbey and to the Chapel Royal in Windsor, and walked on the graves of kings ... I began to think about Christianity and power. At home becoming a Christian meant giving up our own old ways to follow white clergymen and a white Christ. Our religion, in which we approached God through our ancestors and the history of our

[53] *Bantu Mirror*, 30 August 1950.
[54] *Bantu Mirror*, 1 November 1950.
[55] *Home News*, 27 February 1954.

people, was said to be primitive and backward. But here in England the ancestral tombs in the churches signified the continuity of the nation.[56]

'Can any person swear by the living God', asked Ncgebetsha after Nkomo's return, 'that the British people do not *tetela amadhlozi* [honour the ancestors]?' That was exactly what they did at Westminister Abbey and what Rhodesians did at Rhodes's statue in Bulawayo and at his grave in the Matopos. 'We, too, have our dead heroes'.[57]

Nkomo carried this message into Matobo district. In April 1954 he spoke to teachers there on the need to 'preserve customs, language, folklore and traditional song', and called for an annual gathering to praise 'African heroes of long ago who had done wonderful work for the African races before the Europeans came to this country.'[58] In July 1955 Nkomo and the MHS activist, Mazibisa, attended an *umbuyiso* ceremony at Bida to bring home the spirit of Joshua's Christian father, Nyongolo. 'It is a matter for gratification', wrote Ncgebetsha, 'to see that some educated Africans are convinced that African ancestral spirits ought not to be discarded.'[59] There were popular resonances to all this. In February 1956, for example, the Native Commissioner, Matobo, expressed his anxiety over a plan to depopulate the eastern zone of the Matopo Reserve. The Mahlahlandhlela under Chief Bafana, he wrote, would almost certainly resist removal 'because of the attachment of this section to the site of Mzilikazi's royal kraal, at which the Memorial now stands, and to his grave at Entumbane.'[60]

Nkomo's re-evaluation of the graves of Rhodes and Mzilakazi was far advanced, then, before the emergence of mass nationalism with the revived Congress of 1957 and its more radical successor, the NDP of 1960. By this time the new reading of the Matopos monuments was well established. In 1960 Joshua Nkomo's brother Stephen was leader of the MHS, resigning from office in the nationalist movement in order to assume the headship, but explicitly remaining a nationalist. There was no debate in the MHS leadership about their alliance with nationalism – though there was some debate about the exact ways in which the new African nation should be defined by its past. In August 1960, for instance, the MHS publicly rebuked Salisbury leaders of the NDP for unilaterally choosing the name 'Zimbabwe' for the projected nation. This was a name, they objected, which 'promoted tribal feelings'. The Matopos made a better symbol of national unity: 'the Matopos are both historically and traditionally of great significance and attempts to belittle it would be resisted in Matabeleland'.[61]

Even quite explicit attempts to reclaim Entumbane for the Ndebele narrowly defined were employing nationalist language by this time. Thus in July 1960 the Sons of Mzilikazi organised a burial ceremony for Lobengula's son, Sidojiwe, at Entumbane.

[56] *Nkomo*, p. 52. John Lonsdale has described a similar perception by Jomo Kenyatta as a 'brilliant insight'.
[57] *Home News*, 27 February 1954.
[58] *Bantu Mirror*, 17 April 1954.
[59] *Home News*, 16 July 1955. Later in 1955 Ncgebetsha's paper carried a serial story about the adventures of Tshuma and Mary. On 10 December the story told how Tshuma was excommunicated from his church for performing ancestral rites, though this was 'what they do at World's View in Matopos at the grave of a white man, Rhodes, whose spirit they worship for the simple reason that they say he found this country for them.'
[60] Native Commissioner, Matobo to Provincial Native Commissioner, 23 February 1956.
[61] *Bantu Mirror*, 20 August 1960.

It was attended by 'the whole of the Ndebele nation, represented by indunas and tribal elders', a thousand people in all, wailing and weeping for 'the glory that is past and is no more'. In his oration Cephas Hlabangana proclaimed:

> Mzilikazi came seeking freedom. His son Lobengula fought for freedom.... Those of us still alive should fight together for that freedom.[62]

The NDP itself confidently condemned Cecil Rhodes's grave in the Matopos and glorified Mzilikazi's. In June 1961 Robert Mugabe 'told one meeting that Cecil Rhodes had stolen the country from the Africans and that he would dig up Rhodes's grave and send it to England.'[63] In early September of the same year, the NDP condemned 'the reign of terror perpetrated by the Police and Native Commissioners' in Semokwe and other Reserves. Then Joshua Nkomo carried the NDP executive, with its Shona majority, off into the Matabeleland bush. They were to meet secretly to plan new policies of confrontation; to develop 'a militant and hard hitting' party. The *Daily News* tried to pursue them – they were in Gwanda, it thought, or at Antelope mine. Finally, it identified a secret 'house or cave' at Entumbane from which the NDP executive issued a call for confrontation, for a fast of mourning on Pioneer Day and for a subsequent series of 'postive actions.' The forthcoming national congress of the NDP would be presented with a master plan for non-cooperation 'inspired at the national executive meeting held near Mzilikazi's grave at the Matopo Hills'.[64]

In Matabeleland it seemed appropriate that a policy of confrontation should be legitimated by the memory of the Ndebele king. But the NDP's national journal, *Democratic Voice*, appealed to other memories of the Matopos:

> Next came the preparatory hour of the Second Chapter of Positive Action. Out in the serene wilderness of Nyambane, Matopos, President Nkomo and his lieutenants sat in a mud hut for five successive days, making the final greasing to the engine of action before the whistle for the Second Phase was blown.
>
> Apart from its topographical attraction, it was in this same area that the treacherous British adventurer, Cecil Rhodes, found what he called the best World View. It is in the place that the wretched bones of Rhodes lie [so it is ideal for] the launching of a counter-declaration. Where Rhodes and Imperialism lie buried is where a new unparalleled Action and revitalised Nationalism were born.[65]

Meanwhile, much less publicly, the Mwali shrines were coming together with nationalism. As we have seen, in the late 1940s the political leaders of National Park residents made no appeal to the shrines. They did not wish to appear as Nyubi traditionalists. Their whole case against eviction depended upon being Ndebele, heirs to the promises of Rhodes; their whole case against charges that they were ruining the soil was that they were progressive Christian farmers. Yet, at the same time that *Sofasonke* was meeting in Whitewaters to plan resistance, the shrine at Njelele, a few miles further south, was experiencing revival. In 1947 Nkobambwe, a member of the

---

[62] *Daily News*, 21 July 1960.
[63] Federal Intelligence report, 8 June 1961, F120 L 343/No. 3.
[64] *Daily News*, 6 and 9 September, 19 October 1960.
[65] *Democratic Voice*, 23 September 1961.

Venda/Kalanga family which had provided priests to Njelele in the nineteenth century, came 'to re-open the shrine' after years of neglect.[66] He cleared away the long grass which hid the entrance to the cave and replaced the rotting log screen; he organised rain dances; and in 1949 – the year of the Commission of Inquiry into the Park – even the white press became aware of unusual activity at the shrine:

> Weather prophets from their rocky fastnesses in the Matopos have forecast an abnormally wet season this year ... Because of the late rains, more attention than usual has been paid to appeasing the weather prophets. White-haired, goatee-bearded old men, who are sticklers for tradition, have been trekking from their kraals to the sacred hills, and rain dances have been taking place at Njelele.[67]

But *Sofasonke* made a clear distinction between rain rituals and the politics of resistance. At the Commission of Inquiry it was only *Sofasonke*'s lawyer, Lloyd, who appealed to the importance of the shrines. In cross-examining the Director of the Bulawayo Museum and acting chairman of the local National Park committee, R. H. N. Smithers, Lloyd quoted Nobbs's guide to the Matopos, with its reference to 'rain-dance hills'. 'Now that refers to a somewhat uncivilised religion', concluded Lloyd, 'but I suggest that it is a consideration when deciding how many people should be allowed to remain in the hills'. Smithers replied that his committee were 'appreciative of the traditions of the Native peoples and the veneration in which sections of the Matopos Area are held by them and it is their earnest wish that nothing should be done to disturb their sacred character'.[68]

In his closing address to the Commission Lloyd urged that in view of 'ancestral worship and the presence of various holy places' the inhabitants of the hills could establish a right to remain there. On at least one member of the Commission, the long-serving Native Department official, W. R. Benzies, this argument was more persuasive than the appeal to the promises of Rhodes. A draft for a final report found in the Benzies papers runs:

> The Commission is satisfied from the evidence brought before it that these people in the Park have a moral right to the occupation of the land in the Matopo Hills and that by virtue of their natural affiliation with this area both spiritually through the Mlimo cult and socially through their many family ties, those people to be removed from the Park ... should be given special consideration in regard to their future accommodation.

Benzies recommended the purchase of farms immediately adjacent to the Matopos either in the foothills or the *mapani*. In the event, of course, neither his text nor his recommendations were adopted.[69]

---

[66] The arrival of Nkobambwe is documented by oral testimonies collected at Njelele by Leslie Nthoi, 'Social Perspectives of Religion: Study of the Mwali Cult of Southern Africa', PhD thesis, Manchester, 1995.

[67] *Chronicle*, 26 November 1949. The report quoted 'an old resident of Bulawayo' who had tried to visit Njelele some years earlier but been turned back by 'an old African armed with an assegai' and 'shaking with rage'. The 'old-timer' felt that 'Europeans should not idly visit any of the sacred spots, particularly Njelele.... Though the high gods may have fled there is still some jealous secrecy remaining.'

[68] Proceedings of the Commission of Inquiry, 22 and 23 March 1949, S 1561.46.

[69] The draft is in file BE 8/3/2/1.

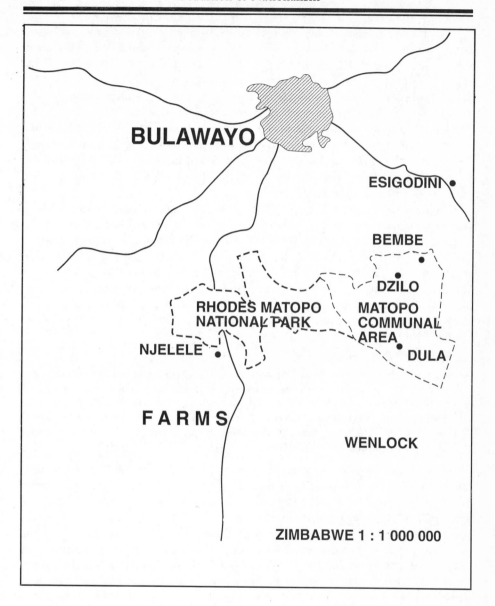

Map 5 The site of the main shrines from the 1960s to the present day

After the Commission's findings in favour of large-scale eviction and resettlement far to the south of the hills, National Park activists no longer trusted in the promises of Rhodes and found that missionary support for their progressive farming had little effect. Increasing official intervention in the Matopos environment meant that the distinction between rain and politics was much more difficult to maintain. In Matopo Reserve the whole cult-sanctioned agrarian economy was under threat; when the peopleless National Park was created Njelele was left outside the Park boundaries and cut off from many subsidiary shrines. Dula and Dzilo and the newer shrines in Matopo Reserve offered a critique of the state's doctrine of how to preserve the environment of the hills; Njelele offered a critique of the National Park's importation of big game and of its creation of a 'wilderness area'.[70]

It was this renewed local sense of the relevance of the shrines, coupled with his cultural nationalist interest in 'traditional religion', which led to Joshua Nkomo's visit to Dula in 1953, a key moment in the cult's nationalist history. Nkomo was taken to Dula by the trade unionist Grey Bango, a member of one of the Kalanga families associated with the cult and very familiar with the shrines – he knew them as well as he knew sadza porridge, says the shrine priest, Sitwanyana Ncube.[71] Nkomo's visit to Dula has become legendary and subject to much later elaboration. But it is seems appropriate to explore the various accounts now since they set up the main themes of nationalist encounter with the shrines.[72]

Nkomo's own account is the briefest:

> As the spirit of Zimbabwean nationalism came to the fore again in the early 1950s, I examined for myself the power of the traditional faith of my people and visited the shrine where Mwali resides in the Matopos hills. Well before dawn, at about 3 a.m., William Sivako and Grey Mabhalani Bango, the nephew of the chief of my father's village, accompanied me to the place called Dula. We were led by a frail old man along an ancient track: some twenty others were with us, each bringing his own problem.

Nkomo heard the Voice from the shrine hailing the three Kalanga/Ndebele by their family names – 'You, son of Nyongolo, and you, son of Sivako, and you, son of Luposwa Bango, what do you want me to do for you? How do you expect me to accomplish it?' The Voice had told Lobengula 'not to fight against his cousins who were coming into the land', but Lobengula had disobeyed. Nkomo replied that he had come 'to ask you to give this land back to your children, the people of the land.' The Voice replied: 'Yes, my children. I will give you back your land. It will be after thirty years and it will be after a big war in which many will die.' Grey Bango urged that Mwali had 'the power to give it back to us now', but the Voice was firm. 'It cannot be given to you now ... because Lobengula failed to heed my word.' For 30 years, Nkomo

---

[70] An account of the complicated shrine politics of the Matopos Reserve in the 1950s and 1960s is given in 'The Shamanism Book' compiled in 1973 by A. Latham, and stamped 'Top Secret' at the top and bottom of every page. I saw a copy in the District Administrator's office, Mzingwane.

[71] Interview with Sitwanyana Ncube, Umgusa, 30 August 1988. According to Sitwanyana, Grey Bango was a descendant of a Mwali priest shot in 1896.

[72] I first explored this subject in 'The Politics of Prophecy in Matabeleland', Fifth Satterthwaite Colloquium on African Religion and Ritual, April 1989, on which I draw for what follows.

concludes, 'I kept the secret that the voice had foretold a long and costly struggle'.[73]

I have been given two other accounts of the Dula visit, one by Grey Bango and the other by Mrs Thenjiwe Lesabe, who was certainly not herself there but who as Nkomo's close political ally in the 1970s and 1980s and as an adept of the Mwali cult claims to have had the story from those who were present. Grey Bango says that when the three Bulawayo men arrived at Dula they were rebuked by the shrine elders because of their urban dress and their youth and refused permission to go to the cave. But when they inserted themselves into the queue to the shrine after darkness had fallen, the Voice wept for half an hour and then rebuked the elders, dismissing them in order to speak for hours to Nkomo and Bango. During these hours the Voice narrated 'history'.[74]

This was the history of the divinely ordained transition of regimes outlined in the first part of this book – the overthrow of Sipundile, the pre-Rozwi ruler of the Matopos, by Mambo, the first Rozwi king;[75] the overthrow of Mambo by the Swazi and the Ndebele; the overthrow of the Ndebele kingdom by the whites. Nkomo and Bango went to the shrine asking how they could bring about the end of white rule. The shrine answered them by telling them of the patterns of the past; of how and why regimes had come to an end; and of how the whole sequence had been controlled by the will of Mwali.

Mrs Lesabe adds to this a number of claims which were probably developed as a response to later exigencies. Nkomo's visit to Dula took place before even the emergence of mass nationalism in 1957 and long before the sabotage campaigns of 1961 and 1962 and the guerrilla war of the later 1960s and 1970s. But the story of his visit went on resonating throughout the decades. Mrs Lesabe insists that Dula was operating in its role as the shrine of the Red Axe 'and giving Joshua support for the war'. 'This is why ZIPRA [Nkomo's guerrilla army] was so much powerful'. She also insists that the Voice promised invulnerability to Nkomo:

> Before you are settled, really settled, in this part of the country, there is really going to be bloodshed. But you, son of Nyangolo, great-son of Maweme, you will lead this nation. When you go into the river, I'll be with you, into the seas, I'll be with you. When you climb trees, I'll be with you.... Wherever you are I'll be with you until this war is over. Nobody will touch your body. I'll fight with you. Let's go to the war together.[76]

Narratives of Nkomo's visit to Dula, which came to be widely distributed in Matabeleland, bestowed a sacred legitimacy upon his leadership. Mrs Lesabe insists

[73] Joshua Nkomo, *Nkomo. The Story of My Life*, Methuen, London, 1984, pp. 13–14.

[74] Interview with Grey Bango, Mpopoma, 29 August 1988.

[75] Bango told me that Mambo had sent a beautiful girl to Sipundile; he could not resist her and took her in; she discovered and destroyed the magical source of his power. Bango said he had heard this story not only from the shrine but also from the medium of Sipundile and that the ancient ruler, speaking through his medium, declared that he would do exactly the same again. 'You should have seen that girl! She was worth it.'

[76] Interview with Mrs Thenjiwe Lesabe, Bulawayo, 24 August 1988. The idea of Dula as a shrine for war is certainly not an artefact of the 1970s and 1980s. The Zimbabwean historian, R. Mwanza, carried out research in Matopo Reserve in the late 1960s. He was then told that 'Dula is for war, Wirirani [Dzilo] is for fertility and misfortunes'. R. Mwanza, 'Mwari: the God of the Karanga', ms, 1972.

that Nkomo's very birth was ordained by the shrines; the anthropologist Leslie Nthoi collected accounts of Nkomo's divine origins in his field work at Njelele; Jocelyn Alexander has often been told in northern Matabeleland that after Dula, Nkomo became 'holder of the calabash', signifying both that he was the senior kinsman and also that he had the responsibility for ensuring rain.[77] Much of this body of myth no doubt developed much more recently, but Nkomo's cult name, *chibwechitedza* – the little slippery rock – was certainly known and widely used as early as 1965.[78]

But of course the influence of the Matopos shrines was not limited to Matabeleland. Many of the scholars who visited Dula or Dzilo in the 1960s were students of Shona society, approaching the Matopos from the east. Michael Gelfand visited Dula in 1963 with messengers from the Nyajena area.[79] Mwanza came to Dzilo in the late 1960s with pilgrims from Gutu, Ndanga, Bikita and other Shona areas, and he regarded the shrine as a 'Karanga' institution.[80] So too did Martinus Daneel who came to Dzilo in 1967 with cult messengers from Gutu.[81] At the time these scholars reported that the eastern Matopos shrines studiously avoided nationalist commitment. Mwanza was told at Dzilo that 'Mwari is totally against bloodshed. He loves peace ... Europeans are troublesome but they should be persuaded not to follow their troublesome way of life. Africans should not fight them'.[82] When Daneel attended a seance at Dzilo in 1967 the Voice hailed him, and all other Europeans, as a *muzukuru*, or maternal nephew, one of the most positive of Shona kin relationships. These reports encouraged students of the Mwali cult who believed that it was incapable of supporting political parties or of endorsing violence.

It now seems likely that elementary prudence was partly responsible for the shrines' pacificism. Mwanza was told that Dzilo was visited by the CID and it is likely that he was himself suspect as a stranger; white visitors like Gelfand and Daneel were hardly likely to be offered a really radical critique of European rule. Daneel's own recent inquiries are producing a rather different picture. In his *Guerrilla Snuff*, a thinly fictionalised account of events in Gutu, Daneel has a chapter called 'Mwari of Matonjeni'. Based on recent interviews with Taziveri, spirit medium of the Makwanya ancestor, Daneel reconstructs the messages brought back to Gutu by Taziveri's close friend, the Mwali messenger Vondo.

'In the mid fifties' Vondo addressed the people at Gutu's 'with the authority of a prophet of Mwari ... addressing a trusted inner circle which contained no informers'.

[77] Jocelyn Alexander, 'Drought and Accountability in Post-War Matabeleland', seminar, Oxford, October 1997.
[78] The *Home News*, then being edited by Charlton Ngcebetsha from the restriction area of Gonakudzingwa, where Nkomo was also held, told its readers on 23 January 1965 that Nkomo was universally known by this name.
[79] Michael Gelfand, *An African's Religion. The Spirit of Nyajena*, Wynberg, 1966. Gelfand did not himself hear the Voice at Dula but the Nyajena medium told him that both blacks and whites had heard the Voice speaking from the shrine in February 1962.
[80] R. Mwanza, 'Mwari: the God of the Karanga'.
[81] Martinus Daneel, *The God of the Matopo Hills*, Mouton, The Hague, 1970.
[82] Mwanza, 'Mwari: the God of the Karanga', p. 8.

What he told them – just as the Voice at Dula told Nkomo – was divine history. 'Mwari punished the bad kings in the Bible by taking their reign from them'; in the same way He 'allowed the Nguni armies from the south to overrun the Rozwi kingdom'. Vondò assured the people that 'Mwari sides with the oppressed. He is always the liberator!' Daneel adds that 'the signs of black rebellion and liberation were there for those who had the courage to see and interpret. The people increasingly heard Mwari's message about liberation in Vondo's account of the past.' So Vondo went on to tell of Lobengula's disobedience of Mwali and his overthrow. Then he drew the contemporary lesson. The whites had disobeyed Mwali by oppressing their black cousins and taking their land. 'We messengers have had to work under cover because we are always watched by the CID. We speak loudly about Mwari's rain and softly about his liberation.' But now 'Mwari says Forward with the Struggle'.[83]

As for his own visit in 1967, Daneel now adds to his published account. The Voice at Dzilo certainly did describe whites as his *vazukuru*, the children of his sister. But it added that these white nephews had abused the relationship:

> They had grabbed the best land and herded their black kinsmen into overcrowded reserves. This Mwari will not tolerate. He warned: 'If the whites keep on oppressing their uncles and enforcing the unfair land apportionment laws, I shall fight them!'

Daneel was told to go back and report this warning to the District Commissioner.[84]

Like Mrs Lesabe's testimony, Daneel's recent accounts bear the mark of the subsequent guerrilla war. But what is certain is that dramatic natural events in the Matopo Reserve took place in 1963 which gave rise to a new shrine and seemed to portend some great transformation. Minye Ncube lived at Dzilo. In 1961 she was possessed by a rain spirit:

> Minye had to set up her own kraal. The site of this had been indicated to her in a dream when she was a child. In the dream she saw a boulder falling down the side of a hill and she knew that when this happened the time would have come to take up her duties. In late 1963 a huge rock rolled down the side of Bembe Hill and Minye set up home at the base of a shrine 'where the boulder fell down'.[85]

The Voice of Mwali spoke from the overhang of the fallen rock. Bembe shrine was close to the *Indaba* site of 1896 and to the perennial rock springs which the Europeans had appropriated as Diana's Pool. The fall of the great rock seemed to portend a major symbolic and cosmological upheaval. Bembe shrine rapidly became a place of pilgrimage, hundreds coming for rain, and in 1967 a delegation from the Nyanga Association of Central Africa who were 'promised extra healing powers'.[86]

All these events were taking place in the eastern Matopos, in the Matopo Reserve.

[83] Mafuranhunzi Gumbo [Martinus Daneel], *Guerrilla Snuff*, Baobab, Harare, 1995, pp. 64–73.
[84] *Ibid.*, p. 79. An account midway between this and the original 1970 version can be found in Martinus Daneel, *African Earthkeepers*, Vol. 1, forthcoming. Here he says that 'in a profound manner Mwari was urging his/her white nephews on the eve of war to heed the laws of the land.... At the same time, Mwari in no uncertain terms added both a rebuke and a warning to his/her backward nephews.' p. 30.
[85] 'The Making of a Rain Goddess', *Sunday News Magazine*, 26 October/8 November 1988.
[86] *Chronicle*, 23 October 1967.

Meanwhile things were also happening at Njelele. Early in the 1960s a woman from southern Matobo, Ngcathu Mayezana Ncube, a descendant of nineteenth-century priests, went to the shrine at Dula with a sick relative; the Dula Voice told Ngcathu to go to Njelele where the keeper had recently died. So Ngcathu went to re-open the Njelele shrine and according to her own account 'the Voice then moved from Dula to Njelele which was senior'. With Ngcathu went her husband, Sitwanyana Ncube, a charismatic healer, ex-Zionist preacher and also a descendant of nineteenth-century priestly families. Sitwanyana came from Semokwe Reserve, was a strong ZAPU supporter and well known to Grey Bango. Once at Njelele there was competition between husband and wife; Bango and Nkomo backed Sitwanyana, thinking that it would be useful to ZAPU to have him as priest. In March 1966 Sitwanyana 'was examined by Chief Herben, accepted, and passed to Chief Garret Masuku, in whose area Njelele lies. Garret consulted the elders and Sitwanyana was accepted.' Ngcathu left Njelele.[87] This key shrine was now in the hands of a dynamic and politically conscious man.[88]

Sitwanyana had usurped his wife's position and even after she left there were many rival claimants for the priesthood. Nevertheless, he claimed pristine and natural legitimacy:

> I was sent by Ngwali, it was not my own will. I was happy being a Christian. You know, once the spirits have chosen you there is nothing you can do. I stayed 3 months in a cave. That cave is known as Sihazabana where my village was. It is at that cave that I was taught the traditions of the shrine. I was talking directly to a snake which is the one that showed me all the caves.

Drawing on this natural legitimacy, Sitwanyana was profoundly critical of the idea of 'nature' represented by the National Park.[89]

In the Park there were monuments where holy places had once been revered. Rhodes's Grave was 'fine for whites but not for us. That is where we were brainwashed.

[87] On 2 September 1996 Dr Jocelyn Alexander and Dr JoAnn McGregor interviewed *Gogo* Ngcathu Ncube at Njelele. A few days before at a cleansing ceremony for ZIPRA guerrillas held at the shrine, Ngcathu had violently attacked Joshua Nkomo for backing Sitwanyana against her. She told them that 'when I was still young I left this place because of a war, because Sitwanyana wanted to kill me'. She denied that she had ever been married to Sitwanyana – 'he wanted a place to live with his family, so I let him stay in my home.' But Nkomo sent cattle to Sitwanyana as her 'husband'; she objected and left; and 'during that time Nkomo enticed Sitwanyana to be in charge.'

[88] The details of this story, and particularly its dating, are very confused. *Gogo* Ncube told Leslie Nthoi that she had first come to Njelele in the 1970s and Alexander and McGregor that she was there in 1962 and already fighting with Sitwanyana. In an interview with *Prize Africa* in April 1985 Sitwanyana himself claimed to have been called to Njelele in 1965; informants at Njelele variously told Leslie Nthoi that he came in 1967 or 1969. Joel Nyathi, whom I interviewed in Bulawayo on 1 August 1988, made only one visit to Njelele, while he was a ZAPU youth activist. Soon thereafter he was detained so he remembers clearly that the visit took place in September 1964. He found Sitwanyana already receiving visitors. Nephas Ndlovu, the first District Administrator, Matobo, after independence, whom I interviewed on 2 August 1988 confirmed the 1964 date. Sitwanyana's formal installation in 1996 is attested by the retired District Commissioner, I. G. Cockcroft, who 'made a penetrating investigation of the Mlimo/Mwari cult'. Cockcroft published an account, 'The Mlimo (Mwari) Cult', in *NADA*, 10, 4, 1972, but my quote is from the fuller version of his findings cited in 'The Shamanism Book' under 'The Matojeni, Mwari, Mlimo Cult.'

[89] Interview with Sitwanyana Ncube, Umguza, 28 July 1988.

That grave is the fontanelle of the nation.'[90] Deserted nature – wilderness – was in fact unnatural; people were needed to perform the rites which made the right balance between environment and humanity. As a result of the boundary between Kumalo Reserve and the peopleless Park, Njelele was cut off from 'the hills inside the Park where some rituals were performed'. People should be resettled in the Park and the rituals resumed. There was confusion between animals long essential for shrine ritual – 'black rabbits which are used by Bango people' and 'three-legged leopards used in issues concerning succession' – and newly introduced beasts. 'Now those animals have been mixed with rhinos – men, it's difficult.' 'Beserk animals' were shot down without inquiring whether they had been poisoned by plants.

> Where does our eagle fly when the whole space is usurped by whites' aeroplanes? We need the guidance of eagles. Whites despise our customs. Whenever we have a cultural occasion they disturb us with their big noisy aeroplanes. How I wish they would pardon us!

The animal kingdom was in anarchy – lions now came to Njelele not as cult creatures but as wild beasts.[91]

The Internal Affairs Department 'expert' on traditional religion, A. Latham, drew up a report on the Mwali cult in 1973. In it he emphasised that 'far from being a remote deity, Mwari was believed to control the fertility of Shona occupied country, to give rain in time of drought and advice on the course of action in times of national crisis.' The Department was right to think that advice was still being given in time of crisis, but they were wrong to associate the cult so closely with 'the Shona'. The families who lived around the shrines and played a key role in determining who should control them had come to define themselves as 'Ndebele'. Moreover, during the time of cultural nationalism Ndebele history was being re-imagined so as to make the Mwali shrines a key element within it.

Nkomo was taking the risk that his 1953 visit to Dula might be interpreted as mere Kalanga cultural nationalism. He had gone with two other Kalanga to a shrine that pre-dated the Ndebele state. But not only did he simultaneously pay public honour to Entumbane, he also took steps to link the Mwali shrines with the monuments of Ndebele history. Ngcathu Ncube says that in the early 1960s she went from Njelele with 'Nkomo and others ... to Mzilikazi's grave to perform a ceremony there. [Nkomo's men] drove animals from the Mzilikazi ceremony' at Entumbane to offer to Sitwanyana Ncube at Njelele.[92]

Sitwanyana, though himself of Venda/Kalanga origin, came to develop a version of cult history much more favourable to Lobengula than the established orthodoxy. Mwali, he said, had willed the coming of the whites, 'the sons of our sisters':

> These children would show the Ndebele the riches of the soil, gold. Lobengula had accepted that advice but his warriors refused ... For some time it looked like Ngwali and Lobengula had been bought. The warriors objected. Lobengula tried to beg them but failed. Then Ngwali

[90] Interview with Sitwanyana Ncube, Umguza, 28 July 1988.
[91] Interview with Sitwanyana Ncube, Umguza, 19 August 1988.
[92] Interview with Ngcathu Ncube, Njelele, 2 September 1996. It was these cattle which were given to Sitwanyana 'under the pretext that we were married.'

said that if that was the case then he would leave, but the whites were not going to capture Lobengula. Ngwali was going to protect him. The shrine said, 'I will hide you. I will go with you and leave you among the reeds.' When the two armies met there was a lot of fighting.... The whites were eager to catch Lobengula. When they reached the river there were some beautiful girls. When they turned round and looked at the girls Lobengula disappeared. When he had crossed, the river flooded. The girls disappeared.[93]

Later Sitwanyana lent his authority to the idea widespread in ZAPU that nothing would go right in Zimbabwe unless Lobengula's remains were brought back and interred at Entumbane.[94]

Thenjiwe Lesabe, a Khumalo reared in Whitewaters and ex-head girl of Hope Fountain mission school, who professes herself a 'convert' to the Mwali cult, also came to develop a version of Ndebele history which gave central prominence to Njelele. When Mzilikazi arrived, she says, 'he asked how people here were living, what their tradition was and how they conducted their day to day life.... He was then directed to Njelele.' The shrine priest sent his son to Mzilikazi and he explained:

> The people in this part of the world worshipped at Njelele. That's where they get instructions on what to do at given times and occasions and seasons of the year. And then Mzilikazi wanted to go and worship too, so as to live well with the people there. He had had trouble; his cattle were dying; people were running short of water. He wanted to know what the cause was. This man explained to him that he had not paid tribute to the Njelele shrine. Mzilikazi was very keen to do so ... so he took out ten head of cattle, black, which the Njelele people in their custom led on top of Njelele hill. They just disappeared there.

Every year thereafter Mzilikazi sent ten cattle to Njelele. 'And then the good spirits of Njelele in turn revealed that it was them that made Mzilikazi come to this part of the country to lead them.... That is why the Ngunis have also the right to go to the shrine.'[95]

Sitwanyana and Thenjiwe Lesabe have been key ideological innovators, he within the Mwali cult and she within ZAPU. But there is no doubt that these ideas diffused widely. In August 1993 I visited Inyathi Communal Area, north-east of Bulawayo. That evening the people produced their oldest man so that they could watch two historians at work. The old man – a high-caste Ndebele – gave me an account of Ndebele history suffused with the agency of Mwali. Njelele had sustained the Ndebele kingdom; neglect of Njelele had brought about its overthrow. And there is no doubt that this version of the past has become orthodox in Joshua Nkomo's own circle.

In January 1995 I interviewed Nzula Ndebele, one of Nkomo's immediate circle, whose ancestors entered the country with Mzilikazi. According to Nzula, his great-grand-father was one of Mzilikazi's advisers. He was sent on a delegation to Mambo to ask him how the country was ruled. 'Mambo said, we have got Njelele, a highly important

[93] Interview with Sitwanyana Ncube, Mguza, 28 July 1988.
[94] It seems probable that 'the river' in Sitwanyana's narrative is the Zambezi. ZAPU came to believe that Lobengula died in what is now Zambia and his spirit is said to have appeared to ZIPRA guerrillas based there in the 1970s asking to be brought home.
[95] Interview with Thenjiwe Lesabe, Bulawayo, 24 August 1988.

mountain'. The hill contained 'the traditions of the various nations of Zimbabwe. Each and every year we sent bulls, twenty or so. They used to come from the whole country. Every chief had got to send some.' Lobengula was 'a cheeky king' to his *indunas* but he continued to respect Njelele – 'he didn't forget what his father had done'. Nzula himself venerates the shrine, having been taught to do so by his father and grandfather when the family was living in Nyamandhlovu. He himself first went to the shrine in 1945. 'I have no doubt of Njelele. I go there as a free man. Njelele is our Sinai'. According to Nzula, Lobengula's eldest son, Nyamanda, leader of the first movement for an Ndebele National Home, used to send regular offerings to Njelele. These offerings went by way of Entumbane. 'All of these shrines – Njelele, Dula, Dzilo – people who visit them don't forget to pay respect to Mzilikazi at Entumbane. The right way to go to Njelele is to go first to Entumbane.'[96]

It is possible that these narratives build on old traditions but there is no doubt that they were developed and elaborated during the nationalist period. They served an important ideological function. In the 1940s the Ndebele political identity had been based on a combination of pride in the nineteenth-century kingdom and profession of 'progressive' Christianity. The cultural nationalist linking of Entumbane and the shrines offered an alternative, or at least a supplement.

Nor was the increasing importance of the Mwali cult in Matabeleland's nationalism the imaginative business only of urban political activists. The cult was not, after all, an archaic institution, freely available for symbolic exploitation. It had always reflected the interests of small peasants.[97] As rural nationalism spread beyond its original founders – the teachers, businessmen and master farmers – to the mass of the small cultivators, so the ideology of the cult was used to rebuke and repress the acquisitive aspirations of the Christian entrepreneurs. This expressed itself mainly through a campaign to enforce the cult's rest days.

One can see the process through the eyes of the Christian progressive readers of the *Bantu Mirror*. Its reports began with a very garbled news item on 27 December 1958, which announced that 'the evangelist' had called all villagers together at Vizhe school in Insiza, at the foot of a mountain, 'for the purpose of praying for rain'. The meeting took place on a Wednesday.

> After the evangelist [in reality a messenger of the shrine] had stated that all Wednesdays will be observed as a day on which prayers will be said to the 'God of Rain' a decision was taken that those people who do not obey the rule of not working on Wednesdays be dealt with. Villagers were allowed to work on Sundays at their fields but not on Wednesdays.

On 10 January 1959 this report provoked both clarification and indignation from the church evangelist at Vizhe school, R. M. Mhlanga. He expressed:

> my greatest horror of my life about what I see here. People here at Insiza have chosen to keep

[96] Interview with Nzula Ndebele, Bulawayo, 28 January 1995. Nzula claimed that he had known Sitwanyana from childhood, since the latter used to visit an uncle in Nyamandhlovu.

[97] Terence Ranger, 'Religious Studies and Political Economy: The Mwari Cult and the Peasant Experience in Southern Rhodesia', in M. M. J. van Binsbergen and M. Schoffeleers, eds, *Theoretical Explorations in African Religion*, Routledge and Kegan Paul, London, 1986.

Wednesday holy whilst working on Sunday. The reason, I am told, is that on Wednesday the goddess of the Matopo Hills ordered them that should they plough or cultivate on Wednesdays they will have offended her and as a result she will not send them rain. The result is that people have taken to ploughing on Sundays. Worse still, the chief has made it a rule, not let me call it a law, that no-one should do field work on a Wednesday.

Mhlanga declared that this was against the Ten Commandments. 'Uneducated chiefs are a danger to the African community', he declared, 'because they do not know how to read the Bible. There is only one God – Jehova – and not Ngwali.'

On 17 January the *Mirror* revealed that the same thing was happening in Semokwe Reserve, Matobo. Chief Bidi, who controlled the area where Joshua Nkomo's family lived, had:

> told a gathering of teachers, church deacons, demonstrators, Christians and non-Christians, and ordinary villagers, that he was one of the people who used to plough on Wednesdays some time back. Chief Bidi Ndiweni said that sometime back a delegation went to a mountain near his Reserve, where it is believed a goddess lives, to ask for rain. The goddess of rain is reported to have told the rainseekers that their chief cultivated his land on Wednesdays. They should go to him and ask him to supply them with rain.

Chief Bidi told the gathering that in the past year 'he had experienced great phenomena which proved to him that he was doing wrong'; he ordered those who cultivated on Wednesdays to stop it and to observe the day as a holy day. They would be made to pay 5/- for the messenger who arrests them'.

The prosperous trader, J. M. Dube, who was secretary of the local branch of the ANC, summoned his own meeting of 300 people to denounce this order:

> Congress did not discourage or despise African customs, tradition or culture. But he takes great exception to the fact that an individual should force people – even Christians – to observe Wednesday. Enough blood was shed in the middle ages.... Mr Dube told the meeting to oppose the Chief's suggestion and to continue cultivating on Wednesdays.

On 31 January 1959 another outraged progressive, P. H. Fandasi, demanded that Africans in Matabeleland obey the law of Almighty God rather than Baal. 'They *must* work on Wednesday, one of the days when a man should sweat in labour'.

These Congress Christian progressives were soon silenced with the ban on their party in February 1959. J. M. Dube was one of the men detained. By the time nationalism got under way once more with the NDP and still more with ZAPU, 'African customs, tradition and culture' were playing an ever larger role in rural nationalism.

Mark Dokotela Ncube, who lives in north Wenlock in the foothills of the Matopos, some three miles south of Dula shrine, a teacher and member of *Sofasihamba*, had been the first secretary of the local branch of the ANC. In February 1959, when the party was banned, he was arrested and held in Khami prison until May. On his release he devoted himself to developing his father's land, a great sponge which he drained to form dams and irrigation channels. Working incredibly hard, he ferried good soil from other parts of the Reserve which he then irrigated; he kept fish in his ponds, grew tomatoes, maize and bananas, and employed twenty men. Dokotela descended from many generations of Kalanga but he was a fervent subject of Chief Sigombe.

He was also pre-eminently the Christian progressive. When I interviewed him in August 1990 he insisted that 'there never has been a God' at Dula. Within sight of his land is a hill where an ancestor of the Dula priests is buried 'and when they had rain ceremonies they came and drummed there'. He attended Dula church and school in the early 1940s. 'I wanted to see the God myself' so he went into the Dula cave and found two pieces of metal which made a bell sound when struck. 'An old lady used to go into the cave. She would strike the metal. It was she too who spoke, in Kalanga, in a foreign language. Her son would translate.' He was completely unimpressed by the whole thing – scraps of metal, a scruffy old woman. Neither his father nor he himself paid any attention to the 'rules' of the shrine. His father told him that the demand to respect Wednesday as a rest day only started in the 1950s 'as a result of confusion'.

But as Doketela developed his land in the 1960s, and as the Wenlock nationalists came more and more into conflict with teachers and Christians, he clashed increasingly with his neighbours:

> Everyone else around here believes in it. They do not farm on Wednesdays and they demand that I do not. I refuse and they call me a Tshombe. I say to them, 'Stores do not close on Wednesday; grinding mills do not close on Wednesdays; businesses do not close. If they close, then I will close. My farm is a business. They hate me for that.

He founded a local school but hornbills attacked the windows and broke several of them. The people said this was because he did not honour the shrines and obey their rules. When guerrillas began to operate in Wenlock, neighbours 'who hated my progress' denounced him to every successive guerrilla group. And, indeed, the centrality of the shrines to rural nationalism increased as opposition to the white regime increasingly took the form first of sabotage and then of armed violence.[98]

[98] Interview with Mark Dokotela Ncube, North Wenlock, 30 August 1990.

III
Violence, Identity
& Environment

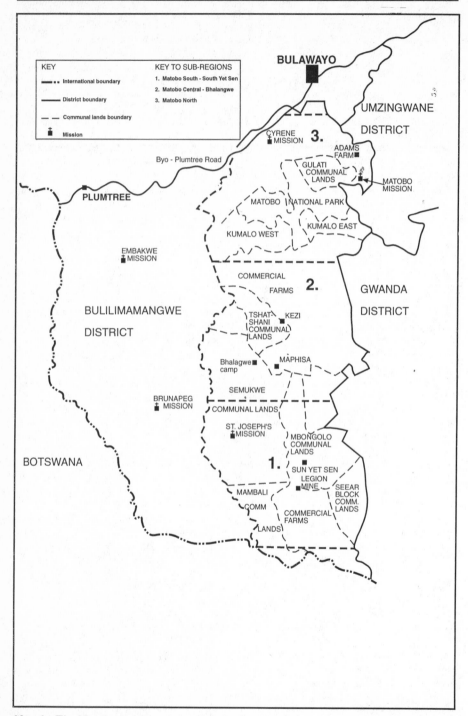

KEY
- – – • • International boundary
- ——— District boundary
- – – – Communal lands boundary
- ⚓ Mission

KEY TO SUB-REGIONS
1. Matobo South - South Yet Sen
2. Matobo Central - Bhalangwe
3. Matobo North

BULAWAYO

UMZINGWANE

DISTRICT

CYRENE
MISSION **3.**

ADAMS
FARM

Byo - Plumtree Road

GULATI
COMMUNAL
LANDS

MATOBO
MISSION

PLUMTREE

MATOBO NATIONAL PARK

KUMALO EAST

KUMALO WEST

EMBAKWE
MISSION

COMMERCIAL
FARMS **2.**

GWANDA

DISTRICT

BULILIMAMANGWE

DISTRICT

TSHAT-
SHANI
COMMUNAL
LANDS

KEZI

Bhalagwe
camp

MAPHISA

SEMUKWE

BRUNAPEG
MISSION

COMMUNAL LANDS

ST. JOSEPH'S
MISSION

MBONGOLO
COMMUNAL
LANDS

1.

SUN YET SEN
LEGION
MINE

BOTSWANA

MAMBALI

COMM

SEEAR
BLOCK
COMM.
LANDS

COMMERCIAL
FARMS

LANDS

*Map 6   The Matobo district as it is today. Motopo Communal Area is now in Umzingwane
District. Mbongolo/Prospect is shown in the south-east.*

8

War & Politics
in the Matopos

1964–87

Introduction

By the mid-1960s the core area of the Matopos had been cleared of Africans much more completely than Rhodes had ever imagined possible when he was seeking to lure the fighting men out of the hills in 1896 and 1897. His own grave was now surrounded by great empty spaces filled with sun. But the price paid for this was that the rest of the Matopos – where much of the fighting during 1896 had taken place – was now thickly inhabited by resentful Africans. The 1896 *indaba* site, at which Rhodes had held his first meeting with the Ndebele *indunas*, now lay in the Matopo Tribal Trust Land close to the new shrine at Bembe, where the falling rock presaged great changes. The area was full of caves and hiding places, as were the newly created Gulati and Kumalo. This difficult terrain lay within striking distance of Bulawayo to the north and of the white farms and ranches to the south, and surrounded the National Park itself.

Of course, the violence that took place in the hills in the 1960s, 1970s and 1980s was not a repeat of 1896, nor a fulfilment of the military intelligence predictions which for decades thereafter had imagined a second uprising in the Matopos. The time had long passed for formal confrontations between armies. But the terrain was ideal for the ZAPU sabotage campaigns of the 1960s, affording abundant hiding places for weapons and dynamite. Later, the peopled Matopos provided an ideal setting for the guerrilla war of the late 1970s, in which both Nkomo's ZIPRA forces and Mugabe's ZANLA were involved. And in the 1980s, when so-called dissidents were hunted by the forces of Mugabe's new Zimbabwean state, 'the mountainous terrain and lush vegetation of this part of Matobo provided ideal cover for the dissidents, who could hide easily and escape quickly from army personnel.'[1]

---

[1] *Breaking the Silence. A Report on the Disturbances in Matabeleland Midlands, 1980–1988*, CCJP/LRF, Harare, 1997, p. 137.

Yet the appropriate environment was not the only reason for the intensity of violence in the Matopos. As this book has amply shown, there were plenty of grievances to which guerrillas and even dissidents could appeal. In the 1970s guerrillas promised that the National Park fences would be torn down and the animals in the Game Park barbecued. Both then and in the 1980s the people of the Matopos cooperated enthusiastically in putting pressure on their old rivals, the white *mapani* landowners, through rustling and poach-grazing. And over and above this, there was the more metaphysical belief – widely held among the inhabitants of the hills – that the Matopos were the key arena in which the fate of states and peoples was to be decided.

In August 1988, less than a year after the Unity Agreement between Robert Mugabe and Joshua Nkomo which ended the dissident war, I met the late Reader Ncube. Ncube, a Banyubi from the Mtshabezi Valley, a junior member of the shrine families, Provincial Chairman of ZAPU and Chairman of the District Council, was dismissive of my saying that the Matopos provided a good terrain for guerrillas:

> Whenever there is any war, when it reaches the Matopos it is near to settlement. In 1896 the war reached the Matopos and there was the Indaba; in the 1970s the war reached the Matopos and there were the Geneva talks; in the 1980s the war reached the Matopos and there was unity. You may say it's the terrain from your understanding of causation but its because the hills are holy.[2]

Two weeks late Reader took me to a group interview with families connected to the shrines at Kumbudzi clinic in Matopo Communal Area. They insisted that the concentration of shrines in their own area made it particularly holy and particularly decisive in struggle. 'That's why you couldn't defeat us because our God is still here.' And Reader repeated: 'The Matopos is the fontanelle of the nation. It is here that everything comes to a climax. You have had to come here to get this information. You are ending here.'[3]

None of this meant, however, that any of the stages in the sequence of violence – sabotage in the 1960s, guerrilla war in the 1970s, dissidence and the deployment of the Fifth Brigade in the 1980s – was unambiguous for the people of the Matopos. As we shall see, most dissidents are remembered harshly – as is, of course, the Fifth Brigade with its terrible record of repression and atrocity against the civilian population. Both the militant nationalist period and the guerrilla war of the late 1970s intensified divisions within the communities of the hills – between strict Christians and observers of Mwali's holy days; between rich entrepreneurs and small peasants. In the Gulati Tribal Trust Land, for example, the relatively prosperous market gardening and cattle-keeping economy allowed the emergence of many African storekeepers and businessmen. By the late 1970s all but one of these had fled to Bulawayo. Only one remained, Moffat Zithatheleni Ndlovu, a local butcher, and he had not been allowed by the guerrillas to buy cattle. His business was closed. 'As you can see', he told a reporter in June 1980, pointing to his large brick-built house, 'business was good before the war.

[2] Interview with Reader Ncube, Esigodini, 29 August 1988.
[3] Group interview, Kumbudzi, Matopo Communal Area, 10 September 1988.

It will be nice to make money again'.[4] In less than two years the businessmen of Gulati and the other Matopos communal areas, now targeted by the dissidents, were once again in flight to the towns.

In addition to the extremities which war involved everywhere in Zimbabwe, the situation in the Matopos was especially dangerous. In the late 1970s both guerrilla armies – Joshua Nkomo's ZIPRA and Robert Mugabe's ZANLA – operated there, clashing with each other and punishing people who too enthusiastically assisted their rivals. With Security Force raids and Selous Scout dirty-trick operations added to guerrilla activities, the hills were awash with armed men, each group forcibly seeking information or support. When I drove around Matopo Communal Area in 1988 my guides showed me the burnt-out or blown-up relics of the violence of all these various groups – the shell of a car here, which had been ambushed and burnt out by ZANLA; there the effects of a landmine which had been planted by ZIPRA; there a school whose walls were pockmarked with Security Force bullets. It was my first realisation that the hills, which had been so quintessentially ZAPU, had also sheltered ZANLA guerrillas during the late 1970s.

Local guides in the Matopos or in the lands to the south of them also pointed out to me the sites of the violence of the 1980s – of dissident ambushes and murders; of Security Force dirty-trick operations; of Fifth Brigade torture camps; of South African-backed 'Super-Zapu' atrocities. The whole landscape of the Matopos was scarred by these visual memories of violence.

The involvement of so many armed groups placed the Mwali shrines in a particularly dangerous situation. The shrines, after all, were both local and regional in their significance. Priests at Njelele, Dula and Dzilo told me that as men they were ZAPU but that Mwali was above politics. At Njelele and Dzilo in particular pilgrims had come before the war – and continued to do so during it – from Shona-speaking areas to the east. It was natural that ZANLA guerrillas should expect support from the shrines and equally natural that ZIPRA guerrillas and local people should resent it when support was given. As a cult messenger from Gutu told Martinus Daneel: 'During the war the shrines were both holy and dangerous: holy because of Mwari's presence, dangerous because so many people of different tribes congregated there for advice.'[5] During the 1980s the shrines continued to be both holy and dangerous.

Rhodesian spies – and later Zimbabwean Central Intelligence Organisation agents – mingled with pilgrims at the shrines and at times both the Rhodesian and the Zimbabwean governments tried to co-opt their priests.[6] The Rhodesian government

---

[4] *Sunday News*, 8 June 1980.

[5] M. L. Daneel, *African Earthkeepers*, vol. 1, forthcoming, p.33.

[6] R. Mwanza visited shrines in the Matopo TTL in 1972. He was told that 'during the Pearce Commission [in early 1972] Special Branch Members visited the Dula/Maswabe shrine.... The priests are aware of the interest of the Rhodesian authorities and as such avoid political discussions.' The Dzilo priests were suspicious of the unknown Mwanza and assured him that 'Mwari is totally against bloodshed. He loves peace ... Europeans are troublesome but they should be persuaded not to follow their troublesome way of life. Africans should not fight them. Mwari was never asked about ANC, NDP, ZAPU and split ZAPU/ZANU.' They told him, however, that 'the rival cave Dula Svavi is for war'. R. Mwanza, 'Mwari: The God of the Karanga', conference paper, Lusaka, September 1972.

carried out detailed studies of the cult and its priests were listed in its official catalogue of significant spiritual leaders, who were to be watched carefully.[7] In the 1980s the contant resort to the shrines by the harrassed ZAPU leadership meant that close attention was paid to them by the Zimbabwean state.

As we shall see, in the 1970s both ZIPRA and ZANLA guerrillas were able to make use of the shrines despite all this. So too were ZAPU politicians in the 1980s. But Mwali's endorsement of the liberation war – or of ZAPU's right to survive – had to be covert and indirect and was always contested, with rival priestly families taking opposite positions. The Voice of Mwali was heard amidst a clamour of other voices.

The greatest peril for the shrines was a complete failure of control over the armed men. If guerrillas or soldiers or dissidents disobeyed the rule that no guns were to be brought to, still less fired within a shrine, the sacrilege would destroy its legitimacy. In the later 1980s it was widely believed that this had happened at Njelele and that guns had been fired inside the shrine cave itself, though this was variously blamed upon guerrillas, the Security Forces, the dissidents or the Fifth Brigade. But the shrines were not the only religious centres placed in peril by the violence of the 1970s and 1980s. The mission stations at Matopo, Mtshabezi and Cyrene were under constant pressure from guerrillas, dissidents and government forces. In June 1980, under the headline 'The Church Comes out of Hiding', the *Sunday News* described the disarray caused by the war. Chimali Mission, near the Antelope mine, south of the hills, was 'in a bad way, with only a few old women meeting for prayer services'. The *News* announced that Cyrene Mission, which had been evacuated in 1978, was returning to the outskirts of the Matopos.[8] But in a year or two Cyrene was in the midst of the violence of the dissident war.[9]

In the middle of all this lay the peopleless Park. During the mid-1960s the Park itself was a major target for petrol bombs, grass fires and other sabotage. There then followed a period of restored 'law and order' during which the Park authorities took advantage of what looked like a victory to enforce more rigorous preservationist policies. Then came the guerrilla wave of the late 1970s and the realisation that a majority rule regime was inevitable. The Park authorities desperately looked for ways to assuage African public opinion.

In the first half of this chapter I shall take up these themes with reference to the 1960s and 1970s. I shall first seek to provide a brief narrative of what happened in the Matopos between 1965 and 1980; then I shall examine National Park responses to the guerrilla war; and finally I shall turn to the symbolic struggle in the Matopos and the interaction of the Mwali shrines with the guerrillas. In the second half of the chapter I shall narrate and then analyse the events of the 1980s.

---

[7] In 1973 A. Latham synthesised the earlier researches of Cockcroft and Hemans for the section on the shrines in the 'Shamanism Book'.

[8] *Sunday News*, 8 June and 18 July 1980.

[9] On 31 December 1986, for instance, the *Chronicle* reported the narrow escape of a kraal-head near Cyrene from 'a hail of bullets'; it was said to be the fourth time his kraal had been attacked by dissidents.

Violence in the Matopos, 1964–80

When ZAPU was banned in 1962 preparations were made for sabotage on a more professional scale than filling in dip tanks or burning school rooms. A group of Bulawayo youth activists received grenades and explosives which were smuggled in from Lusaka. One of them was Daniel Dube's son, Ethan. Together with colleagues who knew the hills, Ethan hid dynamite and grenades in caves in the Matopos. They were then distributed to 'trusted youths' in Bulawayo. The Matopos were also used for practising explosions, and Dumiso Dabengwa, later head of ZIPRA intelligence and now Minister of Home Affairs, began to learn his trade there.[10]

In September 1964 Matobo district was the site of the first ZAPU guerrilla incursion. This has become mythologised in Matopos memory. Many people believe that it was planned in revenge for the evictions from the hills. It took place at Dube ranch in the far south, to which evictees from the Matopos had been moved, only to be evicted once again and resettled in Tsholotsho. It is said that the guerrilla group was led by Mishek Velaphi, one of those forced out of the ranch, who later achieved prominence in ZIPRA.[11] In fact, the operation aimed to capture the Magistrate who had banned an NDP march in Bulawayo in 1960, thereby precipitating riots which led to many African deaths, but had now retired to ranch at Dube. Although two Kezi men were members of the guerrilla group, an urban rather than a rural revenge was planned. But it was enough that it took place in the district to make people feel that their grievances were about to be redressed by force.[12]

The Rhodesian authorities managed to repress these early sabotage and guerrilla campaigns. Thereafter, nationalist energies went into recruitment and training of guerrillas. Many recruits came from Matobo. In 1995 and 1996 Jocelyn Alexander, JoAnn McGregor and I worked with ex-ZIPRA commanders to collect over 50 guerrilla autobiographies. One of these was by Adam Ndlovu of Wenlock, born in 1948, educated at Mtshabezi and Matopo Mission, who left the country in October 1978 because of 'ill treatment by the Rhodesian government.... This war could have been avoided had the Rhodesians listened to our cry of better treatment by them, but every African who showed disgruntlement was hunted down and arrested.' Another Wenlock man, Dama Ndlovu, who studied at Mtshabezi, was among the autobiographers; so too

---

[10] Narrative by Colonel Richard Dube, July 1995. Richard Dube worked with Jocelyn Alexander, JoAnn McGregor and me on collecting guerrilla autobiographies. He was himself born in Matobo in 1943 and was educated at Matopo Mission.

[11] Interview with Zephaniah Moyo, Bulawayo, 14 July 1988.

[12] Interview with Elliot Ngwabe, Esiphezini, 4 September 1988. The story of the guerrilla raid is an extraordinary one. The guerrillas came in by way of a laundry van travelling from Livingstone to Wankie; they then hired a car to drive themselves south. They attacked the ranchhouse; were beaten off by rifle fire; took refuge in the caves of Gwanda; were eventually captured, taken to Grey Street Prison in Bulawayo where ZAPU sympathisers effected their escape, were again recaptured. Elliot Ngwabe was sent to Khami prison, escaped in 1965, nearly got into Botswana, but was taken once again. He remained in prison until 1979.

was Janet Mdaka Moyo, born at Matopo Mission. The longest autobiography yet written by a Zimbabwean guerrilla, Nicholas Nkomo's *Between the Hammer and the Anvil*, tells the story of a boy from Joshua Nkomo's home area in south Matobo who leaves the country to become a key ZIPRA commander.

The District Commissioner, Matobo, compiled reports on all guerrillas sentenced to death and these grim memorials survive in the district files. In January 1978 three Matobo men were sentenced to death, two of them coming from the Matopos and one from the Kalanga-speaking areas to the south. The DC interviewed their families so as to discover the background of such committed enemies of the regime. 'Quite intelligent, not a problem child, always being obedient and respectful', he noted of Nicholas Ndlovu, who tended his father's cattle after school and then vanished into South Africa where he was recruited for ZIPRA. The DC could find nothing in this background to justify suspension of the death penalty.[13]

By the early 1970s ZIPRA guerrillas, better trained and directed than the 1964 insurgents, were penetrating the Matopos. Makhobo Ndlovu, who became a ZIPRA guerrilla and later a dissident, remembers his schooldays. He went to Whitewaters primary school and then from 1973 to Matopo Mission for his O levels:

> I hated the regime of the white man and my father actually drilled this into my mind. My father talked about poor salaries, land issues, etc.... Matopo Secondary School was being run by missionaries. The way they explained the Bible actually tallied with my father's views. Although injustices were noted at school, theoretically the missionaries were enlightening us. I became a prefect in form two and I was actually very vocal and my colleagues liked my talks on politics.... By 1977 soldiers were coming to the school and treating us badly. The guerrillas were sneaking in during the night and preaching to me about socialism and communism. I felt very good about nationalist soldiers. I took it upon myself to rebel against the school authorities and the soldiers who were at the school. I organised the strike.

In 1978 he left the country for Zambia.[14]

In 1978 and 1979 the guerrillas turned the Matopos into a no-go area. Having survived the 1977 strike, the Matopo School was closed down by ZIPRA guerrillas on 16 September 1978. A group came after dark, told the headmaster that 'We have to come to close Matopo', and summoned all the pupils to the hall. They gave 'a display of technical knowledge of dismantling AK rifles'; the contents of the tuck shop were brought for their use; they instructed the students in radical nationalist ideology. Collecting up school texts they asked, 'What use are these books in the new Zimbabwe?', took them out and burnt them. The guerrillas left at 3.30 a.m. and the whole school went to Bulawayo on the next day, where they found an empty factory in which to set up classes.[15]

In these last two years ZANLA guerrillas also arrived in the hills and pressure on their population increased. Between the two guerrilla armies and the punitive raids of the Rhodesians, the people found it hard to manage. Cattle sales were prohibited by the

[13] District Commissioner, Matobo to Provincial Commissioner, 8 March 1978, Box 23673, Bulawayo.
[14] Autobiography of Makhobo Ndlovu, interviewed by Nicholas Nkomo, 30 September 1995.
[15] Interview with Richard Dube, deputy head, Matopo School, 4 July 1988.

guerrillas; travelling to Bulawayo to sell garden produce became too dangerous; all stores closed down and their owners took refuge in the town. Schools closed; roads were blown up by mines; dipping stopped, and a disease called theileriosis was carried into the Tribal Trust Lands by ticks from the National Park game animals. As the *Sunday News* wrote in 1980, 'Gulati TTL in north-west Matopos was devastated. The schools were closed, the roads almost non-existent, and the cattle were dying.'[16]

South of the hills the war was fought with equal intensity. In Wenlock ZANLA operated only in the hills of the north and ZIPRA in the flatter land of the south. 'They hated each other. Guerrillas from ZANLA would pretend to be ZIPRA and vice versa so they could find out who people supported and then punish them'. In north Wenlock ZANLA guerrillas held *pungwes* [political education meetings] and taught Shona *chimurenga* songs.[17] In Prospect/Mbongolo 'both ZIPRA and ZANLA were there in strength. The struggle was pretty hot.' Storekeepers were suspected of distributing poisoned clothes to the guerrillas on behalf of the Rhodesian regime; prominent Protestants were suspected of supporting Abel Muzorewa's Internal Settlement. 'Quite a lot of people, prominent men, died then', says S. M. Ncube, 'killed by freedom fighters, chaps with beautiful houses who were denounced as sell outs.' One Prospect entrepreneur gave a lift in his car to guerrillas who asked him to drive to a particularly posh house which they had come to destroy. It turned out to be his own. He took them well past it and survived on that day, but was killed later. Ncube himself, son of a transport entrepreneur and cattle owner, built his house in Prospect next door to Samson Tshuma's famous mansion, with its polished wood doors. Ncube was a leading churchman. During the 'hot' years of 1977 to 1979, 'things were really bad and forced me to buy a house in town. If I had stayed there I wouldn't be alive today'.[18] Nqabe Tshuma and his brothers – the old radical and the moderate entrepreneurs alike – made their own accommodations with the guerrillas. Nqabe was treated with respect by those who remembered *Sofasonke*.

But if the guerrillas hammered the entrepreneurs – and killed some ordinary peasants as 'sell-outs' and witches – they also responded to many local grievances. In the northern area of Prospect, land was removed in 1976 for the expansion of the government's Antelope Dam cotton scheme, run by the state agency, TILCOR. The old evictees from the Matopos responded with bitterness. A District Assistant's report in December 1976 revealed their opposition:

> The District Commissioner has now destocked his food [said Ndumela Ncube], he will not get enough food because cattle are his daily living, now he has given Tilco to take our grazing area.... We were promised this place by a lawyer when we moved from Kumalo. We came here by a special law. We were told this is our land. Now the DC is taking over our land.... It is very bad to stay with Tilco.

16 *Sunday News*, 8 June 1980.

17 Interview with Abraham Moyo, Bulawayo, 24 August 1990.

18 Interview with S. M. Ncube, Hope Fountain, 3 August 1989. Some of the southern Matobo entrepreneurs were men of real substance. The murdered store-owner, T. F. Ndebele, had at the time of his death 13,000 dollars, 72 cattle, 114 goats, 14 sheep, 12 pigs, a land-rover, a lorry, a scotch cart, and a cultivator. Box 12487, Bulawayo.

'They were given Mbongolo farm and told they will stay there for life', said kraal-head Sivanane, 'but what is done to Mbongolo I don't know. We won't do anything but we cry for cattle and fields.'[19] The old men did not need to 'do anything'; the guerrillas did it for them. TILCOR's cotton scheme came under attack; labour fled; the cattle owners of Prospect were able to graze their herds not only on the land in north Mbongolo but also on the core Antelope estate.[20]

Further to the west, the farms and ranches in the *mapani* veld also came under combined guerrilla and peasant pressure. The records of Matopos South Rural Council, the representative body of the white landowners, reveal a steadily changing balance of power. In the early 1970s its Natural Resources Committee pressed hard for intervention in Matopo, Gulati and Kumalo TTLs, complaining that 'cattle are being permitted to graze the Njelele sponge', calling for destocking, and demanding that steps be taken by the Natural Resources Board. Cattle from the white ranches were allowed to graze in the National Park during the 1970 drought but the Committee was glad to note that 'the Secretary for Internal Affairs refused to sanction the utilization of the Park for alternative grazing for stock on Kumalo and Gulati TTLs, stating that the locals must suffer the consequences of abusing the veldt.'[21]

By 1974, though, with wire-cutting and poaching on their land increasing, the white farmers began to question 'the wisdom of again becoming involved in TTL affairs.... This Council was becoming a most hated group'.[22] In February 1976 the minutes of the Natural Resources Committee note that 'the majority of Committee members were again obliged to report for military duty on March 1st'; they asked that the Department of National Parks send their anti-poaching unit to 'farms on the southern boundary'.[23] By 1978 it was noted that members of the Committee had to travel in protected vehicles and concern was expressed that its membership had declined from seven to three because so many landowners had taken refuge in Bulawayo. In October 1978 the police advised that no further farm inspections be undertaken 'because of the marked deterioration of the Security situation.' In February 1979 'the security situation continued to deteriorate. Terrorist activities were on the increase, total intimidation of labour had occurred and instances of stock theft and fence cutting are on the increase.'[24]

By 1978, indeed, the authorities had abandoned any hope of controlling peasant incursions into the *mapani*. 'The problem is universal', the District Commissioner told a complaining farmer, 'and has been on the increase due to the political and military insecurity which is prevalent. Quite honestly, talking to tribal leaders and getting them to warn their people ... is a waste of time.' At the end of the war, and after the ceasefire had removed most guerrillas from south Matobo, the best that the Secretary of Home

---

[19] District Assistant's Report, December 1976, Box 23672, Bulawayo.

[20] I have treated the case of the Antelope Estates in 'From Paternalism to Privatisation. State Farms in Zimbabwe: The Case of Antelope Estates', Oxford, February 1992.

[21] Minutes of meeting of 6 April 1970. I am grateful to Mrs S. E. Van Vuren, Secretary of the Matopos South Rural Council for showing me these minutes.

[22] Minutes of meeting of 11 September 1974. The chairman was on 'Police Reserve Border Duty'.

[23] Minutes of meeting of 12 February 1976.

[24] Minutes of meetings of 9 February, 7 June and 12 October 1978, 8 February 1979.

Affairs could suggest to protect white ranches against the peasants of the Matopos was 'the employment of large army units on TTL boundary fences', the soldiers to be drawn from guerrillas in the Assembly Points![25]

In this way, guerrillas and peasants turned the tide against the state farm at Antelope and the white ranchers of the *mapani*. Guerrillas also promised the people of Kumalo and Gulati that the fences of the National Park would come down.

The National Park in the late 1960s and 1970s

During the lull between the collapse of the sabotage campaign of the mid-1960s and the opening of intensive guerrilla war in the Matopos in the late 1970s, triumphant environmentalists imposed their ideal pattern on the National Park and the Rhodes Matopos Estate. A select committee recommended that when all the leases on the Estate terminated in 1978 the whole area should be used for agricultural research; in 1978 most of the land was leased to the Department of Agriculture for fifty years. Meanwhile a Wildlife Commission had recommended in 1969 that there should be 'no lumbering, no livestock grazing, no cultivation and no human settlement' in any National Park. These recommendations were put into effect in the Parks and Wildlife Act of 1975. After that the Rhodes Matopos National Park was totally reserved for wild animals and for tourists, virtually all of whom were white.[26] The tamed Park was now quite safe for representations of Rhodesian history and the advisory committee unanimously approved of a film being made there of 'the last stand of the Shangani Patrol'.[27]

Even before the Parks Act of 1975, African cattle were excluded from the Park since officials 'didn't believe the farmers gained any benefit, that none was gained by Parks and that no goodwill had been derived ... So far as Africans were concerned there was no appreciation whatever.'[28] When it was argued that 'facilities should surely be made available for both black and white' since Rhodes had intended the land to be 'for the benefit of the people of Bulawayo', it was countered that 'as the Park was classified as European area under the Land Tenure Act ... only European cattle should be accepted for grazing.'[29]

[25] District Commissioner to Mr Goodwin, 12 June 1978; Secretary, Home Affairs to Provincial Commissioner, 8 April 1980, Box 1971–84, file AGR 6/1–3, Bulawayo.

[26] Monthly Reports by the Regional Warden, Matabeleland South, for the period October 1972 to January 1973 give a picture of life in the National Park in the early 1970s. In September 1972 Ian Smith came to the Park and laid a wreath at Rhodes's Grave; a representative of the World Wild Life Fund spent three days at the Rest Camp; in October, the Chief Nature Conservator of South West Africa visited Rhodes's Grave; members of the Bulawayo Round Table occupied the whole of Maleme Rest Camp and delegates attending a tourism conference visited the Park; African poachers were arrested; staff quarters were being built in Whitewaters; a rhino calf was born in the Game Park.

[27] Minutes of Advisory Committee meeting, 8 January 1969, Ashton Box File, Historical Reference Library, Bulawayo.

[28] Minutes of Matopos National Parks Committee, 2 March 1970.

[29] Minutes of meeting of 14 April 1970. The Park Warden was afraid, however, that if European cattle were allowed grazing 'there might be repercussions in the way of fence cutting and deliberate starting of fires by the African population.'

This resolute rejection of any political or social concessions to Africans could not be maintained into the late 1970s. It become increasingly clear that a majority rule government was inevitable and conservationists began to explore how the Park might be saved. In December 1976 J. H. G. Grobler, Research Officer, Wildlife, drew up 'A Case for Survival':

> We are in a time of ferment, progress and instability where in Africa this has often resulted in the destruction and exploitation of natural resources by the uneducated masses.... In the wake of black extremism there is every chance that the Matopos Park would be given back to the people to abuse as they see fit.

Grobler urged that international Wild Life organisations be asked to help protect the Park. 'The urgency for this action is brought out by rumours already circulating in the neighbourhood areas that "we know once we are in power we will be permitted to move into the Park to live and to kill all the animals".'[30]

Others thought that there must be some belated attempt to win over Africans. In December 1978 C. R. Saunders, Chairman of the Rhodes Matopos Committee, enunciated what he called 'The Matopos Message'. Saunders declared that he could 'fully appreciate the indignation which local [African] leaders expressed during the period 1948 to 1963, when they accused successive Governments of caring more for wild animals than for local people.' He admitted that the Park had not been 'people-oriented in its broadest sense, or at best designed to benefit only a narrow segment of our people. This is not good enough.' The Park *must* be managed in the interests of 'local tribesmen, the citizens of Bulawayo, the whole Matabeleland region and our nation'. Africans must be offered thatching grass; there was 'an ideal opportunity to recreate and maintain an authentic working model of a traditional Ndebele village, as it was prior to the influence of civilisation.' There must be public education so that 'the child of future generations will have the opportunity like the psalmist to lift up his eyes unto the hills, there to find inspiration, not degradation.'[31]

In the same month two Interpretative Officers, one white and one black, produced a report on the Park:

> The Matopos is a very special piece of land. There is probably no other land of equal size in Rhodesia which evokes so much depth of feeling and sentiment.... Tribal and/or spiritual contacts with the Matopos are regularly kept with people from such remote districts as Mount Darwin, Gutu and Wankie.... Because of this the Matopos is reckoned to be our most threatened part of the Parks and Wildlife estate.

But it was to the 'Ndebele people' who surrounded the Park that any plan of action must be directed. If nothing was done, guerrillas and agitators would press arguments 'concerning playgrounds for the white affluent and of animals being more important than people'.

To counter this, there should be licensed fishing, hydrax rearing, 'limited access to resources by registered herbalists', 'active promotion of tribal cultural gatherings or

---

[30] J. H. Grobler, 'The Rhodes Matopos National Park: a Case for Survival', 14 December 1976, Ashton files.
[31] C. R. Saunders, 'The Matopos Message', *ibid.*

ceremonies', even the 'donation of a pair of white rhinos to an appropriate tribal leader.' Above all, ways should be found of satisfying 'spiritual leaders'.[32]

The Mwali Shrines and Violence in the 1970s

There had been previous attempts to recruit African 'spiritual leaders' to protect the fauna and flora of the Park. Rhodesia Front studies of the shrines emphasised that they were devoted to rain and fertility and to propagating Mwali's doctrine of the environment. In the mid-1970s, for example, Ian Smith visited the National Park and chiefs were instructed to recruit 'all people who were familiar with African rain dancing'. Sitwanyana Ncube and other priests and mediums assembled by the Maleme Dam. They danced and there was rain.[33] But, as we have seen, Sitwanyana was in fact deeply critical of the way that nature was managed in the National Park. He was much more available to the Park's enemies than he was to its protectors.

By the time first ZIPRA and then ZANLA guerrillas were operating around Njelele there were two priestly villages competing with each other. Sitwanyana Ncube, the ZAPU stalwart, had been evicted from Njelele by District Commissioner Cockcroft in 1968. But he returned to Halale village on the southern side of the mountain during the 1970s; on the northern side Mayabu Ndlovu took pilgrims to the shrine from his village by the side of the main Kumalo West road. As Japhet Ngwenya, once a teacher at the Seventh Day Adventist school close to Mayabu's village, remembers: 'Njelele was right in the middle of the mountains, it is so remote, it is a good hiding place.' So there were many guerrillas. Moreover, as Ngwenya says, when the war became hot, the guerrillas 'began to pay attention not only to the shrine but to the spirits in general'.[34] Both priests had much interaction with them.

Sitwanyana, with his ZAPU connections, worked closely at first with the ZIPRA guerrillas. Siwani Nyathi of Halale village says that he 'came to be generally known as a priest of war because he used to pray for guerrillas at his shrine'. Sitwanyana himself says that many ZIPRA came to his home. They could not go to the shrine wearing uniform or carrying guns, so he hid their clothes and buried their guns at his kraal, and took them to the cave wearing the black of pilgrims. The guerrillas asked for the protection of Mwali. When the Security Forces came to his home Sitwanyana would deny having seen any ZIPRA men and speak merely of the visit of pilgrims.[35]

Sitwanyana was criticised by the Ndlovus for being too ready to associate with

---

[32] A. A. Ferrar and J. C. Makina, 'An Assessment of the Matopos Problem', 4 December 1978, *ibid*.

[33] Interview with Sitwanyana Ncube, Mguza, 19 August 1988.

[34] Interview with Japhet Ngwenya, Tshatshani school, 30 August 1988.

[35] The words of Siwani Nyathi and Sitwanyana's account come from Leslie Nthoi, 'Social Perspective of Religion: a Study of the Mwali Cult of Southern Rhodesia', PhD thesis, University of Manchester, 1995. Nthoi spent a year between June 1992 and June 1993 residing in the southern and northern priestly villages at Njelele. He argues very sensibly that it is impossible to say either that the Mwali cult as a whole backed the guerrilla war or that it did not. Some officials and some shrines did; other officials and other shrines sought to remain aloof.

armed violence. But in the end it was Mayabu who established the most amicable connections with the guerrillas. Sitwanyana was as always charismatic and controversial; he was criticised by locals for charging fees and for taking his women to the shrine. He says himself merely that 'when the struggle intensified – around 1977 – I left because of the war.' In fact he was chased away by guerrillas. As Ngwenya says, their new concern for the spirits meant that 'if they feared that somebody was abusing certain spirits and certain traditional rules then they didn't like this person.' In the end Sitwanyana's closeness to Nkomo did him no good with ZIPRA guerrillas, who felt 'this man is pushing himself close to Nkomo in order to hide some of these things that people are complaining about.' So:

> He had to run away from the freedom fighters. They didn't like him, they knew he had no right to be there. They didn't want him there. He had introduced wrong things ... too many women.[36]

Sitwanyana left before the arrival of ZANLA guerrillas. Thereafter both ZIPRA and ZANLA approached the shrine by way of Mayabu. The route to the cave from his village passed by the Seventh Day Adventist school and church and in 1978 the tension between these rival religious claims to the holy mountain erupted:

> During the war ... there were some people who were patronising the shrine there and they passed by Njelele school and the church there, and they would say a few nasty comments as they passed by. Some people were beginning to say the church should not be here because this whole place belongs to the Njelele shrine ... and yet because they had no backing from anybody, they couldn't force that one. In 1978 even the guerrillas got involved. I was actually there and on a Sabbath day soon after church, they had been at Mayabu's place, they arrived at my house and they were told that we were in church. Now, after church some of our church-members passed by, they were quite old people and some of their books were burnt and after that the guerrillas came straight to the church and school there, where they found us, they gave us a bit of a beating and burnt our books, saying we were foolish, colonised and shouldn't be doing that.[37]

The war was yet more intense and there were more shrines on the eastern side of the Matopos, in Matopo Tribal Trust Land. The TTL was the site of Dula, the shrine of the Red Axe, to which Nkomo had famously gone in 1953; it was the site of Dzilo, the shrine of Mwali's female principle, to which came very many pilgrims from the Shona-speaking east; it was the site of the new shrine at Bembe, where the rock had fallen. All these shrines had interactions with the guerrillas.

Jonas Chokoto of Dzilo says that the guerrillas came to the shrine saying: 'We are hunting, father, please give us guidance'. They came at night without their uniforms and arms. The Voice told them to venerate the ancestors, and 'where to move and how to avoid dangerous situations'. One group of guerrillas had their base camp close to Dzilo. A landmine was planted near to the cave, which exploded killing three head of cattle. Mwali reprimanded them and they apologised. Meanwhile, Shona-speaking

---

[36] Interview with Japhet Ngwenya, 30 August 1988.
[37] *Ibid.*

240

pilgrims and messengers were coming to the shrine from the east and being given 'a full declaration of war' by the Voice. 'The power to fight', Jonas Chokoto told Martinus Daneel, 'came from the *mhondoro* spirits together with Mwari. That is why we won the land! The people saw it was the truth.'[38]

Minya Ncube, the Goddess of Rain at Bembe, speaks of intense interaction with both ZIPRA and ZANLA. ZIPRA sent gifts of black cloth to the shrine – 'the guerrillas had respect because they wanted to be blessed through ancestral ceremonies until the country was independent'. But by the end of the war her hills had become a ZANLA stronghold:

> When the ceasefire was declared they came but the majority were not Ndebele. It was those from the east, it is those who came. They never gave me problems. When the war was ended they came in very large numbers. Locals were surprised up to today. Even today many people don't like me [because of local hostility to ZANU]. The guerrillas heaped their guns together ... the size of that house. They wanted to find out if it was true there was a ceasefire. They wanted to consult the shrine that genuine freedom had come or was it a ploy to massacre them in camps. I told them that independence would come but that there might be problems.... They filled the whole village. It was during Christmas time 1979. I had brewed some beer and there were many locals. The guerrillas asked for my radio to dance and say goodbye.... They danced very well and in the middle of their dance, a 'manoeuvre' from the army camp arrived. I told him they were present, some in the surrounding bushes, hills and fields. We sent children to call them because there was now peace.[39]

Just as at Njelele, local Christians became the butt of those who believed the whole area was now solely the country of Mwali. Old Mark Dokotela, cultivating his fertile sponge in northern Wenlock, had to deal with band after band of guerrillas. To each group he was denounced by his neighbours as a man who despised the laws of Mwali, who cultivated on rest days, who ran his farm as a business and had a licence for a shot-gun. According to Ncube, he managed to persuade the guerrillas that it would be irrational to kill him, telling them that the only reason there were bananas growing to feed them was because he could guard the crops against thieves and baboons with his gun. If they killed him and took the gun they would have plenty of bananas for the moment – but thereafter none. He survived the war on his land but this was a rare victory of entrepreneurial logic.[40]

The Matopos in the 1980s

The ceasefire and the establishment of majority rule brought immediate signs of a

---

[38] M. L. Daneel, *African Earth-keepers*, vol. 1, forthcoming, pp. 31–4.

[39] Interview with Melusi Sibanda and Minya Ncube, Bembe, 27 July 1989. The open celebration by ZANLA in Bembe village had the immediate consequence of the arrival of Rhodesian soldiers who 'alleged that I was hiding them in my hills. They threatened to kill me'.

[40] Interview with Mark Dokotela Ncube, Wenlock, 30 August 1990. An earlier treatment of the interaction of Mwali ideologies and the guerrilla war is Terence Ranger and Mark Ncube, 'Religion in the Guerrilla War: the Case of Southern Matabeleland', in Ngwabi Bhebe and Terence Ranger, eds, *Society in Zimbabwe's Liberation War*, University of Zimbabwe and James Currey, Harare and London, 1996.

return to 'normality' in the Matopos.[41] All interests in the hills sought to reassert themselves. Thus in January 1980 it was reported that 'Confidence Fills Matopos Resort' and that for the first time in the past three years all the chalets at Maleme Dam were fully booked by white holiday-makers rejoicing that the hills were 'no longer a security risk'.[42] At the same time, it seemed unlikely that the Park could merely return to its old hardline position. In March 1980 the Chairman of the Matabeleland branch of the Wild Life Society and the Director of the National Museum combined to argue that 'the Matopos is a special case. Although small it was a natural "island" and was of great historical, cultural and religious significance to all people in the country. Obviously we are going to have to make some sort of special arrangement.'[43]

The first months of 1980 saw both a public glorification of the Mwali cult and the return of the Christian missions to the hills. On 23 February Joshua Nkomo held a great election rally six kilometres away from Njelele but in sight of the mountain. Some 300,000 people turned out to hear him say that Njelele was 'a major religious shrine of everybody, whatever their tribe or religion. It had been a centre of the uprising in the 1890s. Chiefs came there to announce their triumphs and to see if the ancestors approved.' Nkomo's words were greeted with thunder and lightning and with heavy downpours of rain, leaving many of the crowd stranded as water rose over the bridges. Nkomo himself was lifted out by helicopter.[44] On the other hand, it was not long before the press could announce 'The Church Comes out of Hiding' and that Cyrene and Matopo Missions had returned to the hills.[45] There was even still occasion for belated Christian triumphalism in the Matopos. It was after 1980 that Father Odilo Weeger persuaded a Catholic landowner in the hills to erect the huge metal cross which can be seen rising opposite Rhodes's Grave.

There was a return to order in the Matopos accompanied by a persistence of some forms of popular disorder. In June 1980 the *Sunday News* carried a headline 'Life Returns to Normal in Lucky Gulati'. The article described how the Matopos reclamation plan was starting in the north and working its way southwards. Roads were being tackled first – 'simply filling in the holes, blasting the odd rock, and then grading the new surface is all that is necessary'. Schools reopened and were free; dips reopened and were free: 'On Thursday, 1,163 head, the first for two years, splashed through a dip, all three schools were overflowing and policemen cycled over new roads.'[46] Before long store owners were returning from Bulawayo and butchers were buying cattle once again. But those cycling policemen could not restrain poach-grazing or poaching of animals. There was a 'poaching wave' in the Matopos and especially in Gulati, where

---

[41] There were, however, several reported incidents of violence in the Matobo TTLs by ZANLA guerrillas who had stayed out of the Assembly Points and were using force to coerce people to vote for ZANU/PF in the elections. *Chronicle*, 11 January, 13 and 14 February 1980.

[42] *Chronicle*, 22 January 1980.

[43] *Sunday News*, 23 March 1980.

[44] *Sunday News*, 24 February 1980.

[45] *Sunday News*, 8 June 1980.

[46] *Ibid.*

Morgan Dube was found in possession of as many as three hundred dassie skins.[47]

There was some reason to believe, indeed, that in the new Zimbabwe the populist interest might win out over environmentalists or white ranchers or state farming. Everywhere the African peoples of the communal areas were exerting formal or informal pressure. Kraal heads in Gulati sent a memorandum pointing out that a large area of the Park, east of the Mtsheleli River, was not being used and should be handed over to them:

> The late Chief Nzula had spoken about the Park that it has taken more of his people's land.... We the tribespeople feel it is our right that we have been deprived of to resettle in the area. So we still wish to reoccupy the area. We would mostly welcome resettlement not gates.

'The explanation that this was a Wilderness Area meant nothing to them', lamented the Warden, 'which I feel is understandable as they could see no benefit from this type of policy.'[48]

In north Prospect/Mbongolo political activists were preparing to resist plans to revive irrigated state farming on the Antelope estate and to expand the scheme further into Mbongolo/Prospect Communal Area. In April 1981 the Chairman of the newly elected and ZAPU-dominated District Council, Nyathi, marched into Maphisa township with some of his colleagues and delivered an ultimatum to the TILCOR manager. As the latter reported the next day, Nyathi told him that:

> the Council had taken over the development and control of Maphisa. TILCOR was no longer to vet stand or business applications as that function was the Council's. Antelope Estate now came under the control of the Council and I was their Estate Manager growing food for distribution to the local inhabitants.[49]

Meanwhile, people were raiding the *mapani* farms out of Kumalo Communal Area. The commercial farmers' Natural Resources Committee complained of 'indiscriminate cutting of timber on private land by the locals and the poaching and snaring of animals, incidences of which were increasing at an alarming rate'; dogs were hunting on white farms and ranches, fires were being set, Communal Area cattle were being driven on to the land through fences which had been cut down.[50] Nor did the white owners get much sympathy from Joshua Nkomo when he met them at Kezi in September 1980. They complained of harassment but demanded high prices if they had to sell the land for resettlement. Nkomo replied that:

> We cannot continue with vast areas of land on which no other development is done than drilling a borehole and piping water. No rancher ever developed his land. 'You find it like that; you leave it like that'. The people were saying, 'This is majority government. We must get our land back'. They snared because no native is allowed a gun.... There must be a reorganisation of the hunting laws.[51]

---

47 *Chronicle*, 20 September 1980.

48 Provincial Warden to Hugh Ashton, 24 October 1979, Ashton box file, Historical Reference Library, Bulawayo.

49 Urban Controller, TILCOR to Controlling Secretary, District Administration, 16 April 1981, Box 23672, AGR 16, Bulawayo. In June Nyathi pressed his case. 'People feel deprived of rich soils which they know are theirs. The people must be given a chance to participate.'

50 Minutes of Natural Resources Committee meetings, 14 August, 9 October and 11 December 1980.

51 *Sunday News*, 14 September 1980.

But these appearances of government backing for peasant causes were misleading and a combination of factors frustrated populist expectations. Frustration over the National Park came earliest. The environmentalist appeal to international wild life organisations proved decisive. British negotiators at Lancaster House saw to it that National Parks were entrenched in the new constitution. The new government's position became clear in July 1980. Stephen Nkomo, the ZAPU member for Matobo, asked in parliament whether grazing could be allowed in the Park 'in view of severe drought' and whether certain portions could be 'returned' for farming. The Minister of Natural Resources was himself a ZAPU man, Joseph Msika, but he gave a straight conservationist answer:

> Parks served as reservoirs of wild life; were recreational areas for all the people; had enormous potential for earning foreign currency and in a case such as the Matopos were a vital catchment area. It would discredit Zimbabwe internationally were we to embark upon a programme of reducing our parks and wild life estate.[52]

After this there was no longer any need for the Parks authorities to bother with socially and politically sensitive gestures – free grazing, a traditional Ndebele village, etc. The Natural Resources Board announced that it would implement 'World Conservation strategy in every aspect'. And Joshua Nkomo himself, speaking at a rain supplication gathering at Njelele on 25 September 1982, rebuffed calls for the Park to be returned:

> Many people had approached him on the subject of the National Park and getting it back for the people. He said they must forget about it. Wild life had to be preserved; the authorities had set aside the area and that had to be accepted. Joseph Msika was present when this was said.[53]

Nephas Ndlovu, District Administrator of Matobo,

> went to great lengths in talking to the Minister asking that some concessions should be made. No concessions were made. Although we went out and climbed every mountain there, up and down, trying to see exactly how the boundaries could be shifted, but no concessions. He said the Park was a national thing rather than just to think of the locals. Neither did Joshua say that people should go back to the Park.[54]

At the Antelope estate the TILCOR manager was able to frustrate the Council's takeover by stressing to his ZANU/PF minister that 'the local political machine is anti-government' and that the Matobo peasantry showed 'the suspicion born of perverse ignorance, laziness, disinterest and political quibbling'. No local labour was available for cotton picking, for example, and in the 1981 season 'the National Army was called in to assist, a sad commentary on local attitudes'. Far from being cut back, Antelope must expand; its influence must radiate throughout the district, creating a 'work ethic' for the local population. These arguments won the day and TILCOR – soon to be renamed

[52] *Chronicle*, 31 July 1980.
[53] Interview with Jonathan Maphenduke, Bulawayo, 25 July 1988.
[54] Interview with Nephas Ndlovu, Bulawayo, 2 August 1988.

as ARDA – was given the backing of the Zimbabwean state.[55]

The frustration of other popular demands in the Matopos took longer to develop. The national victory of Robert Mugabe's ZANU/PF in the 1980 elections – while ZAPU candidates won in Matobo and in Matabeleland as a whole – threw Matabeleland's politics into limbo. As the Antelope case makes clear, central government did not pay much attention to popular demands expressed through ZAPU members of parliament and councillors; for their part, people in the Matopos did not trust newly instituted organs of local 'development' like village and ward development committees, which they suspected as ZANU/PF cells. In any case, official development policy was all too reminiscent of the colonial days. People in the Matopos soon began to hear talk of the depopulation of the hills, responding that they had fought a war to prevent this. Official resettlement policies involved moving people yet again. Most people felt that they had been moved quite enough already and instead demanded relief grazing land for their cattle. Popular disagreement with official policies could often be expressed with disconcerting frankness. In June 1982 peasants in Wenlock:

> surprised a visiting deputy minister and district administrative officials when they refused to give security guarantees for resettlement officers operating in the area ... Mark Dube was interrupted by a number of peasants when he started to make his appeal for peace and order in the area. One peasant said they had not come to listen or discuss anything other than the resettlement issue. Another peasant said: 'The intimidation of the resettlement officers is not our responsibility until we get grazing land for our cattle. Don't talk to us about policing this area. We will do it as soon as we have been given more land for grazing.[56]

But it was the 'security' situation which really aborted any changes desired by the people of the Matopos. The political tension between ZAPU and ZANU/PF, fomented by South African agents; the fighting in Bulawayo and elsewhere between ex-ZIPRA and ex-ZANLA soldiers being integrated into the National Army; government attempts to break ZAPU's hold on Matabeleland; the emergence of armed 'dissidents' in the bush and the deployment of massive state forces, including the notorious Fifth Brigade, against them; the assault on the civilian population by the Fifth Brigade, the CIO and other agencies – all this meant that no development took place in Matobo between 1982 and 1988. In particular it meant that the people of the Communal Areas came to be regarded as disloyal and unreasonable. They were held at bay from the National Park by armed poaching patrols. When white ranchers fled from the *mapani* veld and the land was taken over by the state, there was no question of allowing peasant cattle on to the land. Attempts by local councillors to assert their control over the Antelope estate were rebuffed and plans were drawn up to take over yet more of Prospect/Mbongolo for irrigated agriculture. The Mugabe government was as much at loggerheads with the people of the Matopos as the Rhodesians had ever been.

In the remainder of this chapter I shall examine two topics in particular, first the experience of the people of the Matopos with the dissidents and with the Fifth Brigade,

---

[55] C. G. Champion, 'The Future Development of Antelope Estate and Environs', June 1981, Box 23673, Bulawayo.

[56] *Chronicle*, 29 June 1982.

and second the desperate symbolic war that raged in the hills, as both ZAPU and ZANU/PF sought to control the shrines and monuments of the Matopos.

Dissidents, the Fifth Brigade and the Matopos

The recent Catholic Commission of Justice and Peace and Legal Resources Foundation report on 'the disturbances in Matabeleland', *Breaking the Silence*, contains a case study of Matobo district. Most of its detail refers to Matobo South and few interviews were carried out in the hills. Nevertheless, the report believes that they had a special experience:

> From a few in-depth interviews with selected residents of Kumalo West Communal Lands it is clear that this area was not as badly hit by 5 Brigade as areas further south, but was worse affected by dissidents ... The dissidents travelled regularly through Kumalo West and were greatly hated and feared by the civilians, who particularly resented their continual demands to feed them. The notorious dissidents 'Fidel Castro', 'Gayigusu', 'Danger' and 'Idi Amin' were among those who regularly traversed this region. 'Fidel Castro' and 'Danger' were killed in Kumalo. The mountainous terrain and lush vegetation provided ideal cover for the dissidents ... The 5 Brigade made regular excursions through this region during the curfew months of 1984 and there were mass beatings and many young men and women were taken away to Bhalagwe [torture camp]. However, the impact of 5 Brigade seems less intense than that further south.... 5 Brigade would have found it impossible to drive trucks through much of this region, and it is hard work to walk through the bush.[57]

This judgement certainly corresponds to my own experience. I arrived in the hills for field work some two months after the amnesty of April 1988, when the surviving dissidents came in. By then the Fifth Brigade had not been deployed in the area for some four years, though other brigades and forces had continued to operate there. (An early field trip to Matopo Mission on 13 July 1988 was interrupted by inquiries from a Central Intelligence Organization (CIO) carload into what I was doing; when I presented my letter of endorsement from ZANU/PF Minister Maurice Nyagumbo – 'Professor Ranger is a fellow freedom fighter' – and the CIO saluted before they drove off, the old man whom I had stopped to talk to rushed off into the bush in terror). It may be, then, that the recently active dissidents were spoken about in 1988 more than the withdrawn Fifth Brigade. Certainly, dissidents were vividly remembered and I was told many stories of their arbitrary brutality.

The overall judgement, however, was one which condemned dissidents and the Zimbwean forces equally. On 13 July 1988 I went on from Matopo Mission to see old Nduna Ncube:

> We were like a beast between two carnivores [he said]. One carnivore was the army and they ate us from the front. The other carnivore was the dissidents and they ate us from the back. We had nothing left but our bones. The dissidents took mbanje and abused the people. The soldiers also took mbanje and beat and beat you. We were lucky in this more open valley

---

[57] *Breaking the Silence*, p. 137.

because the dissidents didn't like to come here, but among the rocks they gave people a really bad time. The dissidents were very troublesome, the soldiers were very troublesome.[58]

Meanwhile, south of the hills in areas like Wenlock and Prospect and in the south Matobo TTLs – readily open to trucks – the Fifth Brigade rampaged. In Wenlock this period is remembered as more dangerous even than the ZANLA/ZIPRA rivalry of the 1970s. 'The dissidents, they were fierce. It was the worst war. Every night one thought one might not live another day.'[59] When I drove down into Prospect/Mbongolo in September 1988 the District Assistant who guided me told me that the area had been 'dense' with dissidents and that 'thousands' had been killed by the Fifth Brigade. The Tshuma family, whom I had been hoping to interview about Nqabe's long career of protest and his support for nationalism, were determined to give no possible cause of offence to any government. Nqabe had never protested; never been a member of ZAPU – after all, men with profiles like that had been hunted down by the Fifth Brigade.

The chronology of the dissident war in Matobo district ran as follows. From April 1982 on there were reports of robberies and of attacks on government projects – on 10 June, for instance, two dissidents robbed the headmaster at Matopo Mission; on 27 June two storekeepers were robbed in Kumalo; on 21 June two armed men robbed a business in Gulati and a store in Kumalo. And so press reports continued through the rest of 1982 and 1983. By that time government was claiming that Matobo was a core dissident zone. Then, as *Breaking the Silence* records, 'in February 1984 the 5 Brigade launched a systematic campaign of mass beatings and mass detentions in Matabeleland South, lasting several months.' In the first months of 1984 there was a curfew and a food embargo; drought relief was stopped; in parts of the hills the Brigade even punished people who ate wild fruits; those few stores which were allowed briefly to open were not allowed to stock food. 'The food embargo was a significant and effective strategy which proved to ordinary people the power of the State to cause extreme hardship.'[60]

People detained were taken to Bhalagwe camp just west of Antelope mine, which lay between Bhalagwe and Zamanyone hills and the waters of the Antelope dam. The Fifth Brigade swept through the villages of southern Matobo, including those of Prospect, gathering detainees as they went. Bhalagwe's regime of terror was at its most intense from February to May 1984. Detainees were brutally interrogated and beaten. Many were shot. *Breaking the Silence* estimates over 220 deaths in Matobo and hundreds of people tortured and detained. 'Bhalagwe was a torture chamber', says Moffat Dhlamini, an ex-ZIPRA guerrilla who fled into the bush to avoid being picked up by the Fifth Brigade.

Before the curfew I had no problems at home. I was staying peacefully. When the Gukurahundi [Fifth Brigade] arrived, we had our de-mobilisation cards. The Gukurahundi would confiscate the cards, tear them up and take people to Bhalagwe. Old people were

---

[58] Interview with Nduna Ncube, Matopo Mission, 13 July 1988. An account of response to the Amnesty in the Matopos and of people's memories of dissidents is, Terence Ranger, 'Matabeleland Since the Amnesty', *African Affairs*, 351, 1989.

[59] Interview with Abraham Moyo, Bulawayo, 24 August 1990.

[60] *Breaking the Silence*, pp. 118–19.

seriously tortured – boiling porridge would be shoved into a person's mouth; people were forced to burn their beards off in fires.[61]

Although the Fifth Brigade was not so active in northern Matobo, there were still many incidents there. In February 1983 Fifth Brigade soldiers took 12 men off buses near Cyrene Mission, shot them and buried them in a collective grave.[62] In February 1984 many villagers in Kumalo West were rounded up and taken to Bhalagwe. Meanwhile people were being beaten by dissidents, girls were being raped and abducted, old women were being accused as witches.

After 1984 the Fifth Brigade was not deployed in Matobo, though other government units, and particularly the Central Intelligence Organisation, were responsible for the 'dis-appearance' of ZAPU stalwarts. Right up to the Unity Agreement between ZANU/PF and ZAPU in December 1987 violent incidents continued to take place and many parts of the Matopos were no-go areas. In November 1985, for instance, I had a letter from an old student of mine then living in Bulawayo. He told me that on visits to the National Park he had been prevented from entering its eastern third:

> The Warden said that it was dissident country and we could only go in with a National Parks escort with guns and that they were very relucant to enter that area. In October we went out to Mtshelele and briefly stopped at Silozwe bottle store for a drink.... A police support unit arrived and said that it was very dangerous to be in this area and that the people around the bottle store were dissidents or harbourers of dissidents and that we should leave the area.[63]

The Matobo Council ceased to visit its schools in Gulati. P. M. Ndlovu, an ex-ZANLA guerrilla, who became District Administrator of Esigodini between March 1983 and the end of 1986, never managed to get to Dzilo in Matopo Communal Area. 'In that place one could just disappear going into a cave'. Headman Samson Nkala, who was responsible for the shrines, fled to Esigodini township; Reader Ncube, ZAPU stalwart and Chairman of the district council, was arrested several times and threatened by dissidents.[64] Around Cyrene Mission dissidents killed a white farmer and a black farm manager and ambushed the school bus; the Fifth Brigade used part of Cyrene Farm as a 'killing ground'.[65] In north Matobo the first black District Administrator, Nephas Ndlovu, who served there between November 1981 and December 1983, narrowly missed death five times during his period of office. In July 1983 he was ambushed at Ove Store and held for three hours by Fidel Castro and thirty dissidents.[66]

Outside the hills, the 'Ndebele Village' on the road between Bulawayo and the Park was burnt down by dissidents; the eastern Matopos ZAPU activist, Frazer Gibson

---

[61] Jocelyn Alexander and Nicholas Nkomo interview with Moffat Dhlamini, Esigodini, 18 December 1965.

[62] At this point the Fifth Brigade was operating in northern Matabeleland but these soldiers had come as far south as Cyrene.

[63] Robert Newton to Terence Ranger, 27 November 1985.

[64] Interview with P. M. Ndlovu, Bulawayo, 31 July 1989.

[65] Interview with the headmaster, Cyrene, 6 August 1989. The missionaries took photographs of the Fifth Brigade killings, got them developed in England, and then sent them to the Anglican bishops and to Mugabe.

[66] Interview with Nephas Ndlovu, Bulawayo, 2 August 1988.

Sibanda, who made a point of walking the streets of Bulawayo in his 'Father Zimbabwe' T-shirt, showing Joshua Nkomo's portrait, was abducted by the CIO and never seen again.

This period of terror is vividly remembered in the Matopos. The sense of government's arbitrary violence and lack of reponsibility to the environment and people is often expressed symbolically. People say that members of the Fifth Brigade forced their way into the cave at Njelele and fired shots there, thereby destroying the shrine's rain-making powers. Thus not only was drought relief stopped but drought was perpetuated. 'Those Fifth Brigade people were notorious', a junior district officer told me in July 1989. 'They did not respect anything local. They went to Njelele and fired in the cave. This offended the spirits, the people say, and affected our chances of rain'.[67] In September 1986 Njelele was deproclaimed as a National Monument.[68]

But as I have said, dissidents are much better remembered individually than members of the Zimbabwean forces. Sitwanyana Ncube, who had returned to Njelele after 1980, was chased away again, this time by dissidents:

There were dissidents all over. It was bad. There was a lot of quarrelling and it was then that I began to see the dissidents. They did not have respect.... One day Gayagisu and Everest Kumalo came at half past nine at night. The bus [carrying pilgrims] had just arrived. There was a lot of trouble. They went inside the house where the food was kept and began to throw it away. My own money which they took, my own money was 14,000 dollars. It was all taken, it all went. Ah!

A few months later 'trouble came again'; Sitwanyana heard that the dissidents were coming to kill him. On 1 December 1985 he left Njelele for the third time; on 30 January 1986 his village was burnt to the ground.[69]

Gayagisu was active in Matopo Communal Area and in Gulati as well. Young Kevin Nxumalo, son of a Zionist preacher, whom I met near Bembe shrine, says that

there were too many dissidents. You would see one gang there, another gang there. I *lived* with Gayagisu. Ah, he was a fierce man, killing too much. The dissidents said to young boys, go and watch and tell us when anyone is coming. Then the National Army came and arrested these young boys and asked them: 'Where are your older brothers?' and if one was hurt he would say 'They are on that hill. I will show you', but the dissidents on top of the hills could see them coming and go down into the caves.[70]

Jacob Mnindwa Moyo became Headman in Gulati in 1986. He came to know Gayagisu well – 'he put the fire in everything. He just stopped the boreholes'. People could not visit the shrines because 'the dissidents were getting all over the place. Couldn't be sure when you were going whether you'd come back or not.' And:

[67] Interview with Deputy Administrator Moyo, Kezi, 24 July 1989. Moyo told me that there had been no destocking in Matobo and added that 'even the Fifth Brigade didn't confiscate cattle. It was human lives they took'.
[68] *Chronicle*, 12 September 1986.
[69] Interview with Sitwanyana Ncube, Umguza, 28 July 1988. When I drove Sitwanyana back to his kraal later in 1988 it still lay in ruins.
[70] Interview with Kevin Nxumalo, Bembe, 4 September 1988.

it was really dangerous being a headman. Because several times they are approaching me that why are you building a dam, you are building it for Mugabe, what, what. Well, they said to me, you are going to be read in the newspaper one day. I said, 'Ok, if you want me to be read in the newspaper it's fine by me.' I used to be brave anyway. I said to Gayagisu, 'Mugabe will not come and drink water in this dam, but yourself you are the one who is going to drink in this dam.' Gayagisu is the one who threatened me. He really jumped up and walked around.[71]

To the east of Gulati, at Matopo Mission, two of the other most notorious dissidents, Fidel Castro and Danger, came to the school in 1985 and forced all the staff and students to strip naked.[72]

Stories like this abound in the Matopos. I met a man who said that if he ever saw Gayagisu as a civilian he would fetch a spear and kill him on the spot. But there were other dimensions of the people's relationship with the dissidents. In Gulati one dissident was known as Ndevu Esipamula Mankemustho − beard which smashes cups. He had a hero's reputation, often saving people from rough treatment, and once arresting Gayagisu and placing him in handcuffs. In Matopo Communal Area another dissident who had taken the name of the proto-nationalist hero, Tennyson Hlabangana, was equally respected.[73] And dissident activities sometimes furthered populist causes.

P. M. Ndlovu insists that people in Matopo Communal Area made use of the dissidents to cover their own activities. People would enter white farms, kill a beast, take a haunch, and blame it on the dissidents. If the farmers investigated they were threatened with the dissidents. The farmers came to him as District Administrator to complain; for their part, the people came to complain that the farmers shot their dogs. The farmers thought that he himself, as an ex-ZANLA guerrilla, was organising raids against them; they refused a meeting with the locals because they feared he would mobilise the people against them. 'I said, how can I do that, I never go amongst them without a police guard!' The farmers came to the meeting carrying guns − and so did he.[74] Around the Antelope dam, dissidents disrupted the operations of the plantation and portrayed themselves as protectors of Prospect/Mbongolo against further alienation. And above all, dissidents drove out the *mapani* veld ranchers.

There has been some debate about who actually attacked and killed white farmers and why. It has been argued that many of the killings were the work of South African-backed 'Super ZAPU' units. Dissidents interviewed by Jocelyn Alexander 'consistently denied that attacks on white farmers had anything to do with a land redistribution agenda. They said they had simply attacked individual white farmers where they found

---

[71] Interview with Jacob Moyo, Gulati, 21 July 1988.

[72] Interview with Jerry Sibanda, Matopo Mission, 21 July 1988.

[73] Tennyson Hlabangana died in 1948. He is often spoken of as a lost national leader. See Terence Ranger, *Are We Not Also Men?*, James Currey, London, 1995.

[74] Interview with P. M. Ndlovu, 31 July 1989. At the meeting the people said that the farmers defended their herds with guns while they themselves defended their crops with dogs; their dogs got shot if they pursued wild pigs on to the farms or even if they were close to farm fences. Ndlovu tried to persuade them that the Matopos were better for game than for crops and that they should develop the Communal Area as a communally managed tourist attraction.

them particularly hostile.'[75] Some dissidents did take up the land issue, however. Mbacanga Viko, who had been in the Matopos as a ZIPRA guerrilla and who subsequently operated there as a dissident, says:

Land was one of the priorities for us, even at the amnesty we wrote letters to government stressing the point of land. We told villagers that people must be given land. We said you may possibly not get land, but we will because we are fighting for it, and here we are. I wonder what our elders think of how people are living with no grazing and big farms all around. All land is taken by the commercial farms. During this recent war, the local communities were using these commercial farms for grazing because we used to cut the fences. And what about areas like the Matopos which are mountainous with no grazing? You'll find white people possess vast tracts of land.[76]

In any case, whatever the agency or motivation, the effect was undeniable. In late 1982 and 1983 the grip which whites had maintained on the *mapani* veld since 1908 was finally broken. Attacks culminated in the killing on his farm of Rural District Councillor C. W. Loxton and his wife, who was then Secretary to the Council. The Loxtons' daughter was also killed, but managed before dying to phone an uncle, who came to the farm and was himself shot. The death of these four represented a 22 per cent casualty rate among then resident commercial farmers. Those remaining fled to Bulawayo. The Rural District Council was put into commission under the Provincial Commissioner, Matabeleland North, and with one of the farmers' wives, Mrs Van Vuren, as Secretary. When I interviewed her in July 1989 she showed me the Council's filing cabinet, still riddled with bullet holes from the attack on the Loxton farm.[77]

White farmers and ranchers could no longer manage their land. But the Zimbabwean government was determined that the dissidents should not score a propaganda triumph and that peasants who 'supported' dissidents should not be rewarded with land. And in any case there was already a stalemate over resettlement in Matobo district.

In January 1983 District Administrator Nephas Ndlovu wrote to the Under Secretary for Development:

In this District there has been no resettlement exercise whatsoever.... The view held by Matobo District Council [i.e. the elected and ZAPU controlled Council for the Communal Areas] on resettlement was and still is that resettlement should be for the peoples' cattle. The Council envisaged a resettlement pattern that would relieve the present communal lands of pressure on grazing. Land that government will acquire should be utilised for grazing purposes. [But] in resettlement nothing has been achieved. The farms that have been bought are still lying vacant.... The resettlement module/programme has certainly been put to the test in this part of the country. The local people being pastoral rather than agricultural have demanded that resettlement be oriented towards grazing.[78]

---

[75] Jocelyn Alexander, 'Dissident Perspectives on Zimbabwe's Civil War', forthcoming in *Africa*.

[76] Interview between Jocelyn Alexander and Mbacanga Viko, Plumtree, 26 September 1995.

[77] Interview with Mrs Van Vuren, Bulawayo, 26 July 1989.

[78] N. M. Ndlovu to Under Secretary, Deveopment, Matabeleland South, 4 January 1983, Box 23673, Bulawayo.

Government insisted that resettlement meant people moving as well as cattle.[79] And from the beginning the process was also bedevilled by the tension between ZANU/PF and ZAPU. In February 1983, for instance, the Rural District Natural Resources Committee noted that 'the Ministry of Lands was looking at Duta and Gumella as the first farms to be settled in this area. However Zimbabwe Republic Police had warned of the possibility of further [ZAPU] arms caches on these properties.' By August 1983 the Committee remarked on the state of farms hitherto acquired by the government but not yet resettled. 'These properties were found to be in an advanced state of degradation'. In October, two months before the Council collapsed and its members fled to Bulawayo, it noted that:

> Properties purchased in this area for resettlement were now disaster areas. Cattle had been moved in by the thousands, the grass was depleted, fences removed and buildings completely demolished.[80]

With the collapse of the District Council at the end of 1983, virtually the whole of the white commercial farm belt between the Matopos and the southern Communal Areas became available to government and could have been used for relief grazing. Instead it was decided that the land should be leased from its white owners for five years at an annual rate of 6 per cent of an agreed valuation, with option for government to buy at the end of the five-year period. Until that time the land was to be managed by ARDA, the parastatal which had succeeded TILCOR. Until at least 1989, therefore, the peasant owners of cattle pushing west from Wenlock, north from Prospect/Mbongolo, east from Tshatshani Communal Area and south from Kumalo were trespassing on state land. It was now the business of a Zimbabwean government agency to hold at bay a black return to the *mapani* veld.[81]

The 1980s violence in the Matopos, with all its unmitigated terrors and ambiguous advantages, came to an end in April 1988 when the surviving dissidents surrendered under the terms of the Presidential Amnesty. The last day of the dissidents is vividly remembered in the hills. 'Tennyson Hlabangana' called the people together at Diana's Pool to make a formal farewell and to warn them that they were still threatened by the plan to 'turn the hills into a game park'.[82] At Matopo Mission 'Ndevu' brought his band to the school and ordered that all teachers and pupils come 'to take tea' with them. He addressed them in such excellent English that some of the teachers felt ashamed, and, using Marxist terms of analysis, told them that it had not been crazy or useless to go into the bush. His own distrust of the Mugabe regime had been abundantly justified – 'Can you imagine a ruler who sends an army to slaughter part of his subjects?'[83] At Prospect/Mbongolo dissidents called people together and warned them that they had to

---

[79] For an authoritative discussion of the problems of resettlement in Matabeleland, see Jocelyn Alexander, 'The Unsettled Land: the Politics of Land Redistribution in Matabeleland, 1980–1990', *Journal of Southern African Studies*, 17, 4, 1991.

[80] Minutes of the Natural Resources Committee, 10 February, 18 August and 13 October 1983.

[81] Interview with Mrs Van Vuren, Bulawayo, 26 July 1989.

[82] Interview with Kevin Nxumalo, Bembe, 4 September 1988.

[83] Interview with Jerry Sibanda, Matopo Mission, 21 July 1988.

be eternally vigilant against the still threatened expansion of the Antelope estate. Then the dissidents went off to report the police.

There was an explosion of relief and joy as peace returned to the Matopos. When I arrived to do field work just over a month later I found every religious denomination in the hills celebrating and claiming credit. Old men near Matopo Mission told me that peace was the fruit of the prayers of the Brethren in Christ; a great Zionist gathering at Diana's Pool celebrated their staunchness in faith. Jacob Moyo in Gulati organised a service of thanksgiving on 6 July 1988. 'We can even feel the air coming in. We are feeling very free this time', he told me. 'It was really too warm in this place'.[84] And the priests of the shrines also claimed that the survival of the people had been due to the prophetic and protective powers of Mwali.

Shrines, Monuments and Politics, 1980–88

When I interviewed Joshua Nkomo in July 1988 he told me that Njelele was the only possible site for his great rally in February 1980. Njelele was a *national* symbol – as he said in 1980, 'a major religious shrine of everybody, whatever their tribe or religion'. By contrast Entumbane had come to seem both too private and too regional. One could not take hundreds of thousands of people to Entumbane, he told me. Mzilikazi's grave had come to represent merely the Ndebele rather than the Zimbabwean past.[85] Nkomo was in fact still very much concerned with Entumbane and paid a ceremonial visit there soon after the Njelele rally. But his instinct was correct. Where once he had been able to carry the whole NDP executive off to Entumbane and to issue from there a manifesto of confrontation, Mzilikazi's tomb had come by 1980 to symbolise regionalism.

In fact it was being increasingly appealed to not only by Ndebele traditionalists but also by Bulawayo whites. White Rhodesians had always had a fondness for the 'manly' and 'loyal' Ndebele, whom they contrasted with the 'treacherous' Shona. After the 1980 election some of them found it intolerable that Matabeleland whites together with 'the Ndebele' should be under the rule of 'the Shona' and Harare. One of these was the eccentric Bulawayo dentist, Frank Bertrand, who longed for an independent Matabeleland state. In 1981 Bertrand was drawn into a fantastic conspiracy. He went to Entumbane to call upon the spiritual powers of 'the spirit medium, Princess Violet Khumalo, who was to be used to induce ZIPRA members of the National Army to rebel'. Violet, the daughter of Chief Nzula and granddaughter of Lobengula's daughter, Famona, had endured a long illness brought on by her grandmother's spirit 'before a dream told her to settle near the hills of Entumbane, where Mzilikazi lies buried.' She moved there in 1976, building her kraal 'on the slope of a spread of granite that overlooks Mzilikazi's tomb'.[86]

Bertrand told the court which tried him for conspiring to overthrow the state that

[84] Interview with Jacob Moyo, Gulati, 21 July 1988.
[85] Interview with Joshua Nkomo, Blue Lagoon, 29 July 1988.
[86] *Chronicle*, 24 May 1992.

'Princess Khumalo is of royal blood, directly descended from Mzilikazi. We had tried all the orthodox techniques. We had failed. And so I decided to try to obtain the help of Princess Violet to obtain the state of Matabeleland.' Violet obligingly told Bertrand that 'the spirits wanted him to lead the Ndebele'. In September 1981 she assured him 'that within three months things would start moving. And she was right', he concluded ruefully, 'because I was arrested and so were the others in three months'.[87] Although hardly anyone had attended these seances at Entumbane except agents provocateurs and members of the CIO, Bertrand was jailed for several years. Violet herself soon fell ill and died in agony. Her successor was 'blown away' from Entumbane by the displeasure of Mzilikazi's spirit.[88] Entumbane was a dangerous symbol to invoke in the 1980s.

Rhodes's Grave, meanwhile, had lost its power. In January 1980 there was a quarrel between the Ministry of Lands, Water Development and Agriculture and the Chairman of the Rhodes Matopos National Park Committee over the use of water from Lake Matopos. The Director of the Matopos Research Station, H. K. Ward, claimed the right to take as much water as he liked from the dam 'for vital test crops'; the RMNP Chairman countered that 'the water belonged to the people of Bulawayo for recreational purposes, by virtue of Rhodes's will'. Ward won this particular struggle, pointing out quite correctly that 'the dam was built at Rhodes's instigation for irrigation purposes.'[89]

After the electoral victory of Robert Mugabe, however, this kind of appeal to the past could no longer be made. Rhodes's name was dropped from the title of the National Park. His statue was removed from Main Street in Bulawayo. There were calls for his grave at World's View to be dismantled. 'The term terrorist is applicable to Rhodes', wrote Peter Nzimande in December 1981. 'His crew were trained terrorists. He was regarded by the British Government of that time as a hero. He therefore deserves to be buried in any one of Britain's "heroes" acres.'[90] In the event Rhodes's Grave was left undisturbed as a tourist attraction. Entumbane was dangerous; Rhodes's Grave was for show; Njelele, on the other hand, was very definitely for use.[91]

There were three phases in the political history of Njelele, and of the other Matopos shrines, between 1980 and 1988. The first was Joshua Nkomo's attempt in 1981 and 1982 to carry through the cultural nationalist programme he had first enunciated in the 1950s. Njelele was truly to become a National Shrine. Nkomo's focus on Njelele in turn provoked an attempt by ZANU/PF to wrest control of Njelele away from Ndebele-speaking supporters of ZAPU. Then, from 1983 to the end of 1987, Nkomo himself and ZAPU as a whole were in such peril that every source of comfort and support was called upon. Nkomo's use of the shrines became private rather than public as he and his associates called on them to bring Matabeleland's agony to an end. And throughout

---

[87] *Chronicle*, 17 March 1982.
[88] Interview with Joshua Nkomo, 29 July 1988.
[89] *Chronicle*, 14 January 1980.
[90] *Sunday News*, 9 December 1981.
[91] The high point of the tourist commodification of Rhodes has been the recent redecoration of the Rhodes Hotel, Nyanga, by the parastatal which has acquired it. The hotel has been lovingly decked out in high colonial style. Zimbabwean tycoons love to be accommodated in the bedroom which was Rhodes's study.

these three phases, when Njelele was very important in national politics, the local and internal politics of the shrines continued unabated.

Nkomo made a good deal of use of Thenjiwe Lesabe in dealings with the shrine and she has provided the best account of his programme in 1981 and 1982. Nkomo told his associates:

In our ZAPU structure we have a cultural section. I would like you to invite all the people that have some thing to do with the Lozani house, the Mbiba House, the Mayezane house, the Bango house, and Mzilikazi, and all other people who have come to me and claimed that they are possessed by spirits. Because I am not a spirit medium myself nor am I a spiritual leader myself. I am only a political leader. Therefore I want you people to refer these things to the rightful people. You call them together. They will give you all the information and then you construct a committee from them....

I, as Joshua, would have loved to see you people respect Njelele like the old people did, number one. Number two, I'd like you people to make improvements to that place, it's shabby, there's no accommodation ... You should have toilets in that area, and have water, and at least have houses, so that every chief in this country, Zimbabwe as Zimbabwe, should [have a] house so that people who come from a particular chief have no problems.

As Lesabe says, Nkomo was drawing on his memories of Westminster Abbey and his 'impressions and experiences of Jerusalem and Mount Sinai.... And of course before Amin he went to Uganda, there's a burial place, the tombs of the kings of Buganda, they were highly respected and Joshua wanted something of that nature.'[92]

An elaborate structure was set up, with an advisory group, of which Lesabe was one, a group of elected tribal representatives and praise poets, and finally an executive committee under the chairmanship of Jacob Masuku. Meanwhile, Nkomo himself urged people to make respectful pilgrimage to Njelele at all his public meetings in Matabeleland. His injunctions drew even members of Bulwayo's intellectual elite to visit Njelele for the first time. In November 1981 the journalist Jonathan Maphenduka heard Nkomo urge a meeting in Kezi to make a pilgrimage to Njelele:

Like most Ndebeles [wrote Maphenduka], I'm not the greatest worshipper of the people's god – or any other god for that matter. But the urge to go there was so strong that nothing could stop me unless I dropped dead.

Arriving at Njelele, he went to Mayabu Ndlovu's village. Mayabu's brother, Sili, had presided over the February 1980 meeting but had since died; his death seemed

to have ushered the family into a deadly decline. Not only is Bayani Mayabu himself dying; the whole family is in the grip of an inexplicable calamity.... Mayabu is dying and it is said Ngwali bashed his ribs in because he started charging a fee before he would let you into the cave.... Two of his children have become insane.

So 'Ngwali has found himself another messenger, who looms as dominantly among the people as Njelele itself among the hills'. This was no less than Sitwanyana Ncube, recently back yet again at the shrine.

Hardly two months since his installation as Ngwali's usher in face of unyielding opposition by

---

[92] Interview with Thenjiwe Lesabe, 24 August 1988.

local elders, he now dominates the scene.... In his regalia of a brawl of colours, which are dominated by black, he stands a forceful personality, enormously improved by an intelligent, handsome face, a strong build of body carried on an equally strong pair of legs which appear to have been seasoned by a lifetime of pounding the earth during ritual dancing.

Sitwanyana told him the story of his checkered career at Njelele but defied any future enemies. 'Anyone who comes here to kill me will be killed himself', he said, victims of his two leopard watchdogs.

Up to this point Maphenduka had been a detached, ironic observer. But when Sitwanyana took him to the shrine all this changed:

> It was dark in the cave. As soon as he had finished introducing us, the usher asked each one to pray to Ngwali.... I started to ask for something. I think I managed to utter a couple of words before I choked on them as warm tears flooded my eyes and my prayer stopped dead in its tracks.[93]

Maphenduka's emotion was a triumph for Nkomo's advocacy of Njelele. But in most other ways Nkomo's campaign ran into insuperable problems. Jacob Masuku was mainly concerned to advance the claims of his daughter 'who he claimed was possessed both by the Njelele spirit and the Mzilikazi spirit' and this 'caused conflict, a lot, in the committee.' In the end the girl was placed at Entumbane from which, as we have seen, she was 'blown away'. The committee backed Sitwanyana at Njelele, and he too was chased away by the dissidents in December 1985. But it was not merely that the Committee backed unsuccessful candidates. The real problem was that none of the shrine priests or elders wanted the kind of 'modernisations' which Nkomo proposed.

The Committee's efforts really got under way in September 1982. Nkomo had enlisted the support of the District Administrator, Nephas Ndlovu, who included buildings at Njelele in the district development budget.[94] Early in September the Shrine Committee was introduced to the chiefs of Matabeleland at Natisa to tell them that funds were being raised to build a hotel there as well as facilities at Njelele itself.[95] On 25 September 1982 Ndlovu attended a huge 'rain ceremony' at Njelele, together with Jacob Masuku, Joshua Nkomo and Sitwanyana Ncube, 'a kind of St Peter of the shrine'. A 'marathon dance' took place in a makeshift ampitheatre between the hills. Masuku told the crowd that the Voice was no longer heard at Njelele 'because the colonial era reduced the respectability and holiness of the shrine'; he believed 'that the attendance of so many people today has gone a long way in restoring that holiness.' He promised that the shrine would be developed and houses built 'in clusters equivalent to the number of chiefs around the country.'[96] On 28 September Nkomo told the press that Njelele was 'like Mount Sinai in Israel where God speaks to Moses'; on 29 September Nephas Ndlovu announced that 'with the blessing of the spirit mediums' he

---

[93] Jonathan Maphenduka, 'The Dangers of Incurring a Rain God's Wrath' and 'Prayers that Brought Tears at Ngwali's Shrine', *Chronicle*, 23 December and 30 December 1981.

[94] Interview with Nephas Ndlovu, Bulawayo, 2 August 1988.

[95] *Chronicle*, 10 September 1982.

[96] *Chronicle*, 27 September 1982.

was going ahead with 'a permanent residence' for the shrine priest; 'accommodation for the spirit mediums', and 'water and sanitary facilities' for visitors.[97]

On 5 October Jacob Masuku issued a call 'to the traditional chiefs':

> The 'heart', the centre, of the people you are leading is at Njelele. In the past, when all was well and there were good harvests, the nation made sacrifices at Njelele. In times of hardships, epidemics, drought and war, the nation went to Njelele to pray to ancestors for protection, support and love. If we are also to seek guidance, this is our chance to revive the pillar of our nation.... This is for the whole nation, irrespective of whether one speaks Venda, Suthu, Shona, Ndebele, Kalanga, Lilima, Lozwi, Nanzwa, Tonga, Shankwe, Tshangani, Ndawu, Korekore, Karanga, Manyika and even English; or any church or political organisation – the nation's umbilical cord is at Njelele.

Chiefs were to send representatives to Bulawayo for a meeting with the Committee; they should also prepare seeds to be blessed at Njelele.[98]

This intensifying campaign ground to a halt partly because of the opening of the dissident war – Nkomo himself asked the chiefs meeting at Natisa not only to support modernisation plans for Njelele but also to help 'rid the region of dissidents'.[99] In March 1983 Nkomo fled into Botswana to escape threats on his life. He was sustained by Sitwanyana's prayers and advice, but there was no chance that his plans for Njelele could now be fulfilled. In any case these plans had also aroused great opposition around Njelele itself. Many elders there condemned both Nkomo's rally in February 1980 – the thunder and lightning and torrential rain which accompanied it were signs of Mwali's displeasure rather than of good fortune – and the 'rain ceremony' of 25 September 1982, which they rightly regarded as completely untraditional. 'In the old days such large numbers would never have gone. People sent their representatives only. The 1982 gathering was not at all traditional'.[100] 'The attendance of so many people' certainly didn't 'restore holiness'. Rumours spread that Nkomo planned 'to build a township at Njelele and this was against tradition'.[101] 'There were a lot of people who opposed [the plans] on the grounds that they were bringing in Western culture to a shrine that would normally have gone along on traditional lines. Chief Nyangazonke himself was in opposition.' Sitwanyana's readiness to collaborate with such plans intensified the elders' grievances against him and made Nyangazonke his enemy.[102]

Moreover, the government in Harare looked at Nkomo's plans for Njelele with deep suspicion. At the 'rain ceremony' of 25 September 1982

---

[97] *Chronicle*, 28 and 29 September 1982.

[98] Inkundla Yelitshe Lenvelo letter, 5 October 1982, translated from the Sindebele by Mark Ncube, CHK/24, District Administrator's office, Kezi.

[99] *Masiye Pambili*, November 1982.

[100] Interview with Jonathan Maphenduka, 25 July 1988.

[101] Interview with J. M. Moyo, Kezi, 26 July 1988.

[102] Interview with Nephas Ndlovu, 2 August 1988. Hlathi Ndiweni Nyangazonke, grandson of Faku and son of the deposed Tapi, was installed in May 1981. He at once established himself as a resolute traditionalist. In August 1981 he was accused of 'trying to revive his authority and those of his kraal-heads' against the newly elected councillors. The *Sunday News* of 4 August 1981 described him as unacceptable 'within the nationalist spectrum'.

a self-styled prophet, who took part in the ceremony ... claimed the ancestral spirits were angered by the spate of violence taking place in Zimbabwe and made some suggestions as to how the Prime Minister, Cde Mugabe, could end the violence and unite the nation. He predicted Zimbabwe would be plunged into two days of darkness at some time in the future.[103]

Njelele could hardly be kept out of politics. The Mugabe regime began to seek to break Nkomo's influence on the shrine.

The 'self-styled prophet' was one Zumba Ravatatu, who claimed to be the medium of the great Shona martyr, Chaminuka, and wore an extraordinary uniform with a combined gun and cross on his chest. In July 1983, three months after Joshua Nkomo had fled into exile in Botswana, Ravatatu made a bid to replace Njelele as the rain-making centre of the nation. He boasted that he had demonstrated his rain-making capacity to police officers in Gwanda and Kezi and that he had certificates from these Shona-speaking officials attesting that he was 'a Man of God'. Ravatatu claimed that there must be 'a national rather than tribal approach to ancestral worship for rains. The mistake people made at last year's Njelele ceremonies for rain is that people were tribal in their approach.'[104]

It is not clear whether Ravatatu had official backing. But one claimant to power over Njelele certainly did. This was the woman Sipoyana, who seems to have represented Nehanda, the other great Shona spirit. Nephas Ndlovu recalls:

> At the height of it all when we were talking about building rest rooms and all that type of planning, putting water, there came a lady who was called Sipoyana Shoko. She was sent from Harare to Kezi and sent to my office. She was claiming to be a rain medium, a hosana. She was sent by the administration in the name of the then Minister for Home Affairs, Ushewokunze. So she came and claimed priestly powers and she wanted to go over there to take over from Sitwanyana.... She was guarded by police. She had about six policemen guarding her, and we were feeding her out of our drought relief food. We took it politically.[105]

Sitwanyana took it politically, spiritually and personally. As he remembers with indignation, 'she insisted that as she was from Masvingo, she would never be affected by our petty beliefs.... She continued to trespass. Since she claimed her spirit was superior to mine, she readily assumed she could go anywhere.'[106]

Smith Mbedzi, a staunch ZAPU supporter, who was in detention when Sipoyana arrived, firmly believes that she came to recapture Mwali:

> They were saying that Mzilikazi took Mwari from Great Zimbabwe ruins to Matopo Hills. They wanted Sitwanyana Ncube to go back to stay in Mashonaland so the Mwari would also have gone back. They sent a certain woman and made her to be guided by police, so that she could go there and represent people from Mashonaland. They thought maybe that by ruling the country you can rule the Mwali shrine.[107]

---

[103] *Chronicle*, 28 September 1982.
[104] *Chronicle*, 5 July 1983.
[105] Interview with Nephas Ndlovu, 2 August 1988.
[106] Interview with Sitwanyana, 19 August 1988.
[107] Interview with Smith Mbedzi, 5 September 1988.

But Sipoyana did not succeed. According to Sitwanyana, she entered the recesses of the cave. 'Even I cannot set my foot on that sacred place. I had warned her'. She was never seen again. 'The police patrolled the place for nine months. Nothing further unusual happened.'

Attempts to wrest Mwali from ZAPU influence continued, however. In September 1983 ZINATHA, the national organisation for herbalists, diviners and spirit mediums set up by Ushewokunze, announced that it intended to meet at Great Zimbabwe to seek a way of transferring back there a 'speaking stone' which had left Great Zimbabwe for the Matopos; at the same meeting claimants to represent Chaminuka and Nehanda would be tested, and national prayers for rain would be held. Interestingly enough, this meeting was cancelled because the Masvingo provincial committee of ZANU/PF insisted that 'Great Zimbabwe was not the place to pray for rain. Historically the proper place was Matonjeni [the Matopos].'[108] The ruling party was concerned to recapture Njelele itself rather than to undermine it. Enos Nkala, the main ZANU/PF protagonist of a hard line with ZAPU, told a rally in Kezi in 1983 'that Nkomo was using Njelele as a political platform' and that this must be changed. It was certainly an ironic relief to government when Sitwanyana was chased away by the dissidents in December 1985.

Long before that, however, Nkomo's plans for the modernisation of Njelele had given way to desperate ZAPU appeals to the shrines for protection. These appeals were not made at Njelele but at the shrines in Matopo Communal Area. Nkomo had focused on Njelele as a monument. But now that power was required ZAPU traditionalists turned to the shrines where the Voice was still heard. They also returned to the Red Axe at Dula. What they were looking for was not only protection but also understanding and prediction. They asked *why* ZAPU – and Matabeleland – had been subjected to such danger and suffering; they asked *how* danger and suffering might be ended. In reply the shrines returned to the sacred history which Nkomo had heard narrated at Dula in 1953. Mwali was concerned with the transition of regimes – the downfall of a regime which had become objectionable and the establishment of a moral regime in its place. The Rhodesian regime had fallen, but nothing had been done to make its successor morally acceptable to Mwali. The new power had not 'reported to the Rock'; the fighting men had not returned to the shrines for cleansing. This could only be done if Mugabe and Nkomo combined. People began to say that when the Voice told Nkomo in 1953 that 'freedom' would not come for 30 years this had been a prediction not only of the long rigours of the independence struggle but also of the chaos which would follow it.

Mrs Lesabe describes how 'when we had all those problems in Matabeleland, about the Fifth Brigade' she decided to approach the shrines. She went along with various 'experts', including 'Dlodlo, Mtuwane's grandson', the 'owner' of the Red Axe at Dula. 'We did many things. We went to different shrines to try and get our people out of this

---

[108] *Chronicle*, 14 September and 14 October 1983. Martinus Daneel shows that similar attempts to recapture the Voice continued into the late 1980s. The spirit medium Tovera in Masvingo argued at the end of that decade that it was inappropriate for the Voice to be heard only 'in Ndebele territory'; people need not go any longer to Dzilo, he said, but could hear the Voice emerging from Tovera's own pole enclosure in Ndanga. Daneel, *African Earthkeepers*, vol. 1, p. 115.

problem'. Early in 1983 just three weeks before he left the country Nkomo himself accompanied Mrs Lesabe, Dlodlo and the Venda, Mtetwa, back to the Red Axe. The Maswabe brothers who lived at Dula were at first reluctant but when Dlodlo went to talk to the keeper he said 'Ah! Baba, if they have come with you I have no choice. Because you are the King of this shrine. Right, go to my brother'. The crippled brother, priest at Dula, also told them that if they had come without Dlodlo to talk about war they would have been turned away. The brothers said that the Voice had been silent for ten years but when they went into the cave and talked to Mwali about their problems, Nkomo heard a Voice, speaking very low. when they were coming away, he instructed them to give money so that the shrine could be restored, with 'new grass, new blocks and everything else'. They did so; the restorations were made; and then 'the Maswabe children said their spirit has come back to them'.

Mrs Lesabe returned to the revived shrine with Dlodlo, Mtewta and Grey Bango:

> Suddenly there was a very big light ...leading us right to the shrine. We were going to ask for [the planned ZAPU] Congress this time. Since we were banned, we had no money, we had no means of organising, can you please let the people come to the Congress.... There was no Voice, we didn't hear the Voice, but as we walked to the shrine there was a crying voice, you know a new-born baby, when it cries, that's all we heard.... It was crying before we went into the shrine. When we got into the shrine it kept quiet. We talked, talked, talked, talked. As we were about to leave ... we saw a new-born baby at our feet.... I was terrified ... but there is a need for the reading of these things. As we got down I saw the owners of the place who know the customs.... Right, we had that Congress. It was such a success.... We went back – that was the 1984 Congress – to say thank you. Then we found this crippled man. He said to us, go and tell your leaders to bring here a black blanket. There are now about two and a half years before all these problems are over. This blanket is going to wrap all over the atrocities both from the British heart and from the locals ... wrap up the atrocities and the hard thinking of the British against the Matabeles. And of the ruling party against the Matabeles.... Right, for sure, we saw things come out, two and a half years dead, the agreement was signed.

In September 1987, three months before the Unity Agreement, Mrs Lesabe learnt for the first time that the Voice could be heard at Bembe. She went there. The Voice spoke from the rock overhang telling her: 'I have been sent by the elders, that's Njelele and the Red Axe, to tell you who work with our son, Umgabu (Nkomo), to go and tell him to give us water to drink before we can give this country water.' So Nkomo authorised that gifts be made to the shrine:

> We went back and reported. When we were moving towards the shrine the Voice began to laugh. We were walking with this lady. The Voice said, 'Thank you very much for the water he gave us. Go and tell him he has only to wait this month, and the next month and the next month, this month is going to get into agreement. And then I am going to give you rains.... It was an oldish sort of disembodied Voice.[109]

Despite these stories of shrine predictions fulfilled, the ZAPU traditionalists became aware of the many disputes among the priestly families; of the local hostility to Sitwanyana at Njelele; and of the widespread feeling that the shrines had lost their

---

[109] Interview with Mrs Thenjiwe Lesabe, Bulawayo, 24 August 1988.

legitimacy. 'As long as we used them without controlling the spirits no peace would come'. So they dispatched at least two delegations to Venda country, one in 1981 and the other in 1987, 'to control these spoilt spirits here of all the shrines'.[110]

But they also became aware that outsiders – whether ZAPU or the Zimbabwean state – could not really control the shrines. As Mrs Lesabe now says:

> The solution, my dear, is that government should keep away from meddling with the shrine. All politicians out of the shrine matters. Chiefs, all other chiefs except those chiefs that are known to be connected with the shrine. There are certain families who are directly involved, from their great grandfathers or grandmothers, who have continued to do the tradition. But because government, politicians, chiefs are interfering too much these people have decided to fold their hands. You know the background culture of the Abanyubi. They are a very sensitive people.... They don't want you to know the secret.... They will allow you to lead them but just fold their hands, let you do what you think is right and never get things right'.[111]

The late Reader Ncube, that ZAPU stalwart, similarly insisted that only the locals really know. He told me in August 1988 that Mrs Lesabe must have been thinking of him when she spoke of the sensitive and taciturn Banyubi:

> In 1980 the new government had a cultural project to make videos at the shrines but Council passed a resolution that government be given no access and no information. The whites ruled since 1890 and there were secrets they didn't know. Mugabe has ruled for 8 years and there are secrets he doesn't know. Nkomo was born in 1917 and there are secrets he doesn't know. Before unity we never wanted any Shona – or any white man – to know about the shrines.... The Shona who come from as far away as Mutare just came, did homage, and went away. They didn't know about the shrines. The Ndebele ruled for 60 years but there were secrets they never knew. Nkomo is my political leader but when it comes to tradition I am his leader. I tell him straight. I told him when he was planning the 1980 Njelele meeting that he shouldn't do that. Who was he to call people to Njelele and all those young men. Nkomo went ahead and did it, and look what happened – there was lightning at the meeting and everything was bad after it.[112]

There could hardly be a firmer statement that the shrines are ultimately the business of the peoples of the Matopos.

During the 1980s, indeed, the Banyubi and other peoples of the hills did not merely 'fold their hands' and let politicians make their own mistakes. Local struggles and local feelings had a great impact on the fate of the shrines. When Sitwanyana was chased away from Njelele by the dissidents at the end of 1985, for example, this was not merely an example of the 'disrespect' of men with guns. As he admits, the dissidents told him, 'We have been sent to kill you. By who? By the villagers, they said. It was the wish of the local villagers. It was jealousy.'[113] Just as they had used the guerrillas in the 1970s,

---

[110] Interview with Smith Mbedzi, Bulawayo, 5 September 1988.

[111] Interview with Mrs Thenjiwe Lesabe.

[112] Interview with Reader Ncube, Esigodini, 29 August 1988. Reader said that he had himself been to the Red Axe to ask if the Unity Agreement was good. He was told that it was good but that Nkomo would never be the ruler. 'Before Nkomo went out to make war he went to the Red Axe ... He was told to report back when the war was over. Instead he went to Njelele, which is a shrine for rain only, not war'.

[113] Interview with Sitwanyana Ncube, Umguza, 28 July 1988.

resentful local elders now used the dissidents to rid themselves of Sitwanyana.

It was the southern dissidents who acted against him. 'The elders would tell us this man is causing drought by mis-management', says Attempt Siziba. 'We wanted to discipline this man.' But he was not killed because the northern dissidents sent a delegation to Njelele. Langford Ndiwei explains that: 'They were thinking of killing Sitwanyana. So we went to say not to do that, because the government had already fired shots there so we shouldn't also be firing.' Sitwanyana was merely frightened away. He took refuge at Joshua Nkomo's farm outside Bulawayo.[114]

After he had gone the district administration, learning from past mistakes, was anxious to leave the choice of his successor in the hands of local elders. 'Some politicians had interfered with Njelele in 1980/81', Deputy District Administrator, J. M. Moyo, told me. 'They put in Sitwanyana causing many problems which we resolved in 1986 by asking for the history of the shrine and working out family trees.'[115] A series of meetings were held with the chiefs of southern Matabeleland at which Sitwanyana was cross-examined and his legitimacy challenged. In April 1986 Chief Fuyana said that it was not a matter for the chiefs but for the local families. On 9 May at a meeting at Natisa Sitwanyana announced that he was stepping down – 'for reasons best known to the community', added Chief Nyangazonke. Fuyana again insisted that 'the elders used to take the grievances of the people to Njelele and not the chiefs'. A local elder stood up and said that 'the shrine should be used for its purpose' and not for the purposes of outsiders. Other locals suggested the names of those who 'knew'. These wise men told another gathering of chiefs on 20 June 1986 that 'God chose the person responsible for the shrine and not people. Houses should never be built in the vicinity. God did not like people with ancestral spirits to live at the shrine. It was reiterated that the chosen person was not voted for. The clans of Malaba, Bango, Nkala, Mbikwa, Mayezani and Thabane all had their caves at the shrine.' Finally, at a meeting of chiefs and elders of the Matobo district on 6 July 'Mr Nkala from Esigodini told the meeting that the elders of Matobo District were the people involved in the issue'. These elders decided that 'Mr David Ndlovu, who was the young brother to Mayabu and Sili, be the one to take care of Njelele.' Chief Nyangazonke would arrange to introduce him to the people.[116]

Meanwhile the dissidents, having made their contribution to a local solution at Njelele, were anxious to show their concern for the shrines. 'We respected these places, Dula and Njelele, and constantly visited them to inform them about us and why we were in the bush and at the same time asking for protection.... After the amnesty we went to Dula and said we're back home ... so we'd lead a normal life with the locals.'[117]

In its combination of local, regional and national dynamics and in its concern to resolve violence and restore peace, the history of the shrines in the 1980s – as so often before – summed up the contemporary experience of the Matopos.

[114] Jocelyn Alexander, 'Dissident Perspectives on Zimbabwe's Civil War'.
[115] Interview with Deputy District Administrator, Kezi, 26 July 1988.
[116] Minutes of these meetings of chiefs are on file CHK/24 in the District Administrator's office, Kezi.
[117] Interview between Jocelyn Alexander and Moffat Dhlamini, 18 December 1995.

*13   Sitwanyana Ncube with senior wives and acolytes at Joshua Nkomo's farm at Mguza,
August 1988 (Photograph by Mark Ncube)*

14 The author with Headman Jacob Moyo, Gulati, August 1988

15 The author with Mwali believers, Kumbudzi, Matopo Communal Area, September 1988. The man to his left is the bearer of seeds to and from the shrines

16 Mark Ncube with Nduna Ndlovu, Matopo Mission, August 1988

9

Seeing the Matopos in the 1990s

I began archival work on the Matopos in 1986 and was able at last to commence field work after the Amnesty of 1988. I spent a further two seasons in the field in 1989 and 1990. Thereafter my writing up of the Matopos material was interrupted first by my discovery of the remarkable Samkange family archives, which led to the publication of a collective biography in 1995, and then by a joint research project in northern Matabeleland with Jocelyn Alexander and JoAnn Mcgregor.[1] I felt guilty about the long delay in finishing a book on the Matopos but as it has turned out the delay has had some advantages. In 1997 the Minister of Home Affairs, Dumiso Dabengwa, announced that Njelele was to be reproclaimed as a National Monument. He added that the Zimbabwean government was approaching UNESCO to have the Matopos declared a World Heritage Site. This announcement makes a fitting climax to the story told in this book and I shall end by exploring its significance.

I cannot provide the detailed narrative of the previous chapters but there are still things to be said about the Matopos in the 1990s. Since 1990 I have done little formal research in the hills, though I have made annual pilgrimages to the rival priests at Njelele and visits to the District Administrator, Kezi. This chapter, then, is impressionistic rather than fully documented. It focuses particularly on developments which are linked – positively, ironically, or tragically – with the themes that have emerged in this book. I hope that readers will never again be able to see the Matopos with the uncomprehending eyes of white visitors in the nineteenth century. Right up to today the political, religious and symbolic struggles, the aspirations and the frustrations which I have been describing have continued in the Matopos and have continued to give them context and meaning.

---

[1] Terence Ranger, *Are We Not Also Men? The Samkange Family and African Politics in Zimbabwe*, James Currey, London, 1995; Jocelyn Alexander, JoAnn McGregor and Terence Ranger, *Violence and Memory. Life in the Forests of Northern Matabeleland*, forthcoming.

The Hopes of the 1990s and the Programme of Joshua Nkomo

The Amnesty of 1988 ushered in a second period of hope in the Matopos and this time, unlike the expectations of 1980, hope was not shattered by the renewal of violence. It seemed that there might now be a resolution of the problems of the National Park, of resettlement in the *mapani* veld, and even of development.

In July 1988 I met the deputy town clerk, Bulawayo, Moffat Ndlovu, who was also a member of the National Parks Board. Ndlovu was a Gwanda man and a ZAPU stalwart. He told me that policy in the Matopos National Park was undergoing review:

> The whole Park is to be fenced. We hope the people won't take that amiss. It all depends on public opinion policy. At first there was a colonial government, then the people felt oppressed by the army which beat and raped. Only now that the people's representatives are in power can we see a chance for acceptance by the people.[2]

The same argument was being made about development policy. Jonathan Maphenduka, now business manager of the *Chronicle*, told me that Joshua Nkomo's long-held ideas about rural development were now close to official policy for Matabeleland South. Nkomo as Vice President and Senior Minister was at last in a position to push his own development policy, to command the support of his long-standing supporters and to be seen to achieve results.[3] Nkomo himself told me that 'we have delayed six years' and that 'I don't have the energy I had eight years ago'. But he also told me that he was determined to address meetings throughout southern Matabeleland to mobilise support for his development strategy.[4]

At ground-level in Matobo district in mid-1988 there was also preparation for change. The Chairman of the district Council, Joel Nyathi, and the council's finance officer, Mr Manombe, told me that they thought it would take some time to produce a detailed development plan. The Village and Ward Development Committees had been feared and hated as impositions from Mugabe's state. There would be much 'tedious work' to do to persuade people that they could be used. (A chart on the wall was headed: 'District Development Plan – Legend'). But already the Council had a clear set of priorities. As far as the National Park was concerned, the road from Gulati to Gwandavale must be repaired and opened up and there must be negotiation on the social use of the Park's resources. Hitherto people had been frightened to speak out about the Park. Now they would do so. Nyathi himself thought that 'the National Park has messed up all the Matopos'.[5] Farms must be set aside in the *mapani* belt from which the people had long ago been forced into the hills. Council would allow people to move back into this land if they wished; elsewhere resettlement land should only be used for relief grazing. ARDA, they told me, had lain like a lion across their path, but ARDA

[2] Interview with Moffat Ndlovu, Bulawayo, 14 July 1988.
[3] Interview with Jonathan Maphenduka, Bulawayo, 25 July 1988.
[4] Interview with Joshua Nkomo, Bulawayo, 29 July 1988.
[5] Interview with Joel Nyathi, Maphesa, 22 July 1988.

clearly had failed. The farms it had taken over were hardly managed. As the original leases from white farmers ran out, the government should exercise its option to buy. Then the Council could make use of the land. Council would like to take over the Antelope estate; or at least to levy an effective tax upon it.[6]

At the end of July 1988 Nkomo spoke to the Zimbabwe Chamber of Commerce about the land problem. He rejoiced, he said, because 'we are very privileged to have the power of speech and not resort to the savage power of arms'. Whites owned more than 40 per cent of Zimbabwe and the remainder was made up of 'national parks and some dilapidated communal lands'. There must be redistribution of lands. 'It is stupid to buy a country that is yours'; nevertheless they should all consult together 'and solve this problem as a people otherwise we are creating a time bomb'.[7]

It seemed that there would be radical change. And on the ground people were acting for themselves. Cattle moved openly into the *mapani*. 'As for the National Park, they are complaining bitterly, they think it is some kind of expropriation and since this is now their government they should be given the land. They had gone into the bush to fight for the land and had not been given it.'[8]

There was a fundamental paradox at the heart of all these expectations, however. After the Unity Agreement the men in charge of Matabeleland changed but policies did not. Nkomo had now been granted the major role in Matabeleland; councillors, elected as ZAPU candidates, continued in office as members of the newly united ZANU/PF. Local government institutions no longer laboured under the charge that they were 'anti-government'. Indeed, after 1988 Matabeleland became the most secure stronghold of ZANU/PF in the whole country. The men who had been the leaders of nationalism in Matobo for 30 years now emerged in command of the official organs of development. But they still had to deal with the expert agencies of the central state; they still had to respond to government's resettlement models; and when they themselves thought about development it was difficult for them to come up with effective fresh ideas. So far as Matobo was concerned, Joshua Nkomo's own ideas were very different from those of the people; and the District Council, whose ideas were much closer to popular aspirations, effectively only had the power to block official initiatives rather than to take initiatives of its own.

When I interviewed Joshua Nkomo in July 1988 he was very clear about his development priorities. The National Park was a closed issue, as he had told the people in 1982. Indeed, he wanted greatly to extend the National Park to cover the whole of the Matopos. 'In the old days very few people lived within these hills and water was everywhere, even pouring out of caves'. Today 'there was too much trampling around, destroying the kind of grass that helps in rain making. The priests at Njelele can stay. All the rest I want to lure away to developments outside the hills.' He would tour Matopo, Gulati and Kumalo Communal Areas, calling on their people 'to get out completely'. Njelele itself was his responsibility and he would ensure that its legitimacy

[6] Interview with Joel Nyathi and Mr Manombe, Maphesa, 1 August 1988.
[7] *Chronicle*, 23 July 1988.
[8] Interview with J. M. Moyo, 26 July 1988, Kezi.

was restored. So far as development outside the hills was concerned, Nkomo held to what other people were calling 'the traditional Ndebele model' – he wanted people to concentrate into large villages and to manage wide-ranging systems of grazing.[9]

These priorities and policies had varying fortunes over the next few years. Nkomo's view of the National Park prevailed. But he failed to lure people out of the occupied Matopos; he lost control of developments at Njelele; in trying to 'develop' southern Matabeleland he lost the confidence of most of his supporters there. Let us look at each of these questions in turn.

The Matopos National Park in the 1990s

In 1998 there were still people longing to return to the Park but even they hardly believed that it was possible. Zephaniah Moyo had been evicted from the Park when he was a small child; had moved first to Sidube ranch; had ended up in Tsholotsho. He had been a ZIPRA guerrilla during the war. In November 1980 he had written to Hugh Ashton, who was then writing a report on the Matopos:

> In the past and even now the National Park and Rhodes Matopos Estate are regarded as the white man's playground – a luxury – while to the Africans they are the places where their fathers lie buried, and to some, their umbilical cords. These are considerations far more important than economic considerations.[10]

When I interviewed him in July 1988, Moyo told me that

> even today I do not think of Tsholotsho as my home. It isn't good for human habitation. I have always had in mind settling somewhere in Matobo District, somewhere in the National Park. I go there; I like it as a visitor, but I still have a kind of envy. I should be living in this beautiful place. But I don't think any government will open it up.[11]

Government doctrine was that under majority rule the Park *had* been returned to the people. There was no room within this majoritarian ideology for special concessions to locals – such as the agreement negotiated, for instance, at Uluru/Ayers Rock in Australia where the Aboriginal 'owners' of the land share in the management of the Park, determine which parts of it tourists may visit, and are able to impose a total ban on photographs or paintings of the rocks.

As I have put it in a chapter which explores the contrast between the Matopos and Uluru,

> in Zimbabwe the whole country, and not just particularly holy places, has fallen under the authority of a black government. But the Matopos National Park has remained under the National Parks Department of the central government, which regards itself as representative of the people. Unlike Uluru, the national park itself is *not* managed in partnership with locals; the modernist doctrines of international conservation are embraced by the Zimbabwean state, which in the interests of the 'whole community' does not allow locals to collect plants, or

[9] Interview with Joshua Nkomo, Bulawayo, 29 July 1988.
[10] Unsigned letter to Ashton, 28 November 1980, Ashton files, Historical Reference Library, Bulawayo.
[11] Interview with Zephaniah Moyo, Bulawayo, 14 July 1988.

hunt, or visit holy places within the park. The imperatives of international tourism have ensured that the park still presents much the same symbolic face that it did under settler rule.
People still visit Rhodes's Grave and other colonial monuments; still camp out and barbecue;
still photograph indiscriminately; and are still ignorant of the African history and cosmology
of the hills.[12]

In the 1990s the main preoccupations of the Matopos Park management have been
with conservation and tourism rather than with its relation with local communities,
black or white. The Game Park has become a major sanctuary for black rhinos and
Victoria Chitepo as Minister of Natural Resources and Tourism proclaimed the
government's intention to defend the heritage of Matopos wild life to the death, for all
the world as if rhinos had grazed there in the nineteenth century. In so far as 'African'
inhabitants of the area have been commemorated in the Park it has been the hunter-
gatherers. A museum has been opened at Pomongwe cave, designed to show 20
'outstanding example of Rock Paintings by Stone-Age Bushmen', with a 'mini-diorama
showing the Stone-Age people engaged in typical daily activities', so that 'a visitor to
the Matopos will be able to get an overall feel for the area and the Stone-Age people
who lived there.'[13] The long history of Iron Age cultivators and cattle keepers has been
expunged from the record. At Nswatugi cave there is a display about conservation in
the Park which declares: 'Without conservation and protection the animals, plants and
trees you can now see would have disappeared.... Intensive agriculture should never be
practised in this area.'[14] African cultivators are left with the feeling that they should not
be in the hills at all. They are given no sense of their continuity with the hunter-
gatherers. In the occupied and cultivated Matopos, schoolboys, feeling no connection
with the long-vanished cave painters, cheerfully vandalise their work.

Even the custodians of the Rhodesian 'heritage' of the Matopos have felt under
threat. The Park has been much visited by tourists from South Africa whose scathing
comments on the spartan facilities felt appropriate by generations of Rhodesian whites
fill the Visitors' Books of the chalets at Maleme Dam. In 1995 entrance fees were
imposed both for local and for international visitors, though at varying rates. This
caused more outrage among Bulawayo whites than among black peasants. Perhaps for
the last time the terms of Rhodes's will were invoked, as Bulawayo whites angrily
insisted that the Matopos had been set aside in perpetuity for *their* rest and recreation.
The ambiguity and strength of local white feeling about the hills were illustrated by a
Bulawayo man who told me that the ashes of his parents had been scattered in the
National Park which they had loved so much, but that he would not visit them there
any more because he refused to pay the entrance fee!

In these ways the Matopos National Park has become more and more an icon of the
international conservation movement and of international tourism, and less and less
connected with its local history. Yet the growth of tourism has paradoxically brought

[12] Terence Ranger, 'Great Spaces Washed with Sun: the Matopos and Uluru Compared', in Kate Darian-
Smith, et al., eds, *Text, Theory, Space*, Routledge, 1996, p. 161.
[13] *Chronicle*, 29 April 1986. The museum was completed only in the mid-1990s.
[14] Terence Ranger, 'Whose Heritage? The Case of the Matobo National Park', *Journal of Southern African
Studies*, 15, 2, January 1989, p. 249.

both local white and black initiative back into the picture. As the Matopos becomes more famous as an international tourist destination so the modest accommodation at the Maleme Dam has come to seem inappropriate. White-owned 'farms' in the hills, which have never been viable as agricultural or grazing units, have blossomed forth as safari lodges, run by the ecology-conscious descendants of the original owners. With bars in caves and swimming pools in crevices in the rocks; with rock paintings and game on their own land; these lodges have rapidly become a thriving enterprise. Now that scenery is for sale these farms are prosperous for the first time in their history. Amalinda Camp is 'set among rocks. Very scenic'; Matobo Hills Lodge has 'fantastic scenery'; Shumba Shaba Lodge, close to the Matopo Mission, is 'situated on the edge of an escarpment in the Matobo Hills' with 'a truly outstanding' view.

Even though Matobo Hills Lodge also offers 'cultural village trips', and even though all of these farms were originally intended for the exploitation rather than the preservation of the environment, these safari camps enthusiastically represent the Matopos as 'nature'. They offer guests a wide range of illustrated books on the animals and birds and rocks and cave paintings of the hills. At Shumba Shaba Lodge, for example, I picked up Valerie Gargett's *The Black Eagle*, a book which celebrates birds of prey rather than human beings. 'There is not an air of great antiquity at the hand of man in the Hills', she writes, 'for he is too recent a comer by their time scale'. And she offers a selective recent history:

> Evidence of human settlement was still visible in 1984 in the protected National Park, over twenty years after the last peasant farmers and their livestock were moved out. A close observer will notice alien plants, the crumbling remains of mud huts, partly concealed ridges and furrows, cleared areas sparsely covered by grass or shrub, and depleted woodland. The scars left by man are healed slowly by nature but most of the inhabitants were moved in 1953 and where they were nature had responded by increased growth, in the form of lush grass-land, moist vleis, more thickly wooded slopes and taller trees.... [It is] a natural community spared for a time from the impact of man.
>
> Man's hand has fallen most heavily on the adjacent Communal Lands, where degradation of the habitat is plain to see. Grasslands are denuded and eroded, hillsides devoid of trees, streams and vleis dry and the refuges of wild animals stand emptied of life. Man and his domestic stock reign supreme, slowly creating a desert ... Envious eyes are cast at the protected National Park and superficial arguments are advanced for its 'return' to the communal subsistence farming that was its fate for so brief [sic] a period of its history. The Zimbabwe Government has stood firm in its resolve to protect for future generations this small, rich and diverse area which is in fact unsuitable for settlement.[15]

In one respect, however, the safari lodges have drawn upon the despised Communal Areas. If their white owners could sell history, at least the black villagers could sell rocks. In June 1995 the *Chronicle* carried a story headed 'Rocks are Money to Matobo Villagers'. Villagers living in the Silozwi area were 'cashing in on the construction of two motels by selling thin slates of rocks scraped from boulders near their homes.' Matopo Ingwe Lodge and Matopo Hills Lodge were being constructed with 'walls

---

[15] Valerie Gargett, *The Black Eagle*, Acorn Books, Randburg, 1990, pp. 25 and 27.

plastered in stone to make the buildings look like they are entirely constructed of stone'. This 'came as a blessing in disguise for the drought-stricken villagers, most of whom now spend long hours in the mountains collecting the slates.' They could sell two scotch-cart loads for $75. Conservationists were horrified, denouncing the 'ugly white spots' left on rocks 'in the tourist area'. A scientist with the Natural Resources Board, Ngoni Chiweshe, announced that the practice was 'illegal. Cockroaches and scorpions live there. We would not allow people to disturb them'. The villagers, however, were using the money to buy grain to feed their families.[16]

But the 'briefly' settled African peoples of the hills, with their 'alien' plants, may have a longer-lasting and more dignified involvement with international tourism. At least one black entrepreneur has entered the 'eco-tourism' market. This is Mark Ncube, director of the Bulawayo branch of the Zimbabwean National Archives, Oral Historian for Matabeleland, and deeply involved in the field work on which this book is based. Mark has set up Emadwaleni Village, at a site ceded to him inside the National Park and opposite the Game Park. He is selling culture rather than nature – or at least the fusion of the two. 'Do you want to have that unique experience of the Matobo area?', his brochure asks.

> The rocks that have water, shelter and something to eat? Would you like to witness and even to dance to spectacular cultural dances such as hosana/njelele rain dance ... amabhiza – good harvest dance, amantshomane – ancestral spirit inovation dance, itshikitsha – quasi-military celebration dance. These are the dances of the Banyubi, Kalanga and Ndebele people who have lived in the Matobo area for centuries.

He offers a view, 'from a distance' of 'mysterious, spectacular and legendary mountains' including Chitendebudzi, 'the resting place of the rain spirits', and Tombo tjisiposelukwi, 'the rock that is round and revolves, and which when walked round becomes perpetual drizzle'.

Mark Ncube has also been granted land by the Ward Committee in Kumalo West, a rocky area of little use for agriculture but splendid for scenery. There is a spectacular waterfall on his land. 'Here, within sight of the sacred shrine of Njelele Mountain visitors can stay in a thatched rondavel lit by solar power, eating village food and walking in the Matobo hills.' The local community support his plans. Maybe Mark Ncube will be able to bring the history and the present of the Matopos together.[17]

Meanwhile the monuments of the National Park continue to serve a symbolic purpose useful to the state. In mid-1995 the Minister for Home Affairs, Dumiso Dabengwa, took Prince Edward to Rhodes's Grave; a little later he took Chief Buthelezi to Mzilikazi's tomb.[18]

---

[16] *Chronicle*, 5 June 1995.

[17] Margaret Ling, 'News from Nyathi Valley', Britain Zimbabwe Society Newsletter, November 1997, p. 5.

[18] Demands for the removal of Rhodes's Grave have not entirely ceased, however. On 19 February 1998 the *Herald* reported a call from 'local pressure group', Sangano Munhumutapa, for the undoing of colonial sacrilege. 'Such abominations include the presence of Rhodes' grave on top of King Chabata Matosi and the other subsequent Mutapas, who were laid to rest in the holy caves of the Matosi-Po shrines.' The

The Communal Areas of the Matopos in the 1990s

Despite Mark Ncube's enterprise in Kumalo West, the occupied Matopos have remained intensely local rather than international, still rarely visited by tourists, still intensely cultivated and still celebrating the power of the Mwali shrines. It is a particular pleasure of mine to introduce people who have lived in Bulawayo all their lives and who have constantly visited the National Park to the different but equal beauties of Kumalo, Gulati and Matopo Communal Areas, where to my mind the spectacle of the countryside is intensely enhanced by its intimate engagement with humanity.

As we have seen, this continuing interaction – so often threatened under Rhodesian rule – was threatened again by Joshua Nkomo's determination to move the people and their stock out of the Matopos. But Nkomo failed as many before him had done. When I travelled in the Matopos in 1988 I found people outraged by his ideas. Clearance from the Matopos 'would be a breach of faith', said Council Chairman, Joel Nyathi. 'He has not consulted the people. He has forgotten that people gave up their lives for what they considered their heritage, and for the cause that they supported, as they supported him'.[19] Philip Bhebe, the Provincial Administrator in 1988, told me that he went himself to 'people living on rocks near Esigodini and urged them to move to better soil. They replied, "Young man, we were living on these same rocks before you were born. We have sons of your age whom we have educated and who have good positions in government out of the proceeds of these rocks".'[20] When told that Nkomo would allow the shrine priests to stay put, the guardian at Dula asked if they would be expected to preach to baboons when all the people had gone.[21] The people gathered for a communal interview at Kumbudzi Clinic in Matopo Communal Area were insistent that they would not leave the hills. Reader Ncube, who had arranged the interview, said that as Chairman of the Esigodini Council he had been asked to persuade them to move to a resettlement area in Plumtree. 'I am very, very reluctant to do so', he said amidst laugher.

> I shall lose votes. People here cannot be compelled. They object. In the 1980s if they were given ZANU cards they threw them into the dam. When the people here don't want any-thing, they don't delay until tomorrow. They tell you today. We give the District Adminis-trator a hard time. We won't agree with anything he suggests – even if it's good![22]

Most impressive of all was my interview with Michael Ncube, director of the Hlekweni farming centre. Ncube trained as an agriculturalist. But he was deeply opposed to the idea that people should be moved from the hills. It would be a big

---

[18] (cont.) pressure group would call together 'cultural activists, local leaders, civic organisations and indigenous business persons ... to work out plans for the removal of Rhodes' remains from Matopos, before the next rainy season'.

[19] Interview with Joel Nyathi, Maphisa, 1 August 1988.

[20] Interview with Philip Bhebe, Gwanda, 31 August 1988.

[21] Interview with Mayembe Ncube, Dula, 12 September 1988.

[22] Interview with Reader Ncube and shrine adepts, Kumbuzi, 10 September 1988.

political mistake since there still continued so much resentment over the previous evictions. And it would be a metaphysical mistake:

> If Nkomo moves people from the hills, the hills will dry up. There is water there because the people need it. In the hills at Mazhayimbe there is a little hole at the foot of a rock which never runs dry. Everyone drinks from there, people and animals. I said, why not make a cement surround, put in a pump. They said, no, when you do that the water dries up. The water is a gift from the rock.[23]

In any case, there was no question of people being forced out of the hills. Nkomo's plan was to 'lure' them to more attractive land. But as we shall see, no resettlement schemes developed that seemed anything like as attractive as life in the Communal Areas of the hills. Matopo Communal Area continued its intensive gardening production; entrepreneurs continued to build splendid brick houses there. When entrepreneurs went too far they continued to be brought to book by the community. In March 1995 *Parade* ran an article headed 'Farmer puts holy water to good use'. It described how a local man was tapping water 'from the sacred Diana Pools. He is interfering with the pools in a way that has never been heard of in the history of the area – the water from the pool is holy.' Locals had compelled him to stop.

But the passive resistance of the Matopos residents and the prohibitive power of their holy places could not keep the state altogether at bay. The Rhodesia Front government had drawn up blueprints for a dam on the Mtshabezi River as it ran through the eastern Matopos; the water would not be used for local irrigation but for the benefit of ranchers in the lowveld south of the hills. The dam was to be built in a spectacular though rarely visited part of the Matopos:

> The Mtshabezi Valley runs for about 20 km through the Matopos in a gorge that averages 300 m in depth, making it the single largest feature in the Matobo Hills. It is fed by the Mtshashasha river that tumbles down 90 m cascades.

The dam had not been attempted in the nationalist years of the 1960s, the war years of the 1970s, or the dissident years of the 1980s. But in the 1990s it was built. It began in 1991. No compensation was offered to those who had to move and no alternative land was offered. From 1993 onwards the displaced began to move up into the hills. By the end of 1994 the dam wall was complete; it was reported that the dam would take four years to fill and that the water would eventually stretch back over 9 kms. Members of the newly formed Matobo Conservation Society were invited to a field day at the dam site in October 1994, the aim being 'to remove and preserve rare plant species from the dam floor and to record archaeological artefacts.'[24]

---

[23] Interview with Michael Ncube, Hlekweni, 21 July 1989.

[24] Circular letter to members of the Matobo Conservation Society, 4 October 1994. I owe access to the correspondence of the Society to Mark Ncube who is a member. The Society has been much concerned with planning for 'the protection of the valley' and for the creation of Mtshabezi Valley Recreation Park. A proposal for this in November 1994 defined the aim of the new Recreation Park as being 'to make visitors aware of ecology ... to make visitors aware of the history and traditions of Zimbabwe with the help of rock paintings and nearby villages, to give tourists a view of the daily life and struggle of ordinary rural people.' *Notes on Aspects of Mtshabezi Valley Recreation Park*, I, Nordesjo, 28 November 1994.

When I drove to the dam wall site in early August 1996 it soon became clear that the technological project of the dam had overridden local cultural considerations. One reaches the dam wall by turning off the Dula road. I was told that although the shrine, and its subsidiaries, had objected strongly, the blasting operations in the hills had gone ahead. Eventually the road reaches Dondorio Hill, a site of considerable symbolic and religious significance. The road makers had blasted straight through the hill so that one can still see the slope running both above and below the road. As one enters the cut there are two signs, modern and traditional. The modern one reads, all too appropriately, 'Blind Rise Ahead'; the other reads 'Dondorio Holy Pass. Please Go Slow', a case of very belated and rather pathetic symbolic revitalisation. The dam wall itself is a piece of brutalist modernism, rearing up out of the course of the river. Downstream from the wall are the dried up vegetable gardens which the river used to sustain: the gardens on the other side of the wall are already under water. It remains to be seen whether a suggested Campfire project for communal management of the Mtshabezi Dam Recreational Park will compensate local people for their displacement.

The Priests at the Shrines in the 1990s

In 1988 Joshua Nkomo aspired to settle the affairs of Njelele; to restore its legitimacy; and have it reproclaimed as a national monument. He continued to be much involved with the affairs of Njelele and the other shrines in the 1990s. After the Unity Agreement the Zimbabwean government ceased to be worried about Njelele falling into opposition hands. It was conceded that the shrines were Nkomo's business. Having learnt from the failures of the ZAPU shrines committee, Nkomo now sought to regulate the cult through the chiefs of Matabeleleland.

Official policy on chiefs was that they should have spiritual and ritual influence rather than executive, judicial and land-control functions. The Rhodesian state, it was said, had forced chiefs to assume such 'political' responsibilities; but in majority rule Zimbabwe chiefs and headmen were 'freed' from these. It was announced that they could 'now carry out their traditional roles ... with their imbued wisdom drawn from years of tradition'.[25] Ndebele chiefs, in fact, had never possessed ritual authority. But now they were expected to settle the affairs of the shrines.

In the early 1990s the chiefs were asked to help restore Njelele to its proper place. In September 1992, for instance, chiefs and headmen from all over Matabeleland, members of parliament, ZANU/PF officials and government officers met at Mguza. Joshua Nkomo reported that 'a lot of confusing stories were being told about the traditional shrine, Njelele, which was one of those areas of concern where chiefs' advice was most sought.' Dumiso Dabengwa said that Njelele, the Mzilikazi Memorial and the site at Pupu in Lupane, where Lobengula had fought his last battle, had all been

---

[25] Secretary, Local Government to District Administrators, 23 November 1982, PER 5, District Administrator's office, Kezi.

deproclaimed as national monuments. 'Reproclamation could only be done if people came up with some supporting information'.

A committee consisting of one chief for each of the twelve districts of Matabeleland was set up to consult local elders and to make recommendations. Nkomo urged that chiefs should 'consider themselves as our traditional leaders who shall play a vital role in the cultural procedures, with particular emphasis on rain-making ceremonies.'[26]

Some important clarifications were made by using chiefs in this way. In Nkayi and Lupane in northern Matabeleland, for instance, chiefs decided to sort out the confused situation in which some people looked to Njelele for rain and others to the Nevana medium in Gokwe. The Njelele adherents observed Wednesday as their rest days; the Nevana adepts observed Thursday. This made it complicated to schedule meetings of local courts, etc. So the chiefs laid it down that south of the Shangani river everyone should go to Njelele and north of it everyone should go to Nevana.[27] But so far as Njelele itself was concerned, the chiefs found a situation which defied their best efforts and which led them to revolt against Nkomo.

As we have seen, when the dissidents chased Sitwanyana Ncube away from Njelele, chiefs and elders chose David Ndlovu as the keeper.[28] His appointment was announced to a wider public by a story in the *Chronicle* on 15 July 1988, complete with a photo of David 'in his working outfit'. But the story quoted Sitwanyana, 'who now lives at Mguza healing people and invoking spirits'. He 'vowed that he will one day go back to his former post saying the present keeper could not get to all parts of the cave because he was not trained to do so.'

It did not take Sitwanyana long to carry out his vow. By the end of August 1988 he was back at his ruined kraal south of Njelele mountain – in fact I drove him there in my Peugeot 404, with his wives and goats in the back. His local opponents objected strongly to his return, especially to his residence close to perennial pools and to the sacred approach to the shrine. Sitwanyana ignored these objections and began to take pilgrims to the shrine. In January 1989 ex-guerrillas serving in the National Army were driven mad by *ngozi* spirits of people they had killed during the 1970s; 'their spirits told them they must come to Njelele'; they reported to the District Administrator, Esigodini, and asked to be sent to Sitwanyana. The District Administrator's office in Kezi 'persuaded them to go to David'. But David 'was very worried' about Sitwanyana's return. He appealed to local elders. Headman Nqindi came into Kezi on behalf of his people and complained about Sitwanyana: District Administrator Mashingele thereupon ordered Sitwanyana to leave Njelele for good.[29]

Sitwanyana at once appealed to Joshua Nkomo and Thenjiwe Lesabe. Nkomo then

[26] Minutes of Vice-President's meeting with Chiefs, etc., 5 September 1992. I owe this reference to Jocelyn Alexander who copied it from the file relating to chiefs in the District Administrator's office, Nkayi.

[27] Jocelyn Alexander, JoAnn McGregor and Terence Ranger, *Violence and Memory*, forthcoming.

[28] During 1988 David was challenged in his turn by another female claimant from the east but District Administrator Mashingele refused to re-open the case. Interview with Deputy Administrator Moyo, Kezi, 7 September 1988. During 1989 claims were made by people from Nkayi and Masvingo and in July another woman went to Njelele to push her case. Interview with Deputy Administrator, 24 July 1989.

[29] Interviews with Mark Ncube, Bulawayo, 17 July 1989; Deputy Administrator Moyo, Kezi, 24 July 1989.

summoned a meeting of Matabeleland South chiefs in Gwanda on 23 February 1989. He intended to bring to the meeting the Minister of Local Government, Enos Chikowore, and his deputy, Lot Senda. After the meeting the chiefs and ministers would go to Njelele for a rain ceremony. But the chiefs, led by Nyangazonke – 'even Nkomo can't stand against that one' – let it be known that the ministers should not attend and that Nkomo, in particular, 'should never come'.[30] When the meeting did take place a month later under the chairmanship of the Provincial Governor, the chiefs made their discontent clear. Nyangazonke said that he was not clear why the chiefs were supposed to go to Njelele

> and noted that he had not been there and in fact no chief had visited the place to hold a meeting. Rather, there were particular people who went there and the chiefs' role was to facilitate travelling arrangements for those who had to go. The Minister had been mis-informed about the problems and Njelele.

He thought there was no need to involve 'people as senior as ministers when the issue could be resolved at local level'. In any case, the chiefs had already met at Kezi and found Sitwanyana's behaviour 'unbecoming'; they had already chosen David Ndlovu; all that was needed to resolve the problem was for Sitwanyana to leave.[31]

Sitwanyana asked the Deputy District Administrator to get this decision reversed. 'But even if I wanted to, I couldn't. Not even the President could. The people have refused.'[32] Yet it was one thing to uphold David as keeper and quite another to remove Sitwanyana from his kraal. The patronage of Thenjiwe Lesabe and Nkomo was enough to keep him there even if not enough to make him the recognised priest. David Ndlovu felt constantly insecure.

Meetings of chiefs were held in Kezi in October and at Natisa in November 1991. At the chiefs' insistence 140 local people attended this latter gathering. By this time the stalemate at the shrine had disillusioned locals with both Sitwanyana and David. For the first time since her departure from the shrine in the 1960s the name of Ngcathu was raised. Local elders insisted that she was 'the rightful person' to take over the shrine. The chiefs took up this recommendation and in May 1992 Nyangazonke informed his colleagues that he and Chief Nzula Malacki Masuku had been mandated 'to try and bring back Ngcathu Ncube who used to look after the shrine a long time ago'. Mean-while, the shrine was closed and neither Sitwanyana nor David were to take pilgrims there.[33]

Ngcathu agreed to return if both her rivals were removed, but Sitwanyana once

---

[30] Interview with Deputy Administrator Moyo; *Chronicle*, March 25 1989. The *Chronicle*'s headline was 'Keep Out, Leaders told', and its story said that 'chiefs complained that it was not proper for politicians to summon traditional leaders for discussions of affairs relating to the Njelele shrine in modern offices.'

[31] Minutes of the Provincial Governor's meeting with Chiefs and District Administrators, 23 March 1989, CHK/24, Administrator's office, Kezi.

[32] Interview with Deputy Administrator, Kezi, 24 July 1989.

[33] Minutes of meetings of 18 October and 6 November 1991 and of 29 May 1992, CHK/24/86, District Administrator, Kezi. These meetings are fully summarised in Leslie Nthoi's doctoral thesis, which exhaustively analyses the competition between Sitwanyana and David.

again appealed to his political patrons. At a meeting in October 1992 the provincial chiefs, disgusted with constant political interference. decided to wash their hands of the whole affair. The month before, meeting at inTabazinduna, the chiefs of all Matabeleland had expressed their disquiet 'over lack of interest, respect and recognition for Njelele as a long-standing sacred shrine.' It was being used as a political football and there was a desperate need 'to revert to culture.... Njelele would function as before if people only revived their culture'.[34] The great meeting of all Matabeleland chiefs with Nkomo and Dabengwa on 5 September 1992, at which the Ministers urged the need for Njelele to be reproclaimed as a national monument, also saw revolt by the chiefs. When Nkomo told them that there had never before been such frequent and intense drought and that they should focus more on 'rain-making ceremonies', the chiefs 'felt a bit disturbed, saying it was unfair to call upon them to play a role in these difficult times and yet in normal situations chiefs were a forgotten lot.' When the Nkayi chiefs met later to make a list of important ritual sites in their district, they noted that 'politics is responsible for all that goes wrong in the process of praying for rain'.[35]

The monthly *Parade* gave publicity to the Njelele deadlock in December 1992, describing 'a factional fight, with two rival "keepers", now resident on opposite sides of the hill'. *Parade* quoted local people as highly critical of Joshua Nkomo and of other politicians who had made use of Sitwanyana 'for their own personal glory and political ends'. The locals also attacked Sitwanyana's practice as a *n'anga* [herbalist], and the presence at his village of fourteen other *n'angas*. 'Njelele is not a *n'anga*'s thing and never has been. It is purely a rain shrine and efforts must be made to restore it to what it was.' Locals had also refused permission to ex-cabinet minister, Herbert Ushewokunze, now head of his own *n'angas* association, who had tried to organise a rain ceremony at Njelele. Clearly local elders had revolted both against Nkomo, who had persistently backed Sitwanyana, and against Ushewokunze, who as Minister had tried to impose Sipoyana/Nehanda upon the shrine. They now insisted that their own candidate, Ngcathu Ncube, be brought back and installed.[36]

The arrival of Ngcathu Ncube at Njelele in 1995, as the candidate of chiefs and people, was a further manifestation of Njelele's autonomy of politicians. She told Jocelyn Alexander and JoAnn McGregor in September 1996 that:

Nkomo enticed Sitwanyana to be in charge of Njelele [but] Sitwanyana is here illegally. At one time these boulders rolled over him. He was trapped between the rocks. Sitwanyana was assaulted by the guerrillas – he has terrible scars on his body. That's when Nkomo took him to his farm for refuge. Nkomo and I are not in agreement.... I told him he brought all this confusion at Njelele. I told him, 'Whether you like it or not, you will lose your position.' I warned Nkomo that he must come to Njelele and apologise. But Nkomo refused. I told him he would have bitter results.... He refused and had to go for an operation. People asked me to come to stay here. The whole country is praying that I come back here and represent them at the rock.... It is the world that wants me here.

---

[34] Minutes of meeting of 1 September 1992, CHK 14, District Administrator, Nkayi.
[35] Minutes of these meetings are in CHK 14, Nkayi.
[36] *Sunday News*, 26 February 1995.

Ngcathu's claims for Njelele are grandiose enough to satisfy Nkomo himself. 'Njelele is the main power. Njelele's power covers the whole world, England, everywhere. All these mountains – Dzilo – power comes from Njelele. Zimbabwe is very good in farming. You can go to Botswana, but we refer to Zimbabwe as Canaan, the land of honey and milk and that's because of Njelele'. Njelele was 'like Mount Sinai in the bible'. It was properly a Kalanga shrine and properly controlled by women:

> It is traditional in our culture that women were in charge.... Sitwanyana comes from the Vendas – he is nothing to do with Njelele. Originally, my grandfather came from this area. You remember Mambo? I am Kalanga. My father was king of these mountains ... the names of all the mountains here are in Kalanga.

Above all, the shrine must not be subordinated to politics. Today 'everyone wants money'; the politicians were 'crooks'; 'there will be war here. When the worst comes to the worst, then they'll come here. But now they're too busy eating, enjoying their money, but when there's war they'll come running, due to fright, thinking they can get salvation here.'[37]

Things had certainly changed at Njelele when Ngcathu could lead a healing ceremony for ex-ZIPRA guerrillas on the night of 30/31 August 1996, and begin it with a harangue against Nkomo – 'a war cry and assertion of her authority'.[38] This dramatic assertion of Njelele's autonomy and predominance obviously owes a good deal to the disillusionment of ZAPU supporters with the unequal fruits of the Unity Agreement. In their eyes Nkomo and his allies have done only too well out of the economic opportunities of peace. Meanwhile, there has been all too little 'development'. Even Sitwanyana told me that no political leader had been endorsed by Njelele. Mugabe was merely 'king of the schoolboys' and not a traditionalist leader. Nkomo could have been a traditionalist leader and had been invited to enter the very recesses of Njelele cave. But 'alas, he was too fat'.

Development in the Matopos in the 1990s

The time has come, then, to look at the fate of Nkomo's development programme. In July 1989 Mrs Van Vuren, Secretary of the Matobo Rural Council, showed me a map of the farms recently acquired by ARDA from the whites who had left the land in 1983. Twenty-three farms in all had been acquired, a total of 51,173 hectares. Joshua Nkomo's four extensive ranches of Nsambaan, Makwe, Shukwe and Walmer would be restored to him. Together with the three farms, Undza, Gumella and Dera which had been acquired for resettlement years earlier, government now owned a belt of land due south of Kumalo West; government land flanked the eastern boundary of the Tshatshani Communal Area; the northern boundary of Semokwe CA; and the northern boundary of Prospect/Mbongolo. These properties thus acted as a buffer zone between the Communal Areas and the inner core of still functioning commercial farms.

---

[37] Interview between Jocelyn Alexander, JoAnn McGregor and Gogo Ncube, Njelele, 2 September 1996.
[38] Jocelyn Alexander, 'Brief Account of trip to Njelele Ceremony, Friday and Saturday, 30–31 August 1996.

The need for such a buffer was illustrated in August 1989 by a dispute between communal farmers in Kumalo East and the white owner of Manyoni farm, Neil Stone. Stone had extended his northern boundary to incorporate 'a fertile strip of land with a spring' on which villagers grew vegetables for the Bulawayo market. Cde Morris Ndlovu, the village secretary, showed reporters 'vast plots containing sweet potatoes, beans and orchard trees' out of which he supported four children in secondary school in Bulawayo. The boundary dispute

> has also touched on traditional beliefs. On the outskirts of the villages lie some boulders where elders go to appease their ancestral spirits. The boundary is going to fence the area into the farm. According to the villagers, the boulders are one of the many 'satellites' in Matobo District, which surround the sacred Njelele.[39]

But disputes like this affected many fewer people than the fate of the farms acquired by ARDA. By the end of 1989 there had been no agreement between the Matobo Council and the government over what should be done with them. Government was now advocating a development plan not much different from Joshua Nkomo's ideas. Within the Communal Areas there should be 'villagisation'; on the acquired farms there should be Model D resettlement schemes onto which people would move with their cattle. The Council – which had to approve any resettlement model before it could be put into effect – resisted 'villagisation' (which would in any case have been very difficult to effect in the hills) and disliked Model D. It insisted that the *mapani* veld should be used for grazing. Government countered this demand with a stress on the current inequalities of cattle holding. If uncontrolled grazing were allowed it would benefit the families who owned two hundred head and offer no relief to families who owned none. Government was recommending that settlers who moved into Model D schemes should be restricted to 20 head. But Deputy Administrator Moyo in Kezi told me in July 1989 that he didn't think people were conscious of inequality; the *mafisa* cattle loan system was still common; and any implication of culling or destocking made 'people say we are going back to the days of the whites. So government walks very carefully. Even the Fifth Brigade didn't confiscate cattle.' He noted that 'planners are always slow'; that the Council was in deadlock with the government planning agency, Agritex, 'so a stalemate will be there'.[40]

The stalemate was still in effect in August 1990 when I was next in Kezi. The responsible minister, Witness Mangwende, had been in Kezi repeating what Joshua Nkomo had said in 1988 – that Communal Areas must first be reorganised and paddocked before there could be any talk of resettling the commercial farms. Government intended to leave the farms in the hands of ARDA for some time and to use them for raising good stock to provide beef, breeding bulls and plough oxen. Joshua Nkomo, whose farm at Makwe had now been restored, had endorsed this approach. There was to be a 'political process' of persuasion; people were to be weaned away from regarding their cattle as a 'treasury' and towards using them commercially.[41]

---

[39] *The Sunday News*, 13 August 1989.
[40] Interview with Deputy Administrator, 24 July 1989.
[41] Interview with Deputy Administrator, Kezi, 21 August 1990.

One of the many problems arising from this approach was that ARDA was prepared to lease farms to 'big men' – and women – who would raise cattle on them. Meanwhile Joshua Nkomo took a different tack, founding a Development Association which applied to buy ranches in South Matobo on which it would provide employment for the locals. In mid-1992 I gave a talk to the boys of a southern Matabeleland secondary school on the history of land; half-way through reporters from the *Chronicle* arrived, and next day I provided its main headline: 'LET THE PEOPLE DECIDE SAYS RANGER'. That day I drove down to Kezi to meet Lancelot Moyo, Mashingele's successor as District Administrator. He told me that the people could not decide because they were divided into too many interests. 'Listen to the People' would be a better slogan. 'I know you admire the capacity of my Council to say No to everything', he told me. 'But they have to say Yes sometime. I am trying to get them to agree to a resettlement model by threatening them that otherwise I shall recommend that land be given to Nkomo's Association'. By this time the District Council was beginning to see Joshua Nkomo as part of their problem rather than as part of a solution.

In the next two or three years others of the old ZAPU leadership lost the confidence of people in Matobo. In April 1996 *Horizon* ran a story on 'land grab' in the district. This concerned 'government officials and businessmen in Matobo who have acquired leases on several old commercial farms earmarked for resettlement, without notifying the local district council'. Nyathi's successor as District Chairman, Frank Masisa, and the local member of parliament, Ananias Nyathi, attacked such people as 'squatters'. 'I want them out', said Nyathi.

> They think Matobo is their playground. It is time they learnt that they are not the only ones who fought the liberation war. What they are doing now is robbing the people for whom they fought the war, the landless peasants.

Thenjiwe Lesabe was said to be one of those involved.

In its August 1996 issue *Horizon* was able to report that 'there were cheers and joyful singing during a meeting of the Matobo District Council in June when it was announced that 22 farms "irregularly" occupied by government and party chefs had been returned to the people for resettlement.' In December 1996 Stanley Bhebe, the new District Administrator, was telling *Horizon* that 'we are still having problems with the fat cats'; that three farms were being contested; and that 'it was a tough job trying to convince communal farmers in the area that the farms were now theirs.' By January 1997 'the restoration of the farms had still not been completed'.

In that month *Horizon* ran a story which struck many echoes from the history narrated in this book. It concerned land on what had been the Rhodes Matopos Estates, now administered by the Department of National Parks. Until 1993 Honeydale estate and Matopo Vale had been owned by the Chennells family. The land lay adjacent to the Matopos Agricultural Research station and also to the Gulati Communal Area. In 1993 the family offered the land to Harold Ndlovu, headmaster of a school in England but born in the Communal Area; he brought in a retired army colonel, Tshenga Dube, and the Minister of Home Affairs, Dumiso Dabengwa, and the three men bought the farms. Then in October 1995 more than nine hundred 'members of a pressure group calling themselves *Inqama* (Ndebele for ram), moved on to the land. They were arrested and fined $30 each for trespass. Readers will recall that before the 1896 rising the *Nqama* regiment lived along the northern fringes of the Matopos and that they had only later regrouped in Wenlock. According to *Horizon* the *Inqama* pressure group 'claims 4,000 members' and is chaired by Jonathan Moyo, a Bulawayo accountant:

> Inqama is threatening 'war' if the people are not given back the land occupied by politicians. 'We are very angry because our leaders made us fight a war for the land which is still not ours.'.... On October 29 last year, after the Inqama 'squatters' were evicted, a mysterious bush fire sprang up and swept through 5,000 hectares of national parkland and parts of the Matopos Agricultural Research Station land. [42]

Conservation after the Unity Agreement

On 9 November 1988 the *Chronicle* published a guest column entitled 'The Reality of Being Free' by Basil Sibanda. This looked back to the history of conservation in Matobo. Sibanda remembered Noel Robertson, the District Commissioner who was nicknamed *Nkomiyahlaba*, 'the ox that gores':

> Nkomiyahlaba was a name which had become synonymous with Kezi itself. Everything, and I mean everything, was his. My first contact with conservation, for example, was when we were thrashed by a khaki-clad District Assistant who found us 'cutting Nkomiyahlaba's trees'! Since then my friends and I joined the thousands who knew better than to tamper with Nkomiyahlaba's property. And boy, was that man hated! In my area if you want to know who is hated and who hates who, all you have to do is to go and read what is written under the huge Tshatshane River bridge. Obscenities about Nkomiyahlaba headed the list.

Two weeks later Robertson was defended by Father Odilo Weeger, pioneer of Lupane Catholicism and the man who erected the cross opposite Rhodes's Grave. Robertson 'was deeply concerned about ecology' and when one looks at the 'denuded areas like Kezi' how can we say he was wrong?[43] Weeger was in turn rebuked by Benny Lutshani Moyo and asked how he could defend 'a policy that was inherently unjust'. People had been forced to settle 'on sandy and desert areas like Kezi' and *then* asked to be 'conservation conscious':

> What in all honesty were they going to do apart from cutting down trees for the most basic needs of housing, fencing and food? When the people offended by questioning this logic (for trees were growing abundantly in white commercial and state land) they earned the wrath of neo-fascists like Nkomiyahlaba.

The people 'were herded like sheep into a desert'. But 'I am perhaps too harsh',

---

[42] *Horizon*, Christmas/January 1997. The magazine recalls the earlier protest movement of the *Nqameni*: 'In 1952, to reclaim their land, the Ndebele formed an organisation, *Sofasihamba*, which was unsuccessful in its aim to displace the white settlers.'

[43] *Chronicle*, 16 November 1988.

concluded Moyo. Whites 'cannot be expected to understand the depth and pain of our dehumanisation'.[44]

These articulate criticisms of conservation in the Matobo low veldt were followed by symbolic recognition that agricultural rules in the hills had been too rigid. Old Mark Dokotela Ncube, who had cultivated his sponge in north Wenlock despite the official policy of fencing all sponges off, now began to win national and international awards for good farming. The *Sunday News* reported in February 1991 that 'his swamp reclamation project last year won him a medal and citation from the United Nations Environmental Programme'. (As he told me in August 1990, 'You can't do better than Global'). The *News* noted that local farmers had organised a special field day to congratulate him on the award and 'scores of communal famers have been taking educational tours to Cde Ncube's Wenlock farm'.[45]

Ncube's triumph, of course, was a victory not only over rigid agrarian rules but also over the hostility of those neighbours who had accused him of ignoring the precepts of the Mwali cult. But the cult itself was very active after the Unity Agreement in propagating its own environmental ideology. So far in this chapter, and in the last, I have concentrated on the external and internal politics of the Mwali shrines – the rivalries between claimants to the priesthood; their interactions with politicians; their charging of fees and making of profits. All these weaknesses of the priests were highlighted during the drought years of the 1980s. Drought is bad news for rain priests. The closure of Njelele shrine in 1992 and the prohibition placed on both David Ndlovu and Sitwanyana Ncube was precipitated by the terrible drought of that year. But it is important to remember that despite all the rivalry and all the politics, the Mwali cult had its own deep concerns with environment just as it had its own profound sense of history.

As Sitwanyana told me in July 1988, 'the shrine was responsible for everything, animals, grass, trees and people. All living things.'[46] His comments on the National Park revealed the Mwali ideology at work: 'There has been a tendency to shoot down beserk animals. I suggest that in future people should be chosen to stay with these animals to ascertain what would have gone wrong, whether the animals could have fed on poisonous plants, rather than killing them.' Animals were not to be killed except for food or sacrifice. Mwali disapproved, therefore, of the National Park policy of culling.[47] Councillor Smith Mbedzi, the ZAPU activist, companion of Mrs Lesabe on her visits to the shrines during the 1980s, and organiser of the visits to Venda, spoke with passion about the plight of nature:

> The land belongs to the Creator and all its people and everything that belongs to it. There was a time when I was through, I travelled to Beit Bridge, which is my home, during the drought period, when you seemed to see impala and kudus really desperate. And I said within myself, because I was travelling alone, 'God, don't destroy'; even the trees were falling. I said 'Mwari,

---

[44] *Chronicle*, 21 November 1988.
[45] *Sunday News*, 10 February 1991; interview with Mark Dokotela Ncube, north Wenlock, 30 August 1990.
[46] Interview with Sitwanyana Ncube, 28 July 1988.
[47] Interview with Sitwanyana Ncube, 19 August 1988.

don't destroy your creations because of the evils of mankind. Better destroy mankind and leave those others. It was a pathetic story. Because the kudu when it sees you would try to run away but it couldn't, just gets to the fence there to throw itself to the fence and then it falls down. But that was because of the evil of man, who is the super-natural creature of God.[48]

In the late 1980s and 1990s the shrines in Matopo Communal Area were linked with wide-ranging movements of conservation. In 1988 Martinus Daneel, working with ex-guerrillas, spirit mediums and Independent Church leaders, formed AZTREC (Association of Zimbabwean Traditional Ecologists) and AAEC (Association of African Earthkeeping Churches), under the umbrella of ZIRCON (Zimbabwean Institute of Religious Research and Ecological Conservation). Their activities were centred in Masvingo Province and their aim was to move on from political liberation to the liberation of nature. They concentrated particularly on the planting of tree lots. The Associations felt the need for Mwali's endorsement. In January 1989 a delegation went to Bembe, where they heard a 'trance-like female Voice' speaking 'in a combination of ancient chi-Rozvi, Ndebele and Kalanga'; in 1990 a much larger delegation of sixty chiefs and mediums went to Dzilo. The *Masvingo Provincial Star* described how Simon Chokoto took the delegation 'into the sacred mountains' where they heard 'a hoarse voice from the cave ... a hair-raising experience.' At both shrines, and on subsequent visits to Dzilo, they were given the endorsement of Mwali.[49]

In 1992, however, a differently conceived ecological movement, originating at Dzilo itself, swept across southern Zimbabwe. This was led by the prophetess, Mbuya Juliana, whose professed aim was to restore the balance of humanity and nature. In her vision, the Independent Churches, with their drumming on sacred mountains and their direct challenges to the Mwali cult, were largely responsible for ecological crisis. 'Those against my work are the Zionist and Vapostori. The Creator does not like their noise. Jesus Christ did not play drums'. Also resonsible were the modernisers, the builders of dams and boreholes, the layers down of cement. 'The dams are too many and they also use cement to seal the *njuzu's* homes ... They run away because they think they will be killed when they hear the blasting.' Between the drummers and the users of explosives to blast the land for dams it had become impossible for Mwali's water spirits, the *njuzu*, to thrive in the streams of Zimbabwe. A holy silence had to be restored. It seems clear that Juliana stands in direct succession to the line of female eco-prophets which have carried the Mwali doctrines eastwards during the twentieth century.[50]

The Swedish medical anthropologist, Gurli Hansson, interviewed Juliana in November 1993. Juliana explained that she had become a *nyusa*, a messenger of the shrines, when she was taken by the *njuzu* at the age of seven. She had lived under water at Dzilo for four years:

---

[48] Interview with Smith Mbedzi, 5 September 1988.

[49] M. L. Daneel, *African Earthkeepers*, Vol. 1, pp. 115–34.

[50] For an account of some of the earlier prophetesses see Terence Ranger, 'Religious Studies and Political Economy: the Mwari Cult and the Peasant Experience in Southern Rhodesia', in M. M. J. Van Binsbergen and Matthew Schoffeleers, eds, *Theoretical Explorations in African Religion*, Routledge and Kegan Paul, 1986.

The Njuzu takes you under water and it stays with you. You live there just like crocodiles do. There is everything down there. The Njuzu trains and teaches you.... You are taught good manners, how to live well with other people and to be kindhearted. This is my job, to teach people to be humble with each other.... All the elders died – there is no-one to teach people. Nobody knows any more what the causes of all ills in our land are.... The Njuzu said: 'Go and teach the people, so they will live again according to law and order, so the rains will come again.

People now want money; 'greed and desire for money kills the country'. But in the old days people rested content with what Mwali gave them. 'They would ask for rain and get it. They did not need to dig bore-holes.... All that is needed is to blow *Hwamanda* [to perform the ritual] and the water will come out from the rocks.'[51] The Independent Churches must stop drumming; shrines to Mwali must be set up; businessmen should not seek profits; people must share.

As two observers who encountered Juliana's movement in Zvishavane remark:

The cult quickly became a major force across south central Zimbabwe over an area nearly 300 km across and at least 100 km deep; focussing on the causes of drought it challenged state, business, church and traditional power, and significantly restructured local social relations and land use practice.[52]

Flows of tribute went to Dzilo from the area of Juliana's influence. Gurli Hansson herself twice visited Dzilo with authority from Juliana, hearing the voice of Mwali from the cave. She quotes one of Juliana's assistants, Mai Kembo, describing a three-day barefoot journey from Svita to Dzilo, where Juliana 'reported about her work in Mberengwa'. From Zvishavane comes an account of a visit to Dzilo by tribute bearers from all over southern Zimbabwe:

The journey to Matonjeni was conducted barefoot ... and took six days. Each nyusa carried with him the rusengwe tribute that had been collected in their area.... Once they arrived at Matonjeni this sum of money was passed on to Juliana, who delivered approximately $35,000 to the shrine. On arrival at the shrine, Juliana blew her ritual horn and then spoke to the rock, saying 'I have brought the people from where I have been doing mapa [sacred things]. From the rock came a reply.

After a month of beer-brewing, the messengers assembled again at the rock and the Voice ordered them 'to stick to the new rules brought by Juliana'.[53]

Like Ngcathu Ncube at Njelele, Juliana was very critical of the state and of politicians.

I am suffering, frankly, and the Government is not considering, yet the Government has plenty of things piled up. I try my level best to help, so as to prevent drought, but they do not want to listen.... Or when they see the ancestors they call them devilish spirits.... The Government does not want to contribute, not even a single cent, not even a piece of paper or a letter.

[51] Gurli Hansson interview with Mbuya Juliana, Mudavanhu, 3 November 1993.
[52] Abraham Mawere and Ken Wilson, 'Socio-religious Movements, the State, and Community Change: Some Reflections on the Ambuya Juliana Cult of Southern Zimbabwe', Britain Zimbabwe Research Day, 23 April 1994.
[53] Mawere and Wilson, *ibid.*

It seems that after the Unity Agreement the special relationship between the Matopos shrines and ZAPU gave way to a critical autonomy from all politics and politicians.[54]

With all these developments, scientific ecologists had to find new – and more humble – ways of exercising influence in the Matopos. In January 1993 a group of concerned whites in Bulawayo established the Matobo Conservation Society. Some of its members were particularly interested in rhinos and others in cave paintings. But some were anxious about the state of the Communal Areas in the hills, where there was said to be 'severe sheet and gulley erosion due to overpopulation, overgrazing, lack of paddock fencing and grazing schemes, badly placed cattle dips and water points, destructive agricultural practices and badly planned roads.' 'As much as I love wild life and appreciate the efforts of those conserving it', wrote John Moger, 'there is not the same concern politically, publicly and financially for land degradation.'[55] There was also some interest in history and culture, however: 'the Matobo area has many historical and cultural sites including battle-grounds, burial grounds, rain-making shrines and painted caves. They are all part of our history and we must look after them.' But the emphasis still lay with the Stone Age. 'It is especially important that the cave paintings be not touched or interfered in any way. The paintings are an important part of our history. They show how the early inhabitants of the area lived and the animals who used to live there.'[56]

Protection of the land and of culture could no longer be done by compulsion. 'The communal people must be involved', wrote one member. 'It is unfortunate that some of our wild life conservationists tend to ignore the communal people.' Another urged that people from the Communal Areas must be represented on the Society's executive, since 'I can see only resentment from the people we want co-operation from if they are being told or advised by persons who have no idea what it is like to live there.' It was urged that 'the Park's survival in the present climate depends upon the Communal people obtaining substantial benefit from its existence'. In June 1993 the committee discussed how to raise funds for a custodian at Entumbane and in November 1983 it decided to appeal to Ndebele sentiment by replanting 'Mzilikazi's indaba tree'.[57]

These were certainly reformed, 'born-again' environmentalists. But they had great difficulty in bringing in representatives of the Communal Areas or even in finding urban African members. A turn-out of no fewer than 830 people for a slide show on 'Magnificent Matobo Hills' revealed the continuing interest of white Bulawayans. But only the indefatigble Mark Ncube of the National Archives represented African views at committee meetings. Still, the Society began to make contacts with Umzingwane and

---

[54] Mbuya Juliana's movement was still powerful in early 1998. On 1 March the *Sunday Mail* reported her commands to great crowds in Chivi: 'Cease construction of dams. Stop the sinking of boreholes, otherwise there will never be rain in this area because the rain gods do not want to see anything which involves the use of cement'.

[55] John Moger to Dunjey, 21 January 1993; to Richard Myrtle, 4 February 1993, Papers of the Matobo Conservation Society.

[56] Initial statement of the Matobo Conservation Society.

[57] John Moger to Dunjey, 21 January 1993; Peter Genje, 9 December 1992 and 21 January 1993; minutes of the meeting of 17 June 1993; minutes of the meeting of 1 November 1993.

Matobo District Councils whom it advised on possible Campfire schemes. In April 1995 the Chief Executive Officer of the Matobo Council, J. L. T. Gulu, thanking them for literature on Campfire and advice on how to gazette the Council's conservation by-laws, added that 'our association with the Matobo Conservation Society is beginning to bear fruit.'[58]

But the key project of the Society was its desire to have the Matopo Hills declared a World Heritage Site. In February 1993 the executive was told that a previous bid to World Heritage status 'had been rejected as Rhodes's Grave had been included'. In May 1995 the Society's Chairman, G. R. Stephens, attended a meeting of the Zimbabwe Council for Tourism to discuss a World Heritage application. He consulted with Dr W. Nduku, Director of National Parks, and UNESCO World Heritage representative, who told him that 'the geology and the rock art in the area is not enough to gain World Heritage status but the birdlife is.'[59] By the end of 1995 the Society had a draft submission; by mid-1996 it had drawn up a formal 'Submission for the Matobo National Park and Matobo Dam Recreational Area to be recognised as a World Heritage Site Within the Matobo Hills.'

The Matopos and the Heritage of the World

The submission's opening summary began with and laid most emphasis upon the 'unique geological environment ... enormous diversity in flora and fauna ... magnificent unspoilt scenery and wilderness'. Above all, the Matopos was 'the most significant sanctuary for birds of prey in the world'; 'a major recovery and research area for both species of rhino'; and had the 'largest population of leopard, possibly in the world.' On the cultural side, the summary emphasised 'over 3,000 recorded sites' of rock art, 'making the area the greatest rock art gallery of the world'. There followed ten pages on the natural history of the hills, three on their geology, and three on their 'cultural heritage'. This began, of course, with rock art, but added 'numerous Shona (Makalanga), Ndebele and colonial sites of irreplaceable historical value.' It noted that 'the oracle for the Mlimo Cult resides in the mountain known as Njelele', for some reason dating the cult's origins to the seventeenth century. It also noted that 'the two men who most shaped 19th century Southern Africa both chose to be buried in the Matobo Hills.' It added that 'Lord Baden Powell is said to have derived much inspiration for launching the world-wide scouting movement while on military service in the Matobo Hills'. So far, so much like Nobbs or Tredgold. But a note appropriate to independent Zimbabwe was struck:

> The Matobo Hills played an important part in the history of the indigenous peoples of Zimbabwe's resistance to colonial settlement and subsequent efforts to regain Independence from colonial occupation. Fighters from the liberation war returned to Njelele in 1980 to celebrate their home-coming and freedom.

[58] J. L. T. Gulu to John Moger, 24 April 1995.
[59] Meeting of 11 February 1993; meeting of 11 May 1995.

An appended 'History of the Park', however, presented a remarkably bland and even triumphalist account of its development, with no recognition of the long nationalist struggle against its creation.[60]

An ambiguity of the proposal was whether it extended to the Communal Areas of the Matopos and if so, how. The Society certainly hoped that declaration as a World Heritage site would oblige the Zimbabwean government to enforce conservation in the Communal Areas. In its document, however, it contented itself with remarking that:

> Few protected areas in Southern Africa are better conserved and managed than the Matobo National Park ... but ecological deterioration is widespread and serious in many areas surrounding ... particularly the Communal lands.... Nevertheless the knowledge and skills needed to rehabilitate these areas are available, having been perfected within the Park. By virtue of the nature of the habitat recovery can be rapid and almost all-embracing.

Over-optimistically, the submission credited successive governments not only with 'resolute action' but also with 'good public relations'. The impression was left that the peoples of the Communal Lands would be delighted to be rehabilitated by the knowledge and skills of the Park.

Meanwhile, however, a completely different approach to World Heritage was developing within UNESCO itself. In October 1995 the world organisation held its 'first global strategy meeting' on the definition of 'African Cultural Heritage'. This noted that Zimbabwe already had four Heritage sites – Great Zimbabwe, Khami, Mana Pools and Victoria Falls. This meant that the country was relatively well off for Heritage sites, but in general Africa was very badly provided for by comparison with Europe or Asia. A new definition of 'cultural landscape' was needed. The UNESCO office representative in Harare, Anderson Shankanga, stressed the 'almost complete absence of the heritage of living cultures, especially the so-called "traditional" ones.' The old monumentalist approach must give view to an anthropology which looked at the 'entire economic, social, symbolic and religious context'. Dawson Munjeri, Director of National Museums and Monuments – and the only man to have published on the Iron Age oral history of the Matopos – gave a talk on religious and spiritual landscapes in Zimbabwe; other papers emphasised the interaction of belief and physical environment, with titles like 'From Nature to the Spirits in African Heritages' and 'From Managing Natural Areas to African Cultural Heritage'. There was discussion of the 'cultural routes' of pilgrims. Nobody talked about raptors or rhinos.[61]

In this context it was not surprising that the recommendations of the various working groups at the meeting constantly returned to the Matopos as part of African Cultural Heritage. The Working Group on Archaeological Heritage identified five potential sites, among them 'Matopos, suggested for its cultural as well as natural landscape'. The Working Group on Human Settlements considered seven sites as representing 'the living heritage', among them the 'Matopo hills in Zimbabwe.' The

[60] Matobo Conservation Society, 'Submission for the Matobo National Park and Matobo Dam Recreational Area to be Recognised as a World Heritage Site, Within the Matopos Hills.'

[61] *African Cultural Heritage and the World Heritage Convention*, The National Museums and Monuments of Zimbabwe, Harare, 1996.

Working Group on Religious and Spiritual Heritage indicated seven sites of particular holiness, among them 'the Matopo hills in Zimbabwe, which are associated with rain-making ceremonies [and] significant not only to Zimbabwe but also to the people of Northern Botswana and Transvaal.' No other site was so often and variously recommended.[62] Here it was the Matopos as a whole which was considered. The National Park was not even mentioned, and might have been disqualified for recommendation because of its emptiness of people. It was precisely the Communal Areas and their shrines which made the case for the Matopos as an African Cultural Heritage site.

Conclusion: History and the Matopos

By 1997 the Zimbabwean government had been presented with these two strong, though completely different, cases for the proclamation of the Matopos as a World Heritage Site. As we have seen, Nkomo and Dabengwa had been working with the chiefs to collect material to substantiate Njelele's status as a National Monument. In mid-1997 Dabengwa told the Zimbabwean Parliament that Njelele was to be recognised as a national monument and that he had submitted a case to the World Heritage Committee for it to be recognised as an international shrine. Clearly, the Cultural Heritage approach had triumphed over the Natural Heritage one.

Nobody can have read this book without realising that I am bound to be delighted by such a choice. This book has partly been about revealing to people who go to the Matopos for the scenery that the hills have a rich human history and that only in the light of this can the scenery itself be understood. Yet at the end of so many years' research engagement with the Matopos, after my 1996 misadventure there, and at the end of such a long book, I may perhaps be permitted an even more explicit statement of my own position. I have some anxieties over the proclamation of Njelele as a national and international shrine.

The case made at the UNESCO Global Strategy Meeting was certainly that Africa's 'living heritage' should be recognised. But a very deeply traditionalist definition of an African living culture was offered. 'Most anthropologists agree Africa was the cradle of humanity. So it was there that human activity has had an effect for the longest time.' And of course it is true that the Matopos are the product of the Stone Age peoples as well as of the Iron Age peoples who followed them. But the Matopos – and Njelele in particular – are *not* merely a monument to millennia of tradition. They are living culture in the sense that they are various, constantly changing, contradictory, often challenging or confrontational to states. When Jocelyn Alexander and JoAnn McGregor interviewed Dumiso Dabengwa in September 1996 he told them:

> We've been talking to chiefs Bango and Malaba ... asked them to submit suggestions about Njelele and Dula. We asked if they could provide us with a keeper who will be paid by the Department of National Shrines and Monuments. It was a national shrine and we want to keep it as such. It was once deproclaimed and we've since had it reproclaimed.

[62] *African Cultural Heritage and the World Heritage Convention*, pp. 104, 105, 196.

But it is hard to imagine the priest at Njelele as a paid state functionary.[63]

Recent history in the Matopos is currently the subject of intense dispute. When the Legal Resources Foundation researcher was working in Matobo towards *Breaking the Silence*, 'the CIO attended certain interview sessions, remaining visible but at a distance of about 30 metres.... After the news of CIO interest spread, many decided they would rather not get involved with the project.'[64] The older history of the hills, too, might get cleaned up and its awkward edges smoothed away into 'Heritage'. It is not only hard to imagine Sitwanyana Ncube as a civil servant, but equally hard to imagine all the characters which this book has re-introduced to the people of Zimbabwe – Nqabe Tshuma, Nzula Khumalo, Daniel Dube, Sigombe Mathema, and the rest – fitting neatly into any single vision of culture.

I would very much like to see the history of the people of the Matopos recognised as of world importance. I would very much like to see a UNESCO grant bringing together all the academic institutions of Bulawayo in a great research project on every aspect of the hills, and in particular their Iron Age history. But I hope this can be done without suppressing their capacity for surprise.

[63] In February 1998 the Ministry of Home Affairs called a meeting to resolve the guardianship of Njelele. The Minister, Dumiso Dabengwa, announced that Njelele had been re-proclaimed. It was suggested that Sitwanyana be recognised as keeper; there was an immediate hostile reaction from the crowd; the issue was therefore handed over to the Governor, Stephen Nkomo, and to the Matobo chiefs. The National Museum was asked to research the situation. The Museum researcher, Jackson Ndlovu, found a very complicated situation. Njelele had become part of factional disputes among the Khumalo royal family. The party which recognised Lobengula supported Sitwanyana, along with Thenjiwe Lesabe and the *Amakhosi* cultural group. Those who regarded Lobengula as a usurper and insisted that only Mzlikazi be recognised supported Ngcathu. The *Nqama* squatter movement threw its weight behind her and it was their members who demonstrated against Sitwanyana at the February meeting. Meanwhile another female spirit medium arrived at Njelele and stayed at Sitwanyana's kraal. She was possessed by 'the world spirit', which brooded over sacred mountains in Scotland, India and South America as well as Njelele. *Sunday News*, 22 March 1998; interview with Jackson Ndlovu, Bulawayo, 23 March 1998.

[64] *Breaking the Silence*, p. 117.

Bibliography

Note on Sources

This book draws on a wide range of archival and oral sources. Most of the files consulted are held in the National Archives, Harare, which possesses a more or less complete sequence of Annual Reports for Matobo from 1897 to 1961; a remarkable sequence of local criminal court records; and very many subject files – on chiefs, eviction, missions, African religion, land husbandry, army and civil intelligence, conservation and National Parks, etc., etc. The National Archives also holds the full proceedings of the 1949 Commission of Inquiry into the Matopo National Park and the documents associated with it. The footnotes give full indication of the National Archives reference numbers for the files used.

Few files are available in the National Archives for the period after the early 1960s. I was therefore fortunate to be able to supplement this material by means of access to provincial and district records. I consulted files on chiefs, headmen, the Mwali shrines, land, and many other matters at the Matabeleland South Provincial Commissioner's office in Gwanda, and at District Administrators' offices in Gwanda, Kezi and Esigodini. Some of this material – for instance, the files on Njelele – was available into the 1990s.

Archival material relating to missions is more scattered. The London Missionary Society files are in the library of the School of Oriental and African Studies in London; the Anglican material is available in the USPG deposit at Rhodes House, Oxford; Catholic material is available in the Jesuit Archives in Prestage House, Mount Pleasant, Harare, and I was also given access to historical material held at the main Catholic stations in southern Matabeleland. At first I was frustrated by the absence of Brethren in Christ records inside Zimbabwe, but later I entered into a most fruitful correspondence with the Brethren's archivist, Morris Sider, in Illinois. He sent me the complete typescript of Frances Davidson's diaries. Wendy Urban-Mead, a doctoral student at Columbia, who is working on the Brethren in Christ missions, sent me photocopies of material in the *Evangelical Visitor*. I did not track down archival material for the Seventh Day Adventists nor for the Zionists and other churches of African provenance.

I worked on Bulawayo newspapers – the *Chronicle*, the *African Home News*, the *Bantu Mirror* – in the Historical Reference Library in Bulawayo's city hall. They also possess some valuable archival deposits, in particular the text of Hugh Ashton's 1981 report on the National Park and its supporting documents.

The core of the oral material used in this book consists of interviews carried out by Mark Ncube and myself, most often jointly but sometimes by one or other of us only. These interviews have been transcribed – interviews in Sindebele by Mark Ncube and interviews in English by me. The texts are in the oral history collection at the National Archives, Bulawayo. I have also drawn on interviews of guerrillas and dissidents carried out by Drs Jocelyn Alexander and JoAnn McGregor – with whom I am working on a book on northern Matabeleland – and some interviews of my own which arise from the same project. I have made use of Dr Alexander's account of her visit with Dr McGregor to Njelele in August 1996.

Published Primary Sources

Anon., 'The Graves in the Matoppo Hills', *Zambesi Mission Record*, 2, 24, April 1904.

Baines, Thomas, *The Gold Regions of South Eastern Africa*, Stanford, London, 1894.

Barthelemy, M., 'During the Matabele Wars', *Zambesi Mission Record*, 1, 1, May 1898.

Carnegie, David, *Among the Matabele*, Religious Tracts Society, London, 1894.

Clinton, Iris, *Hope Fountain Story*, Bulawayo, 1962.

Clinton, Iris, *'Those Vessels'. The Story of Inyati, 1859–1959*, Stuart Manning, Bulawayo, 1959.

Davidson, Frances, 'Progress of the Work in Mapane Land', *Evangelical Visitor*, 15 December 1905.

Davidson, Frances, *South and Central Africa. A Record of Fifteen Years Missionary Labours Among Primitive Peoples*, Brethren Publishing House, Elgin, Illinois, 1915.

Engle, Jesse, *Evangelical Visitor*, 30 March and 15 May 1899.

Fogarty, Nelson, *Mashonaland Quarterly Papers*, XXV, August 1898.

Gelfand, Michael, *Gubulawayo and Beyond*, Chapman, London, 1968.

Gouldsbury, Cullen, *Rhodesian Rhymes*, Philpott and Collins, Bulawayo, 1932.

Jones, Neville, 'Whitewaters – a "Foundling" Church', *The Chronicle of the London Missionary Society*, May 1937.

Leary, T. W., *Mashonaland Quarterly Papers*, XIX, August 1899.

McDonald, Sir James Gordon, *Rhodes. A Life*, Philip Allan, London, 1927.

Mathers, E. P., *Zambesia. England's El Dorado in Africa*, London, 1891.

Michell, Sir Lewis, *The Life of the Rt. Hon. C. J. Rhodes, 1853–1902*, Edward Arnold, London 1910.

Mohr, Edward, *To the Victoria Falls of the Zambesi*, Sampson Low, London, 1876.

Nobbs, Eric, *Guide to the Matopos*, Maskew Miller, Cape Town, 1924.

Oates, C. G., *Frank Oates, Matabeleland and the Victoria Falls*, Kegan Paul, London, 1889.

Paterson, Edward, 'Cyrene Art', *Native Affairs Department Annual*, 1949.

Paterson, Edward, 'Cyrene Art in London', *NADA*, 1955.

Pitman, Dick, *National Parks of Zimbabwe*, Harare, n.d.

Posselt, F. W. T., *Fact and Fiction*, Bulawayo, 1935.

Roberts, R. S., ed., *Journey to Gubulawayo. Letters of Frs. H. Depelchin and C. Crooneberghs, SJ*, Bulawayo, 1979.

Sykes, Frank, *With Plumer in Matabeleland*, Constable, London, 1897.

Thomas, T. M., *Eleven Years in Central Africa*, Snow, London, 1872.

Tredgold, Robert, *The Matopos*, Federal Department of Printing, Salisbury, 1956.

Wallis, J. P. R., ed., *The Northern Goldfields Diaries of Thomas Baines, 1869–1872*, Chatto and Windus, London, 1946.

Wyatt, Eric, 'School in the Bush', *The Chronicle of the London Missionary Society*, May 1939.

Newspapers

African Daily News, Harare, 1956 to 1962.

African Home News, Bulawayo, 1953 to 1964.

African Weekly, Salisbury, 1952.

Bantu Mirror, Bulawayo, 1944 to 1962.

Chronicle, Bulawayo, 1897 to 1998.

Democratic Voice, Salisbury, 1961.

Horizon, Harare, 1997/8.

Rhodesia Herald, Salisbury, 1962.

Sunday News, Bulawayo, 1980 to 1995.

Sunday News Magazine, Bulawayo, 1988.

Unpublished Theses and Manuscripts

Alexander, Jocelyn, 'The State, Agrarian Policy and Rural Politics in Zimbabwe. Case Studies of Insiza and Chimanimani Districts, 1940–1990', doctoral thesis, University of Oxford, 1993.

Alexander, Jocelyn, 'Brief Account of a Trip to Njelele Ceremony, Friday and Saturday, 30–31 August 1996', Oxford, 1996.

Alexander, Jocelyn, 'Drought and Accountability in Post-War Matabeleland', seminar, Oxford, October 1997.

Anderson, Peter, 'The Human Clay: An Essay in the Spatial History of the Cape Eastern Frontier, 1811–1835', M. Litt. thesis, University of Oxford, 1993.

Ashton, Hugh, 'The Matopos. Socio-Historical Survey', January 1981, Historical Reference Library, Bulawayo.

Cobbing, Julian, 'The Ndebele Under the Khumalos, 1820–1896', doctoral thesis, University of Lancaster, 1976.

Daneel, Martinus, 'Healing the Earth: Traditional and Christian Initiatives in Southern Africa', conference paper, Utrecht, 1992.

Hostetter, John, 'Mission Education in a Changing Society: Brethren in Christ Mission Education in Southern Rhodesia, 1899–1959', doctoral thesis, SUNY, 1967.

Lonsdale, John, 'Kenyatta, God and Modernity', Humboldt University, Berlin, October 1997.

McGregor, JoAnn, 'Woodland Resources, Ecology, Policy and Ideology: an Historical Study of

Woodland Use in Shurugwi communal area, Zimbabwe', doctoral thesis, Loughborough, 1991.

Makamure, Billy, 'Making Sense of Social Forestry', doctoral thesis, Tampere, 1995.

Mawere, Abraham and Wilson, Ken, 'Socio-religious Movements, the State and Community Change: Some Reflections on the Ambuya Juliana Cult of Southern Zimbabwe', Britain Zimbabwe Society Research Day, Oxford, 23 April 1994.

Matobo Conservation Society, 'Submission for the Matobo National Park and Matobo Dam Recreational Area to be Recognised as a World Heritage Site within the Matopos Hills, Bulawayo, 1996.

Mhabi, S. J., 'The Effects of and African Responses to the Land Husbandry Act of 1951 with Special Reference to Ntabazinduna Communal Land', BA History Honours thesis, University of Zimbabwe, 1984.

Mlotshwa, Sibongile, 'The Matopos Research Station: Origins and Contribution to the Agrarian Development of Zimbabwe', BA History Honours thesis, University of Zimbabwe, 1984.

Mwanza, R, 'Mwari: The God of the Karanga', conference paper, Lusaka, September 1972.

Ncube, T. V., 'Aspects of Agrarian Labour in Matabeleland South from 1899 to 1948', BA History Honours thesis, University of Zimbabwe, 1985.

Ngulube, S., 'Crime and Colonial Ideology: a Case Study of the Bulawayo District in the period 1910–1936', BA History Honours thesis, University of Zimbabwe, 1984.

Nkomo, Nicholas, 'Between the Hammer and the Anvil', 1996.

Ntabeni, Faith, 'The Underdevelopment of Mzingwane District', BA History Honours thesis, University of Zimbabwe, 1985.

Nthoi, Leslie, 'Social Perspectives of Religion: A Study of the Mwali Cult of Southern Rhodesia', doctoral thesis, Manchester, 1995.

Nyathi, Pathisa, 'Lawo Magugu: Traditional Ceremonies of the Amandebele', Bulawayo, 1996.

Raftopolous, Brian, 'Problematising Nationalism in Zimbabwe', University of Cape Town, October 1997.

Ranger, Terence, 'The Politics of Prophesy in Matabeleland', paper for the Satterthwaite Colloquium, April 1989.

Ranger, Terence, 'From Paternalism to Privatisation: State Farms in Zimbabwe. The Case of Antelope Estates', Oxford, February 1992.

Ranger, Terence, 'Indigenous Ideas: Accounting for Drought, Making Rain and Healing History in Matabeleland', Oxford, 1992.

Ranger, Terence, 'Criminal Court Records and the Social History of the Zimbabwean South-West: Witchcraft Belief and Accusation', Oxford, 1994.

Ranger, Terence, 'Murder, Rape and Witchcraft: Criminal Court Data for Gender Relations in Colonial Matabeleland', Institute of Commonwealth Studies seminar, London, 23 March 1995.

Ranger, Terence, 'New Approaches to African Landscape', House of World Cultures, Berlin, December 1996.

Ruwitah, A. R. M., 'Matopo National Park and Rhodesdale Estate. A Comparative Study of African Underdevelopment in a Colonial State, Rhodes 1890–1960', MA thesis, History, University of Zimbabwe, 1987.

Stuart, Ossie, 'Good Boys, Footballers and Strikers: African Social Change in Bulawayo, 1933–53', doctoral thesis, London, 1989.

Thompson, Guy, 'Cultivating Conflict: the Native Land Husbandry Act in Colonial Zimbabwe', doctoral thesis, University of Minnesota, 1998.

Urban-Mead, Wendy, 'The Calling of an Unwomanly Woman: H. Frances Davidson and the Brethren in Christ Mission at the Matopo Hills, Rhodesia (Zimbabwe), 1897–1906', seminar paper, Columbia, 1996.

West, Michael, 'African Middle Class Formation in Colonial Zimbabwe, 1890–1965', doctoral thesis, Harvard, 1990.

Wilson, Ken, 'Human Welfare and Ecological Dynamics: a Case Study of Population, Health and Nutrition in Southern Zimbabwe', doctoral thesis, London, 1990.

Yapp, Katri, 'Voices From the Conflict: Perceptions on Violence, Ethnicity and the Disruption of National Unity', Britain Zimbabwe Society Research Day, 8 June 1996.

Zvabva, Oliver, 'Nyachiranga Regional Cult', BA Honours thesis, Religious Studies, University of Zimbabwe, 1988.

Published Articles and Chapters

Alexander, Jocelyn, 'The Unsettled Land: the Politics of Land Redistribution in Matabeleland, 1890–1990', *Journal of Southern African Studies*, 17, 4, 1991.

Alexander, Jocelyn, 'State, Peasantry and Resettlement in Zimbabwe', *Review of African Political Economy*, 61, 1993.

Alexander, Jocelyn and McGregor, JoAnn, 'Modernity and Ethnicity in a Frontier Society. Understanding Difference in Northwestern Zimbabwe', *Journal of Southern African Studies*, 23, 2, June 1997.

Alexander, Jocelyn, 'Dissident Perspectives in Zimbabwe's Civil War', *Africa*, forthcoming.

Alexander, Jocelyn and Ranger, Terence, 'Competition and Integration in the Religious History of North-Western Zimbabwe', *Journal of Religion in Africa*, February 1998.

Anon., 'Gukurahundi – Ten Years Later', *Zimbabwe Defence Forces Magazine*, 7, 1, 1992.

Benzies, W. R., 'Funeral of Cecil John Rodes', *Native Affairs Department Annual*, 1964.

Behrend, Heike, 'The Holy Spirit Movement and the Forces of Nature', in Hansen, Holger and Twaddle, Michael, eds, *Religion and Politics in East Africa*, James Currey, London, 1995.

Bhebe, Ngwabi, 'The Nationalist Struggle, 1957–62', in C. Banana, ed., *Turmoil and Tenacity. Zimbabwe, 1890–1990*, College Press, Harare, 1989.

Cobbing, Julian, 'The Absent Priesthood. Another Look at the Rhodesian Risings of 1896–7', *Journal of African History*, 17, 1977.

Cockcroft, I. G., 'The Mlimo (Mwari) Cult', *Native Affairs Department Annual*, 10, 4, 1972.

Drinkwater, Michael, 'Technical Development and Peasant Impoverishment', *Journal of Southern African Studies*, 15, 2, 1989.

Garlake, Peter, 'The First Eighty Years of Rock Art Studies, 1890–1970', in Gilbert Pwiti, ed., *Caves, Monuments and Texts. Zimbabwean Archaeology Today*, Uppsala, 1997.

Grove, Richard, 'Early Themes in African Conservation: the Cape in the Nineteenth Century', in D. Anderson and R. Grove, eds, *Conservation in Africa: People, Policies and Practice*, CUP, Cambridge, 1987.

Grove, Richard, 'Scottish Missionaries, Evangelical Discourses and the Origins of Conservation Theory in Southern Africa, 1820–1900', *Journal of Southern African Studies*, 15, 2, January 1989.

Hyslop, J., 'Trade Unionism in the Rise of African Nationalism: Bulawayo, 1943–1963', *African Perspectives*, Johannesburg, 1, 1986.

Lonsdale, John, 'The Moral Economy of Mau-Mau: Wealth, Poverty and Civic Virtue in Kikuyu Political Thought', in Bruce Berman and John Lonsdale, *Unhappy Valley. Book Two: Violence and Ethnicity*, James Currey, London, 1992.

Mafu, H., 'The 1991–92 Drought and Some Religious Reactions', *Journal of Religion in Africa*, XXV, 3, 1995.

Massanari, Ronald, 'When Mountains are Mountains and Gardens and Gardens. Explorations into Sacred Space, Nature and Environmental Ethics', *Journal of Developing Societies*, XIII, 2, December 1997.

Moore, Donald, 'Contesting Terrain in Zimbabwe's Eastern Highlands', *Economic Geography*, 69, 4, October 1993.

Munjeri, Dawson, 'Oral Traditions and the Matopo Hills', in C. K. Cook, ed., *The Matopo Hills. A Guide*, National Museums, Harare, 1986.

Ncube, Mark and Ranger, Terence, 'Religion and the War in Southern Matabeleland', in Bhebe and Ranger, eds, *Society in Zimbabwe's Liberation War*, University of Zimbabwe, 1995.

Perham, M. and Posselt, J. W., 'The Story of Ndansi Kumalo of the Matabele Tribe, Southern Rhodesia', in M. Perham, ed., *Ten Africans*, Faber and Faber, London, 1934.

Phimister, Ian and Van Onselen, Charles, 'The Political Economy of Tribal Animosity: a Case Study of the 1929 Bulawayo Location "Faction Fight"', *Journal of Southern African Studies*, 6, 1, October 1979.

Pikarayi, Innocent, 'Research Trends in Historical Archaeology on the Zimbabwe Plateau', in Gilbert Pwiti, ed., *Caves, Monuments and Texts. Zimbabwean Archeaology Today*. Uppsala, 1997.

Potts, Deborah and Mutambirwa, Chris, 'The Government Must Not Dictate. Rural–urban Migrants' Perceptions of Zimbabwe's Land Resettlement Programme', *Review of African Political Economy*, 74, 1997.

Ranger, Terence, 'Religious Studies and Political Economy: the Mwari Cult and the Peasant Experience in Southern Rhodesia', in M. M. J. van Binsbergen and M. Schoffelers, eds, *Theoretical Explorations in African Religion*, Routledge and Kegan Paul, London, 1986.

Ranger, Terence, 'Taking Hold of the Land. Holy Places and Pilgrimage in Twentieth Century Zimbabwe', *Past and Present*, 117, November 1987.

Ranger, Terence, 'Whose Heritage? The Case of the Matobo National Park', *Journal of Southern African Studies*, 15, 2, January 1989.

Ranger, Terence, 'Matabeleland Since the Amnesty', *African Affairs*, 351, 88, 1989.

Ranger, Terence, 'Power, Religion and Community: the Matobo Case', *Subaltern Studies*, VII, OUP, Delhi, 1992.

Ranger, Terence, 'Tales of the Wild West: Gold-diggers and Rustlers in South-West Zimbabwe, 1898–1940', *South African Historical Journal*, 28, 1993.

Ranger, Terence, 'The Invention of Tradition Revisited', in Terence Ranger and Olufemi Vaughan, eds, *Legitimacy and the State in Twentieth Century Africa*, St Antony's/Macmillan, London, 1993.

Ranger, Terence, 'Healing the Land. Mediums Call for National Healing', *Horizon*, September 1993.

Ranger, Terence, 'African Identities: Ethnicity, Nationality and History. The Case of Matabeleland, 1893 to 1993', in Joachim Heidrich, ed., *Changing Identities. The Transformation of Asian and African Identities Under Colonialism*, Centre for Modern Oriental Studies, Berlin, 1994.

Ranger, Terence, 'Great Spaces Washed with Sun: the Matopos and Uluru Compared', in Kate Darian-Smith, *et al.*, eds, *Text, Theory, Space*, Routledge, 1996.

Ranger, Terence, 'The Moral Economy of Identity in Northern Matabeleland', in Louise de la Gorgondiere, *et al.*, eds, *Ethnicity in Africa*, African Studies Centre, Edinburgh, 1996.

Ranger, Terence, 'Making Zimbabwean Landscapes: Painters, Projectors and Priests', *Paideuma*, 43, 1997.

Reeler, A. P., 'Surviving Torture: A Zimbabwean Experience', in Irmler, D., ed., *Old Ways –*

New Theories, Connect, Harare, 1995.

Ian Scones, 'Landscapes, Fields and Soils: Understanding the History of Soil Fertility Management in Southern Zimbabwe', *Journal of Southern African Studies*, 23, 4, December 1997.

Schmidt, Heike, 'Penetrating Foreign Lands: Contestations Over African Landscapes: a Case Study from Eastern Zimbabwe', *Environment and History*, 1, 3, October 1995.

Schmidt, Heike, 'Healing the Wounds of War: Memories of Violence and the Making of History in Zimbabwe's Most Recent Past', *Journal of Southern African Studies*, 23, 2, June 1997.

Shumaker, Lyn, 'Constructing Racial Landscapes: Africans, Administrators and Anthropologists in Late Colonial Northern Rhodesia', in Pels, Peter and Salemink, Oscar, eds, *Colonial Subjects. Genealogies of Practical Anthropology*, Michigan, 1997.

Sider, E. Morris, 'Hannah Frances Davidson', in E. M. Sider, *Nine Portraits. Brethren in Christ Biographical Sketches*, Napparee, Illinois, 1978.

Walker, Nick, 'Late Stone Age Research in the Matopos', *South African Archaeological Bulletin*, 35, 131, June 1980.

Walker, Nick, 'Dassie Hunters of the Matobo Hills', *Zimbabwe Wildlife*, June 1989.

Walker, Nicholas and Thorp, Carolyn, 'Stone Age Archaeology in Zimbabwe', in Gilbert Pwiti, ed., *Caves, Monuments and Texts. Zimbabwean Archaeology Today*, Uppsala, 1997.

Werbner, Richard, 'Continuity and Policy in Southern Africa's High God Cult', in R. P. Werbner, ed., *Regional Cults*, Academic Press, London, 1977.

Werbner, Richard, 'Regional Cult of God Above. Achieving and Defending the Macrocosm', in R. P. Werbner, *Ritual Passage. Sacred Journey. The Process and Organisation of Religious Movements*, Smithsonian Institute, Washington, 1989.

Published Monographs

Alexander, J., McGregor, A. and Ranger, T., *Violence and Memory. Life in the Forests of Northern Matabeleland*, forthcoming.

Amnesty International, *Memorandum to the Government of Zimbabwe*, May 1986.

Aschwanden, Herbert, *Karanga Mythology*, Mambo, Gweru, 1990.

Beinart, William and Coates, Peter, *Environment and History. The Taming of Nature in the USA and South Africa*, Routledge, London, 1995.

Bhebe, Ngwabi, *Christianity and Traditional Religion in Western Zimbabwe, 1859–1958*, Longman, London, 1979.

Bhebe, Ngwabi, *B. Burombo. African Politics in Zimbabwe, 1947–1958*, College Press, Harare, 1989.

Bhebe, Ngwabi and Ranger, Terence, eds, *Soldiers in Zimbabwe's Liberation War*, University of Zimbabwe, Harare, and James Currey, London, 1995.

Bhebe, Ngwabi and Ranger, Terence, eds, *Society in Zimbabwe's Liberation War*, University of Zimbabwe, Harare, and James Currey, London, 1995.

Carver, Richard, *Zimbabwe: A Break With the Past? Human Rights and Political Unity*, Africa Watch, October 1989.

Carver, Richard, *Zimbabwe: Drawing a Line Through the Past*, Amnesty International, June 1992.

Catholic Commission for Justice and Peace and Legal Resources Foundation, *Breaking the Silence. A Report on the Disturbances in Matabeleland and the Midlands, 1980 to 1988*, Harare, 1997.

Cosgrove, D., *Social Formation and Symbolic Landscape*, Barnes and Noble, New York, 1985.

Cousins, Colleen, *A Hundred Furrows. The Land Struggle in Zimbabwe*, Harare, 1991.

Daneel, M. L., *The God of the Matopo Hills*, Mouton, The Hague, 1970.

Daneel, M. L., *Earthkeeping at the Grassroots in Zimbabwe*, Sigma Press, Pretoria, 1991.

Daneel, M. L., as Mafuranhunzi Gumbo, *Guerrilla Snuff*, Baobab, Harare, 1995.

Daneel, M. L., *African Earthkeepers*, Vol. 1, forthcoming.

Dewey, W. J. and Else De Palmenaer, eds, *Legacies of Stone: Zimbabwe Past and Present*, vols 1 and 11, Tervuren, Belgium, 1998.

Drinkwater, M., *The State and Agrarian Change in Zimbabwe's Communal Areas*, Macmillan, London, 1991.

Eppel, John, *Hatchings*, Carrefour, Cape Town, 1993.

Fairhead, James and Leach, Melissa, *Misreading the African Landscape: Society and Ecology in a Forest Savanna Mosaic*, CUP, Cambridge, 1996.

Gargett, Valerie, *The Black Eagle*, Acorn Books, Randburg, 1990.

Garlake, Peter, *Early Zimbabwe from Matopos to Nyanga*, Mambo, Gweru, 1983.

Garlake, Peter, *The Painted Caves*, Modus, Harare, 1987.

Gelfand, Michael, *An African's Religion. The Spirit of Nyajena*, Juta, Cape Town, 1966.

Gjerstad, Ole, *The Organiser. Story of Temba Moyo*, Liberation Support Movement, Richmond, 1974.

Godwin, Peter, *Mukiwa*, Macmillan, London, 1996.

Head, Bessie, *A Bewitched Crossroad*, Ad Donker, Craighall, 1984.

Hirsch, E. and O'Hanlon, M., *The Anthropology of Landscape*, Oxford University Press, Oxford, 1995.

Hughes, A. J. B., *Kin, Caste and Nation Among the Rhodesian Ndebele*, Rhodes-Livingstone Papers, 25, Manchester University Press, Manchester, 1956.

Keppel-Jones, Arthur, *Rhodes and Rhodesia. The White Conquest of Zimbabwe, 1884–1902*, McGill-Queens University Press, Kingston and Montreal, 1983.

Khumalo, G. N. S., *ULobhengula kaMzilikazi ka Matshobana Isilwana Esimayama Sikomabindela*, Longman, Harare, 1987.

Khumalo, G. N. S., *UMzilikazi kaMatshobane. Imbabala Umasile Ngokuthubela*, Longman, Harare, 1989.

Lawyers Committee for Human Rights, *Zimbabwe. Wages of War*, New York, 1986.

Layton, Robert, *Uluru. An Aboriginal History of Ayers Rock*, Aboriginal Studies Press, Canberra, 1989.

Maddox, Gregory *et al.*, eds, *Custodians of the Land. Ecology and Culture in the History of Tanzania*, James Currey, London; 1996.

Martin, David and Johnson, Phyllis, *The Struggle for Zimbabwe*, Zimbabwe Publishing House, Harare, 1981.

Martin, David and Johnson, Phyllis, eds, *Destructive Engagement: Southern Africa at War*, ZPH, Harare, 1986.

Maxwell, David, *The Cinderella People. Christianity and Chieftanship among the Hwesa People of North East Zimbabwe, 1870s–1990s*, IAI, Edinburgh, 1998.

Mitchell, W. J. T., ed., *Landscape and Power*, Chicago, 1994.

Nkomo, Joshua, *Nkomo. The Story of My Life*, Methuen, London, 1984.

Nyathi, Pathisa, *Igugu Lika Mthwakazi Imbali Yama Ndebele, 1820–1893*, Mambo, Gweru, 1994.

Palmer, Robin, *Land and Racial Domination in Rhodesia*, Heinemann, London, 1977.

Phimister, Ian, *An Economic and Social History of Zimbabwe: Capital, Accumulation and Class Struggle, 1890–1948*, Longman, London, 1988.

Raftopolous, Brian and Phimster, Ian, *Keep on Knocking: a History of the Labour Movement in Zimbabwe, 1900–97*, Baobab, Harare, 1997.

Ranger, Terence, *Revolt in Southern Rhodesia, 1896–7*, Heinemann, London, 1967.

Ranger, Terence, *The African Voice in Southern Rhodesia, 1898–1930*, Heinemann, London, 1970.

Ranger, Terence, *Peasant Consciousness and Guerrilla War*, James Currey, London, 1985.

Ranger, Terence, *The Invention of Tribalism in Zimbabwe*, Mambo, Gweru, 1985.

Ranger, Terence, *Are We Not Also Men? The Samkange Family and African Politics in Zimbabwe, 1920 to 1960*, James Currey, London, 1995.

Rotberg, Robert, *The Founder. Cecil Rhodes and the Pursuit of Power*, Oxford University Press, Oxford, 1988.

Schoffeleers, J. M., ed., *Guardians of the Land*, Mambo, Gwelo, 1978.

Schoffeleers, J. M., *River of Blood. The Genesis of a Martyr Cult in Southern Malawi, c. AD 1600*, University of Wisconsin Press, Madison, 1992.

Soule, M. E. and Lease, G., eds, *Reinventing Nature?*, Island Press, Washington, 1995.

UNESCO, *African Cultural Heritage and the World Heritage Comvention*, National Museums, Harare, 1996.

Walker, David, *Paterson of Cyrene. A Biography*, Mambo, Gweru, 1985.

Werbner, Richard, *Tears of the Dead. The Social Biography of an African Family*, IAI, Edinburgh, 1991.

Index

agriculture, (*see also* cattle, crops, farms, markets, peasants, ranches, wetlands)
  African Christian agriculture, 49, 50, 51, 54, 55, 56, 71, 72, 115, 147, 149, 172, 174, 175, 210, 224, 225, 241, 283
  African communal cultivation, 86, 87, 92, 102, 135, 138, 139, 140, 141, 142, 143, 150, 151, 156, 172, 180, 181, 230, 271,
  African cultivation on white-owned land, 90, 111, 112, 119, 120, 122
  capitalist and settler farming, 79, 80, 83, 84, 93, 132, 133, 134
  control by Mwali shrines, 23, 24 fn 55, 138 fn 33, 140, 149, 209, 216, 222, 283
  pre-colonial, 3, 4, 16, 17, 18, 24, 28, 43, 44, 45, 46 fn 56, 63, 130, 270, 271
animals, wild (*see also* birds), 14, 17, 23, 44, 50, 57, 59, 60, 66, 86, 87, 122, 136, 137, 138, 141, 173, 186, 187, 191, 192, 210, 216, 220, 221, 230, 235, 237, 238, 239, 243, 256, 271, 283, 284, 287, 288
army (*see also* Fifth Brigade)
  British in 1896, 27, 28, 29.
  Rhodesian in 1961/2, 183, 188, 190, 203, 204
  Rhodesian in the 1970s, 232, 234, 239, 241
  Zimbabwean in the 1980s, 232, 244, 267, 276
associations (*see also* Burombo, B; Dube, Daniel; Dube, John Sigodo; Ncube, Dokotela; Sigombe, Mathema; Tshuma, Nqabe)
  African Voice Association, 3, 148, 154, 158, 159, 160, 162, 164, 171, 172, 173, 174, 178, 179, 182, 183
  All African Convention, 173
  Bantu Congress of Southern Rhodesia, 123, 182

  Industrial and Commercial Workers Union, 139, 143, 147, 148, 157
  Kalanga Culture Promotion Society, 210
  Matabeleland Home Society, 114, 117, 118, 119, 123, 124 fn 65, 131, 145, 146, 151, 154, 158, 160, 170, 196, 211, 212
  Sofasihamba, 3, 118, 119, 124, 125, 127, 132, 149, 157, 160, 195, 196, 202, 205, 224
  Sofasonke, 3, 132 fn 6, 142, 148, 149, 151, 152, 154, 157, 158, 159, 160, 161, 162, 163, 164, 165, 166, 167, 168, 169, 170, 173, 176, 178, 182, 183, 195, 197, 213, 214
  Sons of Mzilikazi, 188, 212
  South African National Congress, 139, 147

Bango, Grey, 216, 217, 220
birds, 14, 140, 141 fn.44, 221, 271, 287, 288
botány, flora 57, 58, 59, 61, 62, 137, 274
Bulawayo (*see also* cultural nationalism, labour), 27, 51, 57, 65, 66, 71, 72, 83, 87, 91, 102, 117, 123, 124, 125, 138 fn 32, 139, 143, 146, 159, 162, 173, 181, 188, 198, 202, 229, 230, 235, 236
Burombo, Benjamin (*see also* associations, African Voice), 158, 159, 160, 161, 162, 164 and fn 8, 168, 169, 171, 173
buses, 118-19, 139, 143, 158, 202

caste (*see also* ethnicity), 99 fn 3, 102, 119 fn 53, 128, 149
cattle (*see also* agriculture, ranches)
  African-owned cattle, 40, 50, 62, 63, 65, 74, 79, 86 and fn 67, 89, 90, 94, 95, 106, 107, 108, 111, 112, 113, 120, 122, 123, 124, 127, 131,

301

Index

Ncube, Nduna, 139, 151, 157, 160, 168, 183, 246, photo 265
Ncube, Reader, 4, 230, 248, 261, 273
Ndhlovu, Masotsha (*see also* associations, nationalism), 139, 148, 160, 164
Nkomo, Joshua (*see also* cultural nationalism, Thenjiwe Lesabe, nationalism, parties, shrines), 148, 188, 197, 202, 203, 205, 208, 209, 210, 211, 212, 213, 216, 217, 218, 219, 220, 222, 231, 240, 242, 243, 244, 249, 253, 254, 255, 256, 257, 259, 260, 261, 262, 267, 268, 273, 274, 275, 276, 277, 278, 279, 280, 281
Nobbs, Eric (*see also* agriculture, National Parks), 11, 18, 28 fn 68, 30, 39, 42, 59-62, 63, 64, 65, 81, 91, 214, 287

painters (*see also* landscape, prehistory),
  cave paintings, 16, 17-19, 20, 42, 52, 63, 64, 66, 186, 269, 270, 271, 274 fn 24, 287
  water-colours, 11, 12-14, photo 38, 39, 55-6, photo 193, 194
Parties (*see also* nationalism),
  African National Congress of Southern Rhodesia, 176, 177, 178, 182, 183, 184, 200, 201, 212, 224
  National Democratic Party, 176, 182, 183, 184, 187, 188, 190, 198, 201, 202, 203, 204, 208, 212, 213, 224
  ZANU/Patriotic Front, 268
  Zimbabwe African National Union, 208, 245, 252, 254, 259, 273
  Zimbabwe African Peoples Union, 176, 182, 184, 187, 188, 191, 192, 194, 198, 202, 204, 208, 220, 222, 224, 229, 230, 231, 232, 233, 239, 245, 248, 251, 252, 258, 259, 260, 261, 267, 268, 281, 286,
peasants (*see also* agriculture, crops, markets), 1, 2, 44, 72, 126, 138, 179, 196, 223, 235, 237, 244, 245, 251, 252, 271, 281
photography (*see also* landscape), 29, 39, 41, 113, 188, 237, 269, 270
police, 53, 170, 171, 172, 173, 174, 183, 185, 190, 192, 203, 204, 206, 213, 236, 250, 258
prehistory (*see also* San), 3, 16, 62, 63, 64, 137
prophecy (*see also* shrines), 142, 216 fn 72, 258
Prospect/Mbongolo (*see also* eviction), 167, 169, 170, 171, 172, 173, 174, 175, 177, map 226, 235, 236, 243, 247, 250, 252

ranches (*see also* cattle, farms), 59, 102, 108, 119, 120, 121, 151, 175, 179, 198, 199, 203, 229, 237, 245

regiments (*see also* chiefs, Wenlock), 4, 69, map 98, 102, 103, 104, 108, 112, 113, 122, 130, 131, 146, 205, 209, 282
reserves, Tribal Trust Lands, Communal Areas (*see also* agriculture, cattle, eviction, Wenlock),
  general, 58, 66, 71, 75, 82, 92, 93, 94, 96, 97, 101 fn 12, 134, 135, 137, 161, 184, map 189, 190, 191, 203, 235, 242, 268, 271, 286, 288
  Matopos Reserve, 4, 6, 24, 59, 69, 97, map 109, 113, 121, 127, 128, 130, 131, 138, 139, 140, 150, 151, 160, 166, 167, 172, 177-83, map 189, 219, 229, 230, 231, 240, 241, 249, 250, 252, photo 265, 268, 271, 273-5, 286, 288
rest days (*see also* shrines), 24, 209, 223-4, 225, 230, 276
Rhodes, Cecil (*see also* farms, indabas, monuments), 2, 27, 28 fn 64, 30, 31, 32, 39, 48 fn 37, 58, 70-85, 86, 88, 90, 92, 93, 95, 96, 97, 104, 111, 112, 122, 123, 124, 131, 134 fn 14, 135, 146, 151, 156, 157, 160, 161, 163, 166, 170 fn 31, 184, 187, 202, 211, 213, 229, 254 fn 91, 270
Rhodes-Matopos Estate (*see also* cattle, Murray, Charles), 64, 65, 74, 76, 77, 78, 79, 80, 81, 82, 84, 85, 86, 88, 89, 90, 91, 92, 94, 95, 96, 99, 111, 123, 135, 146, 152, 159, 176, 190, 237, 281, 282
Richardson, A. G. S (*see also* Wenlock), 57, 111, 112, 118, 119, 120, 125, 202
rivers (*see also* water), 18, 19, 20, 65, 86, 87, 95, 178, 191, 195, 197, 198, 210, 222 fn 94, 274, 275, 282
rocks (*see also* landscape, shrines), 3, 4, 11, 14, 15, 18, 19, 20, 21, 22, 23, 25, 26, 29, 32, 40, 49, 51, 56, 60, 72, 219, 259, 271, 272, 273, 278, 280, 285

San (*see also* painters, prehistory), 12, 16, 17 fn 21, 20, 56, 63, 64
schools (*see also* missionaries), 3, 50, 51, 52, 53, 85, 101, 111, 116, 142, 146, 147, 148, 192, 195, 196, 197, 204, 205, 206, 207, 210, 234, 239, 241, 248, 250, 252
shrines (*see also* monuments, rest days, shrine priests),
  general, 3, 4, 19, 20, 21 fn 39, 23, 24, 25, 26, 27, 28, photo 33, 45, 52, 53, 84, 105, 110, 131, 138 fn 33, 140, 186, 209, 210, 213, 214, map 217, 221, 222, 223-4, 230, 231-2, 239-41, 254, 261, photo 265, 273, 274, 283, 284, 288, 289
  Bembe, 21 fn 42, 219, 229, 240, 241 fn 39, 260, 284
  Dula, 17 fn 24, 21, 24, 27, map 109, 113, 216-18, 219, 220, 221, 225, 231 fn 6, 240, 259, 260, 262, 275, 290